IN THE SHADOW OF THE GREAT HOUSE

ALSO BY DANIEL ROOD

*The Reinvention of Atlantic Slavery:
Technology, Labor, Race, and
Capitalism in the Greater Caribbean*

IN THE SHADOW OF

THE GREAT HOUSE

A HISTORY OF THE PLANTATION IN AMERICA

Daniel Rood

W. W. NORTON & COMPANY
Independent Publishers Since 1923

Frontispiece*: The old plantation bell. Greene County, Georgia, 1939. Used to mark time and structure the working days of the enslaved in the antebellum era.*
WOLCOTT, MARION POST, PHOTOGRAPHER. BELL ON PLANTATION. UNITED STATES GREENE COUNTY, 1939. PHOTOGRAPH. REPRODUCED FROM THE COLLECTIONS OF THE LIBRARY OF CONGRESS.

Copyright © 2026 by Daniel Rood

All rights reserved
Printed in the United States of America
First Edition

For information about permission to reproduce selections from this book, write to Permissions, W. W. Norton & Company, Inc., 500 Fifth Avenue, New York, NY 10110

For information about special discounts for bulk purchases, please contact W. W. Norton Special Sales at specialsales@wwnorton.com or 800-233-4830

Manufacturing by Lake Book Manufacturing
Book design by Dana Sloan
Production manager: Gwen Cullen

ISBN 978-1-63149-837-4

W. W. Norton & Company, Inc., 500 Fifth Avenue, New York, NY 10110
www.wwnorton.com

W. W. Norton & Company Ltd., 15 Carlisle Street, London W1D 3BS

Authorized EU representative: EAS, Mustamäe tee 50, 10621 Tallinn, Estonia

1 2 3 4 5 6 7 8 9 0

To my fellow historians, without whom this book could not have been written.

CONTENTS

Prologue: The False King of São Tomé   1
Introduction: This Grand Consumer   7

PART ONE: THE DITCH

1. The Great Gulph   27
2. Broken Rice   37
3. People That Can Go in the Ditch   53
4. The Apotheosis of Johann Bolzius   73

PART TWO: SCIONS

5. Counterblaste   83
6. To Dye in Smoke   97
7. Crop Masters   107
8. The Chiefest of My Estates   127
9. The Colonians   143
10. Vlangbengdeng   159

PART THREE: DWELLINGS

11. The Comprehensive Jaws of America   169
12. The Mother of Slavery   179

13.	Bottom Rail on Top This Time	201
14.	Sherman's Reserve	221

PART FOUR: NEW FIELDS

15.	The Bronze Titan	243
16.	The White Whale	263
17.	Percy's Ode	281
18.	Standing	307

PART FIVE: PLANTATION FUTURES

19.	The Slave Empires of History	331
20.	Sinking	351
21.	In Cotton's Wake	371
22.	From Killing Fields to Kill Lines	393
23.	Caindo na Cana	405
	Coda: Burying Ground	423
	Acknowledgments	425
	Notes	427
	Image Credits	473
	Index	477

IN THE SHADOW OF THE GREAT HOUSE

PROLOGUE

The False King of São Tomé

The priest was accustomed to belting the rites of Mass over a chorus of coughs, wheezes, and creaking pews. But on a Sunday morning in July 1595, the groan of the heavy wooden door startled him from his gesticulations. Necks craning to the back of the hall, a hush fell over the small parochial church of Santa María Trinitá on the African island of São Tomé. The priest watched a group of Angolans stride up the aisle, likely clad "in the manner of heathens."[1]

Luxuriant flashes of red and purple cloth rolled up and sank away as the tightly bunched group advanced on the altar. An instant before the attack commenced, and far too late, the priest recognized them as *mocambos*: escaped slaves, sworn enemies of Portuguese rule who occasionally descended from mountain redoubts to attack individual plantations before beating hasty retreats. This time there would be no retreat. Armed with muskets and cane knives, Black rebels "killed as many whites as they could find" in the church, including the priest. With the dead and the wounded sprawled around them, the *mocambos* gulped the wine from the sacramental chalice. Then they torched the building.²

The rebels next turned to the source of their torment: the sugar plantations of the island. During the five-month cane harvest every year, thousands of enslaved people were forced into the backbreaking task of cutting down vast, uniform fields of cane. Teams of oxen hauled the wagonloads of the crop to the boiling house, where more slaves spent countless hours feeding canes into the grinding mills and scooping gallon after gallon of juice through a succession of fire-heated pans to condense the sugar and ready it for drying and packing.

When the Portuguese planters of São Tomé transformed a diverse tropical island ecosystem of thousands of plant species into a uniform landscape dominated by a single crop; when they used merchant capital to fuse agricultural and manufacturing operations into a single top-down organization; and when they imported thousands of slaves from mainland central Africa to undertake the labor, they assembled a kind of economic machine that the world had not yet seen. For the planters, the plantation was a "New-found Eldorado of the West," minting gold for planter and king alike. For the *mocambos*, the plantation was hell.³

On the first day of the revolt, the rebels burned down sixteen sugar mills. A Portuguese scribe reported that, as they engaged in this work, they "gathered to themselves all the people and slaves that they encountered." Recruits "swore loyalty to the death to the Negro who began to be called 'King of the Island,'" a charismatic leader named Amador, who ordered escaping slaves to return to their former plantations and burn them down. The people on whom the planter depended to make his plantation run, Amador probably reasoned, were the same people who were best qualified and most motivated to annihilate it. By the time they were finished with the countryside, Amador's followers, now numbering around five thousand souls, had "burned sixty properties with their sugar mills, and during sugar-making season no less." They had devastated the export economy of São Tomé. In what would become a refrain in the official account of the revolt, the number of dead Europeans was mere background noise: "In all of the island," reported the Portuguese official, "there didn't remain a single property that could make sugar."[4]

Five days after the attack on the church, thousands of rebels-in-arms assaulted the Portuguese capital city on the island. They employed military tactics they had most likely brought from the African mainland. Banners rippling in the breeze, they advanced on various entrances to the city in independent columns of soldiers, each led by a captain. In spite of their organization, better-armed Portuguese "militiamen responded with much ardor," reputedly killing at least three hundred of the attackers. The surviving *mocambos* retreated, burning all the properties they came across.[5]

Two weeks later, to finish off the reign of the Portuguese, and with them their plantations, Amador led another attack on the city with at least twenty-five hundred armed combatants, but then, "both sides being afraid," Amador made a fatal error. He delayed the planned nighttime attack until dawn, giving the city's defenders time to prepare. "Impetuous battle" began around five or six in the morning and lasted until midday, with clear victory for the Portuguese: "At least 500 negros [were] killed," a scribe boasted, with "many taken prisoner." But Amador evaded capture yet again, "fleeing to a property where he had his principal force." That force was then routed, yet Amador still was not caught.

After the successful defense of the city, the Portuguese governor extended amnesty to all rebels who surrendered. Four thousand of them, hoping to avoid torture and execution, declared loyalty to the slaveholding regime, but Amador and many others were still at large. On August 14, 1595, Amador was betrayed by five lieutenants, who captured him and handed him over to the city of São Tomé. Once in the hands of the incensed and terrified Portuguese authorities, Amador was swiftly punished. First, they tied him in a leather sack and dragged him behind a horse. Then they chopped off his hands. Finally, he was drawn and quartered, his remains displayed in the public square. Other leaders were tortured, and a couple sent to prison. The remainder of the ex-rebels were granted amnesty, but we do not know if they were dispatched back to the plantations they had razed. It seems more likely they were sold and chained in ships' holds bound for the newer sugar plantations of Brazil.[6]

During his breathless recounting of these violent events, the same scribe who acknowledged that thousands of people on the island had called Amador "King" began to refer to him dismissively as "the False King of São Tomé." While intending to flatter his primary audience, King Philip II, as the one true ruler of all Iberian possessions, the official may have protested too much. After recounting the revolt that ended with Amador's gruesome execution, he concluded with the same haunting refrain: "And with this the Island rests quiet and secure, there still remaining intact 24 or 25 sugar mills." Even Philip II was not the supreme authority of the island. The plantation was sovereign. Immediately upon regaining control of the lowlands of São Tomé, the Portuguese dedicated scarce manpower and equipment to the resumption of sugar cultivation, the repair of the mills, and the terrorizing of new shipments of captives.[7]

The rebuilding process would fail. While in 1570 the island furnished 70 percent of the sugar in Antwerp—Europe's most important market—the figure had crashed to 2 percent in the 1590s. By 1609, Portuguese officials were fondly recalling the days when the northern third of the island waved its glossy leaves of sugarcane at the sun, and "500 or 600" captives arrived from Congo and Angola every month to labor and die at the "many sugar mills" dotting the deforested coastal plain. The colonists awoke from their dream of lucrative plantations to find churches in ashes and molasses cauldrons rusting in the grass. Sugar, the real false king, the sickly sweet sacrament, had brought São Tomé to catastrophe—but not before it had brought such riches that European elites had already begun the plantation cycle in the conquered Americas. By 1600, 86 percent of the sugar in Antwerp came from Brazil. São Tomé witnessed the first plantation boom and the first plantation ruin in the history of the world.[8]

After the decline of their sugar industry, São Tomé merchants and planters began to redirect their more short-distance slave trade to the

Americas. They transformed the island into the major seventeenth-century stopover point for slave ships beginning the journey to the Americas. Those same merchants and planters were also heavily involved in the first Portuguese incursions into mainland Central Africa, which resulted in the establishment of the colony of Angola in 1575—a key lever for the slave trade's growth. One Portuguese official enthused in 1591 that, even though sugar production on São Tomé was in decline, the Angolan slave trade "would not wear out until the end of the world, because the land is so populated."[9]

The promise of an infinite supply of captives gave Portuguese merchants reason and ability to do something unusual for the time: to concern themselves with the making of goods. Early modern men of commerce rarely did this, but on São Tomé the Portuguese saw a new kind of potential in industrializing agriculture on the basis of racial slavery and conquered land. They saw the plantation system as a new machine for producing wealth by pricking the desires of European consumers, and this entry of merchant capital into the hurly-burly of tropical agriculture was fateful. The plantation offered something much more sustainable than wealth coming from a silver mine—the other engine of European empire in the early modern world. Each coin newly minted reduced the value of the silver already in circulation. The more you made, the less it was worth. By contrast, planters could always seek out new sources of land, and they would never run out of cheap labor. Because the consumers' appetite they promised to satisfy was also bottomless, they could grow the system indefinitely without confronting diminishing returns.

So influential was the "false king" of sugar in the seventeenth century that wars between Protestant and Catholic forces in Europe often became a struggle over plantations in the Americas. A nine-year conflict between the Dutch and Portuguese over the sugar zone of northeastern Brazil was mirrored by their brutal struggle for control of the slave trade in Angola. For the Portuguese, the Dutch capture of the Central African port city of Luanda in 1643 threatened the whole system. As the governor-general of Brazil lamented to the king, "Angola, milord, is completely lost, and without it Your Majesty does not have Brazil, because settlers will lose heart without slaves for the sugar mills." This was probably the first transoceanic conflict over a commodity in the history of modern capitalism, and it highlighted the links between the New World plantation and slave-trading forts of the African coast. Policymakers were well aware that one could not exist without the other.[10]

To regain their burgeoning slave-sugar empire in 1648, Portuguese warships attacked the Dutch-run plantation colony of Pernambuco in Brazil. As historian Geoffrey Parker writes, they "burned so many plantations . . . that the province lost forever its position as the colony's leading exporter of sugar." But new frontiers beckoned. The cessation of sugar shipments out of Brazil provided an unparalleled opportunity for ambitious planters in the new British possession of Barbados.[11]

INTRODUCTION

This Grand Consumer

Over the last few decades, our understandings of slavery, race, capitalism, and modernity have been transformed by the work of many talented scholars. We have learned a great deal about the struggles and victories of the enslaved, as well as the lives of enslavers, and about the histories of major commodities made on plantations. But the plantation itself has received less attention. In fact, it has been thirty-five years since the last full-length study of the New World plantation system was published. *In the Shadow of the Great House* offers an explanation of what the plantation was, where it came from, and how it has changed over time, to help readers understand why plantations not only haunt our history, but inhabit our present as well.[1]

The plantation is still associated, all too frequently and casually, with the distant past. In the summer of 2019, several online reviews written by visitors to Southern plantation sites went viral. In these posts, white tourists hoping to learn about "the house and grounds" aired their resentment at being informed about the real lives of slaves and slaveholders by the guides of plantation heritage tours that have begun to offer a more honest look at their site histories. The visitors left "feeling depressed." But the tour did not lead them to swear off plantation tourism—it only deepened their ambition to admire the sparkling chandeliers and elegant foyers at other carefully preserved Great Houses of the American South.

This kind of historically amnesiac tourism did not end with the "racial reckoning" of 2020. In the summer of 2022, a new controversy erupted after Black vacationers found, openly advertised on Airbnb, several homestays that boasted of having turned former slave quarters into short-term rentals with all the modern conveniences. When entertainment lawyer and civil rights attorney Wynton Yates posted about these ads on TikTok he drew particular attention to the many comments left by satisfied guests, like the one that noted the slave cabin where they stayed was "historic but elegant." Another visitor delighted in the chance to "step into history, southern hospitality, and stay a night or two."[2]

In both cases, the tourist reviews went viral precisely because times *have* changed—because so many people found them small-minded denials of historical truth, and dismissive of the experiences of enslaved people. Cultural practices like "plantation stays" and "plantation weddings" are likely today to draw criticism, and this criticism is absolutely correct. However, critics and boosters share some problematic assumptions. Whether condemning slavery's cruelties or fawning over the genteel luxuries of the Great House, both buy into the falsehood that the plantation belongs to another era—either a dismal one that belongs in the dustbin of history, or a pristine one meriting fond remembrance. While it is certainly preferable to plantation nostalgia, the notion that plantations are a thing of the past aligns too closely with the mythology that the planters themselves constructed.

Those planters, as well as the many antebellum and postbellum writers and filmmakers who composed odes to their "way of life," peddled the idea that the plantation is a place frozen in time. That the compulsive generosity shown to visitors to the Great House proved that planters were not hustling capitalists, but closer to medieval lords, presiding over a premodern refuge from the rushing currents of modern economic life.

The survivors of their violence knew better. When the American abolitionist and former slave Frederick Douglass wrote of the Maryland plantation where he had been held as a youth, he showed that the plantation sat in the vortex of modern society. Indeed, Douglass called it a "destined vortex," because it powerfully attracted the commodities of a unified global economy toward itself. "The close-fisted stinginess that fed the poor slave on coarse corn-meal and tainted meat," Douglass wrote decades after his escape, "wholly vanished on approaching the sacred precincts of the 'Great House' itself." It looked to young Frederick, his eyes shimmering with hunger, that the whole world was but a funnel poised over the master's plate. Not only were the "Fields, forests, rivers, and seas [of Maryland] made tributary." The Great House—which Douglass called "this grand consumer"—pulled the goods of the entire planet into its orbit: "the fruits of all climes and of every description, from the hardy apples of the north to the lemon and orange of the south, culminated at this point. Here were gathered figs, raisins, almonds, and grapes from Spain, wines and brandies from France, teas of various flavor from China, and rich, aromatic coffee from Java."[3]

This was not mere journalistic description of a rich man's spread. Douglass was pointing out that modernity's cardinal values of unrestricted consumption and infinite growth came from the plantation. It exploited and starved people like him to produce the profits that allowed the Great House to suck in the wealth of the world. Indeed, the slave plantation was not just a remarkably formidable producer—it was a consumer unlike any seen before. Ruthlessly mining the soil, the forest, and the worker's body, fully expecting to destroy the resources of one place and move someplace else so as to serve up ever cheaper and more abundant luxuries to consumers—plantations were the earliest and purest examples of all these destructive fantasies of capitalism. The dream of a bottomless supply of cheap labor matched with ever-expanding consumer desire was and is the essence of the plantation.

The plantation started in São Tomé and laid deep roots in Brazil and the Caribbean. During the eighteenth century, these locales, and not the future United States, were on the cutting edge of plantation developments. The British and French West Indies were far more important economically than mainland colonies in North America. Brazil was the destination of several million slaves over the length of the transatlantic slave trade, compared to fewer than four hundred thousand for the United States.[4] The histories of Latin America and the Caribbean indicate that the United States has not been exceptional with regard to its history of plantation slavery. Until the early nineteenth century, in fact, these places mattered more to European powers.

However, the plantation reached its most powerful expression in the antebellum U.S. South. Overseen not by colonial subjects, but by fully enfranchised citizen-planters who occupied the most important seats of federal power, this is where and when it became fully imbricated with a modern, industrializing, and expansionist nation-state. The antebellum cotton plantation Southern planters made with the help of an activist federal government as well as Northeastern merchants and bankers was the apotheosis of the form, a development without which the British Industrial Revolution and hence global capitalism would have had to unfold quite differently. If it would have been possible at all is debatable.

The North American plantation was a key partner for an emerging global hegemon. This partnership, while challenged by antislavery political interests within the United States, facilitated an unprecedented continental spread of the plantation from the Chesapeake Bay to the Rio Brazos in East Texas, nearly making its way into the new state of California in 1850. Though the alliance between the nation and the slavery-based plantation fractured in 1861, the plantation was revived—in a new form—after the cataclysm of the Civil War, thus securing its place in an era of global capitalism shaped by American power.

Across the span of what *Time* magazine founder Henry Luce

famously called "the American Century," U.S.-based conglomerates like the Sugar Trust, nonprofits like the Rockefeller Foundation, and government agencies like the Department of Agriculture laid out the steps for economic development elsewhere in the world. This book shows that they consistently put the plantation approach to agriculture at the center of their foreign investments as well as their economic development programs. The American-led globalization of the plantation continued after the end of the Cold War. For these reasons, while it has seized various regions around the globe, and other empires and nation-states have built their economies around plantation capitalism, to grasp its evolution and persistence requires telling it as an American story.

In the Shadow of the Great House shows how the plantation sparked the development of slavery and the slave trade in the sixteenth through nineteenth centuries, and then survived the destruction of both, retaining its central place in American capitalism on the basis of new forms of racialized labor exploitation in the late nineteenth and twentieth centuries. This book explains why we are still wrestling with not only the legacies of the plantation but its continuing influence over American life.

In our current moment, the vast majority of agricultural products are made on large-scale, monocrop, centrally managed megafarms geared to world markets. One could reasonably argue that *all* agriculture is plantation agriculture. Indeed, capitalism's tendency toward the plantationizing of agriculture in general is one of the arguments of this book. However, such a definition risks being so broad as to lose all meaning. The plantation, as I see it, represents a more specific convergence of forces.

The plantation:[5]

1. Is a frontier-conquering technology, where land and resources like water, soil, and lumber are still considered "part of nature" and can thus be appropriated at little cost.
2. Is highly specialized. It produces one or two goods for long-

distance exchange, typically a commodity crop that is fungible, easily securitized, universally exchangeable, i.e., money-like.

3. Is premised on an ever-expanding consumer market that allows it to function at a large scale. The planter's desire to exploit gang labor on large, uninterrupted fields, whenever and wherever possible, leaves a characteristic footprint on the land.

4. Calls for centralized management, because the planter is coordinating the labor of dozens, sometimes hundreds or even thousands of people, as well as a complicated set of ecological and economic variables.

5. Is a vast ecological simplifier, clearing the land of old-growth trees needed for fuel, pushing out less profitable crops that otherwise competed for laborers' attention, and tending overall toward the ideal of the soil as a pristine, lifeless place dedicated exclusively to nurturing the main commodity.

6. Is not just a producer, but a consumer. Due to its high degree of specialization and the large scale on which it operates, the plantation draws massive amounts of labor, capital, and goods like shoes, hoes, plows, meat, and fertilizer into its orbit.

7. Depends on worldwide market forces for the essential materials it needs, as well as for the pricing and consumption of the things it makes. Linked by sinews of empire, as well as forces of supply and demand, the plantation's particular style powerfully reshapes distant places.

8. Is usually built on the ruins of previous plantation crashes— often quite directly by planters moving from a declining plantation region to a new frontier.

9. Exploits a racialized labor force with an inferior legal status to that of fully enfranchised subjects or citizens. Outright enslavement was the worst—but not the only—form of racialized legal subjugation planters have used to marshal labor and keep it cheap.

10. Both depends on and struggles to contain a dissenting way of life crafted by the enslaved and other workers forced to

live within a space designed for the pleasure of others. What I call the "antiplantation" both holds the plantation together and threatens its destruction. While often taking the form of uprisings, the antiplantation was deeper than that. It was the crafting and maintaining of a whole oppositional view of life, a counterculture that questioned the system of values undergirding the plantation. Plantation workers—whether enslaved or nominally "free"—planted, harvested, repaired, raised children, worshipped, and traded goods in ways more accepting of needs and limits, while planters pushed the labor, the land, and the livestock to exhaustion.

In recent years, economic historians have argued, fairly convincingly, that antebellum plantations failed to create stable, broad-based economic growth in the South, as well as in other parts of the world. Planters too often failed to cultivate the same fields for long periods of time—instead they practiced a "skimming" husbandry always requiring them to relocate and leave ruined soils behind. Sparse cities and towns, underdeveloped transport networks, a lack of industry, education, and democracy, along with widespread poverty and ill health outside the planter elite—such were the shameful marks of the plantation's failure. Those economists diagnose the failures correctly, but rarely grasp the full significance of their discovery.

The ephemeral, self-annihilating essence of any individual plantation boom is not, I argue, evidence of a "noncapitalist" phenomenon. It is precisely what has given the plantation as an institution such endurance. The plantations' monopolization of resources, their narrow specialization, and their rapacious exploitation of ecological resources are precisely the traits that have made them profitable to planters and continually attractive to investors.

Plantations are precarious by design. Subsistence crises, deforestation, crop pests, slave revolt, soil decline, war, and the vagaries of consumer taste—plantation societies had no insurance against any of these, so they were either growing or dying; they had no steady state. The profits they wrestled out of the land and the labor, however, were so compelling, that the next phase of plantation building was already under way in a new locale. A bust in one place was rarely taken as a lesson in caution; instead, to the planters, merchants, and governments who benefited from long-distance trade, that crash simply opened up a space they sought to fill with another round of plantation development.

Though seen in retrospect by many as a site of torture and horror, the plantation was also the setting where dreams of growth and great wealth—of capitalism itself—found their purest expression. While this book is indebted to hundreds of specialized studies of how plantation societies functioned in different times and places, it is the first to tell it as a single story.

In the first part of the book, I explore how the plantation drove—in fact, saved—Britain's foundering colonial project in the seventeenth-century New World. Barbadian sugar plantations, highly specialized and fantastically wealthy, were "grand consumers" whose purchases supported the struggling early economies of New England and Pennsylvania. With sugar planters insisting on every moment of slaves' days being dedicated to making sugar, they imported salt cod, livestock, and lumber from New England, as well as flour from the mid-Atlantic. Because almost all physical objects in the world of the plantation were made not for use but for exchange, and their profits depended upon the import of thousands of captives per year through the Middle Passage, plantation societies and the colonies that fed them put a price tag on everything and everyone in ways that foreshadowed twentieth- and twenty-first-century capitalism. Across vast distances, the plantation has linked the pleasure of some bodies to the pain of others.

São Tomé's swift ascent and equally rapid downfall was soon replicated in the New World. Overcrowded and overexploited by the 1660s, the sugar system of Barbados sparked an exodus of enslavers. Some of the most powerful founded the new British colony of Carolina in 1672. The planters brought their draconian slave code and a burgeoning racist ideology, implanting in North American ground their expectations to make fabulous wealth on the back of enslaved Black majorities. Rice would be the first Deep South plantation crop. Carolina's planters used wealth derived from its sale in Europe to monopolize desirable land in the Lowcountry. The enslaved cooks forced to work in the Lowcountry Great Houses first made "Southern food" by adapting West African rice dishes to their new home. Enslaved "drivers" more or less ran agricultural activities on the plantations. The two groups of skilled workers were proving to be far more than simple brute labor; while their craft expertise was highly desired by enslavers, their resistance would also be formidable.

In spite of a large slave rebellion in 1739, Carolina planters clamored to spread their system to the new colony of Georgia. Established as an antislavery and anti-land-monopoly haven for poor Europeans in 1733, efforts to populate the territory with free white people did not get far. The legalization of slavery and large landholdings in 1751 proved the plantation to be a more effective means of colonial settlement than an independent yeomanry. The rapid transformation of underpopulated Georgia into a bustling export economy in the 1750s shows how the plantation was bound to spread—even into formerly unwelcoming territories.

Part 2 traces back to the early seventeenth century, showing how the plantation also saved Virginia's Jamestown Colony. The first permanent British settlement in mainland North America, Virginia was established in 1607 as a pirates' nest from which to hijack Spanish silver ships, but it came perilously close to failure in the "Starving Winter" of 1610. Tobacco changed the colony's fortunes. Europeans had adopted the smoking and snorting of the exotic Native American intoxicant in the late 1500s, and Virginia planters' shift to the crop drove the transformation of the Tidewater region from a patchwork of farming, semisedentary Indigenous empires like the Powhatans and the Nottoways into legions of English-owned tobacco plantations worked by thousands of slaves under the control of a tiny elite.

Though the story of colonial America usually begins with Virginia and only later gets to Carolina, the large, slave-driven tobacco plantations emerged in a more piecemeal fashion over the course of the seventeenth century—after Barbadian planters had developed a full-fledged system of plantation capitalism and begun implanting it in the Lowcountry. In this way and others, orienting American history around the plantation forces a reorganization of conventional narratives.

Although recent publications have claimed American history should begin with the arrival of the first enslaved Africans in 1619, the form of bondage the 1619 captives found themselves in, while far from enviable, was more an artifact of a fading past than a harbinger of the future. A religion-based form of unfreedom not so different from convict labor, enslavement before the plantation was a much more inchoate status: not lifelong, not inherited from birth, and not determined by race. It was the particular labor demands of the plantation that would transform these premodern forms of bondage into what we know as chattel slavery. Thinking in those terms, American history may properly be said to begin in 1672, with the arrival in Carolina of Barbadian sugar planter John Yeamans, along with his wife, Margaret, and the slaves Jupiter, Tony, Joane, and several others.

We tend to think of the plantation as an adjunct of slavery—with the "original sin" occupying the primary role—but the opposite has been true historically. Skin-color prejudice and labor exploitation certainly preceded the plantations, but it was New World planters insisting on a rightless, eternally available, ever-increasing source of labor who reinvented and magnified human bondage and stamped it onto a single race. The arguments today in quasi defense of American slavery—on the idea that it was no different from slavery practiced in Africa and elsewhere—founder on this shore. Slavery in the British colonies and in the United States was a distinctive practice expanded by, if not produced by, the plantation.

The place of slavery in the American Revolution has been a contentious topic in recent years, as in the dustup around the 1619 Project claiming the revolutionary struggle was rooted in the desire to "defend slavery" from British interference. I agree with the critics who point out this could not have been the case, because there were plenty of rebellious colonists who were also opposed to the institution, and more importantly because the British would not turn against slavery for another half century, but this debate has perhaps masked the ways in which the plantation was central. The plantation South was the main theater of military contest because of the economic importance and precarity of Patriot rule. Backcountry nonelite white farmers hated coastal planters and sided with the British. A slave majority population also threatened planter rule. Plantation owners as a whole exhibited almost no loyalism.

While there were strong opponents of slavery in the Patriot coalition of the 1770s, when it came to formulating the most powerful ideals and political positions of the revolutionary generation, as well as the constitutional framework of 1787, the outsize influence of Virginia tobacco planters like Jefferson, Washington, Madison, and Patrick Henry cannot be denied. Demonstrating how they were molded by their experience as plantation builders, and how they successfully imposed their values on the founding documents of our nation, part 2 argues that the American Revolution and its aftermath cannot be understood fully without plantations at the center.

Shortly after the Revolution, another anticolonial revolt took place—this one in the heartland of plantation capitalism. The French-controlled colony of Saint-Domingue was the world's dominant producer of sugar up until 1791, when the biggest slave rebellion in modern history led to the antislavery Republic of Haiti being founded in 1804. The United States refused to recognize its independence, and Jefferson maintained a trade embargo against the nation during his presidency because what he and other planters feared most of all was a viruslike spread of Black rebellion to their own shores. Contemplating "the horrors" of Saint-Domingue, Virginia planters became more uncompromising in their defense of slavery. Seeking to rid themselves of "surplus" slaves so as to forestall violent resistance, the state's planter-politicians urged a domestic slave trade on a nation that was not initially sold on the idea. The forced transport of over a million enslaved people from the Upper South to the Deep South made the cotton boom possible in the first half of the nineteenth century.

While this connection has often been acknowledged by scholars, it is less apparent that the previous booms of Virginia and the Lowcountry had formed the legal, racial, agricultural, and economic mold that would soon be stamped across the bottom half of the country. While the two centers of colonial plantation dynamism continued to expand in themselves, a process of soil erosion and diminishing returns, and a lack of available land pushed planters' sons west and into cotton, and continued mercilessly to feed men, women, and children into an overland slave trade after the abolition of the Atlantic slave trade in 1807.

Part 3 of the book begins by charting the deep interdependence of Britain's Industrial Revolution and America's Cotton Belt. The mutually reinforcing expansion of factories in England and plantations in Mississippi, rooted in consumer demand for cotton clothing, was premised on the ever-expanding footprint of the land-gobbling cotton plantation—fed by the domestic slave trade. The cotton plantation's impetus to expand led to the American Civil War because the Republican Party, while not outright abolitionist, committed itself to preventing any further expansion of slavery. To the planters who had come to depend—like all their plantation-building forebears—on constant movement to the next frontier, this was a death sentence for their society. Lincoln's election in 1860 was enough to push them into full-scale rebellion.

Plantations are a great way to make money, but they proved as fragile as ever to shifting political conditions during the Civil War. They were also ill equipped to contribute to a nation-building project amid a modern conflict. Their prominence had narrowed the Southern economy, ensuring that its white population remained small and relatively impoverished, while the society's elites focused on raw materials production and spatial expansion, damning the secessionists' efforts to failure in spite of a persistent determination to fight and the faults of a compromised military opponent.

In the early days after the Confederate surrender in 1865, the formerly enslaved were granted large amounts of former plantation territory by the U.S. government. On this land they began, much like Haitians had in the West Indies a half century before, to carve out their own forms of freedom and sustenance. In the end, this version of the antiplantation was reversed by hesitant Northern white policymakers who could not get around their own anti-Black racism. Just as problematic for newly free people: a deeply held modernizing philosophy among many Union officials of the emerging Gilded Age that associated "progress" with large holdings of land, technology, and capital. Small-scale farms focused on family autonomy seemed un-American to them because such a system did not involve modern technology or economies of scale; they produced little surplus that could be sold in global commodity circuits, and thus left little for speculators to invest in.

That Union philosophy, combined with the intransigence of Southern planters, and the guerrilla terrorism of white vigilante groups, curtailed the potential of an antiplantation world being built in the aftermath of emancipation. But the planters' postwar victory was not complete. With some exceptions, slavery was not coming back, no matter how much the white South wished it. The compromise was sharecropping. Free people got what they wanted—freedom from white supervision—even though they were incensed that the version of liberty they were forced to accept was not rooted in independent ownership of the lands they had worked without pay for generations.

This book doesn't end with what is often assumed to be the end of the plantation. Part 4 is about the plantation *after* slavery. Forms of racialized labor exploitation multiplied and modernized with the emergence of an American empire that aimed to remake plantation systems abroad. Cuba's war for independence from Spain was fought by a Black-majority Army of Liberation. American military intervention in 1898 "liberated" them, and then brought a flood of U.S. investment while attempting to force Cubans of African descent out of leadership positions. Conglomerates like Hershey's and United Fruit launched a new sugar boom in the smallholder-dominated eastern half of the island—indeed, Cuba rose to the heights of a global sugar industry after 1900. In spite of the absence of outright slavery, the other hallmarks of the plantation were not only still present, they were intensified with the help of industrial technology and colonial power: deforestation, the expropriation of formerly enslaved small farmers, plantation-to-port transport improvements, and the building of modern sugar factories in the middle of thousand-acre cane fields.

A major shift in the history of plantations becomes clear at this moment: European empires did not set the laws, and European consumers did not drive the expansion of plantations. It was now an intra–New World system under the aegis of U.S. empire. Thus, the postindependence political decisions that placed plantation slavery at the center of American economic development ensured the plantation would survive the death of slavery and the decline of European empire in the New World.

The U.S. sugar companies' conquest of Cuba was made possible by some of the largest postslavery streams of labor migration in the early twentieth century. The story of Ellis Island in these decades we know well. Less familiar are the 200,000 seasonal migrants from Haiti, and another 120,000 from the British West Indies who worked, under intense discrimination and exploitation, to provide sweetness to American consumers, including immigrants from Europe. While the "planter class" was now made up of oligopolistic corporations based in the United States, and European empires no longer called the tune, the fundamental pairing of cheap land and racialized labor with First World consumer pleasure remained in place after the end of slavery.

The plantation did not die in the American South either. It metastasized. In the fertile new grounds of the Mississippi Delta, the sharecropped plantation returned to centralized management, existing for the primary purpose of producing a single export commodity. More surprisingly, vast areas of the "Upcountry South" that had been dominated by independent white farmers before the Civil War were overtaken by a sea of white bolls. By 1900, the United States produced three times more cotton than it had in 1860.

Yet in what had been the antebellum home of the cotton plantation—Piedmont Georgia and "Black Belt" Alabama—Black resistance coupled with ecological decline forced a transformation in the agricultural system. Though sharecropping did evolve into a deeply exploitative system, in hundreds of thousands of cases tenancy was a rung that free people used to climb back into the landownership they had been denied in 1866. By 1921, there were nearly a million Black-owned small farms in the United States, the vast majority of them in the South and owned by the descendants of enslaved people. There were probably even more Black farmers who had risen out of sharecropping and worked as "standing renters." They owned their own work animals, as well as their plows and wagons. They owed rent on land, but otherwise lived independently of white landowners, successfully repelling their managerial interventions for the most part. In some of the South, in other words, the descendants of enslaved people did not let sharecropping decay into a new form of direct management. The efforts of Black rural Southerners to maintain autonomy helped drive the Old South plantation in the eastern states to an unceremonious death even before the Great Depression.

Wherever the plantation was killed, however, the resulting exodus of planters started a new plantation boom elsewhere. Following the path of Georgia cotton planters, part 4 turns to an unlikely place: California. In 1921, Piedmont Georgia planter J. G. Boswell and several of his compatriots decamped for the San Joaquin Valley. There, they made cotton the number one crop in the state, and California the number two producer of cotton in the country by midcentury. California planters pioneered the use of the automatic cotton harvester, and for two decades—and with the collusion of the U.S. Department of Labor, the INS, and Border Patrol—benefited from an international traffic in unfree labor 150 years after the end of the Atlantic slave trade, in the form of the Bracero Program.

Facing the resistance of Black farmers as well as the boll weevil, sharecropped cotton had gone bust in the Southeast by the 1920s. But even this was not the end of the plantation in the region, as Southern merchants saw the opportunity to exploit small farmers in a new way. Capitalizing on the cheap land, low wages, and antilabor legal environment the cotton plantation left behind, poultry capitalists like Perdue Farms, to this day located in the old Cotton Belt, created the system of industrial cheap meat in America. Exploiting small white landowners-become-chicken-farmers, and former Black sharecroppers as processing workers, the integrated poultry system should be seen as a phenomenon that emerged from the ashes of a plantation world after World War II.

Today, plantations are tasked with solving global warming. The final chapter of the book travels to Brazil, where U.S. firms like Cargill and the pension fund TIAA—along with multinationals like Royal Dutch Shell and British Petroleum—have made themselves the largest sugar planters in history. Investing heavily in ethanol-based "alternative fuels," the firms have bought up vast amounts of grassland in Brazil and built huge sugar- and ethanol-processing refineries in the countryside. Thus, some of the same firms that have spent decades worsening global warming while denying the troubling findings of their own scientists are now expected to save the world from climate disaster. Planters continue to exist, though now they are multinational monopolies—still squeezing productivity out of rightless, racialized masses of workers, still grabbing land, still robbing soil of its fertility, and still letting others worry about the cost of their profit-winning destruction.

For half a millennium, the workers caught up in the plantation's machinery have offered the most clear-eyed understanding of how it all worked. A seventeenth-century Barbadian slave who had joined in a rebellion against British enslavers offered a definition of the plantation that could still be used today. He accused the Englishman of having "the Devel" in him. "He makes every thing work, he makes the Negro work, the Horse work, the wood work, the Water work, and the Winde work." Not taken in by the grinding logic of the plantation—that the civilizing of a savage race justified its existence—this individual grasped the plantation as an ecological machine that drew violently into itself the manifold forces of nature and man in the service of making a single product—one that utterly failed to nourish the people forced to grow it.[6]

"The Devel"—a sort of demon possession that caused the planter to push so hard—could only have been the European merchants who lent money, the British state that ruled the seas and collected duties, and the consumers who always craved more sugar. These dark and remote forces had commandeered the rebellious man's life and turned him into a shippable commodity without ever laying eyes on him. But the distant reasons for his torment did not matter as much as the enslaving enemy he faced on a daily basis. Planters' obsession with building mills and making sugar had made his life intolerable. To right the capsized vessel of his world—just as Amador had understood in São Tomé in 1595—required destroying the plantation.

Part One

THE DITCH

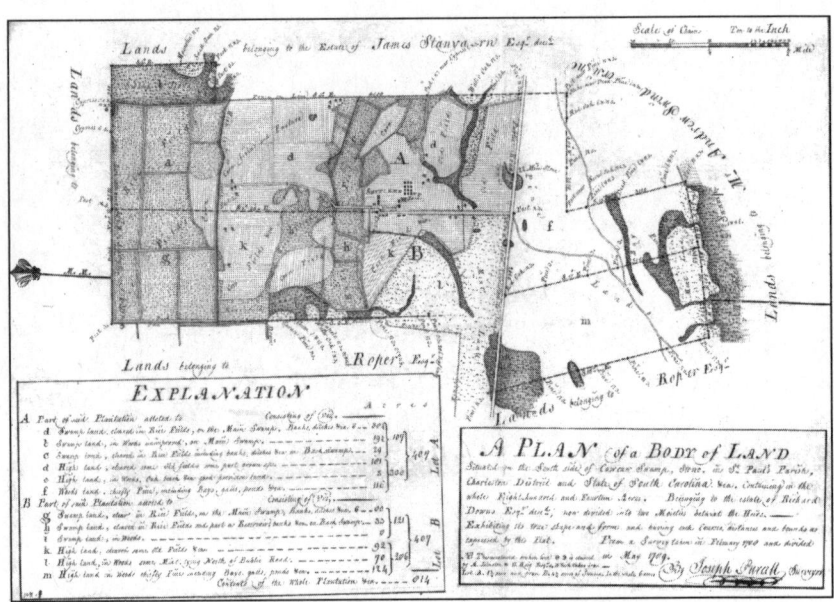

A late eighteenth-century plat showing an 814-acre rice plantation nestled between two branches of Stono Swamp in Lowcountry, South Carolina. The land undulates from left to right, with swampland turned into rice fields on the far left, upland corn fields and pastures protected by a ditch, then another strip of rice fields marked by canals. Most of the eastern half of the plantation is wooded.

CHAPTER 1

The Great Gulph

Even on his deathbed, Benjamin Berringer was not left in peace. In January 1661, as the prominent Barbadian sugar planter lay dying from a mysterious ailment, his former friend and ex–plantation business partner John Yeamans appeared at his side, entreating him to write a new will. Witnesses recalled how these urgings "somewhat offended" the dying man, who "turned to the other side of the bed." Staring for a moment at the curved back of his estranged friend, "Yeamans left him and departed the room." Yeamans's appearance may have particularly vexed Berringer because the two men had feuded over property when they had dissolved their partnership. More importantly, Berringer's wife, Margaret, had in recent years become attached to Yeamans and alienated from her husband. The marriage had been strained for some time. Berringer had become so exasperated by his wife's conduct, in fact, that he often spent the night at the house of a truer friend.[1]

Apparently, Berringer told various people in Barbados he intended to bequeath his entire estate to his family back in England, leaving

Margaret penniless. It was said the two lovers learned of this and conspired to poison Berringer before he could put his new intent in writing. Yeamans, a man of breathtaking boldness, had probably stopped by Berringer's room after the poisoning to procure a new will that would put to rest whispers about the fortune being sent back to England. Berringer expired later that day. Briefly investigated, Yeamans was soon cleared of suspicion in Berringer's death. He and Margaret waited precisely ten weeks to marry, at a quiet ceremony far from their home parish. Then the happy couple moved into Berringer's house—an elegant West Indian manse that now belonged to Yeamans.[2]

This is the stuff of an eighteenth-century English novel: a disputed will, an illicit affair, even rumors of a secret key dangling beneath the nightshirt of a doomed man. Only the stakes were immeasurably higher in this case. John Yeamans had originally gone to Barbados as one of many Royalist exiles in 1650—wealthy men fleeing the revolutionary threat of the English Civil War. He became a major slaveholder during the height of the Barbadian sugar boom in the following decade, was given the title of baronet, and sat on the island's governing council. Yet he felt hemmed in on the small island. When the Lords Proprietor of Carolina—royally connected investors in England—secured a charter from the king to settle the new colony, Yeamans brought fifty settlers with him and established a plantation in Wappoo Creek. He was the first slaveholder in the colony's history.[3]

Appointed governor of the Carolina colony in 1672, Yeamans turned his position into profit by selling desperately needed supplies to hungry English newcomers at inflated prices. The Lords Proprietor, who replaced him as governor for this offense, nevertheless paid him a grudging compliment: "If to convert all things to his present private profit be the marke of able parts," one of them quipped, "Sir John is without doubt a very judicious man." As one of the Barbadian sugar planters who spearheaded the colonization of Carolina in the 1670s, Yeamans planted his ill-gotten fortunes in early North America, along with a merciless drive for profit and the entrenched system of racial slavery that undergirded it. The early plantation in North America is hard to categorize as either a rational or a mad enterprise. It was at once haphazard and calculating. Yeamans's move from Barbados to Carolina was itself a kind of mad calculation about where the future of plantation wealth lay. He was certainly taking a risk leaving the Caribbean, which was in the midst of a plantation boom much larger than even its predecessors in São Tomé and Brazil.[4]

To make their world of sugar, however, English elites first had to push aside small white settlers who grew tobacco, corn, and other grains for trade and subsistence on the island. The capital requirements of sugar meant one needed money to make money, and gentry who had left England during the Civil War drained, improved, built, and destroyed with a degree of freedom they lacked in England. Since Spanish conquistadors had decimated the Indigenous Arawak and Kalinago peoples in the 1490s, English settlers faced no embedded occupants of the land or established legal norms or courts—far from England, the wealthy to a large extent wrote their own laws.

By 1680, a mere 7 percent of the population owned more than half the property. But a pool of labor was the most important factor in the making of England's first plantation boom. The years after 1660s restoration of monarchical power in Britain saw an expansion of the empire across British America, with new colonies in South Carolina, New Jersey, New York, and elsewhere. Three Anglo-Dutch wars, as well as a set of mercantile restrictions known as the Navigation Acts, helped Britain achieve naval supremacy in the Atlantic, commandeering the shipment of goods and becoming the dominant force in the Atlantic slave trade.[5]

Barbados, with its fabulously profitable exports of sugar, was the gravitational center of this new British Atlantic sphere. By 1680, shipments of sugar from the small Caribbean island exceeded in value all the exports from all the mainland colonies of British North America combined. Thus, it is not surprising that 80 percent of the captives shipped through the Middle Passage to all British colonies by the Royal African Company between 1660 and 1688 were sold on the small island. Totaling nearly one hundred thousand men, women, and children, this dwarfed the number of captives who arrived in Jamaica, the Chesapeake, and the Carolinas combined during the late seventeenth century. By 1680, the plantation workforce of Barbados—once a mix of convicts and indentured servants—was 95 percent enslaved.[6]

Early investors in the transoceanic market of plantation products pioneered a new capitalist strategy: While the norm had been for merchants to buy cheap in one place and sell dear in another, now they entered the sphere of production in an effort to *lower* the final price of the commodity, thereby extending the potential consumer base beyond a small elite. The intensive exploitation of enslaved people and depopulated land allowed planters to sell Barbadian muscovado at a much cheaper price than any other muscovado on the markets of London and Amsterdam. By the 1680s, as Barbados's governor observed, "There is not a foot of land in Barbados that is not employed even to the very seaside," and the payoff for a small elite was clear. While most white Barbadians, even professionals like physicians, lived in grinding poverty, the planter elite sweated their days away in sumptuous and stifling English-style mansions attended to by staffs of household slaves.[7]

However, repeated slave rebellions, rapid deforestation, the planting of every acre in sugar, and the need to feed thousands of work animals with imported grain—in other words, the intrinsic precarity of the plantation—did not escape the attention of wealthy planters like Yeamans. As early as 1652, planter Thomas Modyford conceded that "a place must be presently thought upon, where this great people will finde maintenance and employment." Modyford and his cohort would urge the British government to take the island of Jamaica from Spain by naval force, which they did in 1654. A group of Barbadian planters, Modyford included, eventually transformed the island into the next top

This map of the island of Barbados shows how plantations already crowded the southern coast in the 1650s. In the top left of the map, among the hills, the artist has rendered "maroons" being pursued.

sugar producer in the world after Barbadian production tailed off in the early 1700s.[8]

Other Barbadian planters like Yeamans took their enslaved people, their draconian slave code, and their plantation way of "converting all things to present profit" to the new British colony of Carolina in the 1670s. Émigrés from crowded Barbados first envisioned Carolina as a helpmeet of the sugar island. An export-focused monstrosity, Barbados had higher exports per capita than that of any European country, and for that reason it imported much of what it needed. Carolina settlers hoped to provide Barbados with cattle, timber, and other supplies its specialized plantations required. During the first moments of the plantation in the Deep South, then, Barbados was both direct influence and remote force. Spinning like a hurricane in the Caribbean Sea, it flushed new modes of coercion and exploitation outward, while pulling in the products of other lands and encouraging new conquests in faraway places. Thus, in the eighteenth century, the French writer Hector St. John de Crèvecoeur called the West Indian sugar islands "a Great Gulph, perpetually absorbing Men, by the Power of Elementary Heat, of Intemperance by the force of every Excess."[9]

The pull of the "Great Gulph" means plantations were never just a story of what would become the American South. Given its outsize demand on resources, Barbados provided not only Carolina, but the northern colonies, an economic lifeline in their early years. No less a figure than John Winthrop, founder and leader of the Massachusetts Bay Colony, admitted the primary role Barbados played in sustaining the economy of his hoped-for Puritan utopia. Winthrop sent his son Henry to scout the island in 1627. While Henry's own tobacco-growing venture failed, he helped set up the Massachusetts Bay Colony's first profitable export venture: selling barrels of dried mackerel, cod, and herring to planters, who rationed them out to the enslaved. In 1647, John Winthrop recalled the origins of the trade fondly: "It pleased the Lord to open to us a trade with Barbados and other islands in the West Indies, which . . . proved gainful."[10]

This Barbadian exchange was no side business—it was existential for the Puritan colony. In the 1630s, government leaders fretted considerably over Massachusetts's trade deficit with Britain, rooted in the import of manufactures like pots, pans, plows, shoes, shirts, and other things the New England settlers would not succeed in making for themselves until the American Revolution. In spite of the common image of New England's precapitalist yeoman farmers supplying their own needs, they had no choice but to pay for these imports by growing their exports. Indeed, the economic historians John McCusker and Russell Menard conclude that "the prosperity of the entire colonial period rested on the foreign sector, on exporting the produce of farm, forest, and sea." Unable to sell an adequate amount of goods in distant Europe, New Englanders sent the vast majority of exports to the West Indies.[11]

For the period from 1768 to 1772, New England's top export was salt cod, 62 percent of which went to the West Indies. Ninety-eight percent of its livestock exports, the second most important commodity shipped abroad, went to the West Indies, where the animals were used for fieldwork and as a source of meat. Eighty-eight percent of wood products harvested from the old-growth forests of New England went to the sugar islands as well. These provided not only the construction materials for mills, field and pasture fences, and residential structures, but the wooden parts for the barrels and hogsheads in which sugar products were packed. Overall, 67 percent of New England's average annual commodity exports went to the West Indies and Africa, a business worth nearly four times as much as the colony's exports to Great Britain. While early Massachusetts clearly relied on the strength of its West Indian connections, the dependency was mutual: the governor of Barbados admitted that his island "cannot in tyme of peace prosper, nor in tyme of War subsist" without supplies from New England.[12]

By the late seventeenth century, a truly interdependent system had emerged within the British Atlantic world. In 1697, Britain's Council of Trade and Plantations pointed out that "the West Indies and several provinces are almost constantly supplied with . . . bread, flour, beef, pork, etc., [from Pennsylvania] without which they could hardly subsist." The people of Pennsylvania were only able to afford "great quantities of English manufactures," the council reported, because they made basic commodities for "sugar and tobacco plantations." Supplies from Pennsylvania allowed the West Indian colonies, "being supplied with provisions at a very reasonable rate," to concentrate on sugar, a commodity from which the English state benefited handsomely.[13]

Recent historians, noting the dependence of nonplantation regions on the trade dynamism of plantation areas, have relabeled places like New England and Pennsylvania as "hinterlands of the slave economy," without which the imperial trading system would have foundered. This deep interdependence reached back to the mother country. Supplies from northern colonies enabled the plantation colonies to focus on exports to

Europe. In turn, the specialized plantation system dominated Britain's import markets. In 1701, the total recorded imports into London from all British colonies amounted to 838,814 pounds sterling; 507,396 pounds of that was sugar, while another 154,533 pounds was tobacco. Altogether, plantation products accounted for nearly 82 percent of London's colonial imports by the end of the seventeenth century.[14]

The Great Gulph of the British sugar islands, with its massive profits and its deeply specialized character, ignited colonization activities and new settlements around the Atlantic World in the colonial era. The Barbadian planters who had moved to Carolina were well aware that access to a "bottomless" supply of enslaved people kept the Caribbean colonies moving. Thus, their first export as a new colony in the 1670s was neither lumber nor rice, but people.

Even though African slavery was established in Carolina from the start, English settlers were at first more deeply engaged in a new traffic in Native American men, women, and children. With deerskins in high demand among consumers back in the mother country, English traders trying to establish trading agreements in the vast Native-controlled territory beyond Charlestown exchanged guns and ammunition for pelts. Those weapons, however, were also used to hunt human captives, whom the traders purchased from Indigenous slave-raiding nations like the Westo.

With the tacit support of the Lords Proprietor (who wanted a share of profits), English traders fomented conflict among Native societies in order to pump up the demand for weapons and to keep a steady stream of slaves flowing to Charlestown. Most of these enslaved war captives were branded on the cheek with the insignia of the merchant who had purchased them, loaded into vessels in Charlestown, and shipped to Barbados. The Native slave trade to the West Indies was controlled by men like Yeamans.[15]

The Westo, along with other groups like the Yamasee, played along, supplying the English with hundreds of Native captives because they hoped to use the European newcomers as allies in their own geopolitical rivalries. However, the introduction of firearms and alcohol, along with the mass export of slaves, began to give Europeans the upper hand. One of the Lords Proprietor had no qualms in explaining how muskets and ammunition "tyed them to soe strict a dependence upon us ... that whenever that nation ... shall misbehave themselves towards us, we shall be able, whenever we please ... to ruine them." Perhaps inspired by this attitude, English traders operating in Yamasee territory appropriated their land, slaughtered their hogs, plucked ears of corn from their fields, and gulped down watermelon Yamasee women had cultivated. On top of these slights, traders were providing rum in violation of English-Yamasee agreements. They capitalized on the resulting addiction to spread indebtedness, and simply began seizing Yamasee women and children as payment (or more likely as a way to blackmail the Yamasee into supplying more deerskins).[16]

To prevent this ruinous new dynamic from destroying them, in 1715 the Yamasee assembled the most formidable bloc of Native nations the English had yet seen in the Southeast. Warriors from Creek, Catawba, and Yamasee chiefdoms slew hundreds of colonists, burned Lowcountry plantations, and pushed terrified English refugees into Charlestown. They came close to destroying the colony for good. However, they were dependent on the colony of Virginia for ammunition to sustain the nearly three-year war—Virginia eventually cut off the supply in order to aid their English brethren. When Carolinians successfully recruited Native allies from among the Cherokee and Tuscarora, the tide turned, and the Yamasee-led coalition was forced to concede defeat.

Decades of epidemic disease and slave raiding had already created a depopulated "shatter zone" along the coast and into the interior. The Yamasee War accelerated this process, opening new territories to agricultural occupation. Flush with victory over their Native foes, and following years of bitter factional disputes within the colonial government, a new cohort of elite Carolina planters seized power. These Goose Creek men, so named for the location of their expanding rice plantations—

and where "Yeamans Hall" is today a golf course and country club—succeeded in getting the Carolina colonies placed under the direct power of the Crown, ushering the Lords Proprietor off the stage. "Crown rule" translated to settler autonomy and white solidarity. New planters armed with knowledge of rice production and optimistic about striking it rich drove the transition from a frontier economy based on the traffic in captives and deerskins to a policy of land clearance by expulsion. The Creek were pushed westward, while the Apalache and Savannah, their numbers decimated, also lost access to their former grounds. Expulsion was the opening chapter of the plantation in America.[17]

CHAPTER 2

Broken Rice

When she and her husband left Barbados in 1672, Margaret Berringer brought "8 negroes" to Carolina. Among these were a woman named "old Hannah along with her children Jupeter, litle Tony & Joane," who would have been some of the first new settlers to occupy the lands that would become the American South. Until about 1710, nearly all of Carolina's four thousand enslaved people came from the Caribbean—some brought by migrating planters, and some purchased off transatlantic ships in Bridgetown. Frightened by a 1693 slave revolt in Barbados, however, the South Carolina assembly banned the importation of slaves from the island, and later expanded the ban to include all "seasoned negroes," who were feared for their "roguery." Illicit imports surely continued, but across the eighteenth century, and especially after slave imports accelerated in the wake of the Yamasee War, around 90 percent of enslaved Carolinians were brought directly from Africa. Where exactly they came from matters, as their origin helps answer a long-standing question about who is responsible for the success of the plantation in the Deep South. That question is, who brought rice?[1]

Scholars have struggled to pinpoint the precise origin of rice in the Lowcountry region. It would not be surprising if enslaved Africans had played the primary role, as we do have direct evidence of Africans contributing to the first New World cultivation of rice in other parts of the Americas. Decades before the establishment of Carolina, white planters in Virginia were already crediting African slaves with showing them how rice could be grown. West Africans in Jamaica had also been cultivating rice since the seventeenth century.[2]

Africans were credited with introducing other important food crops to the Americas. In 1769, British Royal Society member William Watson shared his research about peanuts, which "are originally, it is presumed, of the growth of Africa, and brought from thence by the negroes . . . cultivated by them in the little parcels of land set apart for their use." As the great Black agronomist George Washington Carver would learn later, peanuts were a good source of oil and animal feed and also fit for human consumption—as well as a marginal-land crop that helped build fertility in worn-out soils.[3]

The colonial naturalist Mark Catesby, who traveled throughout the American Southeast in the early eighteenth century, claimed sorghum was "first introduced from Africa by the Negroes." The renowned Chesapeake social historian Lorena Walsh finds evidence that Africans also innovated "long fallow, hoe-and-hill culture" in the Chesapeake tobacco region. More importantly, black-eyed peas were grown by coastal African farmers and sold to slave traders. Leftovers were taken off ships in the Lowcountry, and enslaved people adapted them to their New World situation. Slaves intercropped the protein-rich legume with sorghum, while its stems and vines were used as cattle feed (hence the English word "cowpea"). Once African slaves had established it, Carolina planters began to force slaves to grow the black-eyed pea on a larger scale for export to food-poor Caribbean sugar islands. This is the most likely trajectory for rice as well.[4]

Taken from rice-cultivating regions on the Upper Guinea coast—which slave traders dubbed the Rice Coast—enslaved West African women and men immediately began growing the grass on the marginal soils of the young Carolina colony before it became a major cash crop. They did so utilizing West African rice-making skills: planting each seed in a hole impressed by the heel, then sweeping soil over it with the foot; making and utilizing the style of wooden mortar and pestle used on the Rice Coast to hull the grains; and separating chaff from grain with woven grass baskets whose style was likewise traceable to the Rice Coast. Swamp clearance, diking, hollow-log irrigation trunks, and awareness of how to manipulate tidal flows were also brought over from the mangrove swamps of Upper Guinea.[5]

While preexisting African knowledge did in fact enable newly arrived people to feed their families and the families of their new masters as well, enslaved newcomers to the Lowcountry achieved something more impressive: They adapted and transformed their expertise—in a hostile environment—to forge something new. As the historian Max Edelson writes, American-born Black people applied new tools to make the rice crop grow on "hilly, sandy, rocky, and watery lands throughout plantation America." Educated planters trying to figure out how to grow rice may have pored over texts to study models of rice cultivation from Asia and Italy, but they also watched slaves transform low-lying "wastes" into gardens and fields. Planters from England would have known how useful drained, leveled, or canaled lowlands could be, especially in tidewater zones. Nevertheless, they were entirely unfamiliar with rice cultivation—Upper Guineans were the only group of people in late seventeenth-century Carolina who knew how to put all the elements together.[6]

English settlers also had to learn how to incorporate rice into their everyday diets, since it was an exotic luxury to most. They quickly learned to use rice flour to whiten looked-down-upon maize bread, which they had been forced to begin consuming after the failure of English-style grain farming in the colonies. So the staple almost immediately was infused with Native American and African ingredients. Other culinary uses for rice began to proliferate. Food historian Jessica Harris describes the "elaborate rice kitchen" created by enslaved cooks in the Lowcountry. They developed a panoply of rice cakes, rice puddings, rice breads, and rice porridges. Hoppin' John and red rice became mainstays of wealthy white tables. They were direct offshoots of Senegambian *thiebou niébé* and *thiebou dienn*, respectively, prepared and served up by enslaved cooks.[7]

Even as rice was being transmogrified into a globally traded commodity and its masters came to consider themselves above adopting African practices, planters quietly relied on Black Carolinians to pass on their hard-won expertise in field, ditch, and kitchen to the next generations of enslaved workers. The more general knowledge of planters required the knowledge enslaved individuals wrenched from season after season of labor in the Lowcountry ground. However, it would take a new kind of white man to translate the small-scale, peasant production of rice into a plantation system that would mirror the achievements of Barbados.

Across the history of the plantation many enslavers painted themselves as judicious patriarchs of multiracial "families." They insisted the real cause of slaves' suffering was the slave trader, that unscrupulous dealer in flesh, who came around unbidden to manipulate caring masters and mistresses into selling their Black dependents. The reality is that the builders of the plantation system in the Southern colonies were often directly involved in human trafficking. After his apprenticeship to a London merchant, Henry Laurens became the biggest slave trader in colonial North America. In league with his partner, George Austin, he sold 7,800 children, women, and men on the wharves of Charleston in the 1750s alone. Laurens rose from slave dealer to rice planter, investing the profits in his first plantation along the Cooper River in 1762.[8]

Georgia's James Habersham followed a similar path. Like Laurens, he made his fortune as a merchant and sold off his trading firm to focus on expanding his plantations. Rising to powerful political office in the colony, Habersham was a fierce advocate of the plantation system, urging the opening up of the slave trade and export-based economy, while expanding his fortunes by exploiting nearly two hundred slaves across three rice plantations. This did not stop him from viewing himself as above all a philanthropist. A deeply religious man, Habersham supported a well-known Savannah orphanage and urged the evangelization of African slaves.[9]

Even if they were not directly involved in the slave trade, early rice planters were likely in the same family as a slave trader. Most of the elite planter families on the outskirts of Charleston were intermarried and first cousins by the late eighteenth century. Both Austin and Laurens were related to the Ball family, which "operated a dynasty of twenty-five different rice farms across a period of two centuries," enslaving thousands. The Balls purchased much of their land at bargain prices after the Yamasee War (in which the family patriarch Elias Ball had served as an officer). Some plots of land that fell into his hands, like a plantation on the Cooper River called Dockum, bore the names of the Indian groups who had been living there before they were violently dispossessed. The smoke from Native fires had barely dissipated when the first gang of Ball slaves tramped in with adzes and spades to begin the work of transformation.[10]

Prone to avoiding wetland areas for large-scale agriculture, English settlers first experimented with rice on higher ground but met with scant success. Then they saw slaves utilizing swampy wasteland to grow small patches of their African food crop. Drawing both on Upper Guinean mangrove swamp techniques brought by enslaved farmers through the Middle Passage and the "floating of the meadows" English precedent, planters started damming inland swamps and cultivating small amounts of rice. But planters' reading in the history of irrigated agriculture in Asia encouraged them to move closer to the sea. They began to utilize flows of fresh water pushed upriver by the movement of ocean tides to more frequently and consistently flood and drain their fields. With the help of improved rice varieties, tidal plantations yielded an average of 1,200 to 1,500 pounds of clean rice per acre, whereas inland properties only put out 600 to 1,500 pounds. New rice-processing machinery as well as shipping improvements further amplified productivity per acre and per slave. At the same time, the low grounds colonized by new rice planters were not well suited for other crops, so they came to depend more on exports of their single crop. On the frontier plantations of the former slave trader Henry Laurens, rice accounted for 98 percent of all commodity sales.[11]

The occupation of tidal marshes required prodigious earthworking, resulting in a new level of demand for labor after 1700. "It was now," planter Richard Drayton recalled, "that importations of negro slaves were made with great avidity." Each new estuarial plot needed a five-foot-high embankment separating it from the river to prevent uncontrolled tidal flooding. About three feet wide at the top, and fifteen at the foot, the embankment was pitched carefully to minimize erosion. Each of the major embankments was penetrated by a hollow-log trunk with a sluice gate that controlled the entry and egress of water to the fields. Ditches ran along the inside foot of each embankment to speed drainage. Smaller embankments had to be erected along the borders between each rice field, while a checkerboard of drainage ditches to carry water down the rows of seedlings subdivided each crop field into precisely measured squares and rectangles that could be used to quantify the work burdens of slaves. As historian Joyce Chaplin explains, "There could be little confusion or debate over a slave's task, since all units could be measured by a 105-foot surveyor's chain: a square to be hoed, 78 trenches to be dug, and so on." Planters used this system to police expenditures of effort among the enslaved.[12]

Control of the unruly marshland became central to South Carolina planters' defense of slavery. Charles Pinckney, enslaver and future delegate to the Constitutional Convention, said that "whilst there remained one acre of swamp-land in South Carolina he should raise his voice against restricting the importation of Negroes." Without slavery, the landscape would revert to a swampy wilderness devoid of profit and security. In other words, it was slavery or barbarism—the wet-or-dry logic hardened into terrifying human fact. It is no surprise that South Carolina enslavers initiated secession after the election of Abraham Lincoln in 1860—any national government that fell short of a full-throated defense of slavery threatened their entire civilization.[13]

The infrastructure of dirt erected by enslaved people in service to rice capitalism extended well beyond individual plantations. The colonial and early state governments conscripted slaves from nearby plantations to produce a network of canals and roads connecting plantations to Charleston, and via the port, to Caribbean and European rice markets. This level of transformation and control was much greater than what would be necessary in the cotton Southwest. Only the sugar regions of the Mississippi River Delta required as much infrastructural work and machinery to make a profitable export-oriented plantation.[14]

Planters faced limitations still. Fens, tidal swamps, marshes, and bogs were the shadow of plantation enterprises' neat plans: they presented opportunities for profit, but only if tamed and redirected. Otherwise, they foiled aspirations for wealth and power. In the case of tide-irrigated rice, a storm or even a strong tide could swamp the dams and inundate the fragile seedlings with brackish water. Environmental blowback was intrinsic to the system of tidal rice plantations: because digging channels upriver concentrated the flow of water, exacerbating the risk of downstream flooding, a new round of canal cutting was required, and eventually the redesign of Lowcountry rivers such as the Ogeechee into "an artificially controlled waterway that needed constant tending." This dynamic of diminishing returns would punish planters over the long term in the rice-growing Lowcountry regions.[15]

In the short term, however, they successfully acquired the political power indispensable to their freedom to build and to wreck the Lowcountry. After the Goose Creek men wrested power from the Lords Proprietor, they passed the Land Act of 1731. The act loosened restrictions on exchanges of property and established the financing of land purchases through mortgages. Mortgage debts were the first link in a more broad-based chain of credit obligations between London and the colony. With the prices of rice and indigo on the rise in the eighteenth century relative to the prices of English imports to Carolina, London investors eagerly established relationships with planters, providing credit on unusually advantageous terms.[16]

Using powers it had gained in the Glorious Revolution of 1689, Parliament established the Bank of England in 1694, which became a lender of last resort for the imperial economy. Thereafter, bills of exchange were discounted with greater ease, promissory notes and bonds were issued more regularly, and marine insurance spread the risk that long-distance trade entailed. Between 1730 and 1759, one British writer pointed out, "[No] People ... carry any commodities in, to, or from the West Indies, for so little money as the English do." Shipping efficiencies of the Western world's foremost commercial empire were refined to deal with plantation produce, and rice planters benefited. Nevertheless, they took extra steps to insulate themselves from oceanic commercial hazards, selling their rice to specialized export merchants in Charleston who in turn sold it to British commission merchants for shipment out of the colonies. Rice planters therefore did not involve themselves in the risky transatlantic trade with its longer turnaround times and frequent accidents. This was a lesson they had learned in Barbados, where the payoff for planters was much larger but where they were also mercilessly cheated by merchants who had the planters' fortunes in their hands when selling and purchasing on their behalf in faraway London.[17]

The years following the passage of the Land Act saw the first major rice boom in colonial America. Carolina's exports grew from four hundred thousand pounds in 1700 to forty-three million in 1740. The half century between the Yamasee War and the Declaration of Independence saw a twenty-five-fold increase of rice exported from the Lowcountry colonies. Planters flush with cash plowed their proceeds into more purchases of people and vice versa: Henry Laurens used proceeds from the sale of captives in Charleston to purchase Carolina rice for shipment to London, where it would be recorded, charged a duty, and readied for reexport. The same vessel would carry British manufactures to the West African coast, where they would be traded for slaves. Once Laurens's partners had filled the hold with captives, the ship would also then be loaded with Guinean rice to feed the captives on their way to North America, where they would be forced to produce more rice, to feed another round of transatlantic transactions. Rice was both the end and the means of this transatlantic circuit of pain. Laurens and his creditors organized it, taking profits off the top and reinvesting them in expanded plantation operations all the while.[18]

Although it paled in comparison to both West Indian sugar and Chesapeake tobacco, rice was the dominant export of the Lower South in the late colonial era. From 1768 to 1772, rice accounted for 55.8 percent of Lower South exports. Indigo contributed 20.4 percent of the total, while naval stores, deerskins, and lumber products each made up about 5 percent. As there was little demand for it in Britain, most of the rice was reexported to Holland, Germany, and Spain. After the Crown began allowing merchants to ship Lowcountry rice directly to the West Indies, "rice became a key export in trade between the American Lowcountry and Caribbean sugar, indigo, and cotton plantations, where it served as a central component of slave diets," though these enslaved plantation workers mostly received a damaged product called broken rice.[19]

The large, integrated plantations of the colonial Lowcountry that took shape after the Yamasee War were a radical historical discontinuity: small-scale peasant cultivation had been the norm in rice production since its early history in East Asia. The burgeoning slave trade, along with a depopulated frontier landscape within easy reach of the larger Atlantic trade routes, allowed planters to imagine a new kind of rice farming.[20]

In one sense, large plantations grew naturally out of the Lowcountry landscape. Since the "good swamp land and tideland" tended to be "concentrated rather than scattered" along the major rivers, as historian Ryan Quintana notes, a small number of elite landowners were able to monopolize rice production. Large units instead of small farms made sense because, without a strong interventionist state like in China, enslavers themselves funded and oversaw the vast landscape transformations required for tide-powered irrigation. They did so as private individuals within the limits of their own properties. That kind of earth-moving project would only be worthwhile for planters processing lots of rice. Likewise, planters who processed large quantities of grain were the only actors able to afford costly rice-pounding mills. The efficiency of these water-powered machines drove small cultivators out of business. Powerful Atlantic elites like Richard Drayton could deploy their large agglomerations of capital, land, and labor to operate in a hemispheric market that required responsiveness and flexibility, while prizing low cost and bulk shipments above all else. The rice enslavers established a thoroughly capitalist enterprise. "And the proceeds of a crop," Drayton wrote, sounding every bit the self-denying captain of industry, "instead of being spent in dissipated living, were economized to increase the exertions of the ensuing year. Hence, fortunes were rapidly made."[21]

Today, plantation heritage tours paint a picture of the plantation as a single "home place," but this is not how things worked in the Lowcountry. Running what would more accurately be described as "plantation complexes," big planters bought up as many as ten different plots of land in different parts of the region, which were fitted together into a single, carefully choreographed system that spread risk while requiring sophisticated management. The planter would keep a sumptuous townhome in Charleston; a showpiece plantation outside of town for vegetable crops, livestock, and social events; working rice grounds in more remote coastal locales; and upland tracts ready to yield lumber, indigo, and grain in the event of price declines on the Atlantic rice market. The planter's scattered properties were linked by what Max Edelson calls "an internal commerce in provisions, cloth, and commodities." Much like in Barbados, enslavers delegated daily management of the engines that produced their wealth to salaried plantation managers, who themselves oversaw the overseers and drivers. Many owners were distant from the plantation experience, including the violence.[22]

Even when they did spend time on their agricultural properties—an act of yeoman virtue for which they gave themselves no small amount of congratulation—planters rarely ventured beyond the more agreeable environs of the showpiece plantations, often within a short carriage or boat ride from Charleston. Drayton lived in what one architectural historian describes as "the most exceptional Georgian-Palladian mansion in British North America." An enslaved brickmason named Carolina had a major role in the construction of the dwelling. Perhaps because Drayton depended on the skills of Carolina and his son to build and maintain structures on several of his properties, Carolina refused to accept his enslaved status. He struck out for freedom a total of seven times, each time being caught and handed over to the Charleston Work House before being returned to Drayton. The colonial mansion he helped build, Drayton Hall, still stands, and the museum workers employed there have been national leaders in investigating and publicizing a full, honest history of their site.[23]

Within the curtained abode of their country manor, the enslaver played the part of the generous paternalist or caring mistress. In 1776, rice planter Jonathan Bryan welcomed the traveling botanist William Bartram to his "villa" eight miles upriver from Savannah. There, Bartram encountered "a very delightful situation, where are spacious gardens, furnished with variety of fruit trees and flowering shrubs." For dinner, Bryan's slaves brought in "horse loads of wild pigeons" they had hunted in the swamps, and Bartram is likely to have tucked into the roasted carcasses with gusto.[24]

Bartram soon departed Bryan's riverside idyll to continue on his botanizing sojourn into the backcountry, where the scene of hospitable and obliging slaves quickly changed. Traveling down an isolated country road, Bartram spotted a group of men coming toward him. Assuming them to be "a predatory band of Negroes," Bartram prepared to spur his horse to a gallop. His concerns were allayed when the group moved to the side to let him pass. The "chief"—probably the driver—"informed me whom they belonged to, and said they were going to man a new quarter at the West end of the bay." What kind of place would this new quarter be?[25]

Much of the plantation landscape of the Lowcountry, which was carved out of tidal mudflats or wooded riverbanks, was hardscrabble and geared to profit. Even some fabulously wealthy planters lived a spartan existence for years. A white family that owned thousands of valuable acres and probably hundreds of slaves along the Waccamaw River in the 1750s dwelled in a posthole cabin with packed-dirt floors. One can only assume that the enslaved people owned by these Dickensian misers lived far worse. Another South Carolina plantation was so exclusively driven by rice profits that it boasted a water-powered rice-pounding mill and the largest harvest in the colony while lacking "even a single structure to house the slaves" who made the plantation run.[26]

This sort of rough-hewn frontier plantation was the profit engine of colonial capitalism stripped bare of its civilizing screen. Away from the relative niceties of the Great House, planters dropped the pretense that they were paternalists creating a familial, Christian salvation as recompense for enslavement (as masters often claimed when challenged about the morality of slavery). On the rice frontier, most slaves were African-born men between the ages of twenty and forty; there were few women, children, or older folks. Their days were filled with onerous physical labor that paid for the excellent gardens and sumptuous feasts Bartram enjoyed at the "villa." On the sprawling plantation complexes, with some properties over a day of travel away, no sale was necessary to tear Black families apart. Enslaved labor was allocated around the circulatory system of planters' integrated plantations as readily as flows of water, cartloads of earth, and barrels of rice.[27]

The more important the plantation sites were economically, the less visible they were to observers. Henry Laurens boasted that his showpiece Mepkin plantation—perched "40 or 50 feet" atop the Cooper River—grew "very little rice." Meanwhile, his slaves were carving a new rice plantation, called Broughton Island, out of the wilder marshes of the lower Savannah. Laurens had not visited the site himself, but he had been informed it was "in fine order & will barring accidents produce me a great quantity of Rice next year."[28]

The showpiece plantation areas closer to Charleston did not produce capitalist-style profit margins, but they did play a key role in establishing the myth of the plantation as an idyll of culture and beauty where profits were secondary and hospitality was the golden rule. Survivor of slavery Charles Ball thus warned his readers not to be taken in by the stories written by travelers who "sojourn for a time at the residences of large planters, and partake of their hospitality and amusements." Such plantation tourists, Ball averred, "know nothing of the condition of southern slaves." To form an accurate view of Lowcountry society, such a visitor would have to "spend a year within view of the rice swamps." Had Laurens made the trip to his own rice swamp of Broughton Island,

Charles Fraser, Mepkin, the Seat of Henry Laurens *(May 1803).*

he would have passed by white neighbors nearly as suspicious of his luxurious lifestyle as Ball.[29]

The Fundamental Constitution that established the colony of Carolina in 1670 was penned in part by the great philosopher of political liberalism, John Locke. Unlike in Virginia, where chattel bondage evolved over several decades of legal and labor experimentation, it firmly established racial slavery and white supremacy from the outset. "Every Freeman of Carolina," the document stated, "shall have absolute power and authority over Negro Slaves, of what opinion or Religion soever." The same legal code that so firmly established the subjugation of Black people granted extensive privileges to whites. Generous land giveaways, tax breaks, the rudiments of representative government, and religious toleration were extended to European settlers. Even those who had begun as indentured servants received "freedom dues" at the end of their term of service, including "a set of clothes, a barrel of maize, an ax, and a hoe . . . a grant of 100 acres." This was more than leaders of the federal government could bring themselves to grant to ex-slaves after the Civil War. Locke's coupling of white liberty with Black bondage succeeded: It spurred in-migration, incentivized ongoing aggression against native landholders, and ignited the plantation system as well as the slave trade, seeming to offer opportunities to a wide array of white men.[30]

But this was only in the early days. As the plantation revolution proceeded apace, the telltale pattern of social inequality emerged in the Lowcountry. After the 1730 Land Law and rice boom, land speculation and high entry costs led to wealth concentration. The retaining dams built by elites often flooded the fields of poorer neighbors upstream. Like their predecessors in Barbados, elites justified their superior claims to the land in terms of "improvement." With an appraising eye, Richard Drayton (whose father had brought the family, along with enslaved people, from Barbados in the 1670s) cast aspersions on lesser planters who left their lands in a "sobby state." Neither adequately inundated nor well drained, sobby fields were redolent of the disorder of the swamp. Malaria-carrying mosquitoes reproduced rapidly in such zones, while weeds that competed with rice for soil nutrients and sunlight grew riotously. A man's rice grounds being "in the grass" could be a deeply personal insult to his ability to manage slaves and accumulate wealth, to manufacture order and flow out of an unwieldy and subtle landscape by force of will, agility of mind, and sheer persistence.[31]

Their lack of slave property, their failure to make planters of themselves or steward the land properly justified excluding nonslaveholding whites from the political process. South Carolina eventually became North America's paragon of antidemocracy, in spite of the perks offered to nonelite whites. The colonial leadership's commitment to consolidated plantation agriculture within a competitive world market all but necessitated their disfranchisement, although they were needed for other tasks.[32]

The colonial plantation was precarious. Settlers' land theft angered Indians, while there was only a small population of Englishmen to aid in defense; slave rebellion was a constant threat if an infrequent reality; and these societies had no peer in the eighteenth-century world in their dependence on imports for survival. The many dangers led to a militarization of society not typically associated with market economies. Elites needed nonelite white settlers to staff the militias and slave patrols for purposes of self-defense. Some white liberties emerged from that balance of power. But these were the Herrenvolk freedoms of a settler society, not the enfranchisement of citizens in a republic.[33]

It is tempting to paint men like the Barbadian transplant John Yeamans as sadists and buffoons. They could certainly be both of those, but if that was *all* they had been, the United States would not have had to fight a costly, bloody, drawn-out war to defeat them. Nor would the exploitative world they made have shaped so many of our institutions and ways of life. These men were formidable, and no one knew this more certainly than the enslaved, whose own survival depended on neither overestimating nor underestimating the master class.

CHAPTER 3

People That Can Go in the Ditch

Lowcountry planters were required by the colony's slave code to have a white presence on the plantations, but finding and keeping white overseers was difficult. One observer called the Carolina law requiring a white overseer for every ten slaves "a bell without a ringer," and most elite planter families, who spent much of the year in Charleston or Savannah, did not just ignore the law; they registered formal protests against it. In some ways the plantation society that emerged in the Lowcountry reflected its Caribbean origins: "In the low country," writes historian Alan Taylor, "blacks outnumbered whites by nine to one, a ratio comparable to that in Jamaica and greater than that in Barbados." How did the system hold together?[1]

Whites maintained only as much control as was necessary to keep the rice barrels floating to port. With its minuscule white population, the Lowcountry was a realm of considerable de facto autonomy for the enslaved, but this arduous norm was broken by acts of terror that made clear the planter's willingness and ability to torture his workers. A white neighbor once witnessed John Drayton shut an enslaved man inside a barrel, hammer spikes into it on all sides, and roll it down a hill. Far more gruesome punishments were also observed. Through torture, the threat of being sold away from kin, and even the widely circulated stories of cruel masters murdering slaves with impunity, white supremacy was made secure.[2]

Charles Ball offered a chilling testimony of how some enslavers maintained order. He overheard a Lowcountry overseer warning two enslaved women he had purchased how he treated runaways: "'When I overseed for Colonel Polk . . . on his rice plantation, he had two Yankee niggers that he brought from Maryland, and they were running away every day. I gave them a hundred lashes more than a dozen times; but they never quit running away, till I chained them together, with iron collars round their necks, and chained them to spades, and made them do nothing but dig ditches to drain the rice swamps. They could not run away then, unless they went together, and carried their chains and spades with them. I kept them in this way two years, and better niggers I never had. One of them died one night, and the other was never good for any thing after he lost his mate. He never ran away afterwards, but he died too, after a while.'" After he finished his sickening tale, the overseer then turned to the women "and told them that if ever they ran away, he would treat them in the same way."[3]

Planters also maintained order by establishing a hierarchy among slaves. According to Swiss immigrant leader Johann Bolzius, colonial rice planters ruled their worlds by installing "the most loyal Negroes as Negro drivers . . . and beaters," whom they gave better accommodations, more varied and healthful food, and certain protection for their loved ones. But was it primarily loyalty that qualified them, and beating that was required of them? In 1764, Henry Laurens paid four times the average price of a field hand for Samuel Massey. Surely Laurens could have purchased a violent and obedient man for less of a premium. Indeed, Massey was far more: he was a skilled builder, and he was literate. He wrote reports to Laurens on plantation operations. He oversaw the overseers and marketed goods in town on Laurens's behalf. In many ways, it was Massey who ran Laurens's sprawling rice enterprise.[4]

Laurens learned important news from his driver. During the British siege of Charleston in 1780, for example, Massey reported to Laurens that "the king troopes have been to mepkin twise in a plundering maner," adding that "they Robd Mr Roddick of his watch and a leven hundred dollars bils and Broaked open Every thing Els they found." After rifling the belongings of the ladies of the house, the eight British soldiers "whent away," but some of Laurens's slaves took the opportunity in front of them and accompanied the British. "Simon mary old Cuffe's daughter, [Augustine] and his wife and child fillis and hamlet and her 3 children Fedrick and his wife fullow prince and Binah tom savage and antelope whent of with the kings people." At another of Laurens's Lowcountry properties, "the negroes . . . most of them can hardly be purSwaided to Stay." In closing, Massey promised "to do all I can My Master for your Intrust who not lost any of the negroes from Santee as yet . . . your Ever humble Slave_Samuel Massey." Drivers were far more than muscle for the planter. They seemed to be a combination of enslaved overseer, plantation manager, informant, and agricultural adviser.[5]

When establishing new plantations, planters used the expertise of drivers like Massey to help them choose the best sites. Seeking to divvy up colonial lands fairly among his relatives, planter Elias Ball asked his slaves to point out "the best pieces of high land on the whole tract" and tell him how it used to be farmed. Another rice planter, relocating in 1766 from Carolina to the banks of the St. Johns River in East Florida, reported that his slaves "wrote several letters to their friends" back home about the fertility of the new property. "They are certain by the trial they have had," he summed up, "that the Land is good." This anxious planter risking capital in an unknown territory took the appraisals of his slaves as comfort: he read what they had written to their kin and repeated it in a letter to his own business associates.[6]

If located too close to the sea, then a rice field would be at too much risk of getting washed out by salt water in heavy weather; if too far from the sea, then the daily tidal push would not deliver enough fresh water for periodic flooding. To choose the correct site for dams and sluice gates, knowledge of plants was indispensable. For example, the dominance of a particular species of marsh grass over others signaled suitable salinity levels for domesticated rice, or simply the appropriate pitch of a piece of ground for easy flooding but rapid drainage.[7]

Once the plantation was in operation, Black drivers "managed the planting" in many cases. The escaped Lowcountry slave and Methodist minister Boston King recalled that his father "had the charge of the Plantation as a driver for many years." Another planter requested from his head driver Ellick "a more full account of Charles' gang," especially "how it is organized—what it has done—how Charles plays the driver." "Playing the driver" involved rousing the gang from sleep and assigning the day's tasks, settling disputes among the enslaved, reporting on the harvest's progress, and even explaining to the master how his own plantation functioned, as is apparent in the case of Ellick. With much more detailed knowledge of the surrounding countryside than area whites, drivers were tasked with the hunting down and castigation of runaways. They were often equipped with a "long shot-gun," which they brandished in the fields.[8]

New arrivals from Africa quickly figured out that they often answered to fellow slaves. In 1766, an African-born fugitive was caught and placed in the Charleston workhouse. When a translator was found to question the prisoner in his own language, it turned out the slave had not the least notion of his owner's name. Instead, he rattled off the names of the Black drivers under whom he worked: Robin and Scipio. Robin and Scipio were the authorities to whom he answered; the planter was a distant, even unremarkable figure. Such episodes begin to shrink the sometimes grandiose image of the plantation patriarch down to a more realistic size.[9]

Modern historians have not looked kindly on drivers. Often portrayed as sadistic traitors to their race, there is certainly evidence that, as historian Robert Paquette writes, "some drivers scourged the weak, played favorites, and sexually abused slave women." However, drivers did not just coerce and capture; they often acted as community leaders, insulating the community from the unwise or shortsighted decisions of white planters. As they aged, their detailed knowledge of not only the laboring capacities of fellow slaves, but of the land itself and the processes of producing rice and associated equipment, made them indispensable to masters, but also respected among fellow slaves. The majority of slave plantations in the American South had no white overseers. The managerial stratum of the plantation complex was Black, and those field managers, the drivers, had few alternatives once the role was foisted upon them, and refusing the role of driver would not have helped fellow captives. Most drivers seem to have done what they could to discourage planters' interventions and to mitigate the damage and the deprivations of slavery. But if they went too far in these efforts, they could be subject to punishment and replacement. It was probably not a very enviable position.[10]

Still, they had material advantages, plus some actual satisfaction in one's own competence—a rare yeoman's pleasure within the strictures of enslavement. These factors would have made the decision to rebel a difficult one. They would be willingly giving up what advantages they had in order to pursue a goal of getting free with odds of success that were vanishingly small. Instead, if conditions were bad enough, they could find smaller ways to protest. One enslaved driver was found to have been "managing the people and their work in a manner skewed from the norm only enough to reduce efficiency and yield but not enough to destroy it."[11]

Drivers stood at the head of a distinctive way of organizing labor that emerged in the Lowcountry and was known as the task system. In it, each slave was given a predetermined amount of work to do each day (say, weeding a certain number of rows in the rice field), and when they completed the job, they were free to do as they wished until the next day. This system has given rise to the inaccurate notion that slavery was more "gentle" in the Lowcountry than in the sugar islands.

Maintaining the artificial landscape required constant labor. Plantation records are replete with notes about enslaved people "ditching, hoeing, and winnowing," "cleaning out the Mill Pond, "cleaning up the 30 acre Square," and so on. This prose of the shovel and the pick captures with great specificity the tasks slaves performed, while obscuring the ache and exhaustion that accompanied such taxing work day after day, year after year. Thanks to the unceasing planning, lifting, and heaving by Black people, a quite ingenious earthen infrastructure was maintained: a graded, trenched, and gated mechanism sculpted out of packed earth, where individual plots could be flooded or drained at different times depending on the prevalence of weeds or uneven ripening times.[12]

Yet, the sprouting of weeds, the gradual slumping of earthen banks, the softening and swelling of cypress wood sluice gates were as inevitable as the brackish tides themselves. Weeds like "bull-grass ... being of singularly rapid growth," appeared almost as soon as the rice seedlings sprouted in freshly drained fields, so slaves were set to work hoeing it out from between the rows, and carefully tugging it out from among the rice seedlings without uprooting the young plants. "Should any be left," the former slave turned author John Brown noted, "the slaves are most severely flogged." Rice work was known as the most onerous of all occupations to which an American slave could be put. The planter's fear of feral nature was beaten into the backs of his slaves. In 1855, Brown, who had experienced both the world of Mississippi cotton and that of Lowcountry slavery, claimed that "more flogging, perhaps, takes place in a rice-field than any other," because the work of weeding required constant coercion. The rice planter Pierce Butler refused to purchase "cotton Negroes," preferring a hardier sort of "People that can go in the Ditch."[13]

After the earthen dams had been laid and quarters divvied out among the enslaved, their work for several days involved hoeing trenches, planting seeds in the furrows, and lightly covering them over with dirt. "When the plant is about half leg high," Brown wrote, the sluice gates were opened to flood the fields for several days, "during which time the slaves are obliged to go into these swamps, grubbing up the grass between the rows ... Men, women, and children are all employed incessantly. ... They work naked, or nearly so, sinking knee-deep into

The laboriously engineered infrastructures of dirt and water in the Lowcountry. The steam-powered threshing mill at top left would not have existed until the antebellum period. The endless shovel work is shown at left. The floodgates at bottom left and top right admit water to the fields and retain it until drainage. The fields during the flooding stage are shown at bottom right, and the drained fields ready for harvest at right.

the muck, which sends up the foulest smell and vapour." To Charles Ball, who had been sold South from Maryland, the flooded fields of the Lowcountry "appeared stagnant and sickly, and swarmed with frogs and thousands of snakes."[14]

Splashing into the water at dawn in March could be freezing. As morning brightened, however, "the sun over-head reflected back into your face from the water" struck many with "giddiness and sun-stroke." Brown also described "the ground-itch, when the flesh cracks and cankers" from being submerged too long in the dirty water. "Chiggers" were another loathsome companion. The Lowcountry insect laid eggs under the toenail, and "breeds in the flesh very fast, causing a great lump to swell up, and an unendurable irritation."[15]

When the sluice gates were opened and the fields drained after a few days, another round of more exacting weeding with the fingers ensued. Fields were flooded and drained in this way three times during the growth period of the crop, leaving enslaved people vulnerable to rheumatism, "yaws," and malarial fevers. Beyond directly work-related ailments, the population was prey to wave after wave of dysentery, typhus, and less frequently, yellow fever.[16]

In spite of its horrors, the task system did provide enslaved people a limited scope of autonomy that would not be replicated in the cotton South. The amount of work expected of groups of enslaved people was in some cases negotiated among masters, drivers, and enslaved communities on a yearly basis. Some planters approached the negotiations of the task system sincerely. In the growing season of 1767, Richard Hutson apologized to a group of slaves for the "unreasonable" amount of work he had imposed on them. They had ceased work to protest the year's hardship, and Hutson rightly calculated that a promise to bring their responsibilities back within the norm would entice many of them back from the woods.[17]

At least one modern historian has asked why a cohort of Barbadian planters who had been content with working slaves to death on sugar plantations willingly participated in the emergence of the task system, with its customary limits on slaves' working hours. Firstly, in a place where white men were scarce and unwilling to work as overseers, tasking through drivers was a more efficient mode of coercion than having to watch each slave working every day and punishing them if they slowed down. Moreover, the task was often set by the planter measuring the capacity of the fastest workers, leaving the rest to "keep pace with the nimbler hands." Finally, with the rice boom of the 1730s, planters had enough power to force enslaved people "into the swamps for more days every year and longer hours every day" over the course of the eighteenth century. The reality of the task system is that in most cases the tasks required were so onerous there was little time or energy left at the end of the day to do anything much.[18]

Sinking large amounts of capital into land purchases and cargoes of enslaved people, the planters of South Carolina moved into competitive market risk and out of the traditional "safety first" farming strategy. The planter's resulting anxiety—an American version of "the Devel" that possessed the Barbadian sugar master—was imposed upon the enslaved. Their lives were partly defined by the ordeal of white people's nervousness about their own success in an unpredictable socioeconomic world.[19]

The enslaved themselves faced more immediate threats. Starvation—if it can be called an incentive—incentivized enslaved people to "accordion time," as novelist Maxine Hong Kingston put it: to work like mad on imposed tasks, or find innovative ways to get one's allotted task finished faster, and allow one's own time to expand and decelerate. The lives of their loved ones depended on their use of ingenuity to manufacture extra time for themselves, so that the time dedicated to working for their own sustenance could then be stretched out.[20]

Enslaved people did get some staple rations, like maize, sweet potatoes, or rice middlings from masters, but these lacked variety and nutrition. Charles Ball got only corn. The plantation mistress Fanny Kemble acknowledged that, for the slaves, the midday meal is "properly so-called, for 'tis *meal* and nothing else." Drayton conceded this, explaining that "to raise something for sale" occupied the "principal attention" of planters. Therefore, "to procure provisions for family concerns . . . is only attended to, as opportunities permit. Hence, skill is chiefly observable in matters relating to primary objects, and, in secondary ones, much is left to accidental circumstances." No surprise that Drayton was the grandson of sugar planters who had come to Carolina from Barbados in 1679, since he brought the attitude that basic dietary needs were a sideline undertaking for planters. They were not farmers—farmers make food. They were planters—planters make money. Therefore, the independent garden plots maintained by the enslaved were not perks granted by generous planters, as owners were fond of claiming—they were central to the survival of enslaved people, and by extension, to the continued existence of the plantation itself.[21]

Not long after Marylander Charles Ball arrived on a Lowcountry rice plantation via the interstate slave trade, he awoke after sunrise on a Sunday to find the slave quarters, typically filled with a couple of hundred people, empty and quiet. Some would have gone to town to hire themselves out for wages. Others would be selling their produce and handicrafts in town; still others would be out in the woods tending their provision grounds. With nothing else to do, Ball accompanied a woman named Lydia to her "patch," which she and her husband had fenced off to protect from wandering animals like cows, pigs, and deer. Recruiting their neighbors to help clear forest when a new garden plot was begun, women and men also shared the labor of watering, weeding, thinning, and harvesting their food crops.[22] It would not have been out of the norm for her to invite Ball along that Sunday. Lydia had prepared for the day by packing bread and a large bucket of drinking water. They walked the mile and a half into the woods and spent the day in Lydia's clearing, tending the patch of onions, cabbages, cucumbers, melons, "and many other things."[23]

An Edisto Island rice plantation of the nineteenth century. Notice the ornamental layout of the front park, the ordered rice fields beyond, and in the distance, the wooded commons.

Women like Lydia also grew gourds that could be used as storage and drinking vessels. They gathered acorns, hickory nuts, and walnuts, and cultivated peaches and grapes. Pigs and poultry were "almost universally kept by plantation bondpeople as an integral part of the domestic economy." Pigs were earmarked by their enslaved owners and allowed to forage in the woods. Annually, when the weather turned cold, they were brought in for killing and processing. Chickens were the most common fowl in the slave quarters, but geese, ducks, pigeons, and turkeys were also kept—both for their meat and for their eggs, which were often sold in town. Roosters, hens, and other birds pecking around the yards gobbled down the juicy caterpillars and snails that otherwise preyed on slaves' garden crops.[24]

Because slave communities were provided with almost no domestic animal protein from masters, enslaved people in the Lowcountry also became expert at trapping, hunting, and fishing. As much as 90 percent of slaves' animal protein diet consisted of wild game like possum, raccoon, deer, and squirrels. Using muskets, as well as homemade traps, hooks, and nets of their own design, Black Carolinians harvested the Lowcountry fauna and created new, African-inflected recipes centered on the bountiful prey often disparaged by wealthy whites. Enslaved people also availed themselves of the turtle, mullet, and catfish in the teeming waters of the Lowcountry. They hewed single-log canoes out of cypress or yellowwood trees, raising a mast or two so as to skip briskly ahead of the breezes that flowed in and out of the marsh zones every morning and afternoon. They would have had to build up considerable familiarity with the complicated and shifting landscape, as well as the tides, the wind patterns for sailing, what to do in storms, and the prime spots for gathering oysters and sweetgrass for baskets and fishing nets.[25]

Even though they lost access to arable lands as masters discovered their potential for rice growing in the mid-eighteenth century, the topography and geology meant Lowcountry slaves had a much higher likelihood of remaining on the same grounds over generations than would slaves in tobacco or cotton areas. The Lowcountry was a far less erosion-prone landscape than other places in America where plantations were established. Slave communities divided land into individual, family, or household plots, carefully husbanding them down the generations. On Lowcountry barrier islands like Cumberland, families enclosed their half-acre plots with small fences. On the mainland, meanwhile, their "private fields" could stretch to more than five acres.[26]

Although the work regime and disease environment were so severe, and the gender ratio so imbalanced, that the population did not become self-sustaining until the second half of the eighteenth century, there was a feeling of permanence for the enslaved community—though it had little to do with the "plantation home" or the enslavers' self-serving notion of a "plantation family." In fact, planters were pushing the slave communities farther and farther away from the Great Houses over the course of the eighteenth century. By the time of the American Revolution, the two halves of the master's "family" lived miles apart, and were even more distant at times, given that many wealthy whites spent much of the year in Charleston or Savannah. The malaria-prone, low-lying areas given over to the slaves were vulnerable to flooding. Drayton reported a spring flood on the Santee River in 1796, during which "some of the negro houses, of the lower plantations . . . were torn up, and were carried by the torrent entirely out to sea." In spite of such dangers, slaves' stark residential segregation from the familial, culinary, and religious life of white Carolinians, along with a constant flow of new captives into Carolina and Georgia, helped create a Lowcountry Black culture that was markedly West African.[27]

Several West and Central West African plants entered the American lexicon carrying the Old World names spoken by the "founding gardeners" who sowed them in the Lowcountry. The Bantu *yambí* evolved into the yam of the Lowcountry and *ñame* in the Spanish Caribbean. The crunchy, slimy seedpod known in Kongo as *okro* became okra, and *kapoke* was Americanized into pokeweed. Embodying the dictum that man cannot live by bread alone, enslaved people turned provision grounds, cabin hearths, and outdoor firepits into arenas of creative expression. They developed new dishes that drew strongly on African traditions. Unfortunately, delicious new recipes like veal and okra soup and Hoppin' John were typically cooked for the planter's family. Cooking that the enslaved enjoyed was reserved for holiday feasts.[28]

The plantation landscape itself came to show traces of African influence. The well-known "swept yards" of the rural South are a tradition imported from West Africa. Kept clear of grass or weeds of any kind, stomped flat, and swept to keep dirt and dust away, these outdoor spaces lent a communal cast to daily life in the slave quarters. Washing, cooking, and music making, as well as the shared burdens and joys of childcare, mostly happened there, as indoor spaces were cramped and smoky. Yards may also have been swept to discourage snakes and other pests like rats from approaching the house. Though the shared yard in front of the cabins was kept religiously clean, behind them was a somewhat wilder-looking space.[29]

Enslaved people densely ornamented their gardens. With castaway blue bottles hung from the limb ends of wrought-iron scarecrows, they sacralized their yards to provide spiritually nourishing alternatives to the disenchanted, profit-driven, rationalized mudscapes where they were forced to spend much of their time. Aesthetically as well as economically, then, the Lowcountry was a Black diasporic space. While the gardens merely looked unkempt to most white observers, Black Carolinians husbanded a messier freedom in gardens that were lovingly maintained over generations by women, probably exhausted, scraping clamshell hoes by moonlight.

Of course, Black Carolinians' notions of "home," and of "mine," and of "ours" only lightly overlapped with the home sense of the enslaver's family. Planters mapped their landscape from a fixed center, the Great House, a promontory from which they tracked the comings and goings of grain, fruit, meat, rice, and people. Plantations bore the names of enslavers' loved ones, of peoples conquered, or of ancestral villages in England—Dockum, Mepkin, Broughton, Drayton. Enslaved people's sense of ownership over the land was equally powerful, but different from the propertied mindset of their exploiters: a grandmother's vegetable patch a half mile into the woods; a burial ground behind the old rice field; a tidal inlet where a cypress canoe hewn by one's father slapped gently against the waves; one's children held at still another place.

While hidden spaces and traces wove together the social lives of enslaved people in the Lowcountry task system, they also used nighttimes, Sunday afternoons, and other "in-between times" to their advantage. They honed craft skills, like learning to use locally abundant marsh sweetgrass to fashion baskets and fishing nets. Many mastered the Lowcountry flora to make healing poultices: planter Pierce Butler claimed that Nanny and Tenah saved him money in this way because he "never ... employed Doctors to my Negroes." The enslaved preacher Boston King's mother also had elevated status and importance. As King recalled, she "was employed chiefly in attending upon those who were sick, having some knowledge of the virtue of herbs, which she learned from the Indians. She likewise had the care of making the people's clothes." Masters sometimes boasted of an enslaved woman's prowess in fowl roasting, bread baking, or keeping the dairy in working order and the cows healthy.[30]

Sometimes enslaved Black women translated these hard-won skills into business ventures. Commonly referred to by whites as "cake wenches," they were the near-exclusive providers of baked sweets in Savannah. As historian Betty Wood writes, "By the early 19th century the mayor and aldermen of Savannah might be claiming that it was they who ran the city's public market, but in fact it was enslaved urban vendors acting in concert with plantation bondpeople and rivermen who organized and controlled it." Enslaved women first gained a place there by selling their master's goods at his behest, but they always trucked on their own account as well, and many came without the master's approval to engage in commerce that was entirely independent.[31]

Whites fearful of Black predominance in the urban marketplace demanded the state's protection. Georgia's slave law dictated that Black people should be restricted from learning any craft save that of the cooper (apparently the need for rice barrels superseded white artisans' anxieties). After all, "since the Negroes learn all kinds of common and useful crafts, the poor [white] craftsmen cannot succeed." Black economic initiative was seen as a threat, pure and simple. It could lead to racial disorder and violent rebellion. It was also thought to encourage slaves pilfering their masters' goods. Enslaved women in particular were just too much for whites in the city's markets, as the former threatened to monopolize the foodstuff trade to the detriment of white entrepreneurs. Colonial-era attitudes that Black people were *too* market-oriented would be conveniently forgotten by later proslavery ideologues, many of whom argued that Black people required the protections of benevolent masters because they were incapable of competing with whites in a market society.[32]

Despite restrictive laws, enslaved people's personal economic activity continued, in part because planters themselves depended on it. For example, although captives often struck out for freedom in homemade canoes, masters hesitated to disallow independent boating because Black people's catching of fish and harvesting of shellfish was so central to keeping the plantation complexes fed. Henry Laurens deputized his overseers to bargain with slaves over the rice and other provisions they grew in their gardens. In return he would market the produce in Charleston on their behalf and purchase the goods individual slaves desired; these often included sugar, molasses, textiles, and ready-made clothing, and only rarely tobacco or alcohol. Many slaves grew tobacco for themselves in their gardens, and they smoked, snorted, and chewed it prodigiously, like working people everywhere. This was an internal economy that Drayton surely saw as just; enslaved people were given few other options. Sometimes, however, this realm of independence, which the planters and leaders of the Southern colonies needed and therefore only unevenly suppressed, was forcefully wrought by Black people into something else entirely.[33]

John Drayton settled on a maxim of sorts to describe a plantation ground out of control. "Withhold the hand of cultivation," he wrote, "and nature immediately causes weeds and plants to spring up again; and, in course of time, covers them with her dark retreats." For Drayton, the disorder that followed from a lax planter's inattention to the tasks of slaves created null zones on the plantation grid. For enslaved people whose extra attention and tired yet persisting hands carved out such hidden spaces, gardens and other "dark retreats" were not just instruments for reproducing the physical life of the body. Physical survival was always central, but it was never the only thing at stake. Calories deprived in one place, and accounted for someplace else, was an enslaver's way of thinking. Through their daily practices and their conversations, enslaved communities populated the value-adding, rational geography of the plantation with ancestors and other forces beyond the control of the master. Newly arrived captives from the Kongo region of Central West Africa, for example, found their "simbi" spirits living around natural springs and wells that sustained the community.[34]

Like a night-blooming Cereus flower, the dark retreats in the wooded, swampy, or fallow corners of sprawling Lowcountry plantations blossomed after sundown. Where planters discouraged their slaves from selling to strange whites, slaves simply waited for planters and their families to go to sleep and slipped out to nearby country stores and taverns whose proprietors kept night hours to host slave entrepreneurs. At these times, the dark retreats of remote provision grounds reached down hidden footpaths and shaded lanes, making contact with white-controlled spaces through illicit trading. Nighttime burials of kin provided occasion for repeopling the land with loved ones lost to the maw of slavery.[35]

The prominence of nightwork in the lives of enslaved people is hard to celebrate. It stands testament both to irrepressible will for survival, freedom, joy, pleasure, intimacy, and faith, but also to the hardness of life under slavery. Having witnessed, as well as personally experienced, physical tortures that were all too common in American slavery, John Brown still held that lack of sleep was one of the institution's worst barbarities. He insisted that the five hours' nightly respite to rice slaves was nothing more than "a broken doze." The descendants of the enslaved are owed reparations for stolen labor, stolen children, and stolen land, but also for less apparent deprivations, among them, centuries of lost sleep—not just from overwork, but from countless nights of anxiety and worry, filled not with slow, restful breathing, but with whispered plans, prayers for sustenance, and wonderings out loud about departed mothers, sons, and husbands. This lack of rest can and should be added to exposure to environmental hazards, and lack of access to medical care and food, as parts of a structural and historical unwellness that has shortened lifespans of Black folk across the generations.[36]

In spite of these limitations, the dark retreats sometimes bloomed into more permanent pockets of Black freedom. Early in the settling of Carolina, captives of the rice planters fled in great numbers into the wooded swamplands, with designs on reaching St. Augustine; they had heard they would be granted freedom there by the rival Spanish. In 1738, a group of freedom seekers perhaps numbering seventy were caught while trying to reach Florida. Carrying axes, hoes, blankets, and other necessities, they clearly had a future in mind of cultivating the land as free people, and of making themselves useful and self-supporting in a free territory.[37]

Black Carolinians also carved out new free communities in the dark retreats closer to home. As in Brazil, Jamaica, Guyana, Saint-Domingue, and other plantation societies, fugitives from slavery known as "maroons" established permanent villages in mountainous or swampy redoubts that were hard for authorities to reach. By the 1760s, a mere three decades after the start of the rice boom, British authorities already recognized one band of self-liberated Africans as the Savannah River Maroons. Fierce campaigns were mounted to crush this living Black alternative to the plantation complex. When one British expedition found a maroon village in the swamps, the village's sentries, posted on scaffolds above the murky waters, fired a couple of warning shots into the air, alerting their companions that their settlement had been discovered. By the time the slave catchers came upon the village, nobody was home, although pots of rice still burbled on the fire, and large stores of rice, tools, and blankets were found. The expeditionaries put it all to the torch.[38]

Multiple slave conspiracies were either uncovered or invented in the early years of the rice boom, a sign of intense suffering and the violation of previous norms. Planter-legislators responded with militancy, legally requiring white men to bear arms in church so as to forestall a Sunday uprising of idle slaves. The planters, outnumbered by the Africans they continued to import, did not hesitate to torture enslaved people to get them to implicate their fellows. Many innocent people were likely accused, and suffered the punishment for guilt: They were burned at the stake.

Yet there was no doubt about the actions taken on the morning of September 9, 1739, when rice plantation slaves quietly attacked a store along the Stono River, commandeering gunpowder, ammunition, and twenty muskets, and executing the two storekeepers who tried to oppose them. Led by a man named Jemmy, they proceeded up the river, not in panicked flight, but in a self-consciously public march, banners flying, drums pounding, with the goal of gathering more slaves about them and making it to freedom in Spanish Florida. From the work many of them had done on the public highways of the colony, they knew they could follow the Pons Pons Road all the way to St. Augustine. Along the way, they were joined by about a hundred freedom seekers. Together, the group destroyed half a dozen plantations and slew twenty white people, including women and children.

A white militia of equal numbers, many of them on horseback, was quickly mustered, and they successfully ambushed the rebels on the second day of the rebellion. Most of the rebels were shot on sight; many others were summarily executed in the field after surrendering. Several were disemboweled and decapitated, their heads mounted on posts at every mile of the Pons Pons Road. The survivors fled into the woods, where most were caught and killed by a massive search party in the following weeks. In a panic, legislators passed an even more repressive slave code that focused on Black property as a particularly potent threat. The new law allowed whites to commandeer slaves' small holdings of land while making it exceedingly difficult to manumit slaves. In a system built on the everyday theft of Black people's labor as well as their parenting labor, their progeny, and their health, white people went still further in perfecting the system of expropriation: legislators taking property from slaves were enjoined to donate it to indigent whites.[39]

Finally scared into reason, planter-legislators placed a prohibitively high duty on slave imports from Africa in the 1740 slave code. However, wooed by the siren song of plantation power and profits, they allowed the duties to expire four years later. Imports of children, women, and men from the African continent resumed. In fact, the panic following the violent uprising presented an opportunity for the hardy: the Ball family of rice magnates and slave traders would snatch up thousands of Lowcountry acres on the cheap from farmers spooked by the Stono rebellion. Taking the lead of bold, heedless planters like Elias Ball, ambitious English settlers were at that moment also attempting to expand the Lowcountry rice complex into the fledgling colony of Georgia.[40]

CHAPTER 4

The Apotheosis of Johann Bolzius

While South Carolina was settled by ambitious planters from Barbados, and later-established states like Alabama and Mississippi were also created by and for plantation interests, the colony of Georgia was founded by the elite English reformer James Oglethorpe as a place for the sickly and poor of England's burgeoning metropolises to eke out a better life. A man thoroughly convinced of the righteousness of his actions, Oglethorpe had roots in England's conservative gentry. He saw modernizing late eighteenth-century London as a godless den of vice, materialism, and social disorder. He and the investors gathered around him, known as the Trustees, wanted to prove that the old English ways of benevolent paternalism would produce a superior society. His example of what *not* to do was neighboring South Carolina. Neither slavery nor large landholdings would be allowed in Oglethorpe's colony. The utopian project, undertaken when both the profits and the evils of slavery and the plantation system were well known from the West Indies, attracted considerable attention from some of the leading evangelical reformers of the day.

The celebrity preacher George Whitefield spent considerable time in the young colony.[1]

Oglethorpe and the Trustees also enjoyed steadfast support from within the early white settler community, particularly groups of Swiss, German, and Irish religious dissenters. Their leader was Johann Bolzius. He urged the Trustees to ignore certain Georgia settlers who complained "that it proves quite impossible and dangerous for White People to plant and manufacture any Rice, being a Work only for Negroes, not for *European* People." The pastor told an associate back home that, "having experience of the contrary, we laugh at such a Talking." Bolzius also proved prescient, worrying aloud in a 1738 letter (only six months before Stono) that a mass of people held in miserable bondage would eventually wreak bloody revenge.[2]

However, the chorus of malignant grumblers, who soon earned the name Malcontents, grew over the 1740s. Most were not poor immigrants but "adventurers" with sufficient resources to pay their own journey and bring enough servants with them to receive the maximum land grant of five hundred acres. They were thus the largest early landholders in the fledgling colony. They had come not for philanthropy but for profit on the Barbadian or South Carolinian model. The Malcontents may have been the spokesmen of the pro-plantation movement, but they found growing support among the ex-servants and charity settlers whom Oglethorpe had brought over in the 1730s.[3]

Their leading spokesman, Patrick Tailfer, penned a lengthy diatribe in 1741 titled *A True and Historical Narrative of the Colony of Georgia in America*. He spared no venom in his attempt to poison the Trustees against Oglethorpe. Dripping with sarcasm, a flowery dedication saluted Oglethorpe for protecting Georgians from "Trade and Affluence." Tailfer also thanked Oglethorpe for securing the "Vertue of Humility" among settlers by preventing them from "procuring, or so much as seeing any *Negroes*." The satirical dedication done with, Tailfer proceeded to explain why he and his comrades were writing from Charlestown, as opposed to their home colony: Oglethorpe's tyranny had forced them to flee Georgia and "Escape to a *Land of Liberty*."[4]

Middling Englishmen without connections to royal power and wealth, the Malcontents had been complaining for years about the Trustees' restrictions on landholding, which included a power to veto any land purchases that might "engross" individual estates. The prohibition on rum, which all but eliminated any chance of settlers trading with the sugar islands, further infuriated them. Finally, without unpaid labor in the form of enslaved woodsmen and sawyers, Georgia's settlers seeking to supply the West Indies found themselves unable to compete with the low costs of Carolina's slave-harvested timber. Oglethorpe's odd fixation on silk manufacture as the anointed path to colonial plenty further vexed and puzzled many "adventurers": colonists had to plant a thousand mulberry trees for every hundred acres they were granted, although no planter had yet produced a decent yield of silk in the Lowcountry.[5]

Beneath all the clamoring about corrupt officials and the lack of a free government, against teetotaling and the mulberry requirement, the Trustees heard two demands from the Malcontents. They wanted untrammeled property rights in land and in Black people. The Malcontent crowd crowed "that they have not Liberty of getting Negroes." They would consider themselves in bondage until they had the right to enslave others. Needing to overcome the Trustees' official resistance, the Georgia Malcontents articulated the first full-fledged defense of racial slavery in North America.[6]

Tailfer claimed "White Servants" would never be the foundation for development of the Georgia colony. Whites could not withstand hoeing the fields under the sun, it being well known that Negroes' "constitutions are much stronger than white People, and the Heat no way disagreeable nor hurtful to them; but in us it created *inflammatory Fevers . . . wasting and tormenting Fluxes, most excruciating Cholicks, and Dry-Belly-Achs; Tremors, Vertigoes, palsies*, and a long Train of *painful* and *lingering nervous Distempers*; which brought on to many a Cessation both from Work and Life."[7]

There was some truth to the statement: English settlers in Georgia cultivated land in ways that promoted the growth of malaria-carrying mosquitos, and many enslaved people carried a resistance to malaria. It is also true that mortality rates among whites in the colonial Lowcountry were somewhat worse than Black, although the rates for Black people were also shockingly high: African-born slaves had only a one in three chance of surviving their first three years in the Chesapeake and the West Indies, and their odds were likely as bad in the Lowcountry. Essential biological distinctions between white and Black races, the Malcontents concluded, made African slavery natural. The growth of plantations made it necessary.[8]

While Tailfer and his fellow rambunctious Malcontents were forced to flee the colony in the early 1740s, their arguments won the day. Having run out of government funding in 1750, and seeing few alternatives, Georgia's leaders conceded to colonists the unlimited buying and selling of land. Not coincidentally, the Trustees legalized slaveholding one month later. The former philanthropists insisted they would limit the number of slaves in the colony, and grant them rights and protections unheard of in Carolina. Georgia would be a beacon of benevolent mastery. Yet this promise of control was an illusion. The old era of patrician reformers controlling events on the ground was fast drawing to a close. Oglethorpe had left the colony in frustration in 1743, hiding on his English country estate, waving away negative reports from the colony with a scowl. The Trusteeship itself ended soon after these fateful political retreats, and the colony would be run by wealthy enslavers from north of the Savannah.[9]

After 1750, a flood of Carolinian planters and slaves crossed into Georgia and remade the old debtor's paradise into the mirror of Carolina. They quickly adopted Carolina's slave code, which itself was an offshoot of the draconian code from Barbados. Oglethorpe's deepest fears were borne out. Within a matter of years, a narrow elite monopolized valuable acreage and braided the Georgia Lowcountry into the Atlantic consumer economy.[10]

Georgia's population exploded, from only two thousand people in 1750 to forty thousand souls in 1775. Nearly half those people were enslaved. A tightly knit, intermarried group of sixty planter clans owned more than half the slaves in the colony. These aggregators drove Georgia's first rice boom in the 1750s, when British armies during the Seven Years' War purchased all the grain colonists could make. Growing demand for people to work the banks of the Savannah and Ogeechee rivers caused a spike in the slave trade. As Henry Laurens warned an aspiring planter in 1767, "It begins to be difficult to purchase good Seasoned Negroes at any tolerable cheap rate as our planters . . . rather want to buy than to sell."[11]

Like South Carolina, Georgia benefited from particularly close connections to the Caribbean that made possible its rice and timber boom in the 1760s. Savannah rice merchants engineered new networks of exchange that linked firms in London and agents in the West Indies. Half of Savannah's shipping in the late colonial period was with the sugar islands. More white Georgia settlers began buying slaves so they, too, could use them to supply cheap timber to the sugar mills of Barbados, Jamaica, and Trinidad.[12]

By the time the thirteen colonies united in defense of their liberties in 1775, Georgia had joined South Carolina to forge a new political bloc more fiercely dedicated to preserving slavery and the slave trade than even enslavers in Virginia and Maryland. The Deep South was commanded by a wealthy elite living in precarity among an enslaved majority. Connected to the markets of the West Indies, Europe, and Africa, surrounded and outnumbered by an "enemy within," the rice planters had made themselves fabulously wealthy and profoundly vulnerable. They would demand an outsize role in shaping the emerging nation. The Malcontents' demand for the "liberty of getting Negroes" would be the region's anthem in the decades to come.

Bolzius, curiously, remained in the colonies after the legalization of plantations and slavery in 1750. He is still remembered for his fervent, and increasingly out of place, antislavery views, but his patrician condescension toward his poor white parishioners grew bitter. He began to blame the white servants of the Trustees for early failures to design a viable colony without slavery, calling them "disloyal, unreasonable, and lazy." By 1751, he had strayed from his original antislavery vision of virtuous colonization. He argued instead, along Malcontent lines, that slavery was the foundation of economic competitiveness: rice was clearly the way to make the colony rich, and it "is planted to great advantage by those who have Negroes." Slaves' perceived needlessness meant feeding and clothing them was much less expensive than doing the same for white servants. "The benefit from their work is great," asserted Bolzius of slaves, "and their yearly upkeep costs very little." Costs of production could be even further reduced with this anti-Black ideology in operation.[13]

Bolzius seemed to see double: on the one hand, "Eternal slavery to them as to all people is an unbearable yoke." Yet, "eternal slavery," he says several pages later in the same report, "of course is required for the safety of the country." Even this dedicated religious leader, who tirelessly though sometimes grumblingly led his flock in the backwoods for thirty years, swallowed the myth and was transformed by the ideology of Black surplus at the heart of the plantation. Whereas in 1738 the specter of slave rebellion was a reason to disallow slavery in Georgia, slavery had perversely become the main insurance against slave rebellion. His reasoning had been twisted. It was at the same time shot through with a new sense of exhilarating possibility. He bowed to the heedless ambition of the Malcontents, who came on the scene at the time of the Stono Rebellion, unfazed and eager to replicate Carolina's dubious achievements. But it wasn't just a movement of the greedy. Georgia was pushed to plantationize by competition with Carolina's low-cost plantation system. They were shut out of lucrative West Indian timber markets by the lack of access to slave labor. Moreover, a high rate of profit was necessitated by the high price of European imports. "Here people do not care for a small profit," Bolzius observed, "but occupy themselves with work which brings in much, since clothing and European goods and many other things are very expensive."[14]

To survive, enslaved communities had to step into the deathly breach opened by the theory of Black needlessness. Sometimes, they fought back with violent resistance. More often, they tried to close the gap with night work, ingenuity, and cooperation among themselves. When Charles Ball was sold to the Lowcountry, he was torn from his loved ones in Maryland. Quartered with a family of strangers in his strange new home, Ball proposed sharing his earnings and his allowances of corn in return for "a portion of the proceeds of their patch." From the moment when the mother of the family, a woman named Dinah, accepted Ball's offer, the group "constituted one community." Indeed, Ball loyally described Dinah as "the head of our family." Such kin-making, Ball knew, was essential to survival. But it was always provisional under the forced movements imposed by the plantation's rule. He added the disclaimer that he was a member of the family only "as long as I remained among the field hands on this plantation." In spite of its severe limitations under the plantation regime, enslaved people crafted a counterculture of American freedom under the noses of enslavers who guarded a much different notion of liberty. Black freedom was not a scarce resource to be monopolized, Ball's story suggested, but a living practice to be joined with. For most prisoners of the plantation, "getting free" would mean claiming kin, repairing soil, and mending garments. It meant the freedom to be safe from harm, and to sleep in more than the "broken doze" of the task system.[15]

When it came to middling and wealthy newcomers from the British Isles, a theory of white deficit seemed to hold true: not only did laws protect white craftsmen from Black competition, but in Georgia, meat, flour, corn, beans, and farm implements "are given to every colonist until he can take care of himself." The Malcontents felt they were owed something. What they were given always fell short of what they then felt entitled to take. The history of whiteness in America has always been bound up with such malcontents: anything short of complete liberty was slavery, and white liberty often meant the right to dominate others, to push, punish, and choke with impunity. Whiteness is a scarcity model: he who makes the mistake of sharing freedoms is doomed to lose them. First articulated in its baldest anti-Black form in the colonial Lowcountry plantation, the exclusionist vision of white liberty spread along with rice.[16]

Carolina, a product of its dominant crop, was itself the seed that germinated early western plantation expansion, in producing a second slave plantation society in Georgia. When Lowcountry planters began to grow cotton in the 1790s, the stage was set for the westward push of plantation agriculture deeper into Creek, Cherokee, and Catawba territory. The territorial ambitions of the Southwestern planters eventually brought tensions between North and South to a boiling point, but it was enslavers back in South Carolina who organized an uncompromising secessionist program in the state and throughout the Deep South in the 1850s.

Long before that, however, a separate plantation system began to emerge a few hundred miles to the north of the Savannah River. Virginia's transformation into a tobacco plantation colony would happen differently than in the Lowcountry. No group of enslaving planters imported their legal code and economic system fully formed. Rather, over the first century of colonial Virginia's existence, the plantation would evolve step-by-step—first to save the colonial project from failure, and then to make Virginia the most politically powerful and influential colony in North America—profoundly shaping the nation that would emerge in the late eighteenth century. To understand how that happened, we must start from English Virginia's initial attempts to set up a small outpost on the fringes of the Powhatan Empire in 1607.

Part Two

SCIONS

Great House as promontory, a place from which to see and be seen. An 1800 painting by Alexander Robertson and Francis Jukes of George Washington's plantation atop Mount Vernon, in Virginia.

CHAPTER 5

Counterblaste

Everybody respected me like a king.[1]

—WILLIAM BYRD II

On June 24, 1710, Betty took to the woods. The next day, her pursuers "found her hoe by the churchland." She had taken her most indispensable gardening tool when she fled. She must have had plans to continue cultivating; or perhaps she intended to defend herself if the need should arise. When Betty herself could not be found, the overseer tasked with finding her reassured her enslaver, the Virginia tobacco magnate William Byrd II: She had probably drowned in the rumbling currents of the James River, which fronted Byrd's Westover Plantation. The overseer was mistaken; she was captured alive a few days later.

To dissuade her from running away again, the overseer put "the bit" on her. The bit was an iron cage fastened on the face with a bar, like a metal tongue depressor, jammed inside the victim's mouth to hold down the tongue and prevent eating, talking, or swallowing. Holes in the face-mask allowed saliva to drip out. Byrd noted, with some surprise, that on July 1 Betty "ran away again with the [bit] on her mouth." He found this so notable that he repeated it in his journal the next day. She must have found ways to take in food and water, because she survived with the cage on her face in the woods for a week. When she was captured again on July 8, Byrd wanted to apply the bit again, but its screw was suddenly missing. Perhaps a friend or loved one of Betty's had secreted it away to spare her further torture. The same mate may have loosed her ropes on the eighth of July, for she "ran away again in the night."[2]

Clearly, the plantation had become an unlivable place for Betty. She refused to stay, regardless of the torture applied. This time Betty remained free in the Chesapeake countryside for over a month, when an enslaved man belonging to Byrd's cousin returned her to Westover. The punishments or restraints to which Betty was subjected at this time are not mentioned in the planter's diary, but he does note briefly on November 6: "The negro woman ran away again." Finally, on November 13, Byrd casually reported "all was well except a negro woman who ran away and was found dead." While he did not mention her by name, this was likely to have been Betty.[3]

Death and freedom lurked together at the margins of Betty's daily existence, beckoning her to the tree line. At some point she probably became convinced she would meet either one or the other, because she would not stay on Byrd's plantation a moment longer. The freedom or death that Betty pursued with nearly unimaginable resolve in 1710 cannot but recall to an American reader the legendary words hollered by a Virginia tobacco planter decades later, in 1776: "Give me liberty or give me death!" Patrick Henry, like Betty, looked out on his world and saw liberty and death as linked fates. Though Betty's actions and Henry's boast emerged from the same social space of the colonial tobacco plantation, Betty's freedom did not require the enslavement of others. Henry's liberty did.

Like his fellow Virginia planters Thomas Jefferson, George Mason,

George Washington, and James Madison, Henry feared emancipated Black people would run riot over white people: the new nation was to be "peopled," he warned, either "with Europeans or with Africans." And though Jefferson talked of building a nation without slavery, he was so terrified that Black freedom would bring about "the extermination of the one or the other race" that he did little to bring it about. Virginia's dominant planter-politicians, who did more in the 1770s and 1780s to shape the principles of the independent republic than the policymakers and thinkers of any other state, diverged from one another on many political issues. But on one fundamental matter all were agreed: there could be no life, liberty, and happiness for whites without Black enslavement. Henry's liberty *required* Betty's captivity. And since Betty refused that captivity, his liberty required her death.[4]

The special kind of planters' liberty the Virginia framers espoused during the American Revolution, as well as the very different freedom Betty and her descendants pursued, each sprang from the nearly two-hundred-year history of the Chesapeake plantation.

That history begins with the first group of settlers who arrived in Virginia in 1607 and claimed the land they called Jamestown—the first permanent British settlement in mainland North America. The hundred-odd settlers were overwhelmingly landed gentry. Many were also seasoned pirates. King James I had approved the original charter and investors had funded the venture with the idea of establishing a forward operating base from which English privateers could launch raids against the silver-laden ships of their Catholic enemies, the Spanish. Romantic tales of Hernán Cortés conquering the Aztec Empire nearly a century before had also raised hopes of finding gold in North America.[5]

English promoters of colonial expansion insisted they would not enact "such strange inventions in mangling, murdering, ransacking, and destroying (as did the Spaniards)." Instead, they would engage in peaceful, mutually beneficial trade with grateful Indian subjects, exchanging sophisticated European manufactures for precious metals. Fantasies of bedding grateful native women also figured prominently in the writings of sixteenth-century colonial boosters like Peter Martyr. "Bewtiful" Indian women, he informed his English readers, consider it "a great matter and an honorable thing yf they be beloved of any [Christian men]. In so much that yf they knowe any Christian man carnally, they keepe theyr faith to hym." With agreeable savages playing the roles of serf and maid, many early adventurers imagined a medieval lordship reborn in the New World. Settlers with plans such as these had little interest in cultivating the ground and fending for themselves. Quickly, they found themselves dependent for their daily survival on gifts of corn from local Indigenous people.[6]

The territory on which they had landed was controlled by Powhatan, a leader who had over the previous decades united a small coastal empire of fifteen thousand subjects at the lower ends of the James and Rappahannock rivers. As paramount chief of the region, Powhatan was expected to dispense gifts of surplus corn to tributary groups. This is precisely how Powhatan viewed his donations of corn to John Smith, the leader of the Jamestown colony. Yet, continuing English requests for food taxed his patience. As he wearily informed his subordinate chief (using the Algonkian term) in 1608, "Captain Smith, I never used anie Werowances so kindlie as your selfe; yet from you I receave the least kindesse of anie."[7]

When denied further gifts of corn, the English took to raiding Indigenous grain stores. At that point, Powhatan and his subordinate chiefs simply pulled up stakes and disappeared into the interior, abandoning their famished but lethally armed guests. Without Native assistance, the winter of 1609 nearly finished off the settlers. When they ventured out of their fort, threatening or begging Native soldiers for food, they "had nothing but mortall wounds, with clubs and arrowes," as Smith put it. In a futile effort to ward off starvation, the inhabitants of Jamestown butchered and ate one another. Smith reported the case of a man killing his wife for meat, joking darkly, "Whether shee was better roasted, boyled or carbonado'd, I know not."[8]

Of the 550 English people who had arrived in Virginia since 1607, only 100 were still living after the winter of 1609. In early 1610, the remaining colonists loaded their few belongings onto a pair of vessels to head home. Jamestown nearly was added to the list of failed colonial undertakings of the English in the Americas. But as chance would have it, a flotilla of reinforcements sailed into the bay just as they were departing. Offered aid by the aptly named Lord de la Warre, the settlers of the Virginia Company turned around and fought against Powhatan's empire over the next several years, seeking to displace his sovereignty with their own.[9]

The survival of the venture was not assured, however, until the colonists could promise returns to Virginia Company investors in London. Unlike the Puritan migrants of Massachusetts Bay, the Chesapeake settlers had been dispatched from England for the sole purpose of earning profits for their wealthy sponsors. When they failed to find gold, tobacco emerged as a likely profit-maker. In the late 1500s, a craze for smoking had spread among the courtiers of King James I. What frustrated him most was that the smoke "blasted" frequently in his face came from tobacco his subjects had purchased from the Spanish realms. The king spearheaded the Western world's first anti-smoking campaign, even penning a pamphlet in 1604 called "A Counterblaste to Tobacco," complete with expert testimony from a court physician. His opposition to tobacco, however, was short-lived.

When Jamestown settler John Rolfe brought seeds from the West Indies and began experimenting in Virginia, with nearly immediate success, James quickly embraced tobacco. He was building an empire, and he had begun to see that commodity production for export, rather than trade with Native Americans or the search for gold, promised the most revenue over the long term. The major trades of the British economy before the seventeenth century, like wool exports and an import trade in Baltic grain, had a low ceiling for growth: A given population can only consume so many pairs of pants or loaves of bread per year. Inflation quickly ate into silver profits. But "drug crops," if they could be brought within the purchasing power of wider swaths of the European populace, had no limit, and the king could tax the booming imports. He went so far as disallowing tobacco farming in England itself in order to protect a more readily taxable colonial import from Virginia.[10]

To encourage more market-minded farmers to head for the New World, the Crown-chartered Virginia Company began to allow private holding of land in Virginia. The company also initiated a system of headrights that granted to potential colonists fifty acres of land for every servant they could bring with them to Virginia for the purpose of growing tobacco. As a final incentive, would-be settlers were told they would continue to enjoy certain cherished liberties of Englishmen, such as trial by jury and representative government through a House of Burgesses.[11]

The population of Jamestown grew from 400 European souls in 1617 to 1,240 in 1622. In response to prices as high as fifteen pence per pound (prices would fall to two pence by 1640), a mania for planting tobacco had taken hold in Jamestown. "The marketplace, and streets, and all other spare places," noted one observer, "[are] planted with Tobacco." Early shipments of Chesapeake tobacco brought large profits to the Virginia Company. Settlers slowly figured out how to grow their own crops as well, mostly by adapting Indigenous farming strategies. For example, farmers took to girdling trees, as well as hilling their crops with hoes. They even began to grow their own Indian corn, though not voluntarily at first. Postfamine governor Thomas Dale passed a law requiring corn husbandry. Violating the law was a capital offense.[12]

While settlers borrowed heavily from native agricultural expertise, they denigrated Indians for their failure to "improve" the land in recognizably English ways. On a sojourn into Virginia's interior, early colonist George Percy sang the praises of the "natural" landscape: "We past through excellent ground full of Flowers of divers kinds and colours," he wrote. The area was "full of fine and beautifull Strawberries, foure times bigger and better than our in England." Without knowing it, Percy was witnessing the results of Indigenous strategies of fire-coppicing—using controlled burns to expose the forest floor to sunlight—which brought a rush of brilliant flowers and berries out of the blackened ground. Percy also noted "many great and large Medowes having excellent good pasture." While he seemed to see them as the work of God, the "Medowes" were in fact hunting grounds carefully and repeatedly manicured by controlled burns to attract grazing deer. Percy perceived Chesapeake plenty as the work of nature alone, as he "could neither see Savage nor towne" during his journey. In fact, he simply missed Native modes of improvement.[13]

Other Englishmen, more attuned to Native Americans' ecological strategies of shifting agriculture, woodland management, and expert gathering, planned to turn that work to their own benefit. "Their cleared grounds ... which are situated in the fruitfullest places of the land, shall be inhabited by us," one of them vowed. This settler openly admitted being drawn to "cleared grounds" because "the grubbing of woods was the greatest labour" the colonists had had to perform. Even when they were not directly enslaving them or stealing their corn, the English still depended on the labors and the ingenuity of Native Americans coaxing fruitfulness out of the Chesapeake Bay's rim. Those fruitful Native lands could be seized with the contradictory justification they were "unimproved": a key British concept of the early modern period that decreed property rights in land to belong to the person who transformed nature in recognizably English ways, with permanent arable fields, permanent homes and barns, and the building of hedges and fences to keep others out.[14]

In 1622, Powhatan's successor decided to rid his people's land of these aggressors once and for all. Chief Opechancanough's lightning offensive left nearly a quarter of English colonists dead. The "trecherie of the Indyans [nearly] Swep us away at once through owte the whole lande," exclaimed the colony's governor, Sir Francis Wyatt. "They have massacred in all partes above three hundred men women and Children ... spoyled and slaine Divers of our Cattell ... burnte most of the Howses we have forsaken ... also enforced us to quitt many of our Plantacons, and to unite more neerely together in fewer places."[15]

Just like the Malcontents in Georgia after the Stono Revolt of 1739, planters in colonial Virginia who could have been discouraged by the attacks were only further tempted by the profits to be made in its wake. One chastened witness of Opechancanough's war later said, "Afterwards coveting quick retornes for profitt they proceeded to new Expedicion without, att all, any regard of Meanes or Redresse of ould defaults." Far from reconsidering their policies of land theft, in other words, the Virginia settlers redoubled their efforts. Whereas previously English expansion was slowed by expectations of "gentlenesse and faire usage" toward the Indians, the colonists were now "set at liberty by the treacherous violence of the Sauvages."[16]

In response to the 1623 massacre, along with reports that the company was mismanaging its affairs, King James revoked the Virginia Company's charter in 1624, taking direct control of the colony. In an era defined by limited imperial governance, this meant in practice increased autonomy for the colonists. Virginia's charter generation of tobacco planters used their newfound "liberty" to orchestrate a brutal ten-year counterinsurgency campaign against Powhatan's people, solidifying and expanding the English presence in the Chesapeake. By "Contynuallie harrowing and burneing all their Townes in wynter," went the plan of settler John Maring, the Indians would be prevented from "settinge Corne at home." At the same time, "spoileinge their weares" (their fish traps), the English would force Powhatan's people and other Native groups to flee to the interior. By decimating the Indigenous food system on which the colonists had depended for nearly two decades, Maring concluded, "our people seacurely may follow their worke."[17]

That is exactly what English planters did. From ten thousand pounds in 1616, Chesapeake exports of tobacco climbed rapidly to about thirty million pounds in 1680. By the 1650s, tobacco had become so central to the colonial economy that most large transactions, and many small ones, used the leaf as currency. Public salaries were paid in tobacco, as were most taxes. In 1656, a man accused of filching tobacco out of a ship captain's casks and filling the hole with "bad tobacco, tobacco stalkes and dirt," was forced to stand at the door of the county courthouse in Charles City "with a paper in his hatt written in Capitall letters these words[:] Be hold and beware by my example how yee cheate and abuse tobacco already received." Tobacco and Virginia had become indissolubly linked, dominating and defining the settlement project, as did sugar in Barbados and rice in the Lowcountry. Yet the tobacco plantation was also distinct, in ways that challenge our notion of the plantation itself.[18]

The shift from subsistence agriculture to sugar monoculture in Barbados was rapid and fairly complete. In Virginia, tobacco farming never displaced other crops as completely as did sugar in the Caribbean. In the Lowcountry, rice plantations depended from the start on economies of scale, requiring a vast reservoir of labor to transform the coastal landscape into a maze of dams, ditches, pounding mills, and sluice gates. Economies of scale were less important in the Chesapeake, at least at first. Tobacco was so labor intensive that one worker could only handle a small amount, and tobacco's high value per acre and low start-up costs allowed small enterprises to be competitive in the early decades of high prices. In early colonial Virginia, in fact, a "planter" was any farmer who grew tobacco—with or without slaves, on farms of any size. A settler in the Chesapeake could set fire to a patch of woodland and put in a crop of tobacco with stumps still in the soil, sharing space with hills of Indian corn.[19]

The labor force of early tobacco plantations also differed from the larger sugar and rice operations of other colonies. While the first "twenty-odd" African slaves were sold in Virginia in 1619, tens of thousands of indentured servants formed the backbone of the tobacco labor force from the 1620s into the 1680s. On small farms, enslaved Africans worked alongside European convict laborers, indentured servants, and members of the landowner's family. There was no clear legal code to distinguish them. Even while still enslaved, they found ways to become integrated into the mainstream of colonial society through participating in churches, registering marriages legally, and suing in local courts. Most poor people in the colony were unfree in some way, and this reality bred a rough but never complete egalitarianism that would fade with the growth of plantations.

Anthony Johnson was typical of this preplantation generation of Black Virginians. Johnson entered the Jamestown Colony as a slave in 1619 under the name Antonio, but gained his freedom, changed his name, got married, began to farm on his own, and received a 250-acre headright from Virginia's colonial authorities in 1651. He became much like other wealthy men, owning his own farm and holding slaves. Small and middling planters made up the majority of tobacco growers for the first sixty years of the industry. Until that changed, slavery would remain an institution not clearly defined by race. Nor did it necessarily consign one to captivity over generations. In fact, manumission was common enough that a large community of free people of color coalesced in the early Chesapeake. As historian Ira Berlin has described, "Free blacks testified on each other's behalf, stood godparents for each other's children, loaned each other small sums, and joined together for after hours conviviality."[20]

Another feature more commonly associated with plantation economies, a cycle of booms and busts, did emerge in tobacco's early years, and this pattern ultimately led to a plantation system more in line with that soon to take shape—from different origins—in the Lowcountry. The first crash in tobacco prices occurred in 1629, and prices remained low for much of the seventeenth century. With smaller planters forced to plant more of the weed to make ends meet, tobacco shipments into London kept lurching upward, from one hundred thousand pounds by volume in 1611, to eight million pounds by volume in the 1660s. Small white men who had been encouraged to dream big were trying to grow more and more tobacco for less and less profit.[21]

In the 1670s, struggling tobacco planters in Virginia, eager for access to western lands still under Indian control, found a dubious leader to rally around in Nathaniel Bacon, a ne'er-do-well son of privilege born in England. His wealthy father had paid to have him educated at Cambridge (it took him two tries to complete his studies), even sending him on a naturalist's tour of the European continent. The young gentleman started practicing law in London in 1668. He was soon thereafter accused of defrauding a neighbor of his inheritance. The father intervened once again, now sending Nathaniel away for good. He crossed the Atlantic in 1673 and purchased a thousand-acre plantation on the banks of the James River. It probably did not hurt that his cousin was married to the powerful governor of the colony, Sir William Berkeley.[22]

Bacon arrived in Jamestown during a diplomatic breakdown between the English and a powerful Chesapeake nation, the Susquehannock. He saw his own substantial tobacco plantation reduced to ashes by a Susquehannock raid that also killed his overseer. Expecting a scorched-earth military campaign to be launched against the savages, Bacon was dumbfounded by the staid reaction of the aging Governor Berkeley. Memories of the brutal anti-Indian war in 1644 fresh in his mind, Berkeley trod carefully when it came to Indian diplomacy. However, he also used tax dollars to build himself a lavish statehouse, doling out huge swaths of land to his well-connected, bewigged friends, while the landless population grew. Bacon accused Berkeley of coddling "his protected and darling Indians," scoffing at the governor's distinction between allied and enemy tribes. He heartily proclaimed his "open and manifest aversion of all."[23]

When Berkeley declined to give him a commission to lead expeditions against Indians in 1676, Bacon took it upon himself to sow chaos in the backcountry. Using his charisma and wealth, he mustered a few hundred small planters, tenants, and landless ex-servants into a private militia. Against Berkeley's explicit orders, Bacon and his men marched to a fort held by the Occaneechee, a small but powerful chiefdom that had positioned itself as a middleman in Virginia's deerskin trade with southern Indian nations. Somehow, Bacon convinced these long-term trading partners of the colony to attack their mutual foe, the Susquehannock.

Occaneechee warriors killed most of the 150 residents of the Susquehanocks' largest town, returning with the chief's scalp and seven captured warriors. Bacon received the prisoners in camp and immediately had them executed. Then, in a chaotic nighttime dispute over spoils from the raid, Bacon's men turned their muskets upon their Occaneechee friends, mowing them down indiscriminately. Many women and children from visiting Indian tribes were shot as well. Maybe these events should have been no surprise, as the new cry of small planters and ex-servants hungry for land was: "Away with these distractions, wee will have war with all Indians . . . wee will spare none."[24]

Bacon's mob, now considered traitors by the colonial government, soon after sacked the capital city of Jamestown. Governor Berkeley fled, and it appeared the Baconites, with their murderous enthusiasm for clearing lands of Native occupants via all-out war, had prevailed. In their eagerness to gain followers, the Baconite movement even recruited enslaved African Virginians into its ranks, promising freedom in exchange for military service. However, a military contingent of one thousand soldiers was sent from England to quash the rebellion. In the meantime, Bacon died of an intestinal ailment, and order was gradually restored; lands stolen from the Pamunkey, a small chiefdom not involved in the conflict, were actually given back to them by the restored colonial government. Governor Berkeley was forced to return to England, having earned the displeasure of the king by letting the rebellion go as far as it did. He passed away before being able to plead his case to the monarch.

Over the past few decades, historians have argued that Bacon's Rebellion should be understood as a "prelude" to the American Revolution, in that it was a first salvo against colonial rule, or even as a radical social movement in which indentured servants and African slaves fought together to overthrow an entrenched elite. It is hard to square either of these interpretations with the image of patrician landlords like Nathaniel Bacon and William Byrd I (the father of the planter we met at the opening of this chapter) ransacking the plantations of their rivals and carrying out exterminationist pogroms against Virginia allies like the Pamunkey.[25]

The upheavals of 1676 are better seen as an explosion of tensions among different groups of English settlers over how best to gain access to Indian land for tobacco production. Berkeley's circle, which already had large plantations along the York and James rivers, counseled steady and slow treaty-making along with the protection of existing trade and diplomacy. Backcountry newcomers, some wealthy like Bacon, most not, insisted that the Virginia colony and Indians could not coexist. It was either us or them. Although Bacon himself had failed, the program of eradication advocated by the Baconites soon became mainstream among colonial leaders. By the end of the century, the Native population of eastern Virginia had decreased by around 85 percent, and Native peoples held precious little land.[26]

Yet it is important to see how this "best poor man's country," with all its faults—including its genocidal foreign policy—did represent a genuine democratic alternative to the plantation system. The small planters who rallied to Bacon's standard did not depend on chattel slaves, but on family labor and small numbers of indentured servants. Their farms were not monocultural; in fact, some early tobacco planters were nearly self-sufficient. While Bacon's Rebellion unmasked the Indian-hating sneer behind the "best poor man's country" idea, its democratic face also died in 1676. From that point forward, small whites would be sated with a psychological wage of increasing legal protections as well as anti-Black legislation, while their economic fortunes continued to slide.

CHAPTER 6

To Dye in Smoke

G iven the persistent downward trend of tobacco prices in the 1670s and 1680s, even large planters found it "more uncertain for a Planter to get money by consigned Tobo. than to get a prize in a lottery." Small cultivators tried to grow bigger harvests to offset low prices, but the resulting glut just worsened the problem.[1]

More notably, land taken from Native Americans was becoming more expensive. Investors with ready cash and the right political connections started buying up large new plots of land farther up the James, York, and Rappahannock rivers. They could rent these lands to tenants who would clear forest, plant orchards, and otherwise "improve" the acreage so it could be sold at a handsome profit. Enough monied men participated in such schemes that land prices rose even while tobacco prices fell, making it difficult for middling planters to amass property.

An ambitious settler and soon-to-be elite planter named William Fitzhugh was instrumental in the transfer of Tidewater farmland from Native hands to those of a small British elite after Bacon's Rebellion.

In 1681, for example, Fitzhugh was awarded the government contract to supply the militia garrison on the upper Potomac with food, arms, and other necessities. His supplies would solidify English theft of Indian land through armed deterrence. Fitzhugh was himself lieutenant-colonel of the Stafford County militia, and in that role supplied and organized the "rangers," a special body of the militia in charge of patrolling the frontier. He continually sought to settle upriver districts "for a watch & Defence agst. Indian Depredations & Excursions." Not surprisingly, perhaps, he was charged with embezzling tobacco by inflating the costs he had incurred to supply the garrison.[2]

Like John Yeamans in early Carolina, Fitzhugh was talented at "convert[ing] all things to his present private profit." An immigrant from England, he attached himself to wealthy and titled men like Lord Culpeper, a British aristocrat and former colonial governor who had been named by King Charles II a "proprietor" of large plots of Tidewater land in the 1630s. As "land agent" for Culpeper, Fitzhugh built up his own impressive portfolio of properties. In one case, he warned Culpeper against purchasing a particular plot of land, listing a number of "scruples and objections," and then tried to purchase the plot for himself.[3]

Fitzhugh was an innovator and pattern setter in colonial land speculation. Whereas lands granted but never improved were supposed to revert back to the Crown's representatives, he established a new policy as land agent for the colony: that "a man may hold 50000 or more Acres . . . without so much as actually Seating or building upon any part of it." English-style improvement of land had justified the transfer of Powhatan's empire into settlers' hands; now Fitzhugh was pronouncing that large pieces of land could be bought up and later sold without ever building a house, clearing a crop field, or anything else. He had legalized the speculation and engrossment of increasingly valuable tobacco grounds.[4]

Were it not for the rapid growth of Europe's consumption of tobacco, however, no speculation would have been possible, for it was the imagined future profits from growing tobacco that gave monetary value to

Chesapeake land. While annual tobacco consumption in England was only 0.01 pound per capita in the 1620s, it climbed to over a pound by the 1670s, and 2.30 pounds by the end of the seventeenth century. Yet, production had grown so much that tobacco prices remained low. Thus, making a profit required producing at scale, which required in turn a greater number of laborers and a greater compliance from those workers. As the secretary of Virginia argued in 1683, the "low price of tobacco requires it should bee made as cheap as possible, and that Blacks can make it cheaper than Whites." But the number of Black captives brought into the colony had never before been sufficient to replace indentured servants. The far greater economic power of the Caribbean sugar planters had drawn most slaving ships to places like Bridgetown and Port Royal first, and the less wealthy ports of the Lowcountry and the Chesapeake only after.[5]

A 1670s crisis in the Barbadian economy—which saw the failure of plantations and the exodus of many planters—forced the slave traders of the Royal African Company to look elsewhere for buyers. They began arriving in the Chesapeake with more frequency. Large planters like Fitzhugh jumped on the opportunity to purchase enslaved Africans. In 1681, he giddily informed a friend that "there are some Negro ships expected into York now every day." He feared that "before I can have notice, they'll be all dispos'd of, or at least none left but the refuse." He therefore asked his associate to "secure me, five or six, where of three or four boys, if can." The land-hungry Fitzhugh was so eager to buy enslaved people because planters had twisted the original intent of the headright system: to populate the colony with free subjects. They were now awarded headrights on the slaves they bought, to the tune of fifty acres per person. So the accumulation of human property had become tied to the monopolization of land in the colonial Tidewater.[6]

A crucial conjuncture had taken shape in the second half of the seventeenth century: Low prices and expensive land increased planters' desire for cheap labor at a time when indentures were becoming more expensive. More and more, news of life in Virginia was reaching

England. The reputation of the colonies as "a hell for the working class" discouraged the rural poor from signing on to indentures. Moreover, the slowing growth of population in late seventeenth-century Britain, along with increased opportunity for domestic employment, pushed the cost of indentured servants out of the reach of small planters.

In the late seventeenth century, as tobacco planters desperate to cut costs battened on to cheap labor aggressively, life for free people of color in Virginia, both rich and poor, got considerably more difficult. Many families were pushed down the ladder into lifelong slavery. Anthony Johnson's descendants fled to Maryland, and then farther north. Other free people of African descent moved to frontier areas, beyond the reach of the law, while some fought to defend their status in colonial courts that were increasingly unsympathetic to their plight. The rise of the centrally managed, large-scale, monocrop tobacco plantation in the Chesapeake was rapidly transforming the institution of slavery, bringing the more flexible Virginia model in line with Barbados.[7]

In a series of laws passed by Virginia's General Assembly between 1660 and 1690, legal paths out of slavery were cut off. In order to force the offspring of white masters and enslaved Black women into lifelong slavery, the lawmakers of the colony boldly inverted centuries of patriarchal English law, in which the status of the mother was immaterial. For "Negroes" only, the status of children was declared by the Assembly to follow that of the mother—if she was enslaved, so was her child, no matter who the father was. Another law reversed a traditional norm in which an individual's conversion to Christianity redeemed them from enslavement. Henceforth, the Assembly ruled, being saved by Christ was irrelevant. In a move further to equate Blackness with slavery and whiteness with freedom, the Assembly passed a law restricting masters' power to free their own slaves. Terrified by the specter of African insurrection, Virginia authorities then made Black Virginians subject to a separate, more punitive criminal code that forbade large gatherings, the bearing of arms, or leaving plantations without a pass. While white suspects were taken to Williamsburg for trial, an act for the "speedy prosecution of negroes and other slaves" stipulated they be tried in the county where their alleged offense had been committed, leaving them prey to the very individuals who held them in slavery in the first place.[8]

Tax law was even transformed to secure cheap labor for the planters. At first, only the working men on a farm were counted toward the tithe a landowner owed the parish. The law was changed to include African women because of the assumption they, too, produced economic value on the plantation. Because indentured European women continued to be untithable, and were also increasingly spared labor in the fields, the law encoded a biological and economic difference between English and African people for the first time. Black women—now synonymous with slave women—were used to define white female domesticity by presenting to the public eye everything it was not. Regardless of sex, Blackness produced value in the fields and should therefore be taxed. Indenture contracts reinforced the assumption that a gender identity that might protect one from economic exploitation was a privilege of white women alone. When a white servant named Margaret Broderick requested a transfer of her domicile from Fitzhugh to a distant relative of hers, she made clear that she would "do no Country work, nor work without doors" for her new master.[9]

Lest we assume the racialization of Virginia society benefited white women in any straightforward way, it is important to recall that the rising tobacco patriarchy was built on the ashes of a "widowarchy"—an earlier phenomenon in which wives of deceased men maintained control over the couple's joint property. Their property-holding status gave older women a voice in the economy and before the law. Therefore, ambitious planters hoping to build great estates out of strategic marriages had to contend with the considerable property rights of the widows they wed (second and third marriages were extremely common at the time). Beginning in the 1640s, white men reshaped the legal system to make fathers and husbands "the masters of family ... responsible for all publique duties, tithes and charges, due from all persons in their family." White women's economic role was thereafter "covered" by a male superior. In

1727, the General Assembly definitively broke the economic power of the white widowarchy by decreeing that slaves belonging to a remarrying widow became the "absolute property" of the widow's new husband, whereas previously she had maintained them as her own property.[10]

Along the banks of the James, York, and Rappahannock rivers, which provided cheap transport from the backcountry into the Chesapeake Bay, a planter class built a mature plantation society in the late seventeenth century. Especially after tobacco prices picked up in the 1690s, large planters in some ways made real the old Virginia Company dream of medieval lordship—not through the obliging serfdom of Indians, but through the violence of the Atlantic slave trade and the growth of an international market in tobacco.

As Fitzhugh distributed vast swaths of the Chesapeake region to himself and his friends at the end of the 1600s, they would promptly entail them, in effect taking hundreds of thousands of acres permanently off the market. Drawing on traditional British law, entailment forbade heirs from selling off inherited property. Once entailed, estates were protected from seizure for unpaid debts. The House of Burgesses—the locally elected but planter-dominated lower house of the General Assembly—passed laws strengthening entailment in 1705 and 1727. Not only did their policies prioritize paternal lines of descent. The new laws paired land monopoly with slave ownership. They stipulated that only fathers possessing more than five slaves could patent more than five hundred acres of land; they also entailed slave property to estates, protecting that "species of property" from repossession.[11]

As they took over the colony's land, as well as its economic and political systems, in the first half of the eighteenth century, planters replaced their humble frontier abodes with sumptuously furnished homes. "Here is an elegant Seat!" enthused the tutor Philip Vickers Fithian when he rode out to John Tayloe's plantation in Richmond County. Tayloe had covered the dining room walls of his mansion with two dozen portraits of

"English Race-Horses." Fithian was equally impressed by Robert Carter III's Nomini Hall. The imposing structure, built at "vast expence," was made of brick and "covered with strong lime Mortar; so that the building is now perfectly white." It sat on "a high spot of Ground . . . at the Head of the Navigation of the River Nomini." The master and mistress of the house could enjoy cooling breezes on the front porch while taking in a view of the plantation from a position of unquestioned mastery. They could also enjoy being admired. Fithian observed of Nomini Hall, "It may be seen a considerable distance."[12]

The plantation home itself had become the scene and stage of the planter's power. A steady stream of visitors bore witness to his public authority, as well as his generosity. Hospitality was the Virginia planters' "most visible indication of gentility and domestic authority," writes historian Kathleen Brown. While many observers attributed the sickliness of the people in Virginia to the "noxious & unhealthy" climate, Fithian blamed the unending cycle of balls, dances, parties, and visits, which invariably involved guests "drinking great quantities of varieties of Liquors," engaging in "Violent Exercise of the Body & Spirits" (dancing), and staying up all night.[13]

Planter families thus cultivated a similar reputation to their counterparts in the West Indies, where the fortunes to be made were larger, but life was shorter, even for people at the top rungs of society. In eighteenth-century Jamaica, European immigrants, lacking resistance to a host of tropical diseases, had a life expectancy of thirteen years. Between about 1700 and 1750, an influx of fifty thousand Europeans into the island increased the white population by only five thousand, because so many of them died. After a yellow fever epidemic ripped through the population of Barbados in 1647, one observer waxed philosophical about the change in circumstances: "Many who had begun and almost finished great sugar workes, who dandled themselves in their hopes . . . were suddenly laid in the dust, and their estates left unto strangers." With sudden death and moldering decay all around them, planters imbibed the lesson that making a fortune required an ambition as shamelessly grand as the outsize powers of life and death in the tropical latitudes. And everything could be taken away just as quickly. With their lives and lifestyles depending on the fickle fortunes of the plantation, they were not savers—they tended to consume everything. Planters' reputation for having an "almost compulsive" generosity owes to this unpredictable reality.[14]

At the same time, the daily habit of mastery over people could fool them into believing that their lives could be made eternal. "Why mama," a colonial planter's daughter exclaimed after her mother listed the new buildings she wanted added to their Virginia estate, "you plan and talk of these things as tho' you should never die!" The new ruling class believed their families would not, at least. With eternal life for Christians available only in heaven, the plantation would bear the patriarch's name in perpetuity on earth.[15]

The gentry home hosted the passing of planters to the hereafter, while broadcasting the enduring quality of their possessions. Contra the old country norm of having the ceremony at the village church, the funeral of a true planter was held at his plantation. As Fithian noted of the Virginia planter community, "Only the lower sort of People are buried at the Church; for the Gentlemen have private burying-Yards." When a neighbor named Mr. Harrison died, Byrd attended. The grand event started at the old man's estate, which was crowded with mourners eager to partake of the wine and cake that the family provided. The coffin was then transported by wagon to the Anglican church for a special sermon. As "the corpse began to move" toward the church, the ship *Harrison*, in the river below the house, "fired a gun every half minute." With the glow of morning wine perhaps wearing off, Byrd's patience in honoring an old rival wore thin. He called the priest's sermon "an extravagant panegyric," which gave the deceased "virtues which he never possessed as well as magnified those which he had." In the afternoon, Harrison's body was returned to the plantation for interment.[16]

The gentry home was also an economic center, rivaling in importance the county courthouses, where merchants, planters, and politicians gathered once a month to conduct trade. William Byrd II ran a sprawling enterprise of plantations, docks, sloops, flatboats, and a tobacco warehouse from his Great House at Westover. Smallholding neighbors and ambitious young planters frequently made appearances to beg favor from the man who controlled so much valuable territory. Byrd, however, may not have been as delightful a host as he assumed: His invitations to stay for dinner were frequently rejected by ships' captains who came to Westover on business. He faithfully noted the slights in his diary.

When securely ensconced at the top of the society they had made, planters refashioned their domestic realm in ways that reflected patriarchal power. Kitchens, laundries, and other domestic workspaces had been part of the living quarters during the frontier phase of Chesapeake life, even for the wealthy. In the late seventeenth century, however, as enslaved women and men took over domestic work from family members and white servants, such tasks were removed to new buildings away from the main residence. The planter assumed the power to redefine his wife as a genteel creature at once stripped of economic power and protected from drudgery, her feminine energies reserved to the duties of "wife, mother, and hostess." Since "labor" was not for true women, the proper home had to be free from it, though of course domestic labor continued—architectural innovations merely masked it.[17]

Many plantation homes, in fact, had hidden hallways, staircases, and "cat walks" above the ceiling, secretly connecting gritty spaces of labor to shimmering spaces of consumption. Forced to fit in these tiny, steep spaces, carrying trays weighed down with steaming, delicious fowl, enslaved domestic workers were like blood circulating through the vessels of the planter's home. As the enslaver's family sat at table discussing the merits of "never dying," ghosts were shuffling all around them, hidden behind walls, in the ceiling, and around the corner.[18]

Gentry plantations also played a key political role within white society in colonial Virginia. The county militia—which was called out to pursue fugitive slaves, suppress uprisings, and defend settler incursions from Native American resistance—was the main form of local "self-defense," as well as an unusual venue for mixing between social classes. Every able-bodied white male living in a county was expected to serve, and this service was an important source of one's place in a society of "free-born Englishmen," yet it reinforced the stratified nature of that society at the same time. While the training, organizing, and equipping of militias was funded largely by planters' tax money, they also monopolized commanding positions, taking titles like Colonel Byrd and Captain Jefferson, which added a martial sheen to their status as planters. The monthly "muster" was often held at an officer's property.

William Byrd recorded one such muster in October 1711, held at the plantation of Captain Jefferson (the grandfather of Thomas). Several of the rank-and-file soldiers failed to arrive on time, so Byrd entered the house to drink with the other officers. Later he came back outside and began to upbraid the troops for performing lackluster maneuvers. One of the soldiers had arrived drunk and was being "rude to his captain, for which I broke his head in two places." The local militia, who wrestled for prizes of pistols and bullets provided by Byrd, drank his liquor, or got bashed about the head by his walking stick, often obeyed such performances of class hierarchy choreographed by planters.[19]

Life for poor white men in the Southern countryside thus combined rituals of obedience with rites of power. As whites and as men, they wielded arms and hoped to join the planter class. They went on slave patrols, worked as overseers, and enjoyed legal control over their household. As the rabble, on the other hand, they wrestled for the jollity of planters and absorbed their blows. Given the much larger white population in the Chesapeake—both the West Indies and the Lowcountry had large Black majorities, while in the Chesapeake, Black people made up at most 40 percent of the population—cultivating the loyalty of lesser white neighbors and incorporating them fully into an orderly hierarchy of power and wealth was a key to the survival of the planter class.[20]

In spite of the panoply of rituals that planters designed to reinforce their new hierarchies of race, gender, and class, in the end their expensive lifestyles depended on what happened in the fields every day.

CHAPTER 7

Crop Masters

Tobacco planters aspired to be "crop masters," a status implying that their own prudent management of soils, tools, slaves, overseers, finances, and all other plantation inputs would yield an abundant and predictable harvest in the face of all the unknowns of premodern farming. Each of the stages of tobacco cultivation—which took fifteen months from start to finish—required considerable care. In January, slaves planted seeds in carefully prepared seedbeds. In February, tens of thousands of small hills were dunged and banked up by the hoeing labor of hundreds of enslaved people. The young seedlings would be transported to the hills in May, when they had attained a height of about six inches. Slaves spent the early summer chopping weeds, as well as deworming, topping, and suckering new shoots to send all the plant's energy into the production of big leaves. August was cutting time, after which the leaves were strung in batches and hung out in the sun. After this process, known as curing, leaves were stripped and stemmed, and finally "prized" tightly into casks for shipment. The casks or hogsheads were taken to wharves on the riverbank.[1]

The operations required to prepare a crop of tobacco for market.

Like in the Lowcountry, crop masters crafted a hierarchy of power, in which enslaved women and men were watched carefully by drivers and overseers, who reported to an estate manager, who reported to the planter—but in many cases the planter was personally involved in the day-to-day operations. The great Tidewater families like the Carters, Fitzhughs, Lees, Byrds, and Jeffersons, were not absentee planters like the proprietors of the Lowcountry in their showpiece plantations. Tobacco enslavers lived close to the land and took a direct role in everyday operations. "Without a constant care & continuall residence thereupon, the labour & care of seven years is destroyed in as many hours," went Fitzhugh's maxim.[2]

Still, much of what they did was for show, no different in this way from their counterparts to the south. Whether or not their guests requested a tour, planters liked to show off their crop mastery. When the Northern tutor Philip Fithian rode out to the fields to get some air, he ran into the planter John Tayloe. "I walked with him among the Tobacco Cotton &c," Fithian recalled. "He gave me Directions for raising the latter.—Cotton must be planted about the middle of May in rich land," and so on. A system of public tobacco inspections at centralized government warehouses, established in the 1730s, provided further opportunity to showcase one's competence as a planter.[3]

While planters hoped that such measures of quality control would help their crop obtain higher prices in Europe, the new system of inspection also helped the elite to marginalize small planters. If the tobacco inspector judged a particular crop wanting in quality, he ordered it destroyed. Given that the inspector was usually of the same social class as the elite planters, it is likely that the shaming ritual, and potential economic ruination of having one's yearly yield destroyed, was most often visited upon small cultivators. This in spite of the fact that small planters, who supervised workers more closely and toiled in the fields with their own hands, often got better prices for their small harvests than wealthy planters got for theirs. As the wealthy planter and father-in-law of George Washington, John Custis, complained to his London factor in 1729, "several of my poor neighbors, whose ground I am sure cannot make good Tobacco," had received a higher price per pound than he had. So their crop mastery was always shaky, and it might be more than coincidence that elites imposed the inspections regime the following year.[4]

The planter gentry literally ruled the colony, passing among themselves the positions of sheriff, county clerk, justice of the peace, and militia captain. Absent a reputation for crop mastery, however, political influence was often out of reach. Their expert operation of their plantations, as well as their subtle domination of enslaved people and of nature, established their local reputation at the county courthouse and in the colonial assembly.[5]

Crop mastery required the planter to control the flows of information across the lands he owned. William Byrd II took daily "walks about the plantation," at least in his younger days, and he also wrote letters to and received letters from overseers at each of his properties. Often, they played billiards or cards and drank together at his home. Yet these relationships could be complicated. The actions of the enslaved community at Byrd's Fall Creek plantation—several miles from his home at Westover—suggest that one Joe Wilkinson may have been a particularly cruel or incompetent overseer.

In July 1710, five Westover cows that had wandered off were returned by two slaves from Fall Creek. They took the opportunity to look in on their master, informing him "that Joe Wilkinson was very often absent from business." In September, another Fall Creek slave was delivering some fruit to Westover. He let slip to Byrd that "Wilkinson carried all the cider away." The Fall Creek slaves got just what they were aiming for in December, when Byrd rode there himself and found Wilkinson absent. When he looked at the condition of the tobacco harvest ("spoiled . . . by house burn") and saw that Wilkinson had taken Byrd's belongings to furnish his own home, he fired the troublesome employee and appointed a replacement. The following month, Wilkinson's wife came to Westover "to beg for her husband but I would not speak to her for fear of being persuaded by her tears," as Byrd recounted. Far from being moved to take mercy on his former overseer, Byrd took Wilkinson to court over the spoiled harvest and was awarded three thousand pounds of tobacco in damages. In this case, the enslaved community had succeeded in ridding themselves of an intolerable overseer without risk to themselves. They understood and utilized class differences between white men to exert some control over their own lives.[6]

In the early colonial era of the "best white man's country," most poor people felt entitled to use wooded or swampy terrain for their own subsistence and that of their livestock. In fact, treating Native American lands as a commons for white folk was one key strategy of colonial expansion throughout early North America: in an endlessly repeated and deadly dance, a free-ranging hog or cow would trample crop fields, a frustrated Indigenous farmer would kill the beast. A white settler would take vengeance on the offending group, and a reprisal by the militia would often result in more land expansion for the English.[7]

Once English land sovereignty was solidified in Virginia, however, planter attitudes toward the property they owned began to shift. As land values rose, and large planters began keeping numerous livestock of their own, they began to worry about the lands they would have to bequeath to their children, and they began to exert a new kind of monopoly control over their sprawling properties. Starting with the passage of a new law in 1662, every four years the landowners in a given neighborhood undertook a "processioning." Together they would walk the property lines, replacing fallen property markers. In the case of any disputes about what land belonged to whom, the county surveyor (usually a local elite) would be called in to adjudicate. The new act of processioning repeatedly affirmed that wooded lands were not a commons—they were private property.[8]

The law was quite permissive toward owners of hogs, basically saying they could graze them in any wooded landscape that was not fenced in. This included the thousands of acres wealthy planters owned without improving. The legal limits of his power over the land vexed Byrd, probably in part because rooting hogs can be very destructive. In 1709, he "found that some of my good neighbors had dug down the bank of my ditch to let their hogs into my pasture." This he would have counted as a crime both because the land was enclosed by a ditch and because it had been improved. Yet the same neighbors may have submitted a petition at the courthouse against Byrd "for stopping the way against the people on the other side the creek." Some of his neighbors felt the construction of the ditch restricted their rightful access to common pasture. In fact, they may have been right, as he soon "wrote a note to forewarn all people from driving their cattle and hogs on my land" without distinguishing between improved and unimproved grounds.[9]

In public declarations and legal actions during the early eighteenth century, elite planters defended a new kind of enclosure mentality in a colony where the customary right to free-range domestic animals was viewed as foundational by small planters and landless whites. It was one thing if a planter owned one hundred thousand acres of woodland on paper; it was entirely another if that planter actually defended his exclusive right to any and all resources on that acreage. While an "open range" for white people persisted in plantation regions until the late nineteenth century, crop masters began to strip away its legal protections to protect the sanctity of their plantation boundaries.[10]

Most fundamentally, crop mastery depended on close policing of enslaved people. While enslavers often flattered themselves with how good their slaves had it, Byrd frequently abused and tortured enslaved people for the offense of finding food for themselves. A man named Caesar ran away from Byrd's plantation because he feared punishment "for killing a hog." On an afternoon "walk about the plantation," Byrd stumbled upon an enslaved man "who had been off the plantation and brought some bacon with him, for which I threatened to whip him." In the spring of 1711, on another "walk about the plantation," a daily activity that Westover's African American community had surely come to dread, Byrd "threatened those of my negroes that stole some eggs from my wife." An enslaved man named John earned himself a threat from Byrd "for giving away the sweetbread of the hog he killed." Even when Byrd received a report of impending "famine" at one of his outlying plantations, he seemed never to conclude that rampant food theft resulted from chronic hunger. Caesar, John, and the others impinged on the master's prerogative to dispose of people and things on the plantation. At the price of severe physical punishment, they insisted on their right to meet their own needs for survival and community.[11]

Many of them were also worthy of the title crop master as well. In source areas of the Atlantic slave trade like Senegambia and Angola, African farmers had already mastered tobacco husbandry in the seventeenth century—they often sold their product to European merchants at the slave-trading forts. Many captives therefore would have been familiar with, and had their own ideas about, such delicate processes as the transplanting of seedlings and the suckering of young plants. Landon Carter, one of the colony's richest planters, enslaved a woman named Sukey, who spoke to him like a peer. On a visit to the fields in July 1770, Carter pointed out the sparse growth in a particular plot. Sukey assured him the area would "see a good crop of tobacco." When he disagreed, she told him that "she knew the ground, knew how it was dunged, and would be hanged if it did not turn out good tobacco."[12]

Sukey was also in charge of the henhouse, where she cared for and kept accounts of around three hundred geese, ducks, chickens, and turkeys. She kept Carter apprised of how many bushels of meal would be needed to feed them all. It is not clear if Sukey kept written notes, or whether she memorized the precise numbers of each species, but she was able to report to Carter with remarkable specificity each species of fowl, along with their sex and maturity. In May 1764, for example, Sukey told Carter there were thirty-three "Old geeses," and seventy-eight goslings, as well as "two geese still to hatch." She also said there were two hundred chickens, with "one hen still sitting on her eggs." Sukey had achieved a level of crop mastery Carter could not replicate, and his overseers rarely did. Many overseers were poor young men with little experience managing labor and often less experience in cultivating tobacco than the enslaved people they were supposed to manage. Surveying his crop field and his henhouse, Carter appealed not to a white overseer but to Sukey.[13]

Sukey's husband, Manuel, was another potential crop master, a skilled plowman. "I went to Manuel plowing my cornrows," Carter once noted. "And to my astonishment I saw clods turning before his plow of near 40 or 50 pounds weight. He goes deep and really it is good work in a prodigious hard soil." It seems Manuel and Sukey could have been formidable Chesapeake crop masters in their own right, but that mastery was denied them by their enslaver, whose own success was premised upon monopolizing the expertise of the enslaved. Indeed, the turning of the soil was of deeply personal significance to a man like Carter, even as he refused to do it with his own hands.[14]

Carter instead invested his energies in surveillance and control. Standing idle in the fields, he watched Manuel like a hawk and recorded his actions in his diary. The relationship between the two men had turned sour by 1770. Manuel had taken to "night walking," and thus begun shirking his morning duties. Another plowman, whom Carter called "mulatto Peter," was soon labeled "a night walker." Importantly, though, he did not go about on foot. "I have discovered he rides my plow horses in the night," Carter wrote. Peter repurposed a working animal to visit friends, family, a lover perhaps, or the nearest tavern. While a "plow horse" was far from an English thoroughbred, riding any mount for one's own purposes provided a fleeting form of freedom, a denial of the abjection forced onto the enslaved.

But Gardner Johnny was the archvillain of Carter's nightmares. On July 25, 1776, Carter caught Gardner Johnny riding back from a fishing hole. As it was for those enslaved by Byrd, the punishment for finding one's own food was cruel: Johnny was "locked up and tied neck and heels with his hands behind him." Soon after suffering this torture, Gardner Johnny broke out, "and has not been seen or heard of since." Manuel, mulatto Peter, and Gardner Johnny, along with five others, fled to British forces in 1776. Their collective flight created a crisis in Carter's patriarchal assuredness, and also confronted him with a plantation brain drain.[15]

Carter must have felt keenly the loss of Jack Lubbar as well, although they had not always seen eye to eye. Halfway through May 1766, Lubbar, put in charge of Mangorike plantation, told Carter the thirty-three bushels of "his Corn," which should have lasted through the year, had all been used up. "He pretends the cattle and sheep eat it," Carter recorded. But he had so few animals this couldn't be true. "He must be a rogue." "Old Jack is both too easy with those people and too deceitfull and careless himself," Carter concluded. "A negroe can't be honest." He called Jack lazy, stupid, and a drunkard who couldn't be redeemed despite his claims to religiosity.[16]

That was in Lubbar's younger days as a field driver. After he aged out of the years masters called "prime," Lubbar spent his latter days at another of Carter's properties, where he was in charge of food production. With only five people to help him, Lubbar yielded "larger crops of Corn, tobacco, and Pease twice over than ever I have had made by anyone, even as high as 12,000 weight tobacco." It seems that Carter had yielded considerable control of operations at the plantation to Lubbar, even though he liked to pretend that the aging man was dawdling contentedly "amongst his melon vines, both to divert the hours and indeed to keep nature stirring."

Carter was wise enough, however, to accept Lubbar's counsel when it came to gardening. The planter "took notice of his Pea vines a good store and askt him why he had not got them hilled." Lubbar gave an interesting answer to the man who had held him in slavery for most of his long life: "The Prudence of Experience, Master." The vines had only just sprouted out of the soil, "and it will hurt too young things to Coat them too closely with earth." "Too young things" were always being violated in the enslaver's world. Lubbar insisted on a gentleness, an amiability with plants, where they are coaxed and not forced into providing plenty. The antiplantation idea that plants ripen in their own time sits uneasily within the plantation ethos of "making all things work," of turning land and people into substantial and predictable profits.[17]

Even as his legs and his eyesight failed him in his final few years of life, Lubbar made himself a master of the woods. Carter described how he became "a vast progger" (expert forager and trapper) of beavers, muskrats, fish, and more. He fed his family of grandchildren, great-grandchildren, and the rest of the community, along with Carter's own household. Carter knew such skills were hard won, as his own nephew Robert Carter IV went to "the Marsh & River" every day to hunt waterfowl, but "never kills any Game." As Lubbar lay on his deathbed in 1774, Carter spoke of Lubbar's progging as a loyal service to himself (in a way, it was). When Lubbar finally passed, Carter eulogized him in his diary "[as] honest a human creature as could live; Who to his last proved a faithful and a Profitable servant to his Master." He had forgotten the discord of earlier years, and he did not record what the loss of the old man meant to the large enslaved community of which he was such an important part. Their private eulogies were likely well out of earshot, but if Carter heard them, he did not think them important enough to write down.[18]

Carter's approximately four hundred slaves worked not just for his own benefit, but for that of his children. In Virginia, planters jealously guarding their patrimony took over and transformed the colony in the eighteenth century. The emerging planter class developed legal codes, landowning patterns, and racist policies that ensured the privileges of mastery would extend down genetic generations, through their own male progeny, which they further ensured by arranging the intermarriage of their children with other children of their elite class.

Tobacco planters knew that their patrimony was replicated through the labor, productive and reproductive, of enslaved people. At a time when there was no domestic slave trade, and arrivals of captives from Africa were scarcer than enslavers would have liked, planters depended on what they euphemistically called "increase." A jubilant William Fitzhugh observed, "My Negroes increase yearly by which I am enabled to settle new quarters and consequently my exports must increase." He equated the reproductive labor of enslaved women to the expansion of his tobacco enterprise. Landon Carter's father, reputed to have been the largest owner of lands and enslaver of people in early eighteenth-century Virginia, willed "my said Slaves & their increase" (five hundred enslaved people) to his three sons. They also inherited about one hundred thousand acres each.[19]

Such planters hoped to force on the women they enslaved a life history like that of a girl named Sharlott. Purchased by a Middlesex County planter at the age of twelve in 1720, she gave birth to at least thirteen children over the ensuing decades. By 1764, Sharlott was the matriarch of a family of twenty-two. Her two-year-old great-grandson, Isaac, was the latest arrival. All were enslaved. All labored for or added to the future value of the master's estate. Sharlott's purchase price had been recouped twenty-five times over.[20]

Behind the illusion of self-replicating value inherent in the notion of "increase" was Sharlott's and her community's caring labor, which kept the children alive. Mothers worked diligently for their own reasons: Because they loved their children, they needed to remain in the good graces of the master so as not to see their little ones removed to a distant plantation. Even though dedicated childcare functioned to the monetary benefit of the master, enslaved people still had to risk punishment to do it: They arrived at the fields late because they had let a baby finish nursing; they smuggled away the sweetbreads of a freshly butchered hog for their own people; they made a few of the mistress's eggs disappear; they even took a hoe when fleeing to the woods. Dangerous deeds like these were required to provide sustenance to young and old alike, and to enrich a spartan material existence with the occasional delight. Planters liked to credit their own crop mastery for the "increase" occurring in the Chesapeake's African American population. They loathed admitting their dependence on enslaved women as well as free, but that dependence was everywhere.

Ambitious white men often depended on strategic marriages to get their start in life. Fitzhugh, who arrived in Virginia as a young immigrant with little wealth to his name, began his social ascent by marrying an eleven-year-old Virginia heiress named Sarah Tucker in 1674. (Sarah first gave birth when she was either twelve or thirteen.) In the marriage settlement with the father of his child bride, the twenty-three-year-old Fitzhugh gained ownership of "a Negro man and woman, three cows, six ewes and a ram, a number of hogs, a bay gelding, a necklace of pearls, and enough dishes, household furniture and kitchen equipment to set up housekeeping at once." He was also granted five thousand pounds of finished tobacco in his father-in-law's will.[21]

With this promising start, Fitzhugh was able to use his position as a lawyer to buy up thousands of acres of property, as well as indentured servants, and scores of enslaved people. He became a slave trader himself in the 1680s. Fitzhugh was a man who kept a close eye on the future, which was tied to the reproductive labor of the women he enslaved. He boasted of one of his several Tidewater plantations that "the Negroes increase being all young & a considerable parcel of breeders, will keep that Stock good for ever." The planter's fantasy of an endless supply of free labor, first seen on São Tomé in the 1500s, lived on in eighteenth-century Virginia, although Fitzhugh's own climb through the ranks of Virginia planters depended less on direct access to African captives and more on the ownership and sexual forcing of minors.[22]

When he sat down with his lawyer and imagined a world without him in it, Fitzhugh focused on treating his own sons justly. Indeed, when Fitzhugh died in 1701, he had over fifty thousand acres to bestow upon his four sons. His sole daughter, Rosamond, received none. The enslaved families, that "parcel of breeders," were sundered in the will, ensuring his own male descendants were supported for life. "Mulatto Sarah & her young Daughter Diana," for example, were given to Fitzhugh's son George, while Sarah's two other children, Esop and William, were given to John. The very idea that Black families would have concerns and dispensations that tied together generations was dismissed in a variety of ways in colonial Virginia, starting with a 1680 law banning "any Solemnity or Funeralls for any Negroes." The patrimony, almost by definition, belonged to white people, not Black, and to men more than women.[23]

The focus on protecting family estates could lead to self-destructive fits of patrimonial overreach. In 1710, Byrd's father-in-law, a powerful West Indian royal governor named Daniel Parke, was murdered in Antigua. A mob led by sugar planters incensed by his abuse of authority and his habit of "debauching" their wives and daughters pulled him from his home and beat him to death. He left to his family a mountain of unpaid debts. Parke's plantation in Virginia was to have been sold to satisfy his creditors, but Byrd assumed responsibility for the debts in order to take the land himself. He would struggle to pay off what Parke owed over the next three decades, trafficking in land and slaves, and even at one point offering Westover for sale. Yet, like Parke, he still had much to pass on when he died in 1744, including 179,000 acres sprawled across the colony.[24]

His sole male heir was William Byrd III, who married a Carter in 1748. He took up residence at a mansion called Belvidere he had built on a hill overlooking the falls of the James River, future site of the state capital of Richmond, which, along with Petersburg, was later built on Byrd land. His grandfather, the founder of the dynasty, had been so wary of contracting debts in London that he instructed his agents there to "abate" purchases of goods if the proceeds from his tobacco "did not come to expectation."[25]

William Byrd III had no such self-control. He squandered his inheritance in the classic planters' pastimes: horseracing and gambling. Plantation business was left to a coterie of managers and advisers, while he chased public power and glory. He served in the House of Burgesses and then the Crown-selected Colonial Council. When the Seven Years' War came, Byrd joined up as an officer, but he never saw combat. In 1760, his wife committed suicide (it is thought) in the Belvidere house. He remarried, was implicated in a major late colonial corruption scandal, and went broke in the credit crunches of the early 1770s.

Early in the independence struggle, he remained a committed Loyalist. A pro-independence newspaper politely warned him to leave the state. Only when the British had begun their offensive did he finally change his loyalty. But he had served the Crown so faithfully that the Patriots did not trust him. Spurned by both sides and isolated at the old family estate of Westover, William Byrd III drew out a pistol and shot himself on New Year's Day 1777. He left behind a will dripping with rancor. He reversed the generosity shown to his children in the "unjust will of my insane mother," and threatened to leave his son Otway only a shilling if he should quit the navy.[26]

Byrd's unflattering final act was an aberration: The half century at the end of the colonial era was a time of unique prosperity for tobacco planters in the Chesapeake. As historian Gordon Wood has noted, "In the years after 1745, colonial trade with Great Britain grew dramatically.... Nearly half of all English shipping was engaged in American commerce," while one fourth of Britain's exports were consumed on the North American mainland. And, since British agriculture could no longer meet the needs of its rapidly expanding population, prices for America's agricultural products in the mother country soared.[27]

After nearly fifty years of lagging prices, the value of tobacco exported from Virginia nearly tripled between 1733 and 1773. Moreover, an influx of Dutch capital into the English financial system created a flush credit market for colonists. Lowcountry rice exports were expanding in the decades before the Revolution as well, from twenty million pounds in 1740 to about eighty million pounds in 1770, but tobacco nearly doubled the exports of rice—it was by far the most valuable export to leave British North America.[28]

The plantation goods from the West Indies, the Lowcountry, and the Chesapeake represented nearly half of England's total foreign trade with the world—including Europe and Asia—at a time when the country surpassed all rivals in international trade. This trade helped make the colonies far wealthier places than Britain itself. By the eve of the Revolution, white residents of the Southern colonies—Maryland,

Virginia, North Carolina, South Carolina, and Georgia—possessed 50 percent of the total private wealth in all of British North America, *excluding the value of their slaves*, which means they held far more than half, as slave property was their most valuable commodity. If slave property is included in the calculations, each white person in the Upper and Lower South commanded four times as much wealth as a free white person in New England. In Jamaica, the per capita wealth of free white people was thirty-six times that in New England, owing to heavy capital investments in sugar factories as well as a population ratio of nine enslaved people to every one white person. Accounting for over one-fourth of England's total global imports, British West Indian sugar exceeded by a factor of ten the value of tobacco exported from the Upper South, and by a factor of ten the value of rice exported from the Lowcountry.[29]

The prevalence of "absentee" sugar planters, who put the day-to-day operations of their massive estates in the hands of salaried "attorneys," in British society and politics made them even more prominent than their wealth suggests. They built palatial estates throughout England. The famed wealth of the "West Indians" even found its way to the heart of British literature. Jane Austen's *Mansfield Park* revolves around the issue of a West Indian fortune. The public schools of Eton, Westminster, Harrow, and Winchester were full of the sons of West Indians. In certain posh districts of London, their carriages were so numerous that they blocked the streets. The story is told of how, on a visit to Weymouth, George III and William Pitt encountered a wealthy Jamaican with an imposing equipage, including outriders and livery. George III, much displeased, is reported to have said, 'Sugar, sugar, eh? All that sugar! How are the duties, eh, Pitt, how are the duties?'" As this oft-told anecdote suggests, the "West India Interest" had a powerful voice in policymaking circles.[30]

While their wealth paled in comparison to their West Indian cousins', an authoritative ruling class had taken definitive shape in Virginia

Trade, Wealth, and Specialization in Colonial American Regions

Region	Major export	Average annual value (in pounds sterling)	Primary destination	Secondary destination	How monocultural (share of total regional exports)?	Per capita wealth for whites, in pounds sterling	Population in 1780
West Indies	sugar products	3.9 million	86% to Great Britain	14% to North America	At least 90%	1,200 pounds sterling (Jamaica)	48,000 white and 489,000 Black
Upper South	tobacco	756,128	100% to Great Britain		75%	132 pounds	
Lowcountry	rice	305,533	66% to Great Britain		55% (most of the remaining was indigo)	132 pounds	297,400 white in "Lower South," mostly NC, and 208,880 Black
Middle Colonies	grain	379,380	47% to West Indies	45% to Southern Europe	72%	51 pounds	
Upper South	grain	199,485	50% Southern Europe	34% West Indies	20%		482,000 white and 303,000 Black
New England	fish	152,155	62% to West Indies		34%	33 pounds	700,000
New England	livestock	89,953	98% to West Indies		20%		
New England	wood products	65,271	88% to West Indies		14%		
New England	total foreign trade	439,101	63% to West Indies (not including slave trade activities)				

This table shows the chief export or exports of each colonial region in pounds sterling. The figures are annual averages for 1768 to 1772. JOHN J. MCCUSKER AND RUSSELL R. MENARD, THE ECONOMY OF BRITISH AMERICA, 1607–1789 (UNIVERSITY OF NORTH CAROLINA PRESS, 1985) by the mid-eighteenth century. The dozen or so Chesapeake planters who owned thousands of acres and controlled hundreds of laborers in 1640 had grown to at least eighty such men in 1763. Much like the richest individuals in our own day, these planters represented the top one tenth of 1 percent of all white males. In one closely studied county, the elite families were forty-six times wealthier than the poorest two-thirds of households in the late seventeenth century, and over one hundred times wealthier by 1750.[31]

Virginia planters advertised their newfound wealth by participating in the most rarefied level of a novel transatlantic consumer culture. The formerly spartan houses of their seventeenth-century forebears filled up with expensive sideboards, velvet-covered settees, and grand oaken bureaus. They saw their faces glimmering back at them in silver sugar bowls and cut-glass chandeliers. They imported hand-tailored coats and choice liquor like the "persico" Colonel Jefferson shared with his fellow officers the day Byrd cracked the militiaman's skull. The new importance of sartorial display made it doubly irksome to planters when luxury goods failed to meet expectations. George Washington was disappointed with a carriage he had purchased from London. He had specified it be built "of well seasoned materials, and by a masterly workman; instead of which it was made of wood so exceedingly Green" that as the pieces of the carriage continued to season, they shrank. The thing had begun to rattle to pieces on the bumpy roads of Virginia, to Washington's grave embarrassment.[32]

They had established larger integrated plantations using slaves. Planters, managers, and overseers wrenched economies of scale out of their captives, with large units yielding far higher revenue per slave than smaller farms. They drove down costs of production by learning how to make tobacco more efficiently. Within the framework of protected colonial trade—a set of arrangements from which they benefited for the most part—they also modernized transport and marketing, with cut-throat competition among British merchants for access to cheap Chesapeake tobacco ushering in a more standardized, high-volume cargo trade after 1748. They also developed a warehouse system in the Chesapeake that ensured that tobacco was collected more efficiently, from a small number of centralized loading points instead of small craft visiting the wharves of individual plantations. Shipowners, captains, and merchants shaved down time at port, reduced their crew sizes, and created regular routes. One of the largest London firms doing Chesapeake business in the eighteenth century was Perry and Lane. They served William Byrd II and many other gentry planters, cutting out middlemen and linking their businesses directly to London investment capital and consumers on the Continent. In London, new tobacco-processing firms struggling for market share in the tobacco-mad markets of northern Europe figured out ways to cut costs, including by rolling cheap grades together with expensive ones and marketing the result as a secret recipe. They also utilized more machinery to press and roll chewing and pipe tobacco. All these new efficiencies pressed consumer prices downward, widening potential markets for tobacco.[33]

In the last instance, of course, the largesse of the planters' golden age was made on the backs of Black families forced to work in the tobacco fields. The competition among elite peers in Virginia, writes historian Lorena Walsh, resulted in "the ratcheting-up of work requirements, the elimination of much of the bound laborers' already scant leisure time, and apparently callous [in]difference to sundering enslaved families by parceling out slave children among widely scattered heirs."[34]

In spite of the surprising "increase" of native-born Black Virginians (a remarkable feat of enslaved families themselves), fifty thousand Africans were brought in between 1730 and 1760. The large imports of enslaved people were both a symptom of increased economic power in the Chesapeake and a lever to raise it further. The rise in tobacco prices, the beginnings of paper money in the colonies, the Seven Years' War that endangered trade between the West Indies and Africa, and the 1739 Stono Rebellion in South Carolina, all combined to make the Chesapeake Bay a propitious market for English slave sellers in the 1740s. At a time when manufactured goods were being brought in from Great Britain in unprecedented quantities, trafficked people from Africa were the Chesapeake's second most valuable import. On the eve of the American Revolution, business was booming for tobacco planters, as well as for all the other beneficiaries of the British-run Atlantic plantation complex.[35]

CHAPTER 8

The Chiefest of My Estates

Just when the system appeared to have been perfected, a shift occurred in the relationship between colonial elites and their British merchants. Planters had been overextending themselves by spending on additional slaves as well as household luxuries for some time, and in 1763, amid the empire-wide recession that followed the Seven Years' War, London merchants began refusing to accept repayment in inflated Virginia money. For many planters, the burden of providing for familial dependents reduced them to groveling before their creditors. "I have [a] large family," Henry Fitzhugh reminded his English consignee in 1764, "& the chiefest of my estates entailed on a few of my children so that I am under a necessity of purchasing Lands for the others."[1]

While such disputes—especially those involving planters paying their debts in dubious colonial bills—had been resolved through personal correspondence in the past, in the postwar recession the merchants were unwilling to absorb the loss. This time they appealed directly to Parliament, which resulted in a law prohibiting colonial legislatures from issuing their own money—the Currency Act of 1764. The planters, feeling that merchants had broken a manly code of friendship by getting the government involved, started to formulate a conspiracy theory: The big-city gentlemen were trying to get them so deep in debt that they would be forced to hand over their land and their slaves.[2]

The bricks of elite planters' self-conception—virtuous independence, enclosed plantations, patriarchal control over women and slaves, and a near-compulsive hospitality—made up carefully constructed facades. Like a Georgian-Palladian mansion, or an "allée" of stately live oaks, maintaining them cost money. Being denied credit was therefore deeply personal, even existential, and now it involved Parliament. Planters began transcribing private financial humiliations into a discourse of public protest. Embarrassed about their debts and unable to secure further credit, the planters helped instigate the colonies' first nonimportation ban in 1769, which allayed their deficits, while registering their opposition to British merchants as well as colonial policy. Exhibiting a new spartan self-denial, the architects of the boycott also hoped to win the sympathy of the nonwealthy white majority of the colony.[3]

A major credit crunch in 1772 further united the gentry and small planters of the colony. Imperial belonging, which had once assured a patrimony in a hierarchical chain of being, now seemed to threaten the same patrimony. Tobacco growers' specific complaints dovetailed with broader colonial discontents: North American colonists were repeatedly used by the British government to solve problems existing elsewhere in the empire. The 1767 Townshend duties were imposed on the colonies partly so that Parliament could reduce taxes on British landowners, who had a much louder voice in the nation's politics.[4]

Even more critically, George III passed a law in 1763 forbidding white settlement west of the Appalachians. Confronting land-poor farmers with added economic hardship, the new "Proclamation Line" also cut off the planter gentry from the land speculation they had long profited from. British officials eventually bowed to pressure from enraged colonists and pushed the Proclamation Line hundreds of miles inland in

1768. When the decision nearly resulted in war with the united Indian nations of the Ohio Valley, the British reversed course, renouncing possession of around ten million acres in what is now Kentucky.

Patrick Henry, together with Jefferson and Washington, had been deeply involved in speculative schemes in those lands. The men planned to flip some of their properties for profit, but also to "hold on to some choice pieces of property, insurance that their sons and daughters would have acreage on which to grow ever more tobacco," as historian Timothy Breen writes. The three Virginian leaders were incensed by the latest restrictions. British dithering on the question of western lands was viewed as an existential threat to planters not only because it rendered their speculative investments a loss. It would also bring the resentments of a poor white majority down upon their heads. Wealth inequality had grown starker in many Tidewater counties, in part because wealthy landowners had entailed as much as 80 percent of the region's farmland. Landless whites, small planters, and second sons had little choice but to demand safe access to western territory. Most viscerally and immediately, though, planters feared being hemmed in by a restive slave population. Without the ability to "diffuse" the growing Black population of the coastal regions across a vast frontier, men like Jefferson thought, their own lives were in mortal danger.[5]

Believing their patrimonies might be snatched from them by scheming British merchants, planters began to revise the very identity of a crop master. Requiring no manufacturing before export, and imposing a dispersed settlement pattern, tobacco kept the colonies in what looked to many a savage frontier state. Even native son Robert Beverley conceded in 1705 that "Sailers for want of Towns there, are put to the hardship of rowling most of the Tobacco, a Mile or more, to the Water-side." Exclusive focus on tobacco became a mark not of mastery, but of slavish subservience to colonial overlords.[6]

Nearly 100 percent of Upper South tobacco exports went to Great Britain. Even though British merchants reexported the majority of that crop to northern Europe, the planters themselves were stuck depending on these merchants for all their income. For many elite planters, crop mastery, mastering one's own destiny, started to mean breaking out of this colonial trap. Many began growing grain along with tobacco, often dealing with a less powerful group of intercolonial merchants instead of consolidated London firms that dominated the tobacco trade. Historians have long claimed that the shift "from tobacco to grain" augured the birth of a more free society. But this was no departure from the plantation system or the slavery that underpinned it.

In the Caribbean islands, flush with sugar money and highly focused on export crops, wheat flour could be sold at a steep markup. Absorbing 34 percent of the grain exports of the Upper South, the West Indian slave plantations were consistently the number one or number two markets during the late colonial period. Grain, which had only accounted for 6 percent of Virginia's exports in 1733, had climbed to over 20 percent by the early 1770s.[7]

In 1774, Robert Carter III proudly took Fithian on a tour of his recently completed grain-milling complex: "He shewed me and explain'd the Plan of his Mill; his Canals; Waste-gates; Toll Mill, Merchant Mill," Fithian wrote. "He told me that his Wastgate as it stands alone cost him 95 lbs." Shifting his investments away from tobacco, building his own manufacturing mills on the plantation, and seeking flour export markets not in Britain, but among the slave plantations of the Caribbean, Carter's turn represented a kind of economic freedom seeking by repurposing his plantation and adding a second crop to his first. Overall, tobacco's place in Upper South exports remained steady at 75 percent between the 1730s and the Revolution. Diversification away from tobacco toward wheat, moreover, only enhanced the power of the planter elite. Carter made this clear by emphasizing how much the set of milling structures had cost him. Much more land intensive than tobacco, wheat husbandry also increased planters' demand for arable acreage, pushing up land prices in the Chesapeake. Wealth inequality grew more stark in many Tidewater counties, as landless whites were cut off from farming.[8]

Virginia's planter elite came to view independence as an opportunity to restore a lost and more virtuous past. The transition to the flour industry did not mean getting rid of slavery but transforming the plantation, making it more industrial, and using its productive powers to remake the relationship with the metropole into something new. This is one of the things that is unusual about the Virginia tobacco system. The planters remained in the same place; they decisively changed their crop and their technology, showing a certain adaptability within the plantation framework. Without moving beyond slavery or plantations, they appeared prepared to move beyond the threats of colonial subjugation. They were investing in the future. They did not intend to "dye in Smoke" as they were born.[9]

Perhaps because their new customers were still within the orbit of the British Empire, and because tobacco still ruled their economy, Virginia planters continued to conflate merchant greed, limits on settler aggression, and the dead end of tobacco monoculture with Parliamentary corruption and monarchical overreach. With orators like Patrick Henry connecting the dots for them, Virginia's whites assembled a horrifying picture of their own looming enslavement. The planter gentry in the early 1770s felt at once supremely powerful and intolerably lacking in influence. That feeling would become more acute for planters in North America over time, with inflexible responses from George III leading to an unhealable break in the colonial tie.

When Thomas Jefferson penned the Declaration of Independence in 1776, the king's effort to "excite domestic insurrections amongst us" was prominent among his list of grievances. He was referring to the fact that when Lord Dunmore, the royal governor of Virginia, was forced to flee his post after trying to disarm rebellious Virginia militiamen in 1775, he immediately issued a public proclamation promising liberty to any slaves or white servants who would join the British side. No move of the British created more Patriots in Virginia than "Dunmore's Proclamation"—to an enslaver like Jefferson, such a measure was quasi-genocidal and made any reconciliation with King George inconceivable. As he looked southward, however, Jefferson noted with alarm that early British efforts to subdue the colonies had also ignited a war among Southern whites.

In the backcountry of Georgia and South Carolina, far from the coastal plantations where independence-minded rice planters predominated, considerable numbers of small white farmers remained steadfast Loyalists. They had long resented coastal planters' stranglehold over colonial policy. Like Nathaniel Bacon's acolytes a century before, many were determined to join the ranks of slaveholders. But coastal grandees denied them representation in Charleston; their requests to have local courts and sheriffs in the backcountry were also rejected by the planter-dominated Colonial Assembly of South Carolina. They were particularly incensed by the ways Lowcountry elites had gobbled up massive amounts of unimproved land on the frontier, preventing them from being able to purchase their own plots.[10]

During the war, these backcountry Tories formed paramilitary groups that massacred Patriot partisans, who in turn tortured, arrested, and harassed their Loyalist neighbors. The cycle of raids and retribution made it impossible for either side to maintain control. Seeing the diehard Loyalism of small farmers in the Carolina backcountry, Virginia's leaders suspected that coastal Carolina rice planters had failed to cultivate the allegiance of plebeian whites. A major concern thus presented itself to tobacco planters who had assiduously elevated themselves above their less wealthy neighbors over the previous decades.

Once the war began, complications related to the social hierarchy thrown up by Virginia's plantation economy arose immediately. The Continental Congress had to create an army from scratch. In 1777, a military draft was therefore instituted for all military-age white men. Yet, sons of the wealthy were protected by "overseer exemptions," the rationale being that people who owned twenty or more slaves had to manage the plantation. Nonslaveholding whites complained that they made a greater sacrifice by going to war, since slaveholders could leave plantations in the hands of an overseer and slaves, while they could not. Moreover, a wide pay disparity existed between officers and enlisted men. When the British began their invasion of Virginia in 1780, the state's General Assembly was forced to go further to entice masses of Virginia's rural white men into military service. In a move that essentially democratized the planters' patrimony, the Assembly offered three hundred acres of land and a "healthy sound negro" from the wealthiest slaveowners to every man who served out his tour. This amount of land was enough to enfranchise them—to induct them into the exclusive society of white male citizens with decision-making powers. The Malcontents' clamoring for "the liberty of getting Negroes" in colonial Georgia—a fateful linking of white liberty with Black enslavement—was echoed in revolutionary Virginia.[11]

So keen were Virginia's leaders on winning the allegiance of nonelite white men by offering to incorporate them into the class of planters that, in the middle of the War of Independence, Governor Patrick Henry took the time to organize the new state of Kentucky into counties. He also "appointed magistrates and militia officers" to administer them, and proposed putting large plots of land on the market. Although the promises of free land for the taking in Kentucky proved illusory, and the thousands of settlers who flooded into the new territory during the Revolution were preyed upon by land speculators and raided by Shawnee and Delaware warrior parties defending their hunting grounds, the wartime Kentucky escapade was one of a series of adaptations the tobacco gentry made to resolve the simmering class conflict in their plantation society. The promise of Kentucky was the promise that independence from Britain would widen the membership of America's planter class.[12]

Dunmore's hastily issued proclamation of 1775 foreshadowed a larger "Southern strategy" concocted by British military leadership in 1778. Seeking to align enslaved majorities, as well as antiplanter Loyalists, against the elite Patriot planters in coastal Virginia and South Carolina, the strategy targeted the weaknesses of a society structured around the plantation, especially its dependence on imports and exports for its very survival. After two years of brutal internecine guerrilla warfare in backcountry South Carolina had failed to yield a decisive victory, British forces retrained on Virginia. In January 1781, the Virginia piece of the

Southern strategy began with a series of British raids on coastal ports to shut down the lucrative tobacco export trade.[13]

Benedict Arnold, the former Patriot general now leading the invading units, traveled up the James River, devastating the countryside and sowing panic among white Patriots. His forces also managed to destroy several major tobacco warehouses across the river from Richmond. They even camped at Byrd's Westover Plantation, preparing to take the state capital of Richmond. They captured the city without facing resistance. Arnold wrote to recently elected Governor Thomas Jefferson, demanding access to the city's stores of tobacco and military supplies. Jefferson had cleverly arranged for the removal of both before the invasion. In response, an enraged Arnold ordered the city put to the torch.

Arnold next focused on destroying vessels, warehouses, and shipyards. He succeeded in seizing small tobacco ports to consolidate his position and used thousands of captured slaves to do the onerous work of digging trenches, without which Arnold's defense of these towns would have been impossible. Petersburg was a particularly tantalizing target. Since its founding in 1733, the riverside town had become the tobacco-marketing capital of the colony. When Arnold's troops occupied it, they burned thousands of dollars' worth of finished tobacco and a number of vessels.

The worst was yet to come for Virginia whites, as British General Lord Cornwallis arrived to reinforce Arnold in May 1781. The prospect of a British-inspired slave revolt so spooked the Patriot enslavers of Virginia that Jefferson begged Washington to return to his native state with the Continental Army. One of the other original architects of the Declaration of Independence, Virginian Richard Henry Lee, even proposed Washington be made dictator of the state until the emergency was resolved. Even if his solution was extreme, his fears were reasonable: Cornwallis led a series of devastating raids up the James River past Richmond, resulting in the flight of white families west into the Piedmont. Many took slaves with them. Lee and George Mason were among the James River planters who packed up their things and fled.[14]

Like the Shawnee militants in Kentucky, the thousands of "healthy sound negros" Virginia elites planned to dole out to white soldiers had a very different idea of the meaning the war might hold. Enslaved people's decisive actions during the British occupation of Virginia transformed a war that expanded the rights of slaveholders into a social revolution that threatened to destroy the tobacco plantation economy that had nourished the revolutionary ideals of their Patriot masters. Many Black people took advantage of the raids to seek freedom for themselves. A white observer watching Arnold's offensive wrote that "the families within the sphere of his action suffered greatly. Some have lost 40, others 30, everyone a considerable part of their slaves."[15]

When the British still could not consolidate control of the region, they withdrew back down the river toward the end of summer—it would be their final time doing so. They went about "sweeping all the slaves and other property and pillaging and destroying houses" on their way. Thousands of enslaved people, seeing their final chance for freedom moving swiftly downriver toward the Atlantic, "flocked to the enemy from all quarters." Though Patriot slave masters had continually filled their heads with half-true stories about Redcoats selling fugitives into an even worse slavery in the West Indies, still they went. Slaves from nearly every plantation along the James River Valley deserted to Cornwallis's army. Jefferson himself had thirty enslaved people run away to the enemy in ten days.[16]

As Cornwallis's army of around eight thousand soldiers marched toward its fate at Yorktown in September 1781, "between four thousand and five thousand men and women of all ages followed behind the baggage train." Many of them had found work in the army as cooks, maids, nurses, and foragers. A Hessian mercenary observed the incredible vision of freedom they embodied on the march seaward. In one case, "a completely naked Negro wore a pair of silk breaches, another a finely colored coat, a third a silk vest without sleeves, a fourth an elegant shirt, a fifth a fine Churchmans hat, and a sixth a wig.—All the rest of the body was bare." Clearly if one man had hoarded this enslavers' costume, he could have clothed himself from head to toe. Instead, they divvied up the loot, each taking one elegant piece and wearing it over their otherwise unclothed frames. Amid the breakdown of slave masters' power, the enslaved displayed a unique vision of bodily adornment and perhaps inside humor, an aesthetic embodiment of the kinds of illicit sharing that underlay the "natural increase" in their own numbers in spite of plantation hardship. It was a lark during a desperate time; after all, they were putting their futures in the hands of a British invading force that until recently had helped keep them in slavery. For once they were not walking in bare feet. In fact, many of them rode their slave masters' beloved horses while donning the masters' finest threads.[17]

At the swampy colonial village of Yorktown, not twenty miles from Jamestown, where the colonial project had begun nearly two centuries before, British attempts to hold on to the North American colonies essentially came to a close. Cornwallis's army was supposed to be reinforced from the sea, but British leaders had become so concerned with reports of an impending French invasion of Jamaica that they had withdrawn their own naval fleet from Yorktown in 1781 in order to shore up their much more valuable sugar islands. Britain's commitment to protecting its most revenue-rich plantation colonies, in other words, damned to failure its Virginia campaign, and with it the whole effort to keep North America.[18]

In the event, thousands of Black women and men fleeing tobacco plantations for an unknown fate with the British entrenched Yorktown under Cornwallis's orders. Soon enough a siege by allied French and American forces, totaling around eighteen thousand men, tightened around the town. When it became impossible for his men to leave the barricades to forage for food, Cornwallis was forced to slaughter thousands of horses. Then, to extend the lives of his own soldiers, he ordered the freedom seekers expelled from the fort. Thousands of Black Virginians were pushed out of the gates to face the wrath of their former owners, or simply to starve in the denuded countryside. St. George Tucker, a Patriot officer under George Washington, coolly recorded their fates:

"An immense number of Negroes have died in the most miserable manner in York." Thousands of other Black Southerners were luckier. They were able to escape on departing British vessels, carving out new lives for themselves as free subjects of the British Empire in Canada, Nova Scotia, England, and elsewhere. Many of them later led efforts to abolish Britain's Atlantic slave trade, which finally happened in 1807.[19]

Tens of thousands more African Americans remained in Virginia. They had been transformed by the wartime experience and the revolutionary calls for human equality. Some enslavers responded to the moment as well. There was a sharp uptick in individual manumissions in the 1780s. In his will, George Washington freed all 123 human beings he claimed to own. A few other scions of the planter elite, like John Laurens and Robert Carter III engaged in similar one-off acts of mass emancipation. Virginia Methodists and Quakers spoke against slavery, and petitions for a general emancipation were considered in the State Assembly. It never passed. Even this small window of antislavery possibility shut after 1800, when an enslaved blacksmith named Gabriel Prosser orchestrated a plan for his fellow captives to rise against their enslavers in towns stretching from Richmond to Charleston on the night of August 30. They intended to kidnap Governor James Monroe to ransom him in return for their freedom. Betrayed at the last minute, twenty-six men were hanged, while eight other suspects were sold out of state. White opinions on slavery hardened against the threat of Black violence.[20]

"Patrimony" had once described the benefits of the colonial relation. Before the Revolution, when colonials felt unfairly treated, they reminded British policymakers of their rights as "free-born Englishmen." The phrase grounded fundamental privileges in a genealogical inheritance. But it also meant that tobacco patriarchs were colonial subjects. Their deferential relationship to British merchants, ministers of Parliament, and the king himself placed them around the middle in a hierarchy of fathers. Planters who sympathized with independence had come to see

George III as an errant patriarch corrupted by evil advisers (Parliament), the flow of dispensations to the planters choked off by a monarch's weakness and courtiers' greed. George's colonial sons were therefore left with no choice but to become fatherless, or more properly, "sons of liberty," and no longer of the king.

Indeed, from the scale of the household all the way up to the scale of Britain's global empire, patrimony was contested during the Revolution. The oft-told story of Jefferson ridding Virginia of entail and primogeniture during his wartime service in the Virginia House of Delegates is a case in point. In the end, however, white Virginia revolutionaries threw off one type of patriarchal power (the king) to reclaim another: their own power to dispense and dispose of western lands, slave property, and profits from trade. The abolition of entail and primogeniture after the Revolution merely widened the base of inheritance, allowing more white men to plot their climb toward American liberty through land and slaves.

As a delegate to the Continental Congress immediately after independence was secured in 1783, Jefferson laid out the basic framework for what would become the pattern of westward expansion south of the Ohio River. Through an orderly process of survey and sale of Indian land—meant to be the inverse of the corrupt cronyism through which Fitzhugh and his ilk had concentrated a tobacco kingdom in the colonial Chesapeake—Jefferson hoped to democratize the patrimony. Thus, the plantation system more than survived the Revolution. It was reordered into something newly powerful and expansive after independence. The "freedom" to buy, sell, and bequeath plantation estates as one wished meant that Black families would be divided among heirs more frequently.[21]

America's postrevolutionary return to protecting and promoting the plantation would become even clearer during the Constitutional Convention, which was dominated by towering political figures from Virginia. Tobacco planter Edmund Randolph, who submitted the famous Virginia Plan to the convention, would soon serve as the nation's first attorney general and as secretary of state. George Washington presided over the closed-door debates in the sweltering summer of 1787. His fellow tobacco planter James Madison was the principal theoretician of the Constitution. The "compromise" he engineered mollified a New England–Deep South coalition that insisted protections for slave traders and slaveowners be forced into the document. Article 1, section 9, extended the already controversial African slave trade for twenty more years. A clause in article 4, section 2, obligating free states to surrender fugitive slaves to their masters, was also included, in essence forcing states to prop up a system of bondage many of their citizens may have opposed. Most fatefully, the Framers inserted the three-fifths compromise that inflated the representational power of Southern states by counting their slaves in census numbers without, of course, allowing them to vote.

But the Constitution went much further than securing the rights of individual masters over the people they held in slavery. Delegates put in place a strong central government in part to ensure the resumption of transatlantic flows of credit and goods on which the planters so deeply depended. Article 1, section 8, for example, gave Congress unprecedented power to tax the people, to control a national currency, and to assume responsibility over the debts previously owed by the states. In the moment, these measures were intended to reassure London merchants and bankers that the new government would make good on its debts. The delegates succeeded in crafting a Constitution that protected the most important nodes of that Atlantic market: the plantations of the Lowcountry and the Tidewater, as well as a new cash crop: cotton.[22]

Even though there were myriad issues at stake when the document was sent to the states for ratification in 1788, the debate in Virginia focused squarely on the slavery question. Not whether enslavement should or should not be allowed in the new Republic, but rather: Had the conventioneers done enough to secure slaveholders' rights over their human property? Nearly all speakers at Virginia's ratification proceedings, regardless of whether Federalist or anti-Federalist, agreed that the Constitution should do this. All were agreed, moreover, that economic prosperity in the near term was impossible without slaves. Madison reassured his colleagues that the compromises over slave property embedded in the document would guarantee the rights of slaveholders.[23]

The tobacco planter and avowed anti-Federalist Patrick Henry disagreed. Governor of Virginia during the War of Independence and for a second term in the 1780s, Henry was the most renowned orator of a state political class known for its oratory, and he was convinced that the Constitution being considered for ratification would put in place a despotic power that could be wielded by Northerners to end slavery. Virginia Governor Edmund Randolph, a scion of one of the more notable planter clans of Virginia, saw in the proposed document "the foetus of a monarchy," which presumably would result in a new patriarch who would squander their patrimony in slaves. Henry's and Randolph's concerns were not merely economic or political—they were existential. Henry informed his fellow Virginians that a general liberation of slaves would create "a picture so horrid, so wretched, so dreadful, that I need no longer dwell upon it." As if his audience was not sufficiently aghast, he at one point shouted, "They'll take your niggers from you!"[24]

Although Virginia ultimately ratified the Constitution over the objections of Henry, Randolph, and others, the concerns of other Virginia planters like George Mason moved James Madison to suggest the Bill of Rights as a compromise to those who thought the Constitution granted too much power to the federal government. The Tenth Amendment, which made clear that all powers not explicitly granted to Congress were reserved to the states, as well as the Fifth Amendment, which underlined the sanctity of "private property," were meant in part to allay the suspicions that prevented enslavers like Henry from supporting ratification. In 1776, Madison, Washington, Henry, Mason, and Jefferson held it as an article of faith that the American liberty now endangered by the actions of Crown and Parliament could not be regained without the continued enslavement of Black people. In 1787, they embedded that premise in the Constitution, or rejected the document for not adequately securing the legality of property in humans.

While many Northern politicians opposed ratification because the Constitution was too proslavery, and others did not see slavery as the central issue, Virginia's influence in the wider conversation is undeniable. It is difficult to imagine an American Revolution without Henry's fiery oratory, Madison's subtle reasoning, and Jefferson's evisceration of the very idea of British authority. Their prominence continued in the constitutional ratification process and well beyond. A Virginia tobacco planter served as president or vice president in each of the first seven presidential administrations in U.S. history: One of them was in the White House without interruption from 1789 to 1825.

Although the Virginia Framers spoke during the 1770s as if George III had forced slavery upon them, two centuries of intentional, strategic, and persistent actions on the part of colonial planters like themselves had rooted tobacco plantations, dependent on a restive Black population of thousands, at the center of their lives. Their roles in suppressing slave revolts as masters and militia officers, in subjecting their chattel to horrifying punishments, and in attempting to extinguish Black community life while depending upon its fruits had borne an unsightly harvest. At a moment of exhilarating revolutionary possibility in 1776, a weed of fear had sprouted in the clean fields of liberty's leading minds. They were unable to tamp it down as individuals, so they harangued the new nation into taking up the task. In 1787, they succeeded in yoking a free republic to the harrow of the enslaver.

Nevertheless, weaknesses in their tobacco economy had been revealed even before the revolutionary struggle; and British occupation during the war had transformed the groaning discontents of the captives into decisive action against bondage. The Chesapeake planters weathered even harder times in the 1790s, when another financial panic exacerbated the impact of the British decision to cut off Americans' access to West Indian markets. Diminished expectations led to a nostalgia for the colonial Golden Age of the 1720s to the 1760s among an aging Tidewater elite. Yet the plantation system they had seized from Powhatan's domain adapted and survived.

Tobacco production migrated south of the James, while Chesapeake and Piedmont planters kept shifting to wheat, maintaining profitability and ensconcing slavery and export agriculture in the Piedmont parts of the state, as milling industries and new cities grew up to serve the flour trade. In the old tobacco grounds of the Chesapeake, along the bottomlands of the James and York rivers, only the most ruthless cost-cutting plantation managers survived into the first decades of the nineteenth century. Among their strategies was the marketing of "excess" captives westward in a new interstate slave trade. With little regard for "the claims of kinfolk," cash-poor plantation heirs and grasping merchants sold hundreds of thousands of Black Virginians to the emerging Cotton Belt over the next sixty years. But how can we blame them? They were just trying to provide for their sons.[25]

CHAPTER 9

The Colonians

In 1787, the former slave and current London-based abolitionist Quobna Ottobah Cugoano presented a blistering assessment of the men who were debating the American Constitution in Virginia. The planters and slave traders of the New World, he argued, were a violent and savage race unto themselves. "The Colonians," he called them. A race with a marked propensity for thieving, the Colonians "do not take away a man's property, like other robbers; but they take a man himself." Refusing to mince words, Cugoano stated plainly that their "foreign settlements and colonies were founded on murders and devastations." Although they flattered themselves that they were improving the land and civilizing the savages, these Protestant enslavers were "as much enamored with any infamous way of getting riches, as the Spaniards were with the Peruvian vessels of gold." The Spanish gold miner's obsession with getting something out of nothing—just like the planter's obsession with extracting as much tobacco from Virginia fields, and from Virginia slaves, as possible—had a hidden cost for him, however. "The longer that men continue in the practice of evil and wickedness, they grow the more abandoned." Just like the sugar, rice, and tobacco flooding back to England, the evil in the colonies would also find its way home, "at last mark[ing] out the whole of the British constitution with ruin and destruction." This was not a threat, but a premonition.[1]

At the time, Cugoano's description of "murders and devastations" was nowhere more accurate than in the French-controlled West Indian colony of Saint-Domingue, which had taken the thieving stratagems of the Colonians of Barbados and raised them to a new level. In the 1760s, the sugar exported annually from the island was nearly five times more valuable than Virginia's tobacco shipments to Britain. Also exporting more sugar than all the British West Indies combined by the 1780s, Saint-Domingue supplied 70 percent of France's raw sugar, thus supporting a refining sector whose sale of finished products abroad accounted for nearly 20 percent of national exports. As the anticolonial priest Abbé Raynal pointed out in 1770, Saint-Domingue was the engine driving the French Atlantic system. "The labors of the colonists settled in the long-scorned islands," he wrote, "are the sole basis of the African trade, extend the fisheries and cultivation of North America, provide advantageous outlets for the manufacture of Asia, double perhaps triple the activity of the whole of Europe. They can be regarded as the principal cause of the rapid movement which stirs the universe." An estimated 15 percent of France's overall economic growth during the eighteenth century came from the empire.[2]

The flow back and forth of goods and money transformed the port cities of the country; as for Paris, it grew from a landlocked administrative capital into a "financial powerhouse." Men like the Parisian financier Jean Joseph de Laborde (reputedly the richest man in France) invested their fortunes in the Caribbean. As two recent scholars write, Laborde "spent 1.2 million livres to acquire a collection of contiguous plantations" in Saint-Domingue, "and 750,000 livres as his share of a complex irrigation system in the region. He populated his estates with thousands of captives, many of them traveling from Africa on his slave ships."[3]

Although Saint-Domingue was strongly influenced by the plantations pioneered in late seventeenth-century Barbados, "by the late eighteenth century," writes historian Paul Cheney, the French sugar island "was the most modern and radical experiment in the international division of labor hitherto produced by merchant capitalism." The colony was a site of the new and the Enlightened. Enslavers read Diderot and exchanged ideas for scientific improvement in a transatlantic "republic of letters." In 1784, the New World's first hot-air balloon launch took place over a sugar plantation south of the port city known as Le Cap-Français. "Black spectators" were present at the event. They were overheard talking about "the insatiable passion" white men felt to "exert power over nature."[4]

They may have been thinking of their own enslavers—sugar planters like Nicolas Caradeux. An avid innovator in enlightened methods of sugar refining, Caradeux was viewed by his late eighteenth-century peers as a man of "great foresight, full of ideas and plans that were useful and advantageous to the colony." Indeed, Caradeux's "passion to make the best sugar in the colony" was so overweening that it "enraged him against his sugar makers and his drivers; it was also against them that he exercised the greatest cruelties." Even the man's admirers reported him "cold-bloodedly having slaves thrown into the furnaces, into the boiling cauldrons, or having them buried alive and standing with only their head showing, and letting them die in this way," often for the crime of making "*vilain sucre*" (ugly sugar). Buried up to his neck in the madness of plantation building, perhaps Caradeux had lost his mind. Literally planting Black workers in the soil like knots of cane and melting them down in the sugar, he seemed to confuse people with things. Perhaps, the enslaver of hundreds seemed to wonder, slaves *were* sugar. Yet Caradeux's madness was just an extreme version of the logic governing Saint-Domingue's plantation system.[5]

In their overheated imaginations, planters rendered enslaved people miracles of hardness, of resistance to decay. The writer Pierre-François-Xavier de Charlevoix claimed that Black people were "machines whose springs must be rewound each time that you want them to move." Automatons who understood only the crack of the whip, they were given little food or clothing, yet they were in "perfect health" compared to a class of well-fed white masters riddled with an "infinity of illness." Black slaves were forced not only to push the plows and wheels of the planters' machinery, but to push the boundaries of Enlightenment thought. Eighteenth-century European "men of reason"—who insisted that equations must balance, debits must match credits, and that every action has an equal and opposite reaction—at the same time pronounced Africans miraculously productive biological machines who turned zero inputs into perpetual motion. They used new rhetorics of anatomical expertise to justify the oppression of Black people—especially the canard they had "thick skin" with a special "subcutaneous layer" that both absorbed light and made them impervious to pain.[6]

Saint-Domingue jurist Michel René Hilliard d'Auberteuil described each slave on a sugar plantation as a moving unit of value generation for the colony: about six hundred livres apiece if the plantation was managed properly. The median slave repaid one-third of their purchase price in a year, he asserted. If that slave lived for four years and no more, the planter profited from the transaction. Voracious consumers of women and men, the planters of Saint-Domingue talked little about "increase," natural or otherwise. Sugar planters profited most from going into debt to purchase slaves, working them to death over a few years, and then buying more. The plantation's self-renewing cycle of consumption, production, sale, reinvestment, and expansion was activated through the medium of spent Black bodies.[7]

As long as the slave trade continued, and large profits from sugar were "put back into the system" as Hilliard advised, the "seed of fortune in the colony" would continue to grow. And it grew remarkably fast, despite mass death. Between 1780 and 1788, the enslaved population of the island increased from 251,806 to 405,528 souls. Almost all these people came through the Middle Passage. French traders had more than doubled their imports of captives from Africa, delivering 41,000 people to the island in 1790 alone, nearly four times the annual average shipped to Jamaica. By that time, a white population of 40,000 stood nervous

The Enlightenment's ideal plantation; or, the interior of a sugar plantation boiling house in the French West Indies.

The Enlightenment's ideal plantation; or, the landscape of a sugar plantation in the French West Indies.

guard over 452,000 slaves forced into confinement in the closely packed sugar districts of the northern plain.[8]

Trade with the United States was indispensable to Saint-Domingue's sugar boom in the 1780s. The rapidly growing sugar plantation economy required lumber for buildings and sugar barrels, salt cod, rice, and flour for food, and coal for boiling the cane juice. North American merchants supplied over 90 percent of foreign imports into the two principal ports of Saint-Domingue between 1785 and 1790. Conversely, the French Caribbean colony became a lifeline to the newly independent United States. The small island absorbed around 10 percent of all U.S. exports in the 1780s, while as late as 1795 the French West Indies sent over $15 million worth of commodities (mostly sugar and coffee) to the United States. With the exception of Britain, Saint-Domingue was the most important trading partner of the United States. Importations of $1 million from Portugal and $1 million from China were more typical for 1795 than the $15 million from Saint-Domingue. "Access to the West Indies is indispensably necessary to us," Thomas Jefferson concluded in 1785.[9]

It was more than simple economic expediency that oriented Jefferson's mind toward the French-speaking world. *Philosophes* in Old World and New were his informants, his bosom friends, and in some ways his mentors in the ways of liberty. Little did he suspect that, over the decade of the 1790s, the hundreds of thousands of enslaved people toiling in Saint-Domingue's sugar mills would turn his waking nightmares of racial apocalypse and Black rule into reality. The events of 1791–1804, later called the Haitian Revolution, would throw American planters and policymakers into an unprecedented panic. Their reactions, which unfolded over years, transformed the future of the plantation in the United States, leading to an ironclad commitment to slavery among white Southerners that had weakened during the American Revolution.

On a Sunday in August 1791, an enslaved driver named Boukman led a Vodún rite in the woods of northern Saint-Domingue. No written accounts of the meeting ever surfaced, but it is said the attendees sacrificed a pig and took a blood oath, binding themselves to one another. The timing of the gathering was no coincidence—indeed, Boukman likely planned to capitalize on the transatlantic upheavals of the French Revolution, which had begun in 1789.

Many free people of color were quite wealthy and had become planters themselves, but were suffering under a racial hierarchy that had stiffened considerably during the 1770s: The typical plantation pattern of a white-Black dyad began to drown a once multiracial society with dozens of racial labels. Therefore, representatives of the free colored population had clamored for legal protection by the revolutionary government. Just months before Boukman's clandestine gathering, representatives in France granted them full citizenship rights. It was a major event in the history of French republicanism. "From that day forward," writes historian Laurent Dubois, "there would be no racial distinctions among the free.... In the heart of the slave societies of the Americas, legal distinctions on the basis of race were outlawed."[10]

White colonists' refusal to accept racial equality on the island triggered a civil war between them and the free colored population. But the instability of the moment ran even deeper, as the 1789 challenge to monarchical rule in France had created a crisis within the white ruling class on the island. Some sided with the revolutionaries, others with the Crown. Alliances were shifting and complicated. Ongoing strife among the free populations of the island, watched carefully by slaves like Boukman, created the possibility for a massive slave uprising to go much further than any ever had before—including Amador's Revolt on São Tomé two centuries before.

Mere days after the secret meeting, the cane fields of Saint-Domingue's northern plain began to go up in flames. One enslaved person captured at the time confessed that "all the drivers, coachmen, domestics, and confidential Negroes [had] formed a plot to set fire to the plantations and to murder all the whites." Both inside and outside the plantations, drivers like Boukman were important leaders in the coming slave revolt. As in the Lowcountry, drivers had unusual freedom of movement. In Saint-Domingue, they went about armed with swords because of their disciplinary roles on the plantation.

The slave rebellion quickly spread, along with news of violence against the planters and their lieutenants. On one plantation, about a dozen slaves went to the boiling house late one night looking for the refiner. Finding only his apprentice, reported one horrified planter, "they dragged him to the front of the dwellinghouse, and they hewed him into pieces with their cutlasses: his screams brought out the overseer, whom they instantly shot. The rebels now found their way to the apartment of the refiner, and massacred him in his bed." Freedom seekers from two neighboring plantations soon joined this group, "and together they burned the entire plantation to the ground."[11]

By late August, the entire northern plain of the island was alight. One planter, peering through his telescope from a promontory above Le Cap, saw only "slaves, ruins, and the most complete devastation." Another waxed apocalyptic. "The fire, which they spread to the sugarcane, to all the buildings, to their houses and huts, covered the sky with churning clouds of smoke during the day, and at night lit up the horizon with aurora borealis that projected far away the reflection of so many volcanoes, and gave all objects a livid tint of blood." As historian Carolyn Fick emphasizes, the rebels made sure to burn "the manufacturing installations, sugar mills, tools and other farm equipment, storage bins, and slave quarters; in short, every material manifestation of their existence under slavery and its means of exploitation."[12]

Maroon villages—powerful communities of fugitive slaves who had built permanent, multigenerational settlements in hard-to-reach pockets of the island over the course of the eighteenth century—were essential for the continuation of the antiplanter campaign in the early 1790s. They taught the newly self-liberated "maroon tactics" that had been developed in military engagements with French slave hunters, like ambush-and-retreat maneuvers to exhaust better-armed pursuers, along with feigned ceasefires and fake retreats. New rebels were also apprenticed in the craft skills of insurgency. They learned how to fashion hidden traps in the ground, and how to hew a tree trunk so it looked like a cannon from a distance. Finally, they adopted forms of psychological warfare perennially practiced by the outgunned. Flying a flag that read "Death to All Whites" and hollering war chants continuously, the rebels played on white fears of African savagery to instill terror in their oppressors. But freedom seekers' frightful defiance in the face of death was real. When one captured rebel was about to face a firing line of white soldiers, he "began to laugh, sing, and joke" and "jeered at us in mockery." As the decisive moment arrived, it was the prisoner himself who gave the order to fire.[13]

Rifling through the dead man's clothes, his killers "found pamphlets printed in France claiming the Rights of Man; in his vest pocket was a large packet of tinder and phosphate of lime. On his chest he had a little sack full of hair, herbs, bits of bone, which they call a fetish." As the island went up in flames, the African majority of Saint-Domingue let fly an explosive combination of French egalitarian radicalism, Afro-Caribbean Vodún, and the codes and solidarities of secret societies. Urged on by the audible prayers, moans, and incantations of those whom the whites called "their priests," Black armies walked into cannon fire with the Rights of Man pinned to their hearts. Saint-Domingue's planters had a difficult time grasping what was unfolding before their eyes.[14]

Over weeks and then months of the spreading rebellion, the planters still perceived the freedom seekers as automatons incapable of independent thought and action. When they took a rebel prisoner, they demanded to know "who . . . incited this odious trance." One sugar planter mused that "there is a motor that powers them and that keeps powering them and that we cannot come to know." They were shocked by the degree of coordination of a rebellion that was now made up of more than ten thousand people. Its leaders, many of them drivers and other favored slaves, had divided the rebels into three armies. Hundreds of them were mounted on horseback. They used the plantations they had seized as "army camps." An increasing number of planters fled the sugar districts of Saint-Domingue's northern plain by the end of the summer, because they saw no way back.[15]

The 1791 slave rebellion, just as Cugoano had foreseen, sent a wave of change back to European shores. By 1793, events in Saint-Domingue had made it impossible to maintain slavery. "Whichever way things turn out," concluded one despondent planter, "our ruin is total. If we do not defeat and destroy the rebel slaves, we will all end up being slaughtered by these monsters, and by destroying them we destroy our fortunes. For it is in these slaves that our fortunes exist." That year, the National Assembly pronounced a general emancipation, the first ever granted in the Colonians' New World.[16]

In the wake of the momentous 1793 emancipation of slaves in the French Empire, former slaves, free people of color, and revolutionary whites allied with France to defend the Revolution in the Caribbean. Led by the former slave Toussaint Louverture, they waged a gritty, decade-long war of resistance against British and Spanish militaries, who, now at war with France, each tried at different times to seize the island and reinstitute slavery. The alliance between ex-slaves and the French state ended in 1802, however, when Napoleon Bonaparte reversed the emancipation decree and reopened the French branch of the African slave trade. He also decreed that all property-owning people of color should be deported from the island, so that the plantation order of white=owner/Black=owned could be made real once again. The Napoleonic state thus retreated from its revolutionary ideals of universal brotherhood at the moment it was about to embark on a mission to spread Enlightened institutions across Europe via war.[17]

Yet in Saint-Domingue, France's mission of conquest would fail. When word spread to the island that Napoleon was dispatching a military force of 100,000 soldiers and 408 ships to "disarm the blacks" and revive the plantation system through mass reenslavement, the freedom seekers set off a new round of plantation destruction as ferocious as the

1791 uprising. Once again, the focus was on the hardware of the sugar plantations as well as the cane fields. One Black woman arrested by the French on suspicion of involvement in burning plantations identified herself as "Brule Les Cayes"—burn Les Cayes. Les Cayes was a region known to be the site of a future sugar boom.[18]

The French soldiers sent by Napoleon to subdue the island fell in horrific numbers to the old Caribbean killers of yellow fever and malaria. Survivors of illness met their deaths in military engagements with well-organized, combat-seasoned Black veterans fighting the prospect of their own return to slavery. The Haitian Revolution ended in 1803 not with the triumph of the mother country, but with the evisceration of France's colonial system and the establishment of the first free Black republic in the western hemisphere. The Black General Jean-Jacques Dessalines promulgated a "Declaration of Independence" for the new Republic of Haiti that took effect on January 1, 1804. The world's richest planter class had been thrown into permanent exile.

After nearly two centuries of being ignored by mainstream scholars, the Haitian Revolution has, in recent decades, finally received some of the attention it deserves—so much, in fact, that the earthshaking slave

French troops fleeing Saint-Domingue at the close of the Haitian Revolution.

uprisings, unheralded anticolonial violence, and ultimate success of the rebellion have overshadowed the later history of the country. Far fewer scholars have shone a light on the more thoroughgoing revolutions that happened after independence, in part because events of the postindependence years raise difficult questions.

Some of the formerly enslaved generals who helped turn the 1791 slave revolt into one of the first successful anticolonial revolutions in the history of the Western world would also be the first to demonstrate that the plantation, which had adapted and expanded premodern forms of bondage in the seventeenth century, was capable of flourishing without chattel slavery. Toussaint Louverture, whom the French had appointed governor-general of the island in 1801, created a system of "militarized plantation production," going so far as to invite French planters to retake their old estates. He promised them the government's help in disciplining former slaves, and in forcing them to participate, as involuntary sharecroppers, in making the sugar and coffee flow again. Not long after, Napoleon decided to reduce all Haitians of African descent back to slavery, betraying Louverture. He tricked him into a meeting, where he was arrested and shipped to France. He died soon after in a frigid prison cell high in the Alps.[19]

After independence in 1804, General Dessalines had himself declared emperor of Haiti. He, too, was unable to resist the siren call of the plantation. Dessalines dispatched military brigades to hunt "fugitives" whom he forced to work on the old sugar plantations of the northern plain. Henri Christophe, another wartime leader, was crowned king of the northern part of the island in 1811 (north and south were divided politically at the time). He distributed the French plantations to his military generals and helped them restart exports by coercing ordinary Haitians back into plantation labor. His lieutenants engaged in mass arrests of poor people in isolated areas. He ordered one military patrol to "burn all of the small houses" of one village and "ruin" the agricultural fields so the residents would have no choice but to return to work. Soon, Haiti was producing nearly half the amount of sugar that colonial Saint-

Domingue had before revolution. Yet the effort to recompose the cosmopolitan nightmare of Saint-Domingue on the ashes of slave revolution was doomed to failure. Louverture had been shot in the leg when he led a force to put down a plantation rebellion in 1795. Dessalines fell to an assassin in 1806. Henri Christophe was defeated in civil war in 1819 and committed suicide in 1820. During the first decades of independence, nevertheless, many former slaves had to continue their struggle to evade a reborn plantation system. They did not share a vision for the future with their new rulers, most of all the idea that liberation from the French would finally give Haitians the chance to become more like the French.[20]

Fortunately for them, the territory of the independent Republic of Haiti was very lightly populated, allowing a large number of small family farms between three and thirty acres to flourish. Often occupying abandoned plantations, these small farmers concentrated on growing everything that had been kept from them during the rule of the plantation: corn, beans, rice, millet, bananas, sweet potatoes, manioc, and yams. As historian Johnhenry Gonzalez writes, they turned much of the old plantation island "into a kind of immense tropical kitchen garden that produced rich surplus of food in exchange for relatively moderate outputs of labor." In many ways, life was restored. When they did need to access cash, they rifled the abandoned plantations for goods they could sell, like coffee beans. They also progged dyewoods, tortoiseshell, and beeswax from the shoreline and the woodland.[21]

The costly imported cauldrons and grinding mills of the sugar plantation had been emblems of their enslavement. Just like for Betty, the Virginia woman whom William Byrd II tried and failed to keep in chains in 1710, the hoe was the primary instrument of their self-emancipation. In new fields and gardens, it kept down weeds and broke up the sod. Having been in wide use in West Africa for centuries, the iron hoe was also symbolically potent. Ancestral farms in the Haitian countryside were anchored by "sacred household trees." Because individual ancestors and spirits dwelled there, one family's plot and the next were utterly distinct, so land could not be bought and sold as a commodity. Roots of the trees were carefully hoed around or left alone. Moreover, "rooted" land also rooted the people who belonged to it. Since there were no masters, they could not be moved hither and yon according to a white person's caprice. Nor could a member of a rooted family be given a second, ghostly existence as a price that circulated through international financial markets.

The hoe had still other uses for rural Haitians. When detached from its handle, the hoe blade doubled as the percussion instrument of a secret society with the sonorous name of "Vlangbengdeng." Worn on the belt and struck rapidly with a short stick, the blade rang out a rhythm that sounded to its hearers like *"vlang-beng-deng-vlang-beng-deng."* The characteristic jogging, ringing sound of the hoe blade identified meetings of the group, which were often called to protect what Gonzalez describes as "the informal land claims of the masses."[22]

After the fall of King Henri Christophe in 1819, the ghost acres of the sugar plantation fell more and more into the hands of the people once enslaved there. The more land became available, the less Haitians wanted to labor on plantations. This raised the cost of hiring a laborer and pushed sugar production out of reach for those still trying to make planters of themselves. Large landowners were forced to leave more sections of their plantations unused, creating yet more land for subsistence farmers. As land prices fell, more acreage was taken up by small farmers. The plantation sighed its last breath in Haiti in the 1820s.

Other than revenues gained from the export of coffee from the southern half of the island, coastal elites—largely people of color who had been wealthy before the revolution—and inland peasants left each other alone for the next century. Cut off from the trade connections and political support of the white world, and having to spend much of the public revenue to maintain an oversize military so they could fend off the threat of reconquest and reenslavement from France, Spain, and the United States, elites lacked the power to force commoners into a market economy. So the plantation died not with the flight of the French in 1803, but in a kind of stalemate between urban elites, rural smallholders, and the dominant Euro-American nation-states. Haiti ended up with what Gonzalez describes as "the most evenly distributed land ownership pattern of any former plantation region of the Americas." Labeling nineteenth-century Haiti an egalitarian paradise goes too far. Some forms of sharecropping, domestic labor, and intrafamilial exploitation persisted in the countryside. Nor was it a particularly wealthy place. But the formerly enslaved victims of the sugar economy had achieved a nation modeled after their own antiplantation ethos.[23]

At a time when millions of people of African descent throughout the Americas were still being held in slavery, the lives Haitians made for themselves in the former hell created by white masters were truly remarkable. Evading taxation, as well as the new forms of plantation labor that early independence leaders attempted to foist upon them, ordinary Haitians founded independent farm communities and rural market towns in the mountainous interiors of the island that carried Africanized names like Bois Nago, Savane Zombi, or Harbe Guinée.[24]

The many small, quiet revolutions of independent Haiti, rooted in but surpassing the achievements of the Haitian Revolution, were an effort at once physical and spiritual to restore the cosmic fabric rent violently by the relentless builders of the plantation. It was not one colossal uprising or even a successful military campaign, but the slow and steady construction of an alternate society. This was another antiplantation not given a real chance. Not protected, promoted, or supported by the state, the peasant market societies of the Haitian countryside were only suffered to exist due to the weakness of the Haitian government in the nineteenth century. If the new Haitian oligarchy had had the resources to "civilize" the underdeveloped countryside and bring their countrymen into Euro-Atlantic modernity, they would have done so.

By the 1870s, peasants around the world, from French colonial Vietnam to the Brazilian Sertão to Appalachia, to the Russian Mir, were forced by powerful national states in possession of railroads, telegraphs, and, when necessary, repeating rifles, into cash-crop agriculture, tenancy, indebtedness, and dependence. Ordinary Haitians' victories after the Revolution insulated them from this process. In the European-dominated world outside the island, however, the achievements of the slave rebels in Saint-Domingue were seen not only as a regrettable triumph of savagery over civilization, but as an unprecedented opportunity by enslavers elsewhere in the Americas to build their own plantation system on the enlightened French model.

CHAPTER 10

Vlangbengdeng

While they tried their best to forget it, the Haitian Revolution lodged stubbornly in the unconscious of European thinkers, surfacing as nightmares of race war, an unthinkable victory of Black savagery over white civilization, and imminent racial apocalypse every time the question of Black freedom was put on the table. Writers, orators, and politicians raised the specter of "the horrors of Santo Domingo" to silence antislavery voices in early nineteenth-century Virginia and to whip up anti-Union sentiment during the "secession winter" of 1860–61. Well into the twentieth century, the Haitian Revolution was dragged out whenever the dangers of Black self-determination needed highlighting.

A Black radical scholar from Trinidad named C. L. R. James breathed fire on this whole tradition in *The Black Jacobins: Toussaint Louverture and the French Revolution.* Published in 1938, James's book is imbued with the urgency of his moment. The fascist forces of white supremacy were unleashing a new age of imperial expansion. While Hitler sputtered about the right of the more "vital" races to subdue lesser peoples, Mussolini's 1936 invasion of Ethiopia was grounded in the supposed legitimacy of a superior civilization controlling Africa and Asia as colonies. In European political thought, ironically, no event was more indicative of this superiority than the democratic revolutions of the late eighteenth century. Except for one thing, James argued. The French Revolution was not a European event.

James insisted that the Black freedom seekers of Saint-Domingue were the most important protagonists of that revolutionary time. They were the real vanguard of human liberation, representing everything that was most egalitarian and radical about the democratic struggle against absolutist power. They took the lofty ideals of the Revolution and made them truly universal. They fought to defend them even more tenaciously than the French masses, who saw the slaves' struggle and were converted to antislavery as a result. What James did not talk about—and what most ensuing scholars have also underplayed—is the fact that most enslavers, as well as merchants and policymakers in the Atlantic World, were so dazzled by the riches to be won by taking the place of Saint-Domingue's vanquished planters that they set themselves to expanding the plantation system in the nineteenth century.

In late 1791, precisely two days after disturbing news of the slave uprising in Saint-Domingue reached the ears of Spain's policymakers in Madrid, Francisco de Arango y Parreño went to work. A notable Cuban sugar planter and leader of Havana's elite city council, Arango was in the Spanish capital promoting the interests of his class. Two years earlier, he had convinced the Crown to allow a free trade in slaves from Africa. Once limited to official awardees of a Spanish monopoly on slaving called the asiento, now any Spanish trader could sell captives in American ports free of duty. Even non-Spaniards could sell slaves in a select number of Spanish colonies, though they labored under other restrictions, such as a requirement to sell all cargo within twenty-four hours of arrival.

Fearful that news of the devastation on the French island would lead

Spanish ministers to back away from their recent moves to expand the Atlantic slave trade, Arango managed to get copies of a new pro–slave trade essay he had composed into the hands of every member of the Council of State, which reported directly to the king. He also wrote up and distributed a report on the late slave uprising in Saint-Domingue, although in truth he did not know more than anyone else in Spain at the time. No matter.[1]

In the essay, Arango argued that slavery itself was not to blame for the violence. French planters themselves bore responsibility. Seduced by revolutionary ideas into betraying their own sovereign, the masters of Saint-Domingue had foolishly paraded egalitarian political innovations before their bondspeople, who adopted the ideals for their own predictably savage ends. Cuba would be different, Arango promised. "Everfaithful" subjects of the Spanish Crown, Cuban planters adored their king. They also treated their slaves with indulgence, giving them no reason to rebel. Not only was bringing more enslaved people from Africa safe, Arango concluded, but the rebellion in Saint-Domingue meant nothing was more urgent at this moment.[2]

Although he sympathized with the hapless French planters "immersed in a disaster that—if it does not destroy all happiness in the colony—will surely set it back considerably," he could not completely suppress his glee at their misfortune. Arango did not wish for "the best of kings" to miss "the opportunity and the means by which to give our agriculture on the islands the advance and preponderance over the French." He proposed that Cuban planters capitalize on the catastrophe in Saint-Domingue and replace "the pearl of the Antilles" as the dominant suppliers of the sugar markets of Europe. But they would require "an absolutely unrestricted slave trade" to do so. Much as James II in London changed his views on tobacco when he was told of the wealth that would flow into his Treasury, the government in Madrid, having the examples of the British and French sugar colonies before its eyes, was convinced to support the growth of slave plantations in order to boost its revenues.[3]

Soon enough, in accord with Arango's urgings, the slave trade to

Cuba was vastly expanded. Between 1790 and 1820, merchants brought approximately 325,000 captives to Cuba, transforming the demography of the island from one in which slaves were a minority and most of them worked in urban, maritime, or domestic occupations, to one in which a majority African-born, rural labor force was working in sugar. By 1800, a legal and economic structure friendly to a plantation boom was in place on the island.

Just as the breakup of the British imperial trading circuits had provided a huge opportunity to Saint-Domingue in the 1780s, the destruction of French plantations in the 1790s set the stage for Cuban sugar planters. Saint-Domingue's exports had peaked at 95.6 million long pounds of raw sugar in 1789. By 1818, exports were a mere 5.4 million pounds. Between 1795 and 1799 alone, exports from the French West Indies to the United States fell from $15.75 million to $2 million. The collapse of sugar exports from Saint-Domingue led to an extraordinary increase in the price of sugar in the 1790s. Moreover, scores of French planters fleeing the revolutionary violence settled in Cuba. The newcomers set about building many of the early sugar mills in the districts south of Havana. French-speaking planters also brought hundreds of enslaved people with experience in the sugar sector, as well as innovative ways of boiling and purifying sugar. Cuban planters followed their lead, avidly reading French sugar manuals their government had had translated into Spanish.[4]

The number of sugar mills around Havana doubled between 1792 and 1806. They also grew in size, from an average annual capacity of 58 metric tons of sugar in 1792 to 136 in 1804. Large cattle ranches were being repurposed to make sugar. Filled with potential fuelwood for the boiling houses and as yet unplowed acres, the sprawling, ancient grants of land from the Crown were gradually colonized by cane fields and mill complexes. The shift from expansive cattle ranches to tightly organized sugar plantations created a plantation-driven dependency on imported foods in Cuba for the first time. Jerked beef, a common staple in the diets of both sailors and slaves throughout the Atlantic World, was a net export in 1761. By 1792, hundreds of thousands of pounds were brought in to feed the population of Cuba.⁵

For three centuries a loyal servant of Castile and dependable supplier of food to the empire's silver fleet, Cuba's position within the Spanish Empire was transformed by the sugar revolution that gathered steam in the 1790s. Sixty-three percent of Cuba's sugar exports in the 1790s went not to the "mother country," nor to neighboring Spanish colonies, but to the newly independent United States. Imports into the United States from the Spanish West Indies skyrocketed from $1.7 million in 1796 to $11 million in 1799, and nearly $13 million in 1801. Breaking free of a limited Spanish market—which lacked a refining industry and experienced slower population growth than the United States—sugar planters in Cuba were the first West Indians to step into the intra-American trading system being born.⁶

While its exports were absorbed increasingly by Americans, Cuba could no longer afford to depend on Spain's transatlantic provisioning system for its imports either. Due in part to the ability of U.S.-flagged "neutral" vessels to export Cuban sugar to all the nations of Europe during the Napoleonic Wars (1790–1815), Cuba's imports of flour, lumber, and rice from the United States increased further. On the strength of a new intra-American exchange that left Spain on the sidelines, Cuba's sugar exports grew from 13,000 metric tons in 1789, to 28,700 in 1800, and 36,200 in 1805. Benefiting from the larger merchant fleet of the North Americans, planters and merchants in Cuba then convinced their Spanish overlords that U.S. vessels be permitted to carry their sugar even in peacetime.⁷

While the United States played the central role in the growth of Cuba's sugar economy, North American observers took notice of their reliance on the Caribbean islands as well. John Adams declared in 1783, "The Commerce of the West India Islands is a Part of the American System of Commerce. They can do Neither without Us nor We without them. . . . We have the means of assisting each other, and Politicians and Artificial Contrivances cannot separate Us." Though he seemed to be belaboring the obvious, Adams was observing the dawn of a new era of the plantation, in which planters would no longer look to Europe for their primary consumers, their merchants, or their shippers. The American Revolution, and the spread of U.S. territorial sovereignty and influence into the circum-Caribbean, meant the plantation's unmooring from political and economic ties to Europe.[8]

The Haitian Revolution had convinced Napoleon to give up the project of American empire altogether. His vast and sparsely populated colony of French Louisiana had been to Saint-Domingue what early Carolina had been to Barbados: a resource base to provide food, fuel, and livestock to an island focused on sugar production. Once the plantation system was destroyed in Saint-Domingue, however, Napoleon lost interest in keeping Louisiana. His attention was drifting back to his dream of Old World conquest, and he needed an influx of cash to pay for it. In 1803, he offered to sell Louisiana for $15 million—precisely the sum that Americans had been paying annually for Saint-Dominguan sugar in the 1790s. The Louisiana Purchase doubled the size of the United States and solidified American sovereignty over the Mississippi River. A continental power less in need of European trade, with enough population to absorb the exports of the West Indies and sufficient military power to exert economic control over the hemisphere, was born on the ashes of Les Cayes.

Just as the Haitian Revolution ushered in this new, postcolonial phase of the plantation, it also radicalized American enslavers. Ten thousand exiles from Saint-Domingue arrived in the United States in the 1790s. Everywhere they went, the former masters cursed the savagery and treachery of the Blacks. The tales they told landed like arrows of terror in the hearts of powerful white people across the hemisphere. Fleeing planters also brought as many as twelve thousand enslaved people into the United States in the first half of the 1790s. Vice President Thomas Jefferson worried that his own country would be caught up in the "revolutionary storm now sweeping the globe." In 1797, he declared, "If something is not done and done soon, we shall be the murderers of our own children."[9]

While Jefferson proposed emancipating and deporting Virginia's slaves in order to head off a horrific fate, most enslavers came to the opposite conclusion. The lesson they drew from Saint-Domingue was similar to Arango's: Loose talk about equality and emancipation would bring catastrophe. Only the firm bonds of slavery could restrain the hand of Black savagery. In Virginia, where the institution of slavery had been up for debate in the 1780s and many Patriot slaveowners freed their slaves, planters now doubled down. Fear of "another Santo Domingo" made them more militant in their defense of slavery. "The emancipation fume has long evaporated and not a word is now said about it," one Virginia enslaver proudly asserted at the end of the eighteenth century.[10]

Immediately after the purchase of Louisiana in 1803, the sale of American slaves into the new territories was debated in Congress. It was not clear that the Lower Mississippi River Valley, which would by the 1820s be the most intense area of cotton plantation expansion, would welcome enslavers. Interestingly, the Haitian Revolution played a key role in how the debate unfolded. The Republicans, led now by President Jefferson, argued that opening the territory to American-born slaves would allow for a safe phasing-out of slavery through the "diffusion" of the Black population across a vast new territory. One New Orleans official in favor of the overland trade penned a letter to Congress in which he warned that if such a trade were not permitted, settlers would bring in slaves "from the French islands." That foreign population would "consist principally of such Negroes as cannot be retained there with safety to their owners or the public peace." Upper South states could sell safer, Americanized slaves to a climate where their labor was uniquely necessary, while preventing "another Santo Domingo" from occurring in Virginia.[11]

Fighting for the end of the African slave trade as well as the end of importations from the West Indies, while threatening to secede if an interstate trade in slaves was restricted, Virginia politicians began to create a more strictly national identity tied to slaveholding. The Caribbean islands, once the envy of North American planters, were recast as the backward, tropical, and colonized aliens to a more advanced American culture. Ironically, wealthy Saint-Dominguan enslavers living in cities like Charleston and Philadelphia came to typify the hypersexualized West Indian incapable of suppressing his desires for women of color—indeed, parading his scandalous partnerships in the streets of the American republic. The tropical commodities that made him rich—intoxicating rum and enervatingly sweetened tea—reeked of colonial subservience, weakening the bodies and undermining the virtues of the new nation's hardy white citizenry. The Haitian Revolution cemented the necessity of a domestically controlled, self-enclosed landed empire. To this end, leading planter-politicians like Edmund Randolph, William Drayton, George Washington, and Thomas Jefferson attempted to replace foreign sugar by planting groves of sugar maples on their plantations.[12]

While this particular effort failed, and the consumption of sugar and rum continued to grow in the United States, the population of the country—which grew from 2.35 million in 1774 to 9.6 million in 1820—together with the growth in its territory did allow a certain nationalization of economic life. The ratio of exports to aggregate U.S. economic output fell from 10 to 15 percent in the 1790s to under 7 percent in the decades after 1815. And the interstate slave trade was central to how the expanded territory was incorporated into the nation. American enslavers, once aspirants to West Indian plantership, began to look westward to their future.[13]

Part Three

DWELLINGS

The Westover mansion of William Byrd II became a headquarters for Union forces during the Civil War.

CHAPTER 11

The Comprehensive Jaws of America

A train rider outside Richmond, Virginia, quietly observed a coffle of enslaved people riding in the "Negro car." Huddled together were a mother and her children who had just been sold into the Deep South, torn permanently away from the husband and father. The mother was "misery's picture," the traveler noted, and "the children cried the whole way." That same year, 1842, on the other side of the Atlantic, the traveler read about a six-year-old coal worker named Mary Davis, who was found sleeping in a mine shaft by a British government inspector. When asked why she was slumbering on the job, Mary said her oil lamp had gone out, and she preferred retreating into a dream over her fear of the dark. "I was frightened for someone had stolen my bread and cheese," she told him. "I think it was the rats." The same man who had shared a train with crying children sold South was soon taking up the cause of young Mary. The man was Charles Dickens.[1]

Mary Davis was pushed deeper into the mine shaft by the fuel demands of the steam-powered cotton textile industry. The enslaved children Dickens saw on the train were torn from their father because their future labor in the cotton fields was worth more than their future labor in the tobacco fields. Mary and these unnamed youths would never meet, but their lives had been drawn mercilessly together by what Frederick Douglass called the "destined vortex" of the plantation system. The cotton industry was chewing up these children at the most elemental levels of body and soul.[2]

Dickens got two snapshots of American slavery in March 1842. He witnessed the domestic slave trade to the Cotton Belt on one day, and on the next, the continuing dominance of Virginia plantations in the nation's tobacco industry: After disembarking at the railroad station in Richmond, Dickens visited one of the city's multistory tobacco warehouses. The building seemed to hold enough tobacco "to have filled even the comprehensive jaws of America." Typically, the story of antebellum America is told with cotton plantations at the center, and "King Cotton" drives American history right into the Civil War. The planters of Virginia, however, were not "falling behind" and selling off their "surplus slaves," as the story usually goes. They were accelerating and diversifying their own plantation system.[3]

Interior of a Richmond tobacco warehouse, 1865.

Historians have often claimed that slavery was on the decline in the Upper South because wheat required fewer laborers than tobacco. However, the state of Virginia still had over half a million slaves in 1860, more than any other state in the Union. The enslaved population grew by 42 percent between 1800 and 1860, the years when Virginia sold more enslaved people to the Deep South than any other state, contributing essential labor to the ongoing cotton boom in Louisiana, Mississippi, Alabama, Arkansas, and Texas. The much larger share of the Black population that remained in Virginia enabled the state's planters to lead the nation in tobacco production straight down to the Civil War. The state's enslaved people also powered the expansion of Virginia's wheat flour industry, which had begun in the late colonial period but grew considerably in the antebellum decades.

In 1860, when the United States was on the precipice of world domination in wheat and flour exports—as the main ingredient of bread, flour made from milled wheat was arguably the most vital life-giving commodity to enter international trade circuits—Virginia produced the fifth most wheat in the nation. That year, the value of its flour roughly equaled that of its tobacco. Growing 13 million bushels of wheat annually, the state kept pace with the emerging global breadbasket in the Midwest, where Ohio produced 15 million, Indiana 16.8 million, Wisconsin 15.6 million, and Illinois 23 million bushels. In line with its plantation history, Virginia's flour industry was unusually export driven. As a Virginia State Assembly committee explained the tight relationship, "The grade of flour manufactured in the city of Richmond (being much higher than the flour made any where else in or out of the state) is the result of a foreign demand for a particular quality of flour adapted to the southern or tropical climate." Nearly all of it was shipped to another booming plantation society newly in need of food imports. In the mid-1850s, more than one in six barrels exported by the United States went from the slave-exploiting zones of the Upper South to Brazil. The roots of this trade, surprisingly, were in America's growing addiction to caffeine.[4]

Framed as a patriotic, anticolonial alternative to tea, coffee first became popular during the anti-British import boycotts of the 1760s. This was ironic, because although purchasing coffee imparted a sense of liberty to American consumers, the new trade reinforced the colonists' dependence on plantations in the Caribbean and Latin America, which would only deepen further in later years. In the 1830s and 1840s, a flood of European immigrants from coffee-drinking regions of Germany and Scandinavia added to the numbers of Americans consuming it with frequency (along with its accompaniment, cheap Cuban sugar).[5]

The taste for coffee grew even faster than the booming population of the antebellum United States. While immigration increased the U.S. population from 5 million in 1799 to 30 million in 1860, coffee imports grew nearly twice as fast: from 200,000 sacks in 1820 to 1.8 million by 1860. Improved railroad and canal connections from New York, New Orleans, and Baltimore to the booming interior of the country connected millions of Midwestern settlers to international supply chains. This helped keep the prices of imports like coffee within the reach of average consumers, ensuring them a steady supply of caffeine.[6]

While railroads and canals helped, the democratization of coffee drinking in North America was primarily made possible by the product-cheapening mechanisms of the plantation. Global coffee prices fell between 1822 and 1849 because Brazilian planters mobilized over a million captive laborers to settle a plantation frontier to the west of Rio de Janeiro. In the first half of the nineteenth century, they pushed out small landholders and plowed under the fertile but erosive hillsides of the Paraíba Valley to make way for coffee trees. By 1830, Brazil was already the largest coffee producer in the world, well ahead of Cuba, Java, and other historically significant growers. From a negligible quantity of production in 1820, Brazil was producing about 175,000,000 tons of coffee in 1860—over half the world total. A continuing transatlantic slave trade made this possible.[7]

With the collusion of the Brazilian government—which had secured its independence from Portugal in 1822—slave smugglers brought a horrifying 738,000 African captives into the country between 1831 and 1850, nearly twice the number of enslaved individuals brought into mainland North America during the entire two-century history of the Middle Passage. Vessels built in the United States and sailing under the U.S. flag accounted for 58 percent of the total slaving voyages from Africa to Brazil. This in spite of the fact that all U.S. citizens involved in Brazil's slave trade were violating a U.S. law that carried a death penalty—although no slave traders suffered this punishment until 1862. Even after the transatlantic slave trade to Brazil was finally stamped out in 1850, "domestic" slaves continued to be taken south from declining sugar plantations in the northern parts of the country. Between 1852 and 1862, 3,370 such captives arrived in the port of Rio per year. North American consumer demand was central to this late revolution in South American slavery, since three-quarters of Brazil's coffee exports went to the United States after 1830.[8]

Slaves going to work on a coffee plantation, Brazil, 1880s.

While Americans' addiction to caffeine fueled Brazil's slave trade, and Brazil's planters profited from delivering tens of millions of pounds of arabica beans to eager U.S. consumers, the coffee trade also created a large U.S. trade deficit with Brazil. It was not a good system from the perspective of North American merchants, who brought ships "in ballast for coffee, paying for it cash at most exorbitant rates of exchange," according to nineteenth-century travel writer Daniel Kidder. Brazilian merchants used that cash to purchase cotton cloth from Britain, buying fewer goods from Yankee merchants. Richmond wheat flour would be used to solve this imbalance.⁹

The tight focus of Virginia wheat planters and flour millers on Brazil might be surprising, given that white bread was eaten in all the former European colonies across North and South America. Southeastern Brazil's own plantation revolution, however, guaranteed that the region's planters would be dependent on outside supplies. Formerly self-sufficient in food production, Rio began to depend on products imported from other regions. Most importantly, writes one Brazilian scholar, "wheat flour that used to come mostly from southern Brazil began to be supplemented almost exclusively by the United States."¹⁰

Coffee monoculture left central-south Brazil dependent on imports of food, just as Portuguese immigrants, accustomed to eating white bread on a daily basis, moved into the cities of Rio and São Paulo. Bakeries multiplied in the cities, but the wheat flour on which they depended often failed to satisfy. In 1841, an Anglo-American import-export firm stationed in Rio complained to North American merchants, "Flour from the United States sometimes arrives here caked, sour, or musty. From whatever cause this may arise, it is a subject which deserves attentive consideration." Richmond millers would solve the problem by the 1850s, successfully capturing the loyalty of Brazil's "fastidious" bakers.¹¹

A new flour trade enabled Baltimore-based firms like Maxwell Wright & Co. to compete in the lucrative coffee business. Maxwell Wright had been, since the early 1840s, one of the top three exporters of Brazilian coffee to operate in the port of Rio. In the 1850s, they became the most successful purveyors of dependably fresh flour to the South American country. At Rio's main customs warehouse, they sold Richmond flour to local brokers for Brazilian milreis. They used that currency to buy coffee, which they sold in Baltimore to westbound merchants for either U.S. dollars or for more bills of exchange. They were able to cut out the British and transform it into an all-American trade circuit.[12]

Between 1847 and 1857, the exports of American flour to Rio increased one hundredfold, while the sales of coffee going in the other direction only grew 10 percent. Brazilian imports of wheat flour more than doubled between 1844 and 1860. In the second half of the 1850s, flour was the second most valuable import into Brazil, more important to the country's domestic economy than any commodity in the world, save cotton cloth from Great Britain. Thus, Maxwell Wright & Co., with unique access to quality flour from Baltimore and particularly from Richmond, began to recover the profitability of its coffee business. While Maxwell and others could have gathered flour from any of fifty-nine mills operating in Baltimore, 58 percent of Rio de Janeiro's flour came from four Richmond mills, while only 11 percent came from the city of Baltimore, 7 percent from New Orleans, 11 percent from Trieste, and 13 percent from all other places.[13]

The flour of particular Richmond mills was highly desired by Brazilian bread bakers, and they paid a premium for recognized Richmond brands. Flour barrels sent by small country millers in New York City's rural hinterland, for example, arrived in Brazil with only "New York" as a label. Those flours sold in Rio at $6.25 per barrel. The flours of large Richmond mills like Gallego, Haxall, and Crenshaw sold, under their brand names, at around $10.50. They successfully captured the disposable wealth and European-inspired consumer habits of nouveau riche coffee planters in the Paraíba Valley region outside Rio de Janeiro, as well as urban immigrants from Portugal.[14]

American merchants' desire to obtain Brazilian coffee, which ignited the antebellum wheat flour boom in rural Virginia, transformed the urban geography of Richmond, 87 percent of whose flour exports went to South America in the late 1850s. In response to the extensive Brazilian demand for dry, white, high-quality flour that would not spoil on a sailing voyage across the equator, about half a dozen American companies built large and technologically advanced flour mills in Richmond, before mills of similar scale or sophistication existed anywhere else in the United States. As the U.S. commissioner of agriculture observed, "the flouring mills of Richmond are probably equal to any in the world, both in perfection of their machinery and in the quantity and quality of the flour produced." Until the Civil War, the transformation of flour-milling technology in the United States was led by Richmond millers overwhelmingly focused on the single market of Rio de Janeiro. Figuratively speaking, these mills were machines for extracting coffee from Brazil's plantation complex.[15]

The quality and familiarity prized in the Brazilian market drove Richmond flour industrialists to make major capital investments. One company, Warwick and Barksdale, ground grain inside a twelve-story building classified at the time as the "largest brick building in the United States." Incorporating the latest in water-power technology, its six "huge wheels designed to use water twice over" spun thirty-one pairs of millstones. Warwick and Barksdale's impressive structure put out 190,000 to 200,000 barrels per year by 1860—nearly seven times the capacity of the pioneering flour mills of early national Baltimore.[16]

Instead of buying flour from millers, as had traditionally been done by international merchants, antebellum firms like Warwick and Barksdale began to make their own. The profits Richmond firms made in Rio encouraged them to consolidate into much larger concerns with large, enslaved labor forces. While the average rural flour mill in Virginia (and throughout the rest of the nation) typically employed two or three people, one of the Richmond milling firms owned 136 enslaved workers in 1860. The firms also invested in the latest machinery for making fresh, long-lasting white flour, improvements that would have been particularly important for firms shipping through the tropics.[17]

Big millers invested in as many as twenty pairs of specialized grinding stones quarried in France and finished in Utica, New York, that yielded a superfine product. They employed additional millstones specifically designed for "cleaning and smutting wheat" before grinding, which discouraged fungal infestation of the flour during shipment. Improved bolting cloths separated the meal more cleanly into different grades of fineness, making for whiter flour with less bran and less propensity to spoil. Finally, automatic packing machines enclosed export wheat flour more securely and cleanly.[18]

The demand in Richmond for more wheat, and for high-quality wheat, encouraged the rise of new capital-intensive wheat plantations in the central part of the state, the area known as the Virginia Piedmont, which lay between the Tidewater counties on the east and the Blue Ridge Mountains on the west. In the Piedmont counties that fed into Richmond, wheat production increased by three times during the years the trade with Brazil took off—from 0.4 million bushels in 1840 to 1.25 million bushels in 1860.[19]

Although wheat husbandry is typically associated with Northern family farms, in Virginia, wheat farming was even more plantation-like than tobacco. "Yields of wheat per acre were low," writes Lorena Walsh, "so more land had to be cultivated for this cash crop than with tobacco." Only those plantations with large populations of enslaved workers could transform the ecosystem in the ways the wealthier wheat planters wanted. They pushed small farmers into tenancy or day labor, while increasing their purchases of enslaved people. The expansion of large-scale wheat production in a state already devoted to tobacco production also harmed the soil. Wheat required permanent, stump-free fields cleared by the plow, so a new generation of "scientific farmers" departed from the existing practice of rotating tobacco with corn, peas, and fallow. They also left fewer acres of woodland standing, drained swamps, and fenced their animals. Such practices increased soil erosion, especially in the rolling hills of the Piedmont.[20]

Flour, coffee, and African slaves: plantation products that linked together an international capitalist network between North and South America. For the first time in its history, it was not European desire that drove the plantation system of the Americas. Enslavers in Virginia revolutionized their own plantation sector in order to create a profit-generating circuit with a new South American trading partner, and Brazilian planters made fortunes by providing North Americans with coffee. The flour-coffee circuit embodied a new dynamic: a bilateral exchange between two independent nation-states that sidestepped European dominance through the brutally efficient, technology-aided adaptation of the plantation, and the weaving together of an intra-American form of capitalism.

The McCormick reaper is typically associated with postbellum farmers in the Midwest. In fact, the labor-saving miracle of a machine was invented by a slaveholding wheat planter in Virginia whose neighbors were eager to supply Richmond mills with the raw materials for the profitable Brazil trade. The reaper, then, was less a result of simple American ingenuity than a product of the Americas-spanning economic demands of plantation capitalism.

Yet the pull of British demand came to influence the system of slavery in Virginia in a different and perhaps more profound way. American participation in the Atlantic slave trade came to an official end in 1808. What emerged in its wake was a domestic trade in slaves that forcibly relocated enslaved people—and broke apart their families—in far larger numbers than the Middle Passage. This mass internal movement of American captives, which began in Virginia, powered the rise of King Cotton.

CHAPTER 12

The Mother of Slavery

Much like the plantation commodities of sugar, rice, and tobacco, cotton cloth was new to Britain in the late seventeenth and early eighteenth centuries. Cheaper than silk or linen, and more comfortable and washable than wool, textiles from India transformed how Britons clothed themselves, democratizing the use of undergarments as well as other formerly elite blandishments. The writer Daniel Defoe observed in 1708 that cotton "crept into our houses, our closets and beds chambers, curtains, cushions, chairs, and at last beds themselves were nothing but calicos or Indian stuffs." By 1766, three-quarters of the East India Company's imports to Britain were finely crafted, handwoven bolts of cotton "calico," so named for its reputed city of origin, Calcutta. Wealthy Europeans had been wearing calico clothing since the Middle Ages, but its use vastly expanded thanks to the commercial conquest of South Asia by the British Empire.[1]

Most of the cotton cloth British merchants purchased in South Asia, however, did not end up clothing British bodies. Merchants were using

India's coveted textiles to pry open new channels of global trade, nowhere more so than on the African coast. Along with the other major exports of firearms and alcohol, merchants of the East India Company traded cloth in exchange for slaves. They offered to slave-selling merchants among the Fante, the Dahomey, and other slave-exporting African states a dizzying array of prints, colors, weaves, and lengths in exchange for the human cargo they would soon sell in Barbados, Jamaica, and South Carolina. These products made the British the predominant human traffickers in the world in the eighteenth century.[2]

British textile manufacturers, who had built up their domestic business by imitating South Asian handmade designs, now wanted the empire's slave-buying merchants to sell *their* product in the slave forts of West Africa as well, facing discerning trade partners like the merchants of the Oyó Empire, who stayed abreast of changing fashions in the interior kingdoms of the Gold Coast. Slave traders were hesitant to try. The British governor of Cape Coast Castle, the most important slave trading center in West Africa, warned British merchants in 1706 that "East India goods only and not those imitated are saleable." In order to succeed in replacing South Asian textiles, English cotton manufacturers would have to increase productivity and quality. As historian Joseph Inikori has written, the effort to displace South Asian products in the slave forts of West Africa drove the invention of the new technologies that would epitomize the Industrial Revolution.[3]

The mechanization of the British textile industry was first carried out not to save on expensive labor, as is often assumed, but to solve quality-control issues. The fine actions of machines were called for because British hand spinners could not replicate the high thread counts achieved by South Asian weavers. But as a side benefit of mechanization, labor costs began to plummet, making British cloth cheaper than similar Indian products. For example, the average Indian spinner took fifty thousand hours to make a hundred pounds of raw cotton into thread in 1790. A British worker manning a steam-powered hundred-spindle spinning mule used up the same quantity of cotton in one thousand hours. A process of what economic historians call "self-sustaining change" began: As mechanization dialed up labor productivity in one sector of the industry, it created a bottleneck in the next phase of production. After the mechanization of thread-spinning, the weaving of thread into cloth had to be improved, as it was so much slower than spinning. Indeed, a power loom, first developed in 1785, emerged two decades after Arkwright's water frame revolutionized spinning. The Atlantic market, centered on the plantation system and the slave trade, propelled British manufacturers finally to overtake their main competitor of South Asian handicrafts.[4]

As the British slave trade reached its apex in the second half of the eighteenth century, the new "cotton checks" made in Lancashire factories became the predominant product of the country's textile industry, accounting for between 48 and 86 percent of all British cotton exports at the time. Nearly 100 percent of those exports went to either West Africa, where they were exchanged for human chattel, or to New World slave plantations, where the cheaper varieties were given to enslaved people in their yearly allotments of clothing. The grand consumer of the plantation system sucked in all the product of the "check" manufacturers of Lancashire and kept demanding more, sparking a revolution in the British economy.[5]

Whereas in 1770, cotton manufacturing only accounted for 2.6 percent of value added in the British economy, by 1831 the figure had reached over 22 percent. The output of the cotton industry was four times greater than the combined output of the iron and coal industries, the other leading sectors of Britain's Industrial Revolution. As historian Sven Beckert writes, "Other industries would be made possible by the rise of cotton: a railroad network, the iron industry . . . [but] cotton was the vanguard. . . . As late as the mid-nineteenth century, the industrial revolution was still, numerically, the story of cotton."[6]

To keep their textiles globally competitive, manufacturers depended not only on new machinery, but on cheap coal to fuel those machines' engines. The coal industry expanded when more coal was demanded by the cotton manufacturers, which happened as Atlantic markets in

Africa and the Americas opened their jaws wider. The expansion of coal production meant the excavation of narrower seams ever deeper underground. Children like Mary Davis, whom Dickens had written about, were the only creatures small enough to fit inside. "Chained, belted, harnessed like dogs in a go-cart, black, saturated with wet, and more than half naked—crawling up on their hands and feet, and dragging their heavy loads behind them—they present an appearance indescribably disgusting and unnatural," read a government report from 1842. When a mine exploded in Felling in 1812, ninety-two workers were killed. Twenty-three of them were under fourteen years of age. The youngest were two eight-year-old trappers named Thomas Gordon and Michael Hunter. Even if most did not die in mining accidents, thousands of children like Thomas and Michael saw their youth, their health, and their education sacrificed to the energy needs of the textile industry.[7]

With the number of spindles multiplying throughout Lancashire in the early decades of the nineteenth century, however, there was rarely enough raw cotton. Early efforts to promote a more flexible and robust source of supply centered on Britain's colonial plantations in the Caribbean. Jamaica and Barbados were the premier "domestic" suppliers of cotton in the 1770s and 1780s. In fact, after the decline of Barbadian sugar production, the island's plantation system was reborn in a cotton-growing craze. Tobago and the Bahamas also turned to the fleecy bolls, while prerevolutionary Saint-Domingue supplied more cotton to British factories than any West Indian competitors. When revolutionaries destroyed the cotton exports of the French West Indies in the 1790s, it became clear that British manufacturers would need a different supply of cheap cotton to keep machines running and prices low. Supplying exactly zero of Britain's raw cotton in 1780, the United States did not seem a promising partner.[8]

The upheavals of independence drove Lowcountry planters to change the focus of their agricultural energies. The British Army's "Southern strategy" as well as guerrilla conflict between Patriots and Loyalists had left the region in ruins. The 1780s was a decade of recession. As many as one-third of South Carolinians held in bondage had escaped during the war. Given British manufacturers' and merchants' increasing demand, cotton was showing increasing promise for the next plantation boom. The approximately twenty thousand captives imported to the Lowcountry after the 1787 compromise that reopened the Atlantic slave trade would largely be forced to produce cotton, as much as rice.

Earlier developments in Virginia were significant in the shift toward cotton. Settlers moving into the backcountry counties of South Carolina and Georgia often had roots in the Chesapeake. They applied tobacco-planting techniques to the growing of cotton. Cotton plants were topped and suckered like tobacco; planters who had "prized" tobacco into hogsheads now pressed cotton into bales, a new practice as of the late eighteenth century; and a version of the tobacco plantation's "gang system" was adopted into the first large-scale plantings of short-staple cotton.[9]

Early U.S. cotton growers, however, borrowed their most important technology from India. To separate seeds from lint, an incredibly onerous task when done by hand, Lowcountry planters adapted the "churka"-style cotton gin widely used in South Asia. But Lowcountry varieties of cotton could not grow in the colder, drier interior where planters had far more room to settle. The new "upland" varieties of cotton that could withstand the harsher climates of the vast Southern interior required a different gin design. One of the key technologies that allowed cotton growing to spread west were the new "sawtooth" gins developed by Eli Whitney in the 1790s.[10]

Just as the spinning and weaving implements of Lancashire were based on Indian technologies, Whitney's gin was an adaptation of East Indian churka gins and roller gins that were already being used in the Lowcountry. The improved gins, and the large-scale textile mills of Lancashire—which also adapted South Asian methods—should be seen not as European inventions but as creative weldings of mechanical implements developed centuries earlier by peasants and craftspeople in

South Asia. The transatlantic cotton industry borrowed, stole, and contracted intellectual debts that would never be paid. Without such unacknowledged borrowings, the cotton plantation complex would have been impossible. In the last five years of the eighteenth century, South Carolina and Georgia rose from global obscurity to capture nearly 25 percent of the growing British market in raw cottons. By 1810, the United States already provided 53 percent of Britain's raw cotton. But the corrupt acquisition of millions of acres of Native land was the fundamental prerequisite for the cotton boom.[11]

After independence, the land hunger of Revolutionary-era enslavers was unleashed. In the 1780s and 1790s, thirty-five million acres of what is now Alabama and Mississippi were sold to "land companies" that included notable founders like Robert Morris and Patrick Henry. They planned to resell them to ordinary white men, promising that they could become fabulously wealthy cotton planters. As one Southern advertiser noted in a Philadelphia newspaper, the cheap land for sale in the fertile Mississippi region would enable the settler, "after buying one Negro, the next year [to] buy two, and so be increasing on." Keen to maximize the purchase of cheap land from the state government before Georgia ceded its western claims to the federal government (it was easier to bribe state legislators), well-heeled investors such as Senator James Garner of Georgia went "swooping down on Augusta, the Georgia state capital, with satchels of cash," as historian Edward Baptist writes. They successfully bribed state legislators into approving the sale. Speculators spent $200,000 to buy sixteen million acres from the state government. Once these "Yazoo" land bonds began circulating in the markets of Northeastern cities, a speculative frenzy ensued, raising prices and creating trouble for the vision of a westward-expanding yeomen's democracy.[12]

While the Yazoo project ended in scandal, much of the new southwestern territories were priced out of the reach of common farmers by similar elite-favoring mechanisms. U.S. Land Offices in the Mississippi territory—which encompassed the region that would be split into the new states of Alabama and Mississippi in 1817—auctioned off plots at two dollars per acre. This was no mean price for an average settler. A group of Georgians hoping to settle on this southwestern frontier complained to the territorial legislature that all the land would be bought up by "the rich," who brought with them "a certain species of population." The euphemism referred, of course, to enslaved people. These settlers tried to use anti-Black prejudice to keep enslavers from monopolizing the new southwestern lands, but they would largely fail, even though their white-egalitarian view was more aligned with the original design of the public land system, initiated with the Northwest Ordinance of 1785.[13]

The Ordinance laid out a process for westward expansion that aimed to forestall the kinds of land monopolization seen during the colonial era. In the new nation, Congress would incorporate western regions into statehood gradually, first establishing "territorial" governments that controlled the distribution of acreage in a fair manner. In practice, as historian Adam Rothman explains, the buy-up of two-dollar plots in Mississippi and Alabama by wealthy investors "facilitated the spread of the plantation system in the Deep South just as a burgeoning cotton economy increased the value of the land and the profits to be earned from slave labor." Even before statehood was established in 1817, it was clear that the white yeomen's republic in the South was falling before the legislative axe of the enslaver.[14]

The Creek War of 1812–1814 was a watershed. While an older generation of Creek leaders engaged diplomatically with white settlers, a dissident faction known as the Red Sticks committed themselves to preventing the arrival of more American citizens. Aware of the forces driving white incursion on their lands, the Red Sticks targeted cotton plantations and military forts for destruction. A massacre of white soldiers and civilians at a fort in the Mississippi territories drew Andrew Jackson, then an Army major-general, into the war. His troops countered with bloody massacres, shooting 186 people "like dogs" in one Creek town in what would soon become the state of Alabama. They killed another three hundred Creeks at Talladega. Then came the notorious Battle of Horseshoe Bend, at which Jackson's men slaughtered at least eight hundred people, "including some 300 who were shot in the Tallapoosa River as they were desperately trying to swim across." With this culminating battle, Creek resistance to the expansion of the U.S. cotton complex was essentially broken.[15]

Oddly, because most of the Red Sticks had fled to Spanish Florida after defeat, Creek who had allied themselves with Jackson in the war were treated like vanquished adversaries. Under intense pressure, they signed away twenty-three million acres. These former allies of the United States were promised monetary compensation for lost property (it only added up to three hundred thousand dollars, a paltry sum), but even this was never paid in full. The massive land cession included nearly half of what is today the state of Alabama. That patch of Creek territory was ground zero of the cotton boom to come in the new state's fertile Black Belt. Jackson, erstwhile hero of the "small" white man, made it clear that the future of these lands would be shaped by the superrich. The newly conquered territories along the Alabama River, he promised, will soon offer "a beautiful view of elegant mansions, and extensive rich & productive farms."[16]

Yet slaveowners' desire for land was unsated. Even after the land theft pulled off by Jackson in 1814, Creeks still controlled a fifth of present-day Alabama. Nearly a quarter of the state of Georgia was controlled by over ten thousand Native Americans, largely Cherokee and Creek. Southern leaders like Georgia Governor John Clark were convinced that divided sovereignty would demonstrate to enslaved Black people that white power was not absolute, inviting rebellion and, ultimately, race war. He therefore advocated, in 1821, a different sort of race war, one that would replace "all the red for a white population." A Savannah newspaper, inciting its readers to defend "the inalienable rights you possess to your slaves and to your Indian territory," explicitly linked ethnic cleansing to enslavers' pursuit of happiness. As in Nathaniel Bacon's movement in colonial Virginia, partisans of land conquest argued that the "best white man's country" was being spoiled by softheaded elites and savage Indians. From the arrival of the first European settlers in North America, stealing Indigenous land to make way for the plantation had been a practice if not a tradition. But the state-orchestrated expulsion of an entire race of people, as historian Claudio Saunt has pointed out, was something new, a terrible innovation that anticipated the racist ethno-nationalisms of the twentieth century.[17]

"Indian Removal" was narrowly approved by a divided Congress and signed into law in 1830 by now President Andrew Jackson. In the ensuing years, the federal government carried out an unprecedented state-sponsored mass expulsion, forcibly transporting about eighty thousand Native American men, women, and children from their historic homelands to territories west of the Mississippi River. Nominally run by the U.S. Army, the task of expulsion was farmed out to private individuals who ripped off departing Native families. Deportees were inadequately fed and housed, and their wagons were robbed in broad daylight by U.S. citizens. Posses attacked the many Native landowners who refused to leave. Thousands died on what later would be called the Trail of Tears. The undertaking ended up costing the government of the United States $75 million. Yet in sales of the stolen land to white men, the government netted around $80 million. While the nation profited, Creek, Chickasaw, and Choctaw landowners lost about $25 million in personal wealth.[18]

With white control of the southwest fast solidifying, and British demand for raw cotton always growing, the massive export of enslaved people from the Upper South began. Between 1820 and 1860, around two million enslaved people across the South were the victims of sale. Hundreds of thousands of them were relocated from the Upper South to the Lower South by slave-trading merchants, who marched them in coffles of forty to sixty people across hundreds of miles of Southern highways and byways. "The men were usually handcuffed in pairs and fastened to a long chain that connected each pair," writes historian Steven Deyle. "The women and children either walked or rode in a wagon, and the white drivers, carrying guns and whips, rode on horseback at the end of the coffle." The journey lasted seven to eight weeks, and the transportees camped out of doors regardless of the weather. "Late in the even's," recalled one survivor, "we stretched the tents and cooked supper and spread out blankets an' slept." If the trader cared to arrange it, people in the coffle might be housed on a roadside farm. One Kentucky farmer remembered, "We had a big haystack outdoors, and all the slaves, men, women and children were chained together and slept on the haystack that night. Some of the women had babies in their arms." The coffles became a too-common sight on the highways, railroads, and steamships of the American South. One former slave recalled the traumatic sight of transportees "come in lines reachin' as far as you kin see." Their presence on the streets of Washington, D.C., often shocked foreign diplomats who had thought themselves visiting the capital of a people's republic. The heartbroken mother and children Charles Dickens saw on the southbound train in 1842 were a drop in the bucket.[19]

The coffle.

Over time, the slow-moving coffle was replaced by more professionalized operations. Franklin and Armfield of Alexandria, Virginia, was the biggest slave brokerage firm in the United States. They kept a standing advertisement in the papers that read "Cash for 400 Negroes," while sending slave-buying agents into Maryland and Virginia to purchase still more people. Those unfortunate enough to be sold would find themselves with scores of other captives in the firm's "slave prison" in Alexandria. Seeking to move their merchandise more rapidly to market, the firm operated a fleet of ships to transport captives down the coast and into the Gulf, then sold them on commission in the Deep South auction houses of New Orleans or Vicksburg. The working populations of an emerging plantation belt in the southwest took shape, coffle by coffle, and ship by ship. While there were only 33,000 slaves in Mississippi in 1820, there were nearly 437,000 in 1860. Alabama was similarly transformed, with 42,000 slaves in 1820 and 435,000 in 1860.[20]

The wrenching experience suffered by the children Charles Dickens saw on the Richmond train in 1842 was all too common. As many as one in ten teenagers enslaved in the Upper South between 1820 and 1860 were sold into the long-distance trade. Planters often were able to justify selling adult slaves as punishment for some misdeed, but enslaved children they simply turned into cash. When a Georgia planter sought to build a new plantation house, he put a ten-year-old boy named John Brown on the market. Another child was separated from his family because the owners wanted money "ter dress young Missus fer her weddin'."[21]

Scholars have estimated that close to half of all enslaved families living in the Upper South witnessed the sale of at least one of the members. The entire family of Charles Ball was sold south except for him and his father, who "never recovered from the effects of the shock." Solomon Northrup, a free Black man who had been kidnapped into the South and would later turn his harrowing experience into the seminal antislavery text *Twelve Years a Slave*, had a partner named Eliza who always spoke to her children "as if they were actually present," even though they had been taken from her by sale. Another woman whose children were sold away continued to "make clothes and knit for them."[22]

The twin tragedies of Indian Removal and family separation powered the new cotton plantation complex. In the "flush times" of the 1830s, a multitude of joint-stock companies were established in major cities. State banks issued paper money not backed up by deposits. Prices for land, slaves, and cotton spiraled out of control. When President Jackson refused to reauthorize the charter of the National Bank in a fit of populist pique, his decision set off a run on small banks around the country, exposing many of the frauds, along with the South's overinvestment in land, slaves, and government bonds. A reckoning took place as the easy-credit moment came to a bitter end in the Panic of 1837. Big planters refused to let a good crisis go to waste. They bought up distressed properties and consolidated their hold on slave property, pushing out small competitors. In older cotton regions like central Georgia, economic depression sparked a rapid demographic transition away from white yeoman farmers who did not own enough slaves to compete. While they were forced to sell, large planters moved in, and the region became majority Black.[23]

The end of the flush times only put more pressure on enslaved people. Elite enslavers in Mississippi "tried to drive the cost of making cotton below its new low price by wresting more labor from slaves," as historian Anthony Kaye put it. These planters filled the preharvest "laying-by" period, traditionally one of rest and socializing, with new tasks. They widely adopted a new strain of cotton, known as "mastodon," that was frost resistant and enabled the prolongation of picking season into winter. Yet, cotton harvesting was only one of many tasks the enslaved had to master in order to survive.[24]

One of the planters' more notable responses to the thin profit margins of the post-1837 years was to try making cotton plantations self-sufficient by dedicating more acreage to the production of corn and livestock. "Self-sufficient" is a misnomer. Far from being simple "picking machines," Black folk cleared swamps, dug ponds, felled trees, spread guano, wove baskets, and drove wagons for cotton planters. They cooked, cleaned, washed, and darned ceaselessly in the Great House. They hunted, fished, nursed fellow slaves back to health, cranked gins, pressed bales with mammoth screw presses, mended hundreds of plows, hoes, shears, pots, pans, pants, and shirts; they raised corn, pigs, and potatoes. Plantation "self-sufficiency" was the result of the competent husbandry, silviculture, gardening, and animal care undertaken by African Americans, many of them forcibly brought to cotton country via the overland slave trade from the Upper South. Although the master ultimately benefited from it, he did not completely control it. And even though planters thought of themselves as the directing mind of the whole system, little of the intellectual property that underpinned the fabulous wealth of antebellum cotton planters was their own.[25]

Plantation "self-sufficiency" depended not only on the skilled and onerous labor of the enslaved, nor on such "borrowings" of existing technology. It also depended on botanical innovations, specifically a process of experimentation with Mexican cotton varieties that "rivaled anything accomplished by northern wheat breeders in the nineteenth century," according to the most well-known economic historians to look at the topic. They estimate that, while the introduction of the automatic reaper-binder onto Midwestern wheat farms—often considered the epitome of high-efficiency nineteenth-century farming—raised labor productivity in the harvest by 50–100 percent, the impact of the new cotton varieties increased the productivity of labor even more. The new cotton varieties developed on slave plantations by enslavers, overseers, and the enslaved "were essential for sustaining the Industrial Revolution."[26]

From the start, planters faced two major challenges: developing crop varieties that were adapted to the varied environments of the Cotton Belt as well as to the new machine technologies in Britain. They had been trying to crack the code for generations. As far back as the colonial period, Southern planters and their slaves had engaged in consistent experimentation with new cultivation methods and hybridized cotton seeds. In 1735, the director of the experimental Trustee Garden in Georgia told James Oglethorpe, "I have meet with Some Cotton Seeds from Guinea which from it I have Raised a Thousand plants, som of which have Shott Eight foot in highth and The Second Season will Come to its Bringing forth Fruits in Abundance so that I shall be Able to send a Large Quantity of Cotton to the Trustees Use."[27]

In the Lowcountry, planters, with considerable input from enslaved people, developed a variety of long-staple cotton known as Sea Island, which was well suited for high-quality handmade goods. Sea Island cotton was limited to the warm-weather environment of the Carolina coast, however, where rainfall was plentiful and there was little risk of frost. Moreover, Sea Island was a long-staple variety of cotton not hardy enough to withstand the pushing and pulling action of the new spinning machinery. Chasing the profits from the British textile industry, antebellum planters would turn the soils of the southwest into a grand botanical experiment to find climate-appropriate, machine-ready, and easy-to-grow cotton plants.

A planter and diplomat from Natchez—a soon-to-be cotton-growing district in the Mississippi Territory—by the name of Walter Burling smuggled the first varieties of *Gossypium hirsutum* out of Spanish Mexico in 1806, thus stealing the multigeneration botanical product of thousands of years of domestication by Mesoamerican peasants, which was guarded by Spanish colonial officials. Flowering during the fall rainy season in the tropics, *hirsutum* would produce its pickable bolls in winter. In the emerging Cotton Belt of the Southern interior, however, plants like this would be killed by frost. Moreover, the Mexican variety was difficult to pick, and the seeds were very hard to separate from the lint. Within a fast-moving plantation system, where cotton needed to be sent to the gin in big batches to keep processing costs down, and was harvested by gang labor, a profitable crop would have to possess the following traits: simultaneous ripening, early ripening, and rapid pickability.[28]

Burling gave the seeds to a planter associate of his named William

Dunbar to solve this problem by hybridizing the import with local cotton varieties. Success in breeding out the flaws required repeated introductions of cotton seeds from different parts of Mexico, with scores of instances of back-crossing, careful seed selection, observation, and replanting. In the rush of harvest season "acclimatizers" like Dunbar planted extra rows of experimental cotton, telling slaves to weed, observe, and pick the extra area. Each year, the seeds from the best bolls were painstakingly collected so they could be planted again, replicating the best characteristics for the plant's new environment. It was a repeated, piecemeal, collaborative project that spread over several decades and was never finished because soils kept changing, markets kept changing, and most importantly, the pests that plagued monocultures continued to attack, evolve, and flourish in areas of year-over-year cotton cultivation.[29]

Plant breeding, and the ensuing marketing and sale of proprietary seed varieties, became a new line of business for a small number of Southern planters. By the late 1820s, Deep South seed breeders started getting summer-ripening, disease-resistant, higher-quality cotton that ripened in the field simultaneously. They rarely patented their hybridized, Mexican-origin seeds, but they did sell them under brand names like "extra prolific."[30]

The transatlantic cotton complex welded together the "world technologies" of textile machinery in Britain with Whitney's gin, hybrid cotton, and steam transportation to create a revolutionary new phase in the history of the plantation. Planters naturally kept the benefits for themselves. Louisiana's Natchez District was home to more millionaires per capita than any other region in the nation in 1860. The median plantation held sixty slaves, while one in seven lived on plantations with more than two hundred fifty people. The "Natchez Nabobs" formed a grand aristocracy of cotton. Intermarried clans of superelites owned hundreds of enslaved people working tens of thousands of prime acres divvied up into distinct plantations in the fertile but erosive loess hills around Vicksburg. As they built a consolidated agro-industry in the decades before the Civil War, the Nabobs also diversified. Profits from cotton and the traffic in enslaved people were sunk into banking, railroads, and the stock market. They bought up far-flung plantations in Louisiana, Arkansas, and East Texas. They boasted of business connections in Europe, but their wealth came out of the work enslaved people put into the Mississippi mud.[31]

In an in-depth study of cotton plantations in the Natchez District, Anthony Kaye shows that in the 1850s, the number of acres each enslaved person worked shot up 20 percent. The development of higher-yielding, early-ripening, disease-resistant cotton types enabled faster picking, but it also allowed planters to order the planting of more acres in cotton because more could be harvested in a single season. The extra acres of cotton added new labor burdens to all the nonpicking tasks, none of which had been transformed by similar innovations. Slaves had to plow more rows with mules, "chop" more cotton with the same "plantation hoes," and use ever more delicate hands and keener vision to remove worms and weevils by hand. Far from easing the burden of field workers, then, rapid pickability simply ramped up the pressure on enslaved people to engage in more kinds of labor and to work faster.[32]

They could also feel more distant pressures at work in the capitalist markets of the nineteenth century. The cost of transportation fell with the introduction of increasingly powerful and safe steamboats. As river transport got cheaper and faster, shippers needed more bales of cotton to fill their boats to the brim to guarantee they cover their own costs. Overall, as historian Dale Tomich notes, "more cotton required more steamboats, and more steamboats required more cotton," which translated not only to the breeding of better cotton varieties, but to the intensified coercion of enslaved people, who were frequently whipped at the daily "weigh-up" for falling short of the enslavers' escalating picking expectations. The acceleration of British industry, along with the linked demands of a system of steamboat transportation for full freight, and of planters to sell enough cotton to pay off their own debts, meant that the need for land also intensified.[33]

The footprint of cotton plantations was far bigger than the acre-

Steamboats and bales of cotton near the foot of Canal Street in New Orleans, ca. 1858.

age planted in cotton at any one time. This was due in part to the credit-land-slaves-cotton cycle of the plantation, and in part to the character of Southern soils. Even in the most fertile parts of the Cotton Belt, soils were highly erosive and acidic, meaning that fields planted for more than a few seasons rapidly lost their fertility. Planters had to keep a large amount of land in reserve. This is another surprise in the history of plantations: We envision it as a controlled property, fenced in and fully settled, but most of it was actually woods or swamps. Slaves practiced "slash and burn" husbandry within plantation boundaries, "fertilizing" new cotton fields by burning the undergrowth and trees. In other words, even after Alabama and Mississippi were granted statehood, and after the Cherokee were expelled, the frontier character of plantation agriculture persisted within the bounds of each property. One Southerner bemoaned how "prodigal" planters left their mark on the landscape: "Where, twenty years since, there was an unbroken pine forest, now in places there is a scarcity of timber for fencing . . . not unfrequently will one planter deaden and destroy a thousand acres in one season." The thousands of "unimproved" acres that show up in Southern census records were not old-growth forest—they were worn-out crop fields abandoned to weedy growth. Piedmont Georgia and South Carolina regions had already lost much of their soil fertility by 1840, which was one reason so many cotton planters were making a beeline for Texas, Louisiana, Mississippi, and Alabama.[34]

While enslavers have often been blamed for their "soil mining" ways, opportunities to maintain soil fertility over the longer term were limited in cotton-growing regions. Common Anglo-American fodder crops like clover, which returned nutrients to the soil, did not do well in hot climates. The southern cattle tick stunted the growth of cows and decreased their supply of milk, so it made little sense to invest in leguminous pasture grasses that also could have put nutrients back into the soil. Since it was much cheaper to allow cattle and hogs to forage in their vast tracts of unimproved land, planters were unable to preserve manure for the fields. The "open range" required massive amounts of labor and lumber for fence building to protect crop fields from wandering livestock. In one year alone, Alabama spent $22 million on fencing.[35]

The antebellum cotton plantation, with its shifting cultivation, its free-range livestock, and its cotton quasi monoculture, was labor intensive but cheap. Planters used lots of land and exploited lots of slave labor, but they skimped on everything else because the annual cycle of credit, and the decadal cycle of removing to a new plantation, made short-term returns vital. Most plowing for cotton was done on newly cleared ground that was full of roots, stumps, and rocks. As a result, the one-mule plow, which dug only a few inches under the surface, was ubiquitous. A six- or seven-inch plow, which brought more nutrients from lower strata within reach of the seedlings, was impractical. Critics called such agriculture "skating" or "skimming" husbandry. Later historians would say that "planters bought lands as they might buy a wagon—with the expectation of wearing it out."[36]

Between 1850 and 1860, nearly two-thirds of slaveholders in the Cot-

"Skimming husbandry": Enslaved people picking cotton among the girdled trees and stumps characteristic of shifting cultivation.

ton Belt moved at least once. In fact, because only the wealthier planters could afford land-saving inputs like guano and could afford to spend their slaves' valuable time on other work, smaller enslavers and family cotton farmers were even more prone to relocate than wealthy planters.[37] That said, the skimming system required any cotton plantation that was going to produce profit for more than a few years to keep a large reserve of unimproved land, thus keeping the majority of cotton-plantable Deep South acreage out of the hands of other aspiring planters.

To continue the cycle, elite planters needed continuous extensions of credit. To fund more land purchases, they mortgaged their slaves, who cleared square miles of swamp and woodland, plowed it, and planted it in cotton and corn in order to pay for the planter's next round of credit, land, and slaves. Southern planters became creatures of the market, because once they decided to careen down the path of big land purchases, slave purchases, and cotton planting, there was no escape. They were perhaps not any less "self-sufficient" than rice and tobacco planters of the colonial era, but their purchases of slaves and of land were out of all proportion to what their predecessors had done. The destined vortex of the cotton plantation was the distant attractive force pulling so many enslaved Virginians away from their kin and into the market.

Not since West Indian sugar in the eighteenth century had a plantation crop, or any crop at all, so dominated the economic outlook of a nation. While tobacco had accounted for over one-quarter of British North America's total exports in 1770, by the 1830s, cotton accounted for 58 percent of total U.S. exports. Tobacco had dropped to 8 percent, although its absolute production had grown because far more of it was now sold domestically, destined for what Dickens called America's "comprehensive jaws." By the eve of the Civil War (1859–60), direct exports of raw cotton totaled $173 million, tripling the value of grain and flour exports, even though these had come to play a transformative role in a globalizing food system.[38]

The United States was a rapidly growing economy in the antebellum years, but still an agricultural one. Manufactures only accounted for 12 percent of total exports, and nearly three-quarters of those were cotton and tobacco manufactures. Even in industrial production, then, which Northerners are often assumed to have dominated, the most important sectors depended completely upon plantation supplies of raw materials. While helping prop up U.S. industry, the plantation's cheap raw materials were also proving indispensable to the world's leading manufacturing nation. In 1860, 80 percent of the raw cotton that British factories consumed came from the American South.[39]

Up to their collars in debts often payable in bales, however, planters would have ceased to exist without new soils. Maintaining the status quo was not an option. Expansion of their territory was as necessary to the life of the plantation as was the expansion of the lungs of the enslaved. The combined economic and ecological pressures of the cotton system drove the plantation westward. As future Confederate nationalist Edmund Ruffin said, "The system of slave labor requires more *space*." Another antebellum planter identified the "expansive principle" as the key to the South's future success.[40]

Never had the potential profits been this large. Cotton kept drawing planters from elsewhere to the Deep South; thousands of planters' sons, brothers, and nephews from Virginia packed their belongings and their slaves and headed to Georgia, Alabama, and Mississippi in the 1820s and 1830s. But too much was never enough, given a historically unprecedented British industrial sector. In the 1840s, the U.S. government as well as private interests would use every practicable method to make the vision of a country stretching from sea to shining sea come true. In reaction to the onslaught, one Mexican president lamented: "Poor Mexico: so far from God, so close to the United States."

Cotton planters fleeing their creditors after the Panic of 1819 had immigrated into the Mexican state of Tejas, where their help in stabilizing government authority in a territory largely at the mercy of Comanche raiding parties was initially welcomed. The Mexican Congress had abolished slavery in 1829, but the government exempted Tejas so Anglo-American settlers (known as "Texians") would be able to keep their slaves. Immigrant cotton planters from the U.S. side of the border constantly worried that the federal government of Mexico would end the exemption and free their slaves. For this and other reasons they joined a broader revolt against the central government of Antonio Lopez de Santa Anna in 1836. After being defeated by Mexican forces at the Alamo, the Texians won the decisive Battle of San Jacinto in what is now East Texas, and secured independence.[41]

When the Texians drafted their own national constitution in 1836, they explicitly sanctioned slavery. The document, presaging the Confederate constitution of 1861, made the rights of slaveholders unquestionable, going so far as requiring the consent of Texas's Congress for any individual slaveholder to free a person they owned. The slave population of the new Republic grew from five thousand in 1836 to thirty thousand in 1846, outpacing the growth of the free population. In seizing Texas, the Texians expanded the geography of slavery and shrank the New World's geography of freedom. Driven forward by expansionist politicians from both Northern and Southern states, the United

States annexed Texas in 1845, although the expanded territory of the United States was not secured until victory in the controversial Mexican-American War in 1848.

In signing the Treaty of Guadalupe Hidalgo that year, Mexico surrendered more than half of its territory to a foreign aggressor. That aggressor, the United States of America, gained what is now Texas, California, Utah, and New Mexico, as well as most of Arizona and parts of Colorado. In the congressional wrangling over the newly incorporated territories, all became new territories for pro- and antislavery forces to struggle over. The two-party system of Whigs and Democrats, which each had Northern and Southern wings, seemed ill-prepared to contain that conflict within old compromises over slavery.[42]

The cotton plantation's volatility was both its strength and its vulnerability. Fueled by global demand for cotton, a national supply of credit, and above all an export machine of enslaved people from the Upper South, the institution was hyperresponsive to botanical and mechanical change. Mobility was an elemental part of its character, however—it had to move to survive. Soon enough, this imperative of plantations to expand would ignite a civil war that transformed the world of both enslavers and the enslaved. That war—and the emancipation that came with it—did not, as is often assumed, mean the end of plantations in American life. The plantation would persist even after the defeat of the South and the abolition of slavery, still shaping understandings of race and still expanding under the relentless logic of modern capitalism.

CHAPTER 13

Bottom Rail on Top This Time

In 1861, the Confederate States of America established itself as a new barrier securing the Great House. As one Alabama secessionist fulminated in the year the Civil War began, independence must be won, lest "our wives and our little ones . . . be driven from their homes by the light of our own dwellings." Another Southern orator denounced abolitionists' desire "to light up the fires of a servile insurrection, and to give your dwellings to the torch of the incendiary." Remaining in the Union under a Lincoln administration could only result in all-out war between the races in the South, concluded one Georgia secession advocate. If slavery were to be abolished, "our men will be compelled to wander like vagabonds all over the earth, and as for our women the horrors of their state we cannot contemplate in imagination." Only an independent nation by and for slaveholders could beat back from the front gate the hordes of fanatical Yankees and savage Negroes.[1]

In the antebellum South, the patriarch's domain was everything the slave quarter was not. For nearly two hundred years, enslavers had the power to choose who could live with whom. Slaves could only marry with their blessing. Masters and their sons trespassed slave quarters at night, assaulting and raping women and girls. They kept the children of such forced unions in bondage. They forced enslaved women to care for white children before their own. They reached into the enslaved's dwelling and stole countless hours of labor, as well as innumerable nights of sleep, from the folks who lived inside. They entered Black homes to snatch family members away for sale.

Thus, it is no surprise that Black southerners pursuing freedom during the Civil War also spoke of dwellings—and especially of the fences that protected them. In 1865, amid the chaos of Confederate collapse and the end of slavery, a former chattel turned Union soldier squinted at some gray-coated prisoners he had been assigned to guard. Among the throng was a nearly unbelievable sight: his former enslaver, disheveled, dishonored, and reeking of defeat. "Hello, massa," the guard called out. "Bottom rail on top dis time!" This was no mere turn of phrase. In the social revolution that saw slaves and an invading army overturn the plantation order, fences were a key part of the struggle. As planters' power disintegrated in spectacular fashion, and the fog of their invincibility cleared, freed people crossed, broke through, took apart, or simply burned down the plantation barriers that had contained them in slavery. A former slave recalled of 1865: "After de war my marster come back home. De fences was gone, de cattle was gone, de money an' de Niggers was gone, too."[2]

After emancipation, Black women and men quickly put up fences of their own to insulate their loved ones from a market that had long treated them as commodities. For the first time, a Black family's hearth and home could provide a bulwark against the depredations of white people, and those gates were fiercely defended. One Lowcountry planter complained to newly arrived Union authorities in 1865 that his former slaves Harry Gant, Limas, Jim, John, Carolina, Horace, and Jacob, "armed with sticks & clubs, marched to the overseers house and used abusive language because the hogs had broken the fence and got into the cornfield." So incensed were the freedpeople by this violation of *their* property rights that they passed to "the back gate to my dwelling" and addressed the mistress with "a great deal of insolence mixed with threats and brandishing their clubs at her." Planters interpreted the new sanctity of Black dwellings as an emblem of their defeat and a direct threat to their own hearths and homes.[3]

The Civil War and its aftermath, then, is a story of competing enclosures. Planters desired to reenclose the space of the plantation, as well as their region of the country, where their word was law. The most important part of this reenclosure was a reconstituted right of forcible entry into the homes of former slaves, to extract their fieldwork, their domestic labor, and perhaps most importantly, to force the freedpeople to acknowledge the absolute supremacy of the planter's needs over their own.

For good reason, the newly liberated insisted on new enclosures of their own. Small crop fields, gardens, and swept yards, all neatly fenced in, appeared around abandoned plantations late in the war. There were new spiritual fences as well. Scores of independent Black congregations such as the Colored Methodist Episcopalian Church were established in the 1860s to replace the white-run churches where slaves had been forced to worship from the balcony. Thousands of couples who had "jumped the broom" in informal antebellum ceremonies formalized their marriages and went on the road to find and reconstitute families torn apart by the slave trade. However, enslaved people knew, long before the Union invading forces recognized it, that Black dwellings would never be safe unless the plantation was destroyed.

The plantation's destruction would begin mere acres from where it had first touched North American shores in 1672—along the coasts of South Carolina and Georgia. Easy to reach from Union shipyards, and only haphazardly defended by a nearly nonexistent Confederate Navy, the Lowcountry fell quickly. The suddenness of the upheaval for the enslaved of the old "Rice Coast" must have been bewildering.

After nearly two centuries of captivity, after decades of compromises between North and South that had left the master's boot on the neck of the slave, Black folks looked on as an armored Union gunboat steamed up the Combahee River in early 1863. Jubilant, they waved and hollered. But there was much they could not yet know. Many of them read the events through the lens of Scripture. The young white men gazing stone-faced from the decks of the hulking craft were ship caulkers from Falmouth and farm hands from Pennsylvania, many of whom had never seen a Black person before. Would such men, boys really, be ready to believe they marched to the cadence of biblical time? Could they be convinced that theirs was an army of liberation? Was the Pharaoh's painted world finally quaking? In the book of Exodus, Yahweh tells the great emancipator Moses, "When you go [out of slavery], you will not go emptily . . . you will despoil Egypt." It was probably not coincidence that determined freedom seekers on the Combahee signaled their welcome

2nd South Carolina Infantry Regiment raid on a rice plantation, Combahee, South Carolina.

to the Navy by setting fire to the pumphouse next to the rice field. Then they torched the mansion.

Black people insisted from the start that the war was a war against slavery, helping Northern whites make up their minds. Actions like those of the freedom seekers on the Combahee taught the Union seamen: Your army is an army of liberation. Many of them needed the lesson. Naval officer was among the most aristocratic and conservative professions in antebellum America. The head of the Union Navy was Rear Admiral Samuel Francis DuPont, a scion of French royalists and American industrialists. He had "never been an abolitionist" before the war. But the scenes he witnessed during his service in the South changed his mind. "Oh my!" he exclaimed. "What a delusion . . . The degradation, overwork, and ill treatment of the slaves in the cotton states is greater than I deemed possible, while the capacity of the Negro for improvement is higher than I believed." Among his officers, none had been opposed to bondage in 1860. Two years later he could write, "There is not a proslavery man among them."[4]

Their way of seeing the world was being transformed by the flood of escapees from the plantation. Particularly influential on DuPont were fifteen freedom seekers who stole a Confederate barge in heavily fortified Charleston harbor and rowed it quietly out to the Union blockade. Until their escape, they had been compelled to work in the logistics operations of the Confederate military. Thus, they possessed crucial knowledge of "the various defenses, forts, entrenchments, bridges, etc.," which they duly shared with the admiral. The Union Navy was a full year ahead of the Army in establishing a policy for protecting "contraband of war" from their former masters and utilizing the labor of these self-liberating captives for Union ends. But for the plantation to be seriously weakened, confiscation of labor had to be paired with confiscation of land, an issue nearly as controversial as slavery itself in a nation built on settler expansion.[5]

On the eve of secession, planters had grounds for confidence. In spite of their shrinking representation in Congress, an increasingly militant abolitionist movement, and the rise of a new political party that opposed the expansion of slavery, they had won important concessions in the previous fifteen years. The invasion of Mexico had added new slaveholding territories. The Kansas-Nebraska Act of 1854 nullified the Missouri Compromise and raised the possibility of spreading slaveholding nationwide. The *Dred Scott* decision of 1857 revealed that proslavery interests controlled the Supreme Court. Planters also maintained a firm grip on legislatures in their states. These significant political advantages bore fruit in the heady atmosphere of an economic boom in the 1850s, which brought rising prices for slaves and land, along with record cotton harvests.

Between 1850 and 1860, foreign trade leaped to new levels. Gold rushes in California, Colorado, and Australia raised prices globally, encouraging lending and investment, the credit stringency of the post–1837 Panic period loosening considerably. Total railroad miles in the United States went from 9,000 in 1850 to 30,635 in 1860. The postal system—and telegraphs too—integrated coastal ports with interior farms throughout the country. At the same time, in Great Britain food production was no longer keeping pace with population growth. This inexorable fact, coupled with disastrous crop failures in Ireland, meant the British Parliament could no longer afford to continue discriminating against slave-grown products like Cuban sugar; they also slashed all duties against American grain and raw cotton. These concessions by Britain greatly increased foreign demand for American farm products, leading to consistently high prices from 1846 until the Civil War.[6]

Nationally, agricultural production boomed. Cotton led the way, with output increasing from 1.4 million bales in 1850 to 3.8 million in 1860. Manufacturing also grew. U.S. cotton mills consumed 126 million pounds in 1850 and 423 million in 1860, out of 1.5 billion pounds of total cotton production by the plantations. While 72 percent was shipped to Britain, 28 percent of Southern cotton was purchased and used in Northern factories. In the fifteen years prior to secession, total demand continued to outpace supply. Just to keep up, planters and manufacturers installed larger cotton gins and screw presses, many of them powered by steam engines.[7]

The boom of the 1850s, which saw skyrocketing prices for cotton as well as the monetary value of slave property, was abetted by a boom in Southern railroad construction, which was funded by state bonds floated on the London money market. Enslavers' fortunes were also shaped by the New York Stock Exchange, which grew at breakneck speed in the 1850s. Overexuberance led to the Panic of 1857, a market correction that did not dampen investors' spirits for long. The years 1859 and 1860 saw the largest cotton harvests and the largest profits in the history of the South. Thus the plantation's conquest of new territories felt not like a desperate gambit, but a birthright of the nation's wealthiest men of capital.

John Brown's 1859 attack on Harpers Ferry, and the election of Abraham Lincoln in 1860, did not find a planter class that was worried about the vigor of its civilization. The events simply affirmed planters' belief that slavery, and with it the plantation, could no longer spread within an American empire. It would be fenced in by the Republican Party's opposition to any further expansion of slavery. Even though many planters were convinced Republican encirclement presented an existential threat, they did not immediately exit the powerful transcontinental empire they had helped build. They tried to calculate how they would forge a new nation around their plantation way of life. Some Southern leaders called for domestic industrialization to face the new era. Writers such as William Gregg indulged in a fantasy that they could transform their economy into something it was not without giving up the plantation. Others had a more clear-eyed view of what the South really was.[8]

In expanding the plantation since the 1670s, planters had committed the American South to a specialized role as raw material exporter. As much as they resented the "Yankee merchants" for siphoning off their profits, they required Northerners to ship, finance, manufacture, and sell their crops. But planters had profited marvelously from this arrangement. Thus, leading Southern intellectual George Fitzhugh—a descendant of the seventeenth-century tobacco and land magnate William Fitzhugh—

assured his readers that a safe future for slaveholders would not require building factories at home. Instead, independence from "enemies" like Northern merchants and British mills could be secured simply by forging a new set of trade relationships. "Persia, Arabia, India, and China" will soon constitute a world-girdling "confederacy of trade" centered on Louis Napoleon's reactionary monarchy of France, he wrote in 1861. The future of the Confederacy lay in becoming part of an illiberal world system: "By a canal from the James River to the Ohio, [France] will connect the trade of the Mediterranean with the trade of the Chesapeake, and extend continuous and various water communication from the interior of Asia, Europe, and Africa, to the Rocky Mountains, the lakes and the Gulf of Mexico, in America."[9]

As fanciful and retrograde as such a notion appears today, it was the South's full integration into an international capitalist economy that gave "fire-eaters" like Fitzhugh the confidence that their influence would be magnified if they left the Union. However, he failed to understand the particular vulnerability of a plantation society in wartime. Secessionist blowhards such as South Carolina Senator James Henry Hammond thundered with great self-assurance that the global economy would be brought to its knees without Southern cotton. On the contrary. The sinews that had long bound plantation America to world markets made the economic amputations of secession painful and ultimately fatal to the Confederate States of America.

While self-sufficient in basic foods like corn and hogmeat, citizens of the South had long imported means of agricultural production like horses, plows, hoes, nails, shoes, and clothing for slaves. On the eve of secession, 97 percent of the country's firearms and 93 percent of its iron were produced in Northern states. The fledgling war machine of the South required gunpowder, lead, rifles, and cannon. It needed salt to cure meat. It needed flour, medicine, and tents for soldiers. Not surprisingly, the parts of the South where plantation slavery was least embedded would be the most essential in equipping the region for modern war. The South's eight border states held over 75 percent of the its industrial capacity, 50 percent of its horses and mules, and 60 percent of its livestock and food crops.[10]

Unfortunately for Confederate war efforts, those were the parts of the South that, having the fewest slaveowners, were least enthused about seceding from the Union. Kentucky, which Confederate President Jefferson Davis tried desperately to recruit into the secessionist bloc, remained loyal to the Union throughout the conflict. After a minority of cotton planters in the "Boone's Lick" region of Missouri failed to accomplish its secessionist aims, the state was mired in guerrilla violence throughout the war. In all, two hundred thousand whites from the border states fought for the Union, and only ninety thousand for the Confederacy. The Confederate military apparatus was deprived of vital supplies and manpower from all the more economically diversified Southern states for the duration of the Civil War.[11]

Thus, the Confederate States of America needed to develop new industries and diversified agriculture from scratch, but a majority of planters believed their newly created nation was meant to safeguard and promote their own vision of liberty. Many refused to turn cotton acreage over to corn during the war. They also took advantage of the "twenty-slave law" that allowed slave masters to avoid military service. Their land and slaves were not subject to tax levies by the Confederate government until three years into the conflict.

However, as the war dragged on and put increasing pressure on the limited resources of the seceded states, the Confederate military apparatus subjected planters to unheard-of extensions of (Southern) federal power. Officers commandeered planters' slaves to build fortifications, told them what to plant and purchased it at fixed prices, while hungry soldiers carried away their harvests. The plantation mistress Mary Milling observed in early 1864, "I do not think planters will take an interest in their farms as formerly—Now they have nothing that they can call their own—all property at the disposal of the government."[12]

Even though the majority of white Southerners lacked the wealth to join the planter class, their society was still a reflection of the plantation's priorities. Given the "skimming" mode of land use, the South's population was scattered. It lagged behind that of Northern states, which built their populations on small farms and a cohesive system of villages, towns, and cities increasingly tied to one another by rail. Lower average wages in the South meant the vast majority of European immigrants to the United States were drawn to cooler climes. The plantation-dominated parts of the South thus had a small tax base and less manpower, as well as fewer urban centers, than Northern regions.

The railroad system of the South underwent a major building boom in the 1850s, but its layout was shaped by planter hegemony. With thinly settled populations, many of which were not involved in wider markets, most regions of the South lacked the customer base or a quantity of potential freight sufficient to justify a denser network. Instead of trunk-and-branch networks that spiderwebbed densely across entire regions as in Northern states, Southern railroads consisted mostly of single lines connecting plantation neighborhoods to terminals at the coast. Nonplantation areas experienced little in the way of transport modernization. Even where they were more common, the railroads were managed by different firms that sometimes had different gauges, meaning the lines could not be connected. All these factors resulted from the rule and geographic demands of the plantation system. This approach reinforced a continuing dependence on the rivers, which suited a plantation economy well in peacetime. But it turned out to be a problem when the superior Union Navy seized control of most of the major rivers by the midpoint of the war.[13]

Hampered by the railroads' intrinsic inefficiencies, as well as the occupied rivers, the Confederate Commissary Department struggled mightily to get food to where it was needed. Some of the supplies rotted in warehouses while awaiting railroad transportation, which averaged a sloth-like one mile per hour throughout the Confederacy by 1864. Some shipments were intercepted by railroad workers who took it home to feed hungry families. Exasperated Confederate officials reported the disappearance of 617,000 pounds of bacon in a single year. To make up for the shortfall, the government offered outlandish rewards to blockade runners who could bring meat from abroad for its troops. Many of the smugglers brought luxury items like silks and port wine instead. As matters turned desperate, however, they brought an estimated 3.5 million pounds of meat through the Union blockade in the second half of 1864 alone. Some of this was illegally sold to speculators who offered it to everyday people at inflated prices. In response to widespread food theft, Confederate guards were placed on supply trains with orders to shoot would-be thieves on sight. Because basic food was so hard to come by, Lucius Northrop, the head of the Confederacy's Commissary Department, became "the most cussed and vilified man in the Confederacy."[14]

Confederate soldiers craved military engagements because it would give them a chance to grab Union rifles and ammunition, as well as food, shoes, and blankets after a victory in battle. More frequently, however, they obtained such things from their own civilian population. Many units—especially the vaunted Confederate cavalry, whose horses needed fodder—took to raiding Southern farms. Crestfallen white farm women were left with hastily scrawled IOUs or worthless Confederate greenbacks. To make matters worse for civilians, the Confederate government levied a 10 percent tax-in-kind on crops. This was hardest on small farmers, in many cases women without the aid of slaves, who had little surplus to spare beyond what they were able to grow to feed their family. In order to escape this levy, many farmers turned their low-value, high-volume grain into liquor they could sell to passing soldiers, much to the chagrin of their officers. There were also droughts in the South in 1862 and 1863.[15]

By 1864, in spite of bleeding the Southern populace dry, Confederate soldier rations were a pittance, and the "dwellings" that secessionists had promised to protect were in ruins. The hospitable "groaning table" of the plantation kitchen had been smashed up and burned for warmth. White Southerners turned to eating mules and rats. In 1863, a Richmonder was arrested for selling puppy meat. Beggars became a common sight all over the South. "Deaths from starvation have absolutely occurred," admitted one group of Alabama community leaders in a letter to Jefferson Davis. Yet the war was not yet done, as thousands of white soldiers, fearful of "Black Republicans" and loyal both to their comrades as well as to beloved leaders like Robert E. Lee, refused to give up the fight for Confederate national independence—a victory that would have cemented the status of four million Black Southerners as slaves in perpetuity.[16]

After Union General William Tecumseh Sherman successfully took Atlanta in the fall of 1864, his troops burned all industrial resources within town limits. Northern observers crowed about the imminence of victory. But Southern capitals had been changing hands for three years. The sacking of a city was certainly lamentable for its residents. The rebel heart of the Southern white man, however, dwelled not in cities and towns, but in his peculiar version of home: the slave plantation. Even if he did not own one, he insisted it defined his civilization. When one Confederate private explained in a letter home why he fought, he painted a dreadful picture of Yankees breaking up "the large estates into ten acre lots with a two-story framed house on each with ginger bread and apples in the window." For this infantryman, a humble Yankee homestead was downright dystopian. Few Northern white men understood this more instinctively than Sherman. When he vowed to pursue the rebels "to their inmost recesses," he was referring to the plantation dwelling, not just the society and economy that had grown up around it.[17]

The March to the Sea began on November 15, 1864, when Sherman turned his sixty-thousand-man army east. Four columns of battle-tested and well-rested troops swung out of Atlanta like a scythe, cutting a 280-mile swath through the plantation heartland of Georgia, from the upland cotton tracts of the Piedmont to the rice swamps of the Lowcountry. When word spread that Sherman's army was coming, recalled former slave Nettie Henry, "it soun' lak a moanin' wind" in the slave quarters.[18]

While he instructed his soldiers to destroy factories, mills, and cotton gins (thousands were put to the torch), as well as railroads (nearly 450 miles were torn up), what made the March to the Sea and the subsequent Carolinas Campaign unique "was the enormous destruction of private homes," especially those of wealthy planters who had played leading roles in the rebellion. It was as if Sherman had been eavesdropping at the secessionist brouhahas of 1861, taking notes during the fiery orations urging war for the purpose of protecting white "dwellings."[19]

Sherman's route was carefully planned to punish planter elites who had driven their states out of the Union to safeguard plantation slavery. As historian William G. Thomas notes, "Sherman had studied his maps, pored over the latest census data, and interviewed dozens of locals about the buildings and property on the route." In the regions of central Georgia his army marched through, landholdings and slaveholdings were much larger than the state average. In Morgan County, Georgia, 70 percent of a total population of ten thousand lived in slavery. Nearly half of the county's bondspeople lived on large plantations. In Putnam County, meanwhile, 71 percent of slaves were held by planters who enslaved twenty or more people; in other words, they lived not on small farms but on plantations. In some counties in Sherman's path, three-quarters of white families owned slaves—a higher proportion than in most of the South. Those who did not own slaves often had wealthy kin or employers who did, and aspired to join the master class. Eager to punish planters in particular for supporting treason and waging a war against democracy, Sherman's men darkened the skies of plantation Georgia with smoke.[20]

In his memoir of the March to the Sea, Sherman fondly recollected stopping to rest at a large plantation one night. Fiddling with the owner's things, his eyes alighted upon a candlebox with the name "Howell Cobb" engraved on it. When he confirmed that he was indeed occupying the plantation of the onetime treasury secretary of the United States, leading ideologue of secession, and current Confederate general, Sherman instructed his subordinate officers "to spare nothing. That night huge bonfires consumed the fence-rails, kept our soldiers warm, and the teamsters and men, as well as the slaves, carried off an immense quantity of corn and provisions of all sorts." Whatever could not be carried away was turned to cinders.[21]

Camped outside Cobb's big house that night, an infantryman from Illinois disparaged Cobb's haphazard fencing and poorly organized fields. Crop masters like Cobb were accustomed to looking down on their poorer neighbors. Now a grimy Yankee farmer traipsed over the planter's property, subjecting his self-professed mastery of the landscape to withering criticism. Not only were the sacred dwellings of the planter class scrutinized and found wanting; they became the playgrounds of Northern conquerors, who smashed up the master's fine furniture, threw it in a pile, and cooked their dinner on it.[22]

One Union officer, in the middle of assuring a planter's family that their private property would be respected, was interrupted by a fellow soldier barging into the room with an armload of valuables. As the embarrassed would-be protector was walking out, he noticed a fire had already been started at the back of the house. In an anguished diary entry, Georgia mistress Dolly Burge recalled the night the Federals came. She "went to the gate to claim protection & a guard. But like Demons they rush in! My yards are full. To my smoke-house, my Dairy, Pantry, Kitchen & Cellar, like famished wolves they come, breaking locks & whatever is in their way." The act of secession had fulfilled fire-eaters' paranoid prophecy of what would befall the region if the plantation states remained in the Union. In the furious words of one North Carolina woman whose farm had repeatedly been ransacked, abolitionists and slaves had become "desecrators of our homes."[23]

Indeed. The carefully kept records of Sherman's army show a shocking haul from Georgia farms and plantations: 6,871 mules and horses, 13,294 head of cattle, 10.4 million pounds of grain, 10.7 million pounds of animal feed, and "six million rations of beef, bread, coffee, and sugar." Five weeks after leaving what remained of Atlanta, and 25,000 bales of cotton heavier, the blue-coated troops walked into Savannah, which the Confederates had abandoned, knowing they could not defend it.

By attacking "the industrial resources of the South"—not primarily factories, but farms and plantations—Sherman's army had made clear that Jefferson Davis's "promises of protection" were hollow. Sherman famously telegraphed the president on December 25, presenting Savannah to Lincoln as a Christmas gift. Georgians' support for the war had been destroyed.[24]

The free people knew that setting fire to plantation homes was a key part of destroying slavery. For many, Sherman's acts of destruction combined with their own fires brought liberty: "We work on," recalled a former South Carolina slave, "till Sherman come and burn and slash his way through the state in the spring of 1865. I just reckon I member dat freedom to de end of my life." After the taking of Savannah, Sherman continued his march through South Carolina, the seedbed of secession. His army encountered little resistance as it torched, scavenged, and scarfed its way northward. Another ex-slave, reflecting on the destructive march through the Carolinas, wrote that the "people of the South needed some such a dose as that—they needed to learn war is a serious thing.... And Sherman seemed to be the man for that kind of teaching." By this time, around ten thousand fugitives from slavery were in train behind Sherman's marauding troops. An observer from a hilltop must have seen something like the River Jordan itself in majestic flood, cutting through the valleys to wash the enslavers' army away.[25]

In March 1865, Robert E. Lee's Army of Northern Virginia was the last major rebel force in the field. Huddled in trenches around Richmond and Petersburg, Lee's "diehards," even the horses and mules, had been living rough for over three years. While Union animals received at least 23 pounds of feed per day, those in Lee's army were put on a daily ration of 2.5 pounds. Fed on sticks and dirt, they became too feeble to lug caissons into battle. When there was nothing left to eat, Lee was forced to divide his supplies of animal feed between his horses and his men. While there were plenty of soldiers who never gave up the fight, desertion in Confederate ranks was rampant by late 1864.[26]

In a speech in Macon, Georgia, Jefferson Davis acknowledged that two-thirds of the soldiers supposed to be in the field were absent, the majority of them "without leave." As one historian of military strategy notes, "The Confederate armies were simply breaking down, and some of this was due to the collapsing home front as families pled for their absent men to return and save them from chaos and starvation." On April 1, 1865, the president of the Confederacy was informed the defenses around his capital city could no longer be held. He fled Richmond disguised in his wife's clothes. As Lee's malnourished soldiers retreated toward Appomattox Court House, many simply collapsed on the roadsides to await their fate.[27]

Faced with the demands of modern war, a society superrich in land, slaves, and money turned out to be brittle. The rage and desperation with which hundreds of thousands of die-hard white men fought off Union conquest for four years do not change this fact. The fruit of the plantation was abundant, but it was never meant to last.

Large numbers of Confederate men named white women as the cause of the war. In 1861, the loudest secessionist voices had blared that the virtue, innocence, chastity, and racial purity of white women were being endangered by Northerners whose foolish zealotry would unleash the avenging fire of the slaves. For the sake of defending wives, daughters, and sisters from "an unspeakable fate," as much as 80 percent of white men left Southern communities to serve in the military. As death tolls mounted in colossal battles like Shiloh and Gettysburg, and the Confederate military draft went into effect, the plantation became more and more a world of women. Not only in the house, but in the fields, woods, and quarters, many mistresses who had been promised protection were suddenly called on to assume the mantle of plantation mastery.[28]

As if matters were not challenging enough for them, enslaved women opened what historian Laura Edwards calls a "second front" of the Civil War within the plantation household. Determined to set boundaries around their work, to care for their own children instead of white ones, and to fight back against the violence of mistresses, Black women engaged in daily low-intensity conflict from the start of the war in 1861. Slaves were called "impudent" and "saucy" because they finally abandoned the coded language that had been forced upon them in bondage. As one mistress noted during the war, "The negroes are worse than free, they say they *are* free." The true feelings of enslaved people often came as a profound shock to their enslavers. "The conduct of the Negro in the late crisis of our affairs," lamented one ex-master after the war, "convinced me that we have all been laboring under a delusion.... I believed for a season that these people were content, happy, and attached to the master. I have lived to change all these opinions."[29]

Even their most beloved mammies and uncles, the ones they had long thought of as "pets" and "favorites," despised them. When the illusory threads of familial affection between owner and owned began to fray, some mistresses reacted with violence. "When she hear'd de Niggers talkin' 'bout bein' free," Sam McAllum recalled of his enslaver, "she wore 'em out wid a cowhide." When another ex-slave's mistress would fly into a rage about "the Yankees," she "would take me by my ears and butt my head against the wall." As daily life on the plantation became more difficult, as "the Negroes" proved their perfidiousness, and as the prospect of victory grew remote, waves of self-pity crashed over the Great Houses of the Lowcountry. "I think it is a pity," wrote one mistress of her recalcitrant captives, "they cant be made to feel a little of the care which oppress white people [in] these hard times."[30]

People like these found it difficult to imagine any society existing without slavery. *Somebody* has to be a slave, they reasoned. Thus, if Lincoln frees "the Negro," that must mean the Black man is going to enslave "us." Such twisted logic helps explain why so many Southern whites fought so stubbornly for as long as they did. The lie led mistresses to entertain genocidal fantasies. Mary Jones of Savannah comforted herself with the belief that "with their emancipation must come their extermination." "I want the power of extermination," echoed plantation mistress Anne Pope.[31]

After the war—after they had challenged enslavers' authority for four years—free women demanded what historian Thavolia Glymph calls "free homes." Free homes were to be a place where nobody would be "cussing fire to my black heart," as survivor of slavery Katie Rowe put it. Nancy Johnson would have known exactly what Rowe was talking about. When Johnson was forced by circumstance to return to her former plantation, "my old Missus ask me if I came back to behave myself and do her work and I told her no that I came back to do my own work." The next day, "my mistress came out again and asked me if I came back to work for her like a 'nigger'—I told her no that I was free & she said be off then & called me a stinking bitch." During slavery, the decidedly ungenteel character of the mistress would have remained the private knowledge of the community of Black women on her plantation. Now it was in the public record, thanks to Johnson's testimony to Union occupying forces.[32]

Small freedoms mattered. A free woman named Peggy tied "pink ribbons" and a "dozen bows" into her children's hair to illustrate "the pride of their freedom." No longer would these young people walk around with invisible price tags affixed to their bodies, but emblems of self-possession instead. For Josephine Lampkin, freedom meant nursing her own child when it grew hungry—not when a master or mistress should deem it convenient. In November 1865, a white man named Newton Hagar told her to put down her baby and "unload a wagon full of corn." Josephine refused, explaining that her baby "was not done sucking." Hagar immediately flew into a rage, drawing his pistol and shooting Josephine through the hand. Next he pulled out a knife. "He began cutting her and stabbed her in several places," including her breast. At the first opportunity, Josephine "ran to save her life." Hagar then chased her with a club, but she outran him. However, she could not escape her assailant without "leaving her sucking child behind." The day after these horrifying events, a distraught Josephine appeared at the Lowcountry office of the Freedmen's Bureau to report the assault. Josephine had not seen her child since fleeing her attacker. Ex-enslavers like Hagar raged at the new sanctity of the relationship between mother and child that had not existed in slavery, but that Josephine insisted on.[33]

While hundreds of thousands of Black folk risked their lives by departing plantations during the Civil War, many more defined their freedom as the power to remain in the old place. Black women were particularly likely to stay on the plantations where they had been enslaved, even though they were in the majority of cases excluded from the possibility of landownership. As writer and scholar Angela Davis has noted, taking to the road is what freedom often felt like for men; for women, flight carried the additional burden of caring for children, as well as the risk of sexual assault. Many women and girls fled anyway. The majority who remained on plantations and farms felt a keen and justified attachment to the land. The plantation was a site of struggle. They did not want to leave it. They wanted to wrest control of it from their former enslavers and divide it up among themselves. One group of former slaves hoping to return to the plantation they had lived on before 1861 were described as "the old Founders of the place." A freedman pleading their case wrote, "Those that wos taken away wos Born & Raise on that Iseland & there parent is stil there furthermore they has a knolledge of the Soil what it Can Produce . . . the houses & all improvement on the place is there labor . . . these people knoes Evry thing In Regard to the plantation." Thousands of women and men fought for a right of return to the plantation ground, not because they were nostalgic for "slavery times," but because they considered themselves as having legitimate property rights—the exercise of which would require bringing about the end of three centuries of the planter's enclosure.[34]

The antiplantation subculture they had nourished during slavery—an insistence on autonomy, self-provisioning, and privacy over profit—would be their most prized weapon in the coming struggle.

CHAPTER 14

Sherman's Reserve

Early in 1865, two weeks after Major-General Sherman had finished devastating the heartland of the South and had strolled into its second-oldest city at the head of a conquering army, he found himself shifting in his seat as a Black man gave him advice. Garrison Frazier had been held in slavery for the first sixty years of his life. In 1856, he purchased his freedom and that of his wife for a thousand dollars. He quickly rose to local prominence as a pastor for Black congregants in Savannah. When Sherman had sought counsel as to what to do with the ten thousand fugitives trailing his army, Frazier was one of a small number of notable Black men in Savannah to be consulted. Some officials within the Union bureaucracy saw their job as tutoring ex-slaves in the ways of modern economic life by urging them to sign formal labor contracts with landowners to make wages and to prevent idleness. However, Frazier knew that employment contracts between ex-masters and ex-slaves provided insufficient guarantees that real freedom would take root. He advised Sherman to put former slaves "where we could reap the fruit of our own labor." Black Southerners needed "to have land."[1]

Partly in response to Frazier's advice, Sherman issued Field Order 15 before the end of the war, which divided up the plantations of traitors and redistributed them in forty-acre plots—along with a government mule—to ex-slave heads of household. The measure set in motion an unprecedented federal intervention in the plantation's property regime. Under military authority, thousands were settled. After Lee's surrender and the effective end of the slaveholders' rebellion, the Field Order was formalized under the Freedmen's Bureau, which had been established to help newly freed slaves adjust to freedom and destitute Southern whites to recover from the ruin of war.

By the fall of 1865, forty thousand freedmen possessed farms in South Carolina, as did twenty thousand in southeastern Virginia. Black families had settled on sixty-two thousand acres in Louisiana, and tens of thousands more acres in Mississippi. Across the historical plantation belt, ex-slaves were getting cotton and rice production back under way, a priority of the federal government trying to reconstruct devastated societies after four years of war. The most important territory, however, lay in rice country. Dubbed Sherman's Reserve, four hundred thousand acres of valuable Lowcountry land stretching from North Carolina to northern Florida was set aside for Black settlement.[2]

As soon as the Reserve was announced, "former slaves rushed to take up tracts." A planter who had fled his plantation during the Carolinas Campaign returned to find that his former slaves "had occupied every rich lot I had and monopolized all the rice bottoms save one.... They refuse to rake fence to preserve it from fire or to split rails.... They raised & appropriated all the melons which grew on the place, threshed before they were perfectly ripe the peaches from every tree and three orchards did not leave me a single apple tree out of 750 grafted trees.... The melons and peaches and apples were carried to the bluff and sold to the steamers... the men except one refused to cut steamboat wood for steamers at $.50 per cord." He painted them as idlers who "were not inclined to work on their part or my own." Yet they cared for, harvested, packed up, and sold thousands of pieces of fruit while letting the old master's beloved fences rot in the tall grass. The planter worried that "without some change the plantation will go to waste." This statement would probably have been met with hearty nods from his former captives.³

The free people did more than take up plots as individual cultivators. They began building the institutions of an independent civil society. On St. Simons Island off the coast of Georgia, which had been controlled by rice and cotton enslavers until the war, former slaves chartered a town, ratified a constitution, and appointed officeholders to run their government. While Sherman's Field Order required the coming together of four male heads of household in order to trigger the turnover of plantations, former slaves throughout the South took the initiative by forming themselves into cooperatives to purchase land. Black veterans of the Union Army, having been paid in cash over more than two years of war, were prominent in such ventures. They had also been politicized through military service. They had wielded arms and risked their lives to emancipate their people. They had pressed for social change within Union ranks, demanding equal pay, as well as the right to take part in combat. Many had learned to read and write during their service—an act that had been a crime in most Southern states during slavery.⁴

After the Confederate surrender, Black veterans also organized armed self-defense units to safeguard their democratic rights. In December 1865, one white planter beseeched the hated Union occupiers of South Carolina to "spare us only a few white troops . . . [because] my negroes . . . have organized a company near here of 75." He noted the democratic character of the unit, pointing out that the rank-and-file had "elected their Capn (Wesley Jones colored) and other officers." The militia demanded "land or blood." Although the militia represented the duly constituted authority at the time, the planter, falling back on old habits, called their efforts to enforce federal law an "insurrection."⁵

Another militia of former slaves called itself the Ogeechee Home Guard. They informed one recalcitrant planter seeking to reassert his authority that "they would have the land & nothing but the land would satisfy them . . . they *would work for no man.*'" For former slaves, working for a wage, especially under extended contracts, amounted to a new form of bondage. Land was the foundation of independence. The logical conclusion of this line of thinking was clear: democracy and the plantation could not coexist.[6]

Free people settling in Sherman's Reserve did not seek to establish a "commons" in place of the plantation's regime of private property. Having been a key part of the planter's power during slavery, the commons did not necessarily have the feeling of freedom. Throughout the antebellum era, enslavers free-ranged their livestock on wooded areas of the plantation, and these hogs and cows were surely a nuisance to the enslaved gardeners. And what recourse would an enslaved person have had if her corn was trampled by the master's hogs? Worse, planters had treated the slave quarters like a commons. No property rights in the person, the work, or the family were respected. All were freely appropriated by the master, who tyrannically defended his own property rights. Thus, freedom seekers were not likely to conceive of freedom as an absence of fences. On the contrary, the social revolution of the 1860s involved the claiming of boundaries that could never have been defended in slavery. When the U.S. Navy set its livestock to graze on the Sea Islands, for example, destroying the newly plowed fields of the free people, residents confronted the naval officers responsible.

Free people fought for a new way of carving up and cultivating the Lowcountry that reflected their values as American cultivators, while also echoing the antiplantation landscape built by ordinary Haitians in the decades after 1804: a smallholders' world of fences protecting privately held family farms, but with strong neighborhood linkages that often overlapped with long-standing kin groups. One planter reported that the free people on his plantation "set apart a portion of the land under cultivation, which they termed theirs; the other they denominated mine. . . . They devoted almost their whole attention to that portion they

Springtime labors on a free people's farm: setting up a trellis for pea vines, feeding chickens. Notice the maze of fences in the backyard, though the sense of property was not absolute, as a neighbor appears to be climbing over one of the barriers.

had chosen to call their own." At the same time, "the whole of my part of the crop—corn, potatoes and all—have been gathered by them and appropriated, and I myself, left destitute. . . . And so it is now, that while they have an abundance, I have not . . . a solitary ear of corn." This planter's world had been turned upside down. The ex-slaves defended their fields, while the old Lowcountry crop master went progging in the commons, his family surviving on "the wild hogs I have managed to have cought in the Ogeechee River swamps."[7]

Five days after Robert E. Lee's surrender at Appomattox Court House in Virginia, President Lincoln was assassinated by a member of a pro-Confederate terrorist cell that had been hiding out in Northern cities during the war. Andrew Johnson, who had been a planter and enslaver in Tennessee before the war, and who hated secessionists but was very sympathetic to them as planters, was hastily sworn in. Soon, he issued blanket pardons to ex-Confederates who took a loyalty oath. Deep South whites were so quickly ushered back into power after surrender that Radical Republicans in Congress insisted on a more thorough Reconstruction of the South. The die was cast: It was Radical Republicans in Congress versus the president, but the president's powers of pardon and especially his powers of appointment of high officials gave him the advantage in shaping the postemancipation social arrangements in the defeated South. Because of the shift from Lincoln to Johnson, thousands of planters were quickly allowed to return to their properties, even though who now owned them was in many cases an open question.

When the defeat of the Confederacy sank in for the Virginia enslaver and Southern nationalist Edmund Ruffin, it was too much for the old man to bear. As the *Petersburgh Express* reported in June 1865, the old wheat planter "seated himself, and placing the muzzle of the musket in his mouth, sprung the trigger and landed his spirit into the eternal world, with a desperate and unnatural coolness." The headline read, HE PREFERS DEATH TO LIVING UNDER THE GOVERNMENT OF THE UNITED STATES. Although this graying mascot of the "Southern Rights Party" died in utter defeat, his prescriptions for prolonging the power of the Southern plantation would win the day.[8]

Since the 1840s, Ruffin had been advocating "Ring Fence Associations" in which planters in a given neighborhood would collectively build a single fence encircling all their properties, so they would not have to build fences to protect individual crop fields. They would keep their livestock in fenced pens and barns so they could collect the manure. Ruffin advocated for laws that would have forced poor farmers to fence in their animals so they would stop trampling planters' valuable crops, but he failed. The commons persisted, perhaps because nonelite white men with voting rights insisted on it. After the war, however, the large-scale enclosures Ruffin had desired would be made real. This would make things difficult for the freed people, because, while they keenly desired enclosed family farms, they knew that access to commons resources was an essential complement to landed property. From catfish, gar, and possum, to firewood, building timber, and fence rails—and most important, the mast and grass on which free-ranging livestock subsisted—the yeoman's enclosed domestic sphere required the resources of the unregulated commons in the South.⁹

Ironically, it was not ex-enslavers of Ruffin's ilk, but well-meaning liberal modernizers in Union blue who initiated the enclosure of the commons of the South. Postemancipation legal codes outlawed progging, squatting, free travel, and other modes of peasant-like independence, while discouraging nonnuclear kin networks, non-Protestant worship practices, and voluntary self-removal from the official economy. Otherwise sympathetic Union officials imposed their nineteenth-century reformist ideology on the postslavery societies they had been deputized

Harvesting the commons after emancipation.

to control during Reconstruction. Most planters favored the moves, as they stood to benefit from the creation of an ex-slave population with no alternative but to accept wage work on the plantations.[10]

Freedmen's Bureau assistant commissioner Rufus Saxton, from an influential family of Massachusetts abolitionists, served as military governor of the occupied Sea Islands during the war. The brigadier general had recruited some of the first regiments of Black soldiers from among the formerly enslaved of the Lowcountry. During Reconstruction, he fought admirably against the highest authorities in his own government to maintain Black people's access to land.

Yet, he had also been schooled in a very nineteenth-century philosophy of Western freedom centered on property ownership. As an antislavery youth, Saxton had absorbed reams of abolitionist rhetoric designed to sway white Northerners through sentimental appeals. Harriet Beecher Stowe's *Uncle Tom's Cabin*, Frederick Law Olmsted's *Journey Through the Seaboard States*, *Narrative of the Life of Frederick Douglass*, and other texts helped create a set of bedrock assumptions about slavery. Slavery was wrong because it violated the fundamental rights of a man to treat the labor of his own hands as his property, and the issue of his loins as something akin to property. If the mainstream argument against slavery was right, which a dyed-in-the-wool New England abolitionist like Saxton firmly believed it was, then individuals coming out of slavery had never had a chance to cultivate a sense of responsibility for their own survival. They needed to be introduced to the civilized ways of property owning and personal responsibility.[11]

During his tenure with the Bureau, Saxton issued a remarkably condescending circular to the free people of South Carolina that reflected mainstream abolitionism's problematic assumptions. "In slavery you only thought of to-day," he wrote. "Having nothing to hope for beyond the present, you did not think of the future, but, like the ox and horse, thought only of the food and work for the day. . . . You must have an idea of the future, and have a plan and object in life," Saxton droned. In addressing former slaves as if they were stock characters in a New

England children's schoolbook, he echoed former slaveholders' refrain on the "improvidence of the Negro." He also discounted the entire history of Black people in the Lowcountry, including their mastery of the land.[12]

But the free people had worse problems than Saxton, who was in fact one of their most steadfast white allies in the postwar South. Brigadier-General Davis Tillson of Maine, a Johnson appointee who headed Freedmen's Bureau operations in Georgia, was a true believer in the "talisman power" of hard work. He assumed slavery had made Black people lazy and that they needed to be forced to work—now by the obligations of a wage contract instead of a fear of the lash. He believed Black people needed the "education" of working for wages. Most importantly, a "harmony between labor and capital" in the postwar South would show the world that emancipation and capitalism could coexist. For Tillson, "capital" was represented by ex-Confederate planters restored to their antebellum properties, and "labor" was Black people shorn of land. So concerned was Tillson about the health of the plantation economy that his patrols harassed Black children on their way to school, telling them "they should be out picking cotton."[13]

Trained as a professional engineer in industrializing America, Tillson could not but oppose the smallholder agriculture taking hold in the South after the war. Large agglomerations of capital, land, and labor under a single directing force were relatively new phenomena in Northern cities. Their efficiency and productive power had helped win the Civil War. They were also making the United States a global power. In the wake of Union triumph, the rational logic of technology and business seemed unshakably superior—not only to quasi-feudal slave plantations, but to small family farms. To officials like Tillson, free people's pursuit of independent lifeways seemed hopelessly backward looking.

As it aimed to revitalize the staple crop system that had long been the bedrock of the Southern economy, then, the federal government wanted free Black people to work like slaves. Officials were convinced that the "mighty experiment" of slave emancipation would only appear to be a success if macroeconomic indicators, like bales of cotton produced or exported, continued to increase after the end of slavery. Their own abolitionist faith was fired by the belief that free people driven by wages worked harder, smarter, and more efficiently than oppressed beasts of burden. But they could not deny the economic achievements of the planter class of the 1850s. The desire to outperform them by encouraging the rebirth of plantations revealed the limitation of their worldview. It was not long before they conceded the necessity of forcing some people to work.

For example, the infrastructures of dirt in the low-lying grounds of the Southeastern Rice Coast had to be maintained, and the Freedmen's Bureau could only see this happening under compulsion. "I feel confident that unless this work is performed," a disconcerted Bureau official named A. J. Willard wrote his superior, "the health of the district will be seriously affected another year.... I am of opinion that, regarded as a Sanitary measure the Military Authorities will be justified in using proper measures to compel its performance." In other words, "imperfect drainage" justified compulsion by occupying Union forces, the former army of liberation. This is not so different from the vow of rice planter and Constitutional delegate Charles Pinckney in 1787 that "whilst there remained one acre of swamp-land in South Carolina," he would defend the African slave trade. Free people had no interest in the maintenance of a rice plantation landscape that had been the source of their oppression for two centuries. Wherever they settled, Willard noted, they "subdivided the lands among themselves and great difficulties have arisen from their unwillingness to do anything except cultivate and harvest their own little plots."[14]

Keen to remedy what he called the "evil" of smallholding, Willard issued a circular to guide his subordinate officers, whose job he understood to be "inducing the freed people to contract for another year." The urgency of establishing a disciplined, modern proletariat was apparent in requirements like a six-day workweek, along with the unheard-of notion of "the usual working hours." Ditching was explicitly required in the new circular, reintroducing one of the worst tasks under slavery into the "free labor" system of the Lowcountry. Willard placed most agricultural decision-making power in the hands of the planter, who "will determine how much land, and what land shall be prepared for the next year's cultivation." Rather than applauding the independent action of free people, he lamented that "labor has been left without an Intelligent head," due to the continuing habit of absenteeism of the planters. Like Saxton, he failed to understand who had run the plantations during slavery. Willard's circular also demonstrated his desire to reestablish the plantation as a cohesive space, under the control of the planter, designed for a single purpose. Thus, only people who signed labor contracts with the planters and worked according to the provisions of those contracts were allowed to live on the plantations at all.[15]

The Bureau would assist planters in having recalcitrant workers "peaceably removed" from the premises. Willard emphasized that the owner of an "enclosed plantation" has the right to determine who is permitted on the grounds to "hunt or trade." Anyone found "hunting or roaming about with firearms, will have their arms taken from them." In other words, independent methods of using the environment to feed one's family or make ends meet were criminalized—in fact, they were regulated more closely than they ever had been during slavery. The plantation was now to be a site of contractual obligation instead of the lash—in all other ways, it closely resembled antebellum realities. For officials like Willard, this was the only path forward.

The actions of the Reconstruction authorities from 1866 to 1872 were the first steps in the closing of the open range in the American South. In the ensuing decades, Ruffin's vision of a planter's rational landscape was realized in the laws of the Southern states. Protection of woodlands by Northern timber companies who flocked to the South in the late nineteenth century, and the need to replace all the fences that had been removed or had fallen into decay during the war, led policymakers to force small farmers to pen their cattle and hogs so crop growers would not have to fence their fields. The wealthy, who could afford pasture and feed, had to use their own properties more intensively and to depart from shifting agriculture. Once Southern elites lost interest in preserving a commons, those commons were doomed. Without woodland, small farmers both white and Black could not afford to keep animals. Without animals, they could not afford to preserve their own woodland. Now having to purchase things like meat and fertilizer, they were forced gradually into depending on planting and selling cotton, though no enslaver was now ordering that they do so.[16]

An entire culture of the open range was stamped out in the late nineteenth century, especially for poor people. Hunting and fishing became tightly regulated; wealthy men who killed sport quarry like quail on exclusive "hunting plantations" were protected while those who hunted for food in the open woods were tarred as layabouts and regulated out of existence. Laws against setting fires (a particular insistence of the timber companies coming South, who lobbied for new range laws to "conserve" and privatize common woods) made it difficult for labor-poor farmers to open new fields to cultivation, as well as to maintain grasslands as hunting parks. Swamps, which had often been hidden domains of Black people's autonomy, were recast as health hazards, drained, and often privatized. Free people knew they needed not only independent family farms, but access to the sprawling, wooded wilds of the rural South. The reenclosure of rural free people within the bounds of an intensified though "free labor" plantation was one midwife of the reborn plantation after the Civil War. The other would be theft.

Even though Saxton failed to understand some aspects of the struggles of the free people, he and the coterie of military officers around him did what they could to secure ex-slaves' acquisition of their own farms. One by one, they were removed from their posts, as Andrew Johnson appointed more conservative officers like Tillson and Willard to take their place. On Sapelo Island, Black military veteran and Bureau agent Tunis Campbell led resistance to planters' reconstruction of their antebellum property regime. Appointed agent for several islands, including Sapelo, Saint Catherine, and Ossabaw, he worked for the Bureau from

March 1865 to March 1866. He made sure the free people had access to land. Campbell also encouraged peat gathering and fishing in the marshy commons, as well as furniture making from trees harvested in open woodland. He established schools on the islands that served a couple of hundred students. He supported the free people in their refusal to work on Saturdays. He approved as they continued to sell surplus crops at their own convenience. Once Johnson began to constrict the operations of the Bureau, however, Campbell was investigated for "dishonest practices," cleared of charges, then removed anyway in the spring of 1866. He remained in the Sea Islands, doing his work informally.[17]

The community of free people on Sapelo continued to withhold their labor from the planters, who had been allowed to return since Johnson's wave of pardons. Tillson blamed the free people for leading "a precarious kind of existence, fishing, hunting, etc.—and laboring under no guiding head." He was right that vast progging under a democratic system of organization precluded a return of the plantation to Sapelo. But he was wrong in calling it "precarious." It was the slave plantation, with its exposure to fickle distant markets, its practice of family separation, and its ecological ruination that was precarious. In 1865 and 1866, former slaves fashioned a fully fledged independent yeomanry, the kind Thomas Jefferson had long dreamed about (though his vision would have been of white farmers). Tillson's soldiers arrived on Sapelo, arrested a dozen community leaders, and forced them to do hard labor at Fort Pulaski for their refusal to sign contracts with the planters.[18]

Rufus Saxton was dismissed in January 1866. In sworn testimony before Congress later that year, he speculated that he "was removed through the influence of the late rebels in South Carolina." Saxton had earned the enmity of some very powerful ex-Confederates. He was bold enough to name Governor Aiken, "who came to my office and desired me to restore to his possession the lands formerly belonging to him." To Saxton, being removed by the machinations of a man like this former Confederate blockade runner was a sign of everything that was going wrong with Reconstruction in the Lowcountry. Black South Carolinians who had remained loyal to the Union and helped it win the war were now being abused, terrorized, and murdered. Meanwhile, all those who had led the state out of the Union and profited from the rebellion quickly retook control of their plantations as well as the government of the state. History, for Saxton, was moving backward.[19]

By the time Saxton was dismissed from his post, 221,500 of the 435,000 acres of land in Sherman's Reserve had been restored to Confederate rebels. Following instructions from President Johnson, Tillson signed Special Order No. 6 in the summer of 1866, which ended any recognition of free people's landownership rights on the islands under his jurisdiction. The formal restoration of property to antebellum owners became official with this order on January 19, 1867. The experiment in land reform as punishment to traitors and as reparation to those held in slavery was woefully brief.[20]

Holdouts on Cumberland Island and St. Simons were forcibly dispossessed by restored planters between 1868 and 1871. Things were different on the Ogeechee Neck, a coastal Lowcountry peninsula with a large Black population. In 1869, two hundred members of the Ogeechee Home Guard took up arms to clear the peninsula of white people. They occupied a planter's house, making it the headquarters of their resistance, erected fortifications, and established a watch. Leaders issued the "Ogeechee Manifesto" on New Year's Day. They were joined by free people from adjoining counties. For five days they held the region, commandeering thousands of bushels of rice from the Neck's large plantations, calling themselves independent "rice planters." In response to the panicked missives of whites in Savannah, a U.S. Army detachment was sent to complete the dispossession of the free people. The Ogeechee Home Guard tried to stop the soldiers' arrival by destroying the bridge over the Ogeechee River and destroying the major plantation homes under their control—a Shermanesque suite of tactics. The Sixteenth Regiment of the U.S. Army arrived nevertheless, successfully quelling the revolt and arresting 143 free people. The leaders were sentenced to five years of hard labor, though they only served two months before being pardoned by Georgia's Republican governor. Most of the Ogeechee Neck was "restored" to the plantation owners.[21]

In 1865, the free people had insisted, correctly, that they needed land as a basis for self-government, education, rice and cotton cooperatives, church congregations, and domestic life. Land reform would have been the only way to enact a true reconstruction of the South, but it required the federal government actively supporting an interracial class of small rural proprietors. In the nearer term, it required the crushing of the planter class. Former slaves were not alone in this opinion. William T. Sherman was not particularly political, but once he had seen the South up close and heard the advice of Garrison Frazier, he also recognized that lasting victory would require stamping out the master class. "There is great danger of the Confederate armies breaking up into guerrillas," he wrote at the end of the war. "And that is what I most fear. Such men as Wade Hampton, Forrest, Wirt Adams, etc., never will work and nothing is left for them but death or highway robbery. They will not work and their Negroes are all gone, their plantations destroyed, etc."[22]

He got exactly right the inviolable code of honor guiding men like Wade Hampton, who would sooner cinch a hundred nooses than raise a hoe with his own hand. For Hampton, it was plantations or blood. Sherman had a plan in mind for them all: "I will be glad if I can open a way for them abroad." Only enlisted men would receive amnesty—not guerrilla fighters or Confederate leaders. Such men, whether Wade Hampton or Jefferson Davis, who had dragged the rest of the white South into rebellion, can "go abroad or get killed in pursuit." Sherman insisted that complete annihilation of the planters was the only way to secure victory. If federal policy had continued along its 1865 track of settling "freedmen and refugees" on lands formerly controlled by the plantation order, if the Confederate elite had been dead, in prison, or abroad, the history of the plantation in America, and of the country overall, might have looked very different.[23]

But there was far too much opposition in powerful places. Within a few weeks of surrender, Sherman's tone had softened. "Our power is now so firmly established that we need not fear again their internal disturbances," he wrote in May 1865. He was not in favor of a full-scale peacetime military occupation of the South. His own soldiers shared his overly forgiving new stance, considering the intensity of destruction they had wrought in the plantation heartland. Soon after surrender, one Union veteran wrote that if Confederates "are willing to admit that we have whipped them . . . that is all we want of them."[24]

Meanwhile, the insurgency Sherman had feared was already under way. Nathan Bedford Forrest, a former Confederate general, went on to play a major role in the founding of the Ku Klux Klan in 1866. By 1868, Wade Hampton was leading a white supremacist paramilitary group with around thirty thousand members in South Carolina. Resuming the practices of antebellum slave patrols, white men suppressed Black folk's political organizing, as well as their preaching and educational activities. Night riders stole Black farmers' tools, food, and money, then lambasted them for not being able to support themselves. Hell-bent on getting the top rail back in place, they trespassed the free Black homesteads whose proprietors had taken the planters' fence rails for their own use.[25]

One night in 1871, a group of eleven hooded men rode up to the house of the freedman Hampton Mitchell and his family. The invaders yelled, "Open the door," but before anyone in the Mitchell family had a chance to respond, they had wrenched it open. One of the men took Mitchell's firearm away, ordered him to get on his knees outside the front door, and began to question him: "Is this your house?" they asked. Then they repeated the question. As if answering the question for him, some of the intruders beat Mitchell. Others "severely whipped" his son-in-law outside the house and beat Mitchell's wife with their weapons. When they had finished assaulting several members of the family, they ordered Mitchell to go back inside the house and close the door. The political message of this murderous visit was clear. White vigilantism was more legitimate than Black property rights. Black fences were violable.[26]

Harriet Simril was raped as punishment for her husband's political participation in York County, South Carolina, where Black Republicans had won several important offices in 1870. As she reported in federal court, "They came after my old man and I told them he wasn't there. They searched about in the house for a long time. They were spitting in my face and throwing dirt in my eyes.... After awhile, they took me out of doors and told me all they wanted was my old man to join the Democratic ticket... after they got me out of doors, they dragged me into the big road and ravished me there." Several nights after the assault, the Simril home was put to the torch. The attack was one of dozens carried out across York County that night, in a pogrom against households whose owners dared act like citizens. In carrying Black women outside their homes and raping them, the night riders made the point that only white men had "dwellings": an abode where a man's authority over his wife and children, and his protection of them, could not be challenged. As in slavery, Black people might have quarters, a roof under which they might settle down for a "broken doze," but never homesteads.[27]

The postbellum wave of home invasions formed part of a sustained campaign of white terrorism perpetrated primarily against free people, but also against white Republicans, teachers, Jews, and other groups seen as a challenge to the restoration of planter power. In 1870, a mob of 2,500 men launched another pogrom in Laurens County, South Carolina, in the Lowcountry. They succeeded in chasing 150 free people from their homes, assassinating nine Republican Party activists in the process. While a series of acts of Congress placed parts of the South under military rule to try to stem the tide of such violence, not enough white Northern politicians had the political will to keep those mobs from fulfilling the aim of their crimes.[28]

The story of Reconstruction's end is often told as a brutal, utter triumph for the ex-Confederates and a shocking retreat by a federal government that had promised to protect and support free people. Yet, the redemption that the planters won in the old Cotton Belt was far from complete when Reconstruction came to a formal end in 1877. In the immediate post–Civil War years, ex-masters had tried to reconstitute a labor system that was slavery in all but name. They desired a system in which they would work a gang of hands who had no say over their own labor and no claim to the land. With the Freedmen's Bureau forcing wage contracts on ex-slaves, however, planters would need a supply of cash to pay plantation workers. But they had none. Land was worth so little that they could not get equity out of their property either. A man living on his ex-enslavers' plantation after the war said that "Mr. Getlin would promise to pay us fer our work an' when de time would come fer to pay he said he didn' have it an' kept puttin us off. . . . Old Missus would cry an' she was good to us but dey had no money."[29]

With the planters lacking cash, and the free people refusing gang labor, a system emerged in which the landlord divided up his cultivable land among individual families. He furnished each of them with land, food, fertilizer, and mules, taking in exchange half the proceeds from their cotton crop. This sharecropping arrangement was not part of a master plan to subjugate ex-slaves. A Department of Agriculture report from 1870 insisted that the system represented an "unwilling concession [on the part of the planters] to the freedman's desire to become a proprietor."[30]

Under oppressive conditions, sharecropping was a partial victory for the free people. While it did devolve into a deeply exploitative system in many cases, sharecropping could also be a rung that allowed free people to climb back into the landownership they had been denied in 1866. By 1921, there were nearly a million Black-owned small farms in the United States, the vast majority of them owned by the descendants of enslaved people living in the Cotton Belt who had engaged in a multigenerational struggle for landed freedom, first during the Civil War, then during Reconstruction and its aftermath.

In his 1935 masterwork *Black Reconstruction in America*, historian W. E. B. Du Bois labeled the slaves' collective refusal to work or to fight for the enslavers during the Civil War a "general strike." In the 1930s, that term carried considerable freight, as a strike of all workers across a national economy was widely thought to be the most revolutionary of anticapitalist actions. Du Bois noted the tragedy that the great Northern railroad strikes in 1877 took place as Reconstruction sputtered to its sad end. If these two groups of the American working class had seen their common interests, a general strike of agricultural workers in the South and industrial workers in the North could have launched the nation down a new path. In isolation from one another, both groups were crushed.

But does a metaphor drawn from industrial labor leave something out? Strikes are inherently temporary—usually, striking workers *need* to get back to work for companies and bosses. The majority of slaves fought not by ceasing work but by staying on the plantation and insisting on the right to continue husbanding that ground for their own ends. Black Southerners' collective actions during and after the Civil War might better be described as a *gran toma*, rather than a general strike. A *toma* is Spanish for a "taking," an occupation of a site of labor involving a redirection of effort rather than a cessation of work. During the Mexican Revolution in the 1910s, the Chilean Socialist Revolution in the 1970s, and the Landless People's Movement in Brazil in the 2000s, poor people took action by occupying haciendas and plantations and putting them into operation. Land occupation, if not successfully beaten back, is permanent. It lays the basis for a permanent, voluntary self-removal from the labor market. And it represents a takeover of the means of elite power.

Republican Party leaders—not Southern forces of reaction—were the most powerful force undoing the *gran toma* of Reconstruction. They increasingly positioned themselves as the party of big business in the Northern states, and the rapid resumption of economic growth required the resumption of what might be called a "rule by employers" in the South. The reversal of Reconstruction's gains was as much class driven as race driven, and power concentrated in the hands of white planters also resulted in the disfranchisement of working-class white people in the South. The *gran toma*, on the other hand, was the taproot of an interracial democracy sprouting from Southern dirt. This commitment to growing the antiplantation was not yet strong, and it needed tending. It held out the promise of a world not based on racialized labor, low wages, cheap food, and the destruction of nature. In the minds of modernizing reformers, independence for the rural poor, whether white or Black, was bad for business, so even had they not been captive to a virulent racial ideology, the rebirth of the plantation would still have seemed the safest bet for the revival of the South.

While planters and free people fought to a penurious stalemate in the main grounds of the Cotton Belt, opportunities for taking over and expanding plantations were appearing in the Caribbean heartland of the plantation long coveted by North Americans. After 1898, the newly independent republic of Cuba would become ground zero of U.S.-controlled experiments in the postslavery remaking of the sugar plantation.

Part Four

NEW FIELDS

Interior of Central Hershey, pan floor.

CHAPTER 15

The Bronze Titan

In November 1895, about a month before the sugar harvest in western Cuba, "eight negros" showed up at the Soledad plantation of the American investor Edwin Atkins. They had come to torch his fields, but Atkins's managers succeeded in fighting them off. The following year, a Black general named Quintín Bandera rode into Atkins's property at the head of 150 cavalry and infantry. This time, there was little Atkins could do. Bandera's soldiers quickly commandeered the estate, though military order was maintained. The emaciated rebels took nothing without asking permission. The fears of marauding Africans had been exaggerated, Atkins concluded, though he had "heard from various sources that with the leaders are a few negroes supposed to have come from Haiti . . . who wear rings in both their ears and noses."[1]

The occupation of Atkins's plantation in 1896 signaled the final phase of Cuba's independence struggle. In 1868, small planters in the underdeveloped eastern side of the island, vexed by Spain's rule, tried to throw off the colonial yoke without sparking slave rebellion. While thousands of enslaved people gained freedom by joining separatist ranks over the next decade of conflict, the war was limited to the eastern half of the island. There was no uprising of Cuban patriots in the western region, where sugar plantations dominated. Spanish power there was largely unchallenged for the duration of what came to be called the Ten Years' War. In fact, Cuba's sugar exports increased in the 1870s. The popular revolutionary general Máximo Gómez pointed out that "as long as the exportation by the enemy of the production of its great sugar plantations is not impeded . . . the revolution is destined to last even much longer. Cuban resources will be drained, and lakes of blood will run unfruitfully in the fields of the island."[2]

Gómez was right. By 1878, a stalemate had been reached. Both sides signed a peace treaty that included neither independence for Cuba nor abolition for the enslaved. Even after the efforts of former slaves forced the Spanish government to put a definitive end to slavery in 1886, planters' continuing control of the sugar economy and Spain's continuing control of Cuba limited the horizons of newly free people.

While most plantations were still owned by Spanish and Cuban planters at this time, nearly nine-tenths of the island's sugar exports went to refineries in the United States. So, U.S. consumers, demanding cheap and sweet foods and beverages at an ever-increasing rate, ultimately held the sword over the plantation system of Cuba and its labor arrangements. The U.S. Congress, along with its major newspapers and powerful interests like the Sugar Trust, were keenly aware of this interdependence. Having long thought of Cuba as naturally belonging to the United States, they kept a close eye on how the proceedings of war and emancipation affected the island's export economy.[3]

After Britain abolished its transatlantic slave trade in 1807, it convinced Spain to sign on to an agreement, in 1817, ending its own traffic in captives from Africa. But enforcement was lax. Between 1821 and 1866, a secretive but powerful network of Cuban, Spanish, and Portuguese traders smuggled over half a million enslaved Africans to the island. The illegal slave trade abetted Cuba's domination of a skyrocketing international market in sugar. By the time of the Ten Years' War, world production of sugar had soared to 2,360,000 metric tons, a threefold increase over the 1830 total. Cuba alone supplied nearly 30 percent of the whole. During the inglorious dusk of chattel slavery, planters in Cuba catapulted beyond the dubious high-water mark of Barbados two centuries earlier: Total exports from all the British West Indian islands equaled 27,000 tons in the late seventeenth century; in 1868, Cuba alone exported 720,000 metric tons.[4]

Planting a thousand acres in sugar at any one time, the sugar plantation in mid-nineteenth-century Cuba was an ecological monster. Three to four hundred slaves worked in the fields, while hundreds of oxen hauled overloaded carts of cane to the threshold of the boiling house. The canes were loaded onto conveyor belts as long as eighty feet and fed into a steam-powered grinding mill. The largest boiling houses had twelve rows of pans to process 4,800 gallons of juice simultaneously. The fire that created the steam for the engines ran continuously through the grinding season, consuming as much as 200,000 gallons of water per day, as well as cord after cord of Cuban lumber, dried-out cane, and finally, imported British and American coal. Steam-powered centrifuges introduced in the 1840s shortened the drainage and claying time from one month to a matter of hours. Between 1792 and 1860, the average production per plantation went from 27 tons to 406 tons per year.[5]

This acceleration took place across the Cuban economy. Cuba's transportation network was unrivaled in Latin America and much of the United States. By 1860, 1,281 kilometers of railway were in operation. No spot in western Cuba was more than twelve miles from a railroad. Boxes of sugar traveled by rail to the port of Havana, where slaves loaded them into the city's new sugar warehouses, which ranked as the largest cast-iron structures in the world at the time. The components of the buildings were prefabricated in New York and assembled on-site in Cuba. Planters had pulled all the accoutrements of industrial modernity to the island and hitched them to the slave plantation. Cuban sugar production increased 1,450 percent between 1819 and 1868.[6]

Beginning in the late 1860s, the system came under immense new strain. Amid war and emancipation, the large planters of western Cuba tried desperately to hold on to their slaves. Yet their production numbers held steady in spite of shedding their enslaved workforces. They were coming to realize the plantation might have a future beyond slavery. This was a fateful realization for the rural workers of the world, and an epochal transformation in the history of capitalism. The idea that large-scale, centralized, labor-intensive yet mechanized agrarian enterprises could function without the prop of chattel slavery was no certainty at the time. It was in Cuba that the first attempt was made.[7]

At the high point of what has been called "slavery's capitalism," Cuban planters were already building a plantation system in which outright enslavement was only one of a number of forms of labor control. Cuban and Spanish merchants with experience in the illegal African

Interior of a Cuban sugar mill, 1850s. Right to left: steam-powered grinding mill and conveyor belt; enslaved people using oxen to deliver tons of cane to the mill; clarifying pans; about twenty Dumont filters; three domed vacuum pans; a row of Derosne condensers; and on the left, steam-powered centrifuges. In the center background, a row of eight boilers produces steam that drives the rest of the system.

slave trade also reached across the globe to secure a complementary source of cheap labor, pioneering a traffic in indentured servants from China. They brought tens of thousands of men from China to the sugar districts of Cuba between 1834 and the 1870s. While "coolie" laborers never constituted a majority of plantation workers, they helped influential colonial advisers like Ramón de la Sagra imagine a postabolition world that did not repeat the sorry fate of Haiti, with its decayed plantation system.[8]

Sagra loathed slavery, but he was not an emancipationist. He did not seek primarily to liberate Black people from the plantation, but to liberate the plantation from Black people. The mass importation of indentured workers from China was central to his vision of a modernizing plantation. Sagra paid homage to the "free Asiatic laborer, intelligent, dexterous, active, and above all not prone to routinism, but on the contrary, to innovation." Peering into one of Cuba's large boiling houses, Sagra watched "a double file of Chinese, rapid in their movements like a driving belt, carrying out the filling of the molds, with the mathematical regularity of the pendulum." Being machinelike themselves, he opined, Chinese workers would do well as servants of the plantation's machinery. Once again, the plantation was making race.[9]

Yet Chinese workers in Cuba challenged Sagra's fantasy of obedient "Orientals" brought in to avoid the hazards of savage and frequently rebellious Black slaves. Also subject to physical punishment and material deprivation, indentured sugar workers lodged hundreds of formal complaints against planters, mobilizing the support of a proactive Chinese embassy in Havana; after 1868, Chinese Cubans would also join the Cuban Army of Liberation in the wars against Spain.[10]

Nevertheless, for a sugar mill improver like Sagra, the supposedly machinelike Asiatic laborer allowed him to put "*los negros*" where they belonged: in the fields. As he put it, although planters had already initiated "reforms that require perfected instruments, machines, and above all care and reasoning on the part of workers, it was not possible to hope for these qualities from workers brutalized by a system that completely eliminated the intelligence of the operative, so that muscular power predominated exclusively in them." In other words, mechanization demanded precisely the skills that had been allegedly, and purposely, erased by slaveholders: care and reasoning.[11]

This was patently untrue—skilled Black workers had been central to the operations of Cuba's sugar industry from the beginning. Slaves with artisan skills and apprenticeships under their belt, known as *negros oficiales*, also dominated the urban crafts in the eighteenth and early nineteenth centuries, as well as the "fine" arts of music, sculpture, and painting. But the truth did not matter. Spurious notions of racial characteristics facilitated a clearer division between agricultural and industrial phases of sugar production than had been seen since the joining of those spheres in São Tomé three hundred years before.[12]

When war and emancipation destroyed the labor system of Cuban planters, they were ready to make a more radical change. Reacting to emancipation as well as ever more serious globalized competition, and propelled by the late nineteenth-century "Second Industrial Revolution" in materials and chemicals, planters turned away from old practices. When the sugar plantation emancipated itself from chattel slavery—while still deeply dependent on various forms of racialized coercion and unfreedom—it also morphed into something entirely new.

Deprived of their accustomed control over agricultural workers in the 1880s, planters in Cuba began selling off or renting their cane fields and building rural factories, known as sugar *centrales*. Focusing their resources and expertise on the mass production of raw sugar, *central* builders took up and improved upon the state-of-the-art technologies installed by elite Spanish and Cuban planters in the slave plantations of the 1850s. They added other technologies that had not existed during slavery, like steam-powered cranes to dump canes by the truckload into the grinding mill. Cheap, high-quality steel from America and Britain replaced the iron parts of the cane-grinding mills. Mills with as many as twelve steel rollers subjected each batch of cane to multiple juicings. Hydraulic pressure regulators ensured that the right amount of pressure was applied to the sugarcane; they also ensured the right strength of vacuum in the sealed boiling pans, which cooked off the water content of the juice by the thousands of gallons and brought the batch to grain. The factories shipped out bags of centrifuged raw sugar by the trainload, pushing smaller mills out of business. In 1860, 1,365 integrated sugar plantations had produced a total of 2,968,000 bags of sugar (2,200 per mill). In 1904, 174 *centrales* produced 7,253,000 (41,700 per mill).[13]

Once the expensive equipment of the factory was in place, the risks undertaken, and the daily costs assumed, a reliable flow of cane to the mill became indispensable. The sugar mill owners retired as "crop masters." Guided by the modern principle of specialization, *central* builders like Atkins rented out their cane fields to a new class of tenant farmers called *colonos*, who took charge of farming and harvesting on the *central*'s land. Beginning in the 1880s, plantation railroads, which carried carloads of freshly cut cane from the fields to the mill far more efficiently than the old teams of oxen, broke the old spatial limit on the size of cane plantings. While the biggest plantations in 1860 grew between 900 and 1,400 acres of cane—already the largest in the history of Caribbean plantations—by the 1890s, new companies like United Fruit controlled more than 150,000 acres, an increase of nearly 1,000 percent.[14]

The disaggregation of the integrated plantation happened just as Cuba was falling under the shadow of U.S. imperial power, a development the island's planters had alternately embraced and resisted for nearly a century. The more Cuba geared its economy to the production of sugar in the early 1800s, the more it depended on North American supplies. Parts for sugar boxes, barrels, and hogsheads came from the lumber mills of the mid-Atlantic states. Barrel hoops, nails, and other iron goods left eastern ports for the island. As the formerly diverse subtropical economy of Cuba plowed more resources into the export of sugar, it also became a net importer of daily staples like textiles, salt, corn, lard, flour, and rice. New England merchants established houses in the port cities of

Havana, Matanzas, Cienfuegos, Cárdenas, Sagua la Grande, Trinidad, and Santiago de Cuba. Increasingly, they "provided credit, purchased the sugar crops, and . . . expanded their control over the carrying trade [to] . . . New Orleans, Savannah, Charleston, Baltimore, Philadelphia, New York, and Boston," as historian Louis Pérez has written. American women opened inns, bars, brothels, restaurants, and billiard rooms in Cuban port towns, which provided spaces for Cuban–North American interaction. Although the island was legally an extension of Spanish power, it had far more important trade relationships with "El Norte" by the time of the American Civil War.[15]

This was mostly raw sugar and molasses. Up until the war of 1868, English consumers across the Atlantic still digested most of Cuba's white sugar. Britain's "empire of free trade," centered on the financial colossus in London, largely conducted the movements of world trade, shaping the value of rival currencies. "The City" was the clearinghouse for bills of exchange used to lubricate transactions all over the world. After Parliament reopened England's market to slave-grown sugar in 1846, much of the expansion in Cuba's white sugar exports went to the British Isles. Even in Cuban ports where New York merchants already dominated, white sugar products were bound for Britain.[16]

Cuban planters were living through the last gasp of the multipolar world initiated long before by Barbadian enslavers, who violently built a world in which Spanish, American, British, and French merchants competed over finite supplies of sugar. Colonial-era West Indian planters were the most ostentatiously wealthy businessmen in their respective empires. By the 1860s, big planters' ability to make white sugar for European markets enabled them to evade a U.S.-dominated trade dynamic governed by New York bankers and industrialists.

Together with emancipation, new policies in Europe designed to protect its beet sugar industry finished breaking down the European–Caribbean nexus that had helped define plantation America for over two centuries. As late as 1864, 22 percent of Cuban sugar still went to Britain. By 1877, this number had fallen to 4.4 percent. By 1890, when the abolition of slavery was complete, and the *central* highly developed, Cuba's sugar industry had become entrapped. While Cubans and Spaniards still owned most of the *centrales* and cane farms, the American Sugar Trust absorbed 90 percent of their sugar exports. Because of the United States' own tariffs on refined sugar products, future growth in the Cuban sugar industry would be in raw sugar, with the profits from value-added phases of refining accruing to refiners in the United States. As Cuba was on the precipice of gaining political independence from Spain, its economy began to look downright colonial.[17]

Although the technology used in the refineries of Boston, New York, and Baltimore was largely the same as that in Cuban *centrales*, the dynamic in which a Caribbean nation exported "raw material" to be refined and made table-ready by U.S. industrial technology reinforced the notion that Cuba was backward. In fact, tariffs actually *pushed* Cuban technology backward. Now merchants and bankers in New York, with the help of a neomercantilist American state, could steer a global system of raw sugar–producing peripheries, preserving the more profitable end of the business—the making and selling of white sugar—to refiners based in the United States. As the comprehensive jaws of America opened wider, there was little Cuban planters could do to escape the grip of the new empire.

The U.S. population consumed 426,000 tons of sugar in 1860, and 2.5 million tons in 1900. Because sugar consumption among Americans was growing so fast, a single market could at least accommodate massive amounts of Cuba's raw production. Refined sugar had become widespread in a rapidly urbanizing nation with plenty of cheap, factory-made commodities. Formerly a preserve of the very rich, mass-produced "family silver" like sugar tongs, and "wedding china" like sugar bowls, became obligatory accoutrements of a middle-class home. The mass migration of Southerners to the urban North, and of European immigrants to towns and cities, increased families' dependence on store-bought foods. While consumption of table sugar grew, shoppers also purchased Cuban sugar indirectly in new processed foods like condensed milk and prepackaged baked goods. New factories preserved Hawaiian pineapples in cane syrup, packed them in tin cans, and shipped them across the nation by rail.[18]

No icon of American consumer culture was more important to the rebirth of plantations in Cuba than Coca-Cola, which was founded in 1886 and consumed more sugar than any company in the world by 1910. Eager to maximize the consumer's dependence on the dopamine rush of sucrose consumption, bottlers packed as much sugar into each bottle as they could. The resulting beverage was so hypersweet they had to add a heavy dose of low-pH phosphoric acid to make it drinkable. Although most Americans did not know it, as they sipped the official soft drink of industrial modernity, they were ingesting concentrated Cuban plantation sweetness.[19]

The new plantation economy of Cuba—the *central-colono* system under the aegis of U.S.-based multinational trusts with refineries and distribution networks in the United States—brought considerable profits. Owners of the new *centrales*—some of them Americans, but still mostly Cuban and Spanish—had no intentions of letting go. After abolition in 1886, they still monopolized the arable land as well as the capital, but they needed thousands of cane cutters and scores of factory workers. They struggled mightily to prevent ex-slaves (known as *libertos*) from obtaining farmland.

In Cienfuegos, J. S. Murray, who managed Edwin Atkins's Soledad *central*, complained that the *libertos* had only been working "when they feel like it and keeping up a constant loafing during the day." Murray suspected the economic autonomy they had built for themselves explained such behavior. Recognizing that mules, horses, and pigs were crucial to former slaves trying to become independent farmers, Murray first gave "orders to Negroes to sell all their hogs, prohibiting in the future the raising of hogs." Clearly the free people at work on the plantation paid the manager no mind, for three months later, he had some workers tear down the stone wall that enclosed the animals. He noted with satisfaction that he had left the "negros pig styes without protection so they will have to sell or have them stolen it is imeterial to us which."[20]

Of more concern were horses. Murray complained that "almost every Negro on the estate owns a horse, and they are a source of constant trouble in some way." When he ordered the *libertos* to sell their mounts, they ceased working. Not only was the horse a marker of dignity and masculinity in the aftermath of slavery, but the mobility they provided helped cement social connections in the foothills of the region. They were also a crucial aid in establishing new farms: they pulled plowshares through deep soils and dragged large trees to nearby rivers. By expropriating their animals, the manager was defining for the formerly enslaved what freedom meant: diligent, obedient drudgery in exchange for a measly account at Edwin Atkins's company store. The *libertos* clung to a different vision. One of the estate workers, Felipe Criollo, purchased a cape and a saddle in 1886. It seems he was joining the ranks of horse-owning men. Yet, the promise of a more expansive life was becoming more precarious: As the sugar economy recovered in the wake of the Ten Years' War, more and more of the arable acreage in the area around Soledad was planted in cane.[21]

Even though it was Spain that pronounced the end of slavery in 1886, workers like Felipe Criollo became aware that emancipation would never be fully realized without Cuba's liberation from the mother country. Since the disappointing end of the Ten Years' War, leaders of the independence struggle had come to a similar conclusion. In his poetry and essays, the independence hero José Martí advanced the notion that the national soil was suffering under the boot of foreign-owned sugar companies. As relics of Spanish colonialism, racism and plantation agriculture could only be undone with full decolonization. Racism, however, also struck deep roots within the patriots' movement. It would have to be confronted in order for the struggle against Spain and the planters to succeed.[22]

To their great credit, in the three decades between the start of the Ten Years' War (1868–1878) and the final War of Independence (1895–

1898), white revolutionary leaders like José Martí articulated a vision of race-transcending Cubanness that managed to counter Spanish propaganda and numbed, at least for a time, conservatives' fears of a race war. This hard-won vision of racelessness made the mobilization for the final war possible. At last having the manpower for an invasion of the western half of the island, white generals were in overall command, but men of African descent had key leadership roles. Most notably, the African-descended general Antonio Maceo, known admiringly as "the Bronze Titan," was second-in-command of all independence forces. Separatists and Loyalists alike considered him the most fearsome leader, strategist, and soldier in the war.

When the new insurgency began in 1895, Supreme General Máximo Gómez vowed to "plant the triumphant flag of the Cuban republic on top of the ruins" of the plantation. This required an unprecedented invasion of the much more profitable (and heavily fortified) western half of the island. The fact that the Cuban Liberation Army was a predominantly Black institution with an officer corps that was 40 percent nonwhite added to the dismay of western sugar planters, who had never seen an independence fighter in person. It was not long after Gómez's declaration of war on the sugar plantation that Atkins received word his *central* had been shut down by an army headed by the Black General Quintín Bandera.[23]

Determined to usher in the end of "King Sugar," the Army of Liberation announced a land reform policy in 1896. As in the American Civil War, the independent Cuban government would confiscate all properties being used for the maintenance of colonial power and distribute them to veterans. First, however, victory had to be secured. To speed along the dissolution of Spanish rule, Gómez ordered all activities related to the production of sugar ceased. Any plantation found growing or processing cane "will be destroyed, the standing cane set fire and the factory buildings and railroads destroyed." Any worker caught violating the moratorium would be executed. By enforcing the ban on sugar production, the independence army could burn the roots of colonial capitalism. To a far greater extent than in the Ten Years' War, former slaves recognized the separatist cause as their own. Thus did Spanish counterinsurgency chief Valeriano Weyler correctly grasp that he was now fighting against a multiracial Cuban people.[24]

At a historical moment when even second-rate powers like Belgium ruled massive colonial empires, Spain, the empire that had set the pattern and standard for all others with its conquests in the Americas, was now held up for ridicule as "the sick man of Europe." The butt of the racist taunt that "Africa ends at the Pyrenees," Spain was ready to defend its most remunerative colonial possession to the last, shipping 190,000 military personnel to Cuba—the largest military force ever mustered to defend European rule in the Americas. Spanish authorities did not just want to protect their tax base; they were determined to devastate the insurgency, which they viewed as a Haiti-like race war against civilization.

They gave command of Spanish forces to General Weyler, who was known as "the Butcher" for his brutality and efficiency. Just as the plantation was recognized by the insurgents as the beating heart of colonial rule, Weyler recognized peasant farms as the core of the insurgency. Under Weyler's orders, Spanish soldiers roamed the rural precincts, setting fields of corn, wheat, and plantains ablaze. They dug up garden crops. They arrested small farmers and commandeered their livestock. Between the depredations of the insurgents and the police actions of the Spanish, the entire countryside was laid waste. One observer who traveled by rail from Havana to Matanzas reported that "I did not see a house, man, woman, or child, a horse, mule or cow, nor even a dog. I did not see a sign of life, except an occasional vulture or buzzard sailing through the air. The country was wrapped in the stillness of death and the silence of desolation."[25]

The wartime traveler did not exaggerate. Weyler's forces carried out a brutal policy that forcibly transferred rural families to the twentieth-century's first concentration camps. As many as two hundred thousand people, many of them women, children, and the elderly, died in Spanish custody. While "reconcentration," as the policy was called, created an immense amount of suffering, as a counterinsurgent strategy it backfired. The Black General Antonio Maceo boasted that "the Revolution does not have a better ally than Weyler himself." The Butcher's violence made any return to colonial rule out of the question.[26]

Across nearly four centuries, Cuba's white elite had clung to the mother country, cementing the legend of the "ever faithful isle." White property owners' fear of the race war that might accompany any change in the status quo kept most of them on the Loyalist side until the final months of the war. Now their confidence in Spain's mastery of the situation wavered. As they had done in the 1850s, when many planters supported having the island annexed by the United States, they let themselves imagine a better-equipped savior sweeping in. One group of conservative planters confessed, "The mother country cannot protect us. . . . Therefore, we want the United States to save us." Some leaders in the United States were contemplating exactly that.[27]

American consuls in Cuba were sending word home that Spanish control of the island was nearing its end. While the American Civil War had quashed proslavery U.S. desires to acquire Cuba as a slave state, now, without slavery, Cuba looked attractive again—especially since its planters had sorted out how to expand and improve the sugar plantation after slavery was abolished. The violence of the independence war in Cuba was used by expansionist U.S. politicians as evidence that islanders lacked the "capacity" to establish a modern nation on their own. Bit by bit, the logic of American military intervention became unassailable. The military, technological, and naval power of the United States was many times greater than it had been before the Civil War. The threat of setting off an armed confrontation with Britain had faded. Besides, the old champions of abolition in London were now deep in their own global project of colonial conquest—how could they muster the military might or moral furor to stop the United States from doing the same?

The white conquest of less-white populations across the world, and especially across the central and western United States—the so-called

Indian Wars in the American West having been won—had become so common a pattern as to seem like common sense itself. The historical entanglements of Cuba with the United States had led many to believe, since the 1780s, that Cuba would at some point become part of the United States. The time seemed auspicious.

While Cuba, although certainly not free of anti-Black racism, was in the process of securing Black men's democratic rights in 1898, in the same year the last vestiges of interracial democracy in the U.S. South were stamped out with a violent election day coup d'etat in Wilmington, North Carolina. North Carolina had followed other Southern states in the disfranchisement of African Americans and the removal of Black officeholders, but the Black-majority city of Wilmington had been a holdout.

A multiracial coalition that included white and Black Republicans as well as members of the profarmer Populist Party governed what was then the state's most populous urban center. Democratic leaders like the newspaperman and racist demagogue Josephus Daniels openly called for a "white supremacy campaign" and the lynching of Black men. On election day, Black officeholders were threatened with death if they did not leave the state. A fascist, white supremacist group called the South Carolina Red Shirts (which had been started by Wade Hampton) led a white mob that killed as many as sixty Black Wilmingtonians. Company K of the all-white Wilmington Light Infantry had just returned from service in Cuba, and they brought two cannons along with military discipline to support the actions of the mob and the Red Shirts. Focusing their wrath on community leaders and property owners, the killers enabled white Democrats to secure one-party white rule in North Carolina. President William McKinley, who was at the time already managing the United States takeover of Cuba, slow-walked an investigation into the massacre, and it never went anywhere.[28]

The Lost Cause—the myth that Southern white men had bravely fought for honor, liberty, and states' rights against the abominable forces of industrial modernity—had by 1898 become the dominant historical interpretation of the Civil War in the United States. Empowering African American men with the vote and with political office during Reconstruction was viewed by most white historians, Northern and Southern, as a colossal mistake. White supremacists had successfully made the pro-slavery fiction of "the utter incapacity of the negro for self-government" gospel truth in the American republic. Because the social Darwinist ideologues of "fitness" believed that white people were destined to win the "race of life" in a modern, capitalist democracy, anything that challenged the American version of racial hierarchy also threatened disorder, inefficiency, and failure.[29]

Thus it is appropriate that a man by the name of Fitzhugh Lee looms so large in the American invasion of Cuba. He was the nephew of Robert E. Lee, the great-great-grandson of George Mason, and a descendant of the Virginia tobacco planter and land magnate William Fitzhugh. His world was turned upside down by the South's defeat in the Civil War (Lee had been a Confederate cavalry officer of little note), but he landed on his feet, receiving a patrimony from enslaver ancestors: an inherited fortune that freed him from the necessity of making his own. His annual income assured, he turned to burnishing the memory of the Confederacy through his role in the newly founded Southern Historical Society. He penned numerous articles promoting the Lost Cause, but he made his public reputation as an orator. Before rapt audiences across the South, Lee told of a noble, brave, and outnumbered army of unified white men fighting for its constitutional rights. He wrote a fawning biography of his uncle. As president of the Lee Monument Association in the 1870s, he was largely responsible for the gargantuan statue of Robert E. on a horse, which towered over a major thoroughfare in the state capital of Richmond until it was finally removed in 2020.[30]

Fitzhugh Lee served as consul-general to Cuba from 1896 until the United States declared war in 1898. He took charge of the military departments of Havana and Pinar del Rio after enthusiastically championing the U.S. occupation of Cuba, which lasted from 1898 to 1902.

In the intervention, which was one part of a world-spanning Spanish-American War, U.S. forces supposedly sided with the Cuban Army of Liberation against Spanish rule, although once they had defeated the Spanish in a few brief months, they quickly tried to pull back on or reverse many of the antiracist measures put in place by the rebels.

After his brief tenure in Havana, Lee published a book offering his views on the history of Cuba and its present status (with former Confederate General Joseph Wheeler as his coauthor). His days as a booster of Confederate heroes had made Lee an expert at ignoring inconvenient facts. He would need every ounce of self-delusion he had mustered in defense of the Lost Cause to support his interpretation of the war in the Caribbean. For him, the struggle of Cubans ran parallel to the galloping adventures of the Confederates: dashing, passionate, white men astride steeds, hollering about their constitutional rights through dangling moustaches. Spanish tyranny and Spanish tariffs were the great villains of his Cuban story. Worst of all, the Spanish had maintained their rule by inverting the natural racial order. Lee approvingly quoted a work from the 1850s that fumed, "the whites have been disarmed," while "colored men" had been mustered into colonial regiments, "thus holding before the unfortunate inhabitants the constant threat of a war of races, a renewal of the horrors of San Domingo."[31]

To reassure his North American readership (and comfort the investors soon to be plundering the island), he explained that the natural order would reassert itself when the island was freed of the Spanish yoke: "As there are no more than half as many Negroes as whites in Cuba, and the proportion of Negroes steadily growing smaller and will continue to do so at an increasingly rapid rate, all fear of 'Negro domination' in the island may be dismissed as idle." Wheeler echoed the idea later in the book: "There is no danger that Cuba will ever pass from the control of the white race." While these leaders of the intervention harbored reservations about particular aspects of the U.S. administration in Cuba, they were sparklingly clear on one thing: Rumors of a Black revolution were unfounded. Lee and Wheeler repeatedly reassured their

American readers that white people were, and would remain, on top. U.S. intervention would ensure it.[32]

The intervention was not launched initially to shore up white rule, whether of the Spanish or of the Cuban planter class. In 1898, President McKinley told Congress that the blowing up of the USS *Maine*, which had killed 236 seamen, had made a military intervention unavoidable. Whether or not the vessel had actually been attacked by the Spanish navy in Havana—it had not—an armed peacekeeping mission would "secure in the island the establishment of a stable government, capable of maintaining order and observing its international obligations." Although the very real horrors of reconcentration were used to justify the intervention as a humanitarian act, McKinley's address expressed not a whiff of support for the self-determination of the Cuban people. Nor did he acknowledge the military situation that preceded the intervention: the soldiers, officers, peasants, nurses, and other supporters of the Army of Liberation who had been in the field for three years, and who had fought the Spanish to a stalemate at the cost of hundreds of thousands of lives.[33]

The United States toppled the old Spanish Empire in a four-month war that stretched from the Philippines to Puerto Rico. They arrived in Cuba supposedly as allies of the Army of Liberation. When the occupying forces saw that the revolutionary ranks were racially integrated and often led by Black officers, however, they quickly recast the freedom fighters as "a lot of degenerates . . . no more capable of self-rule than the savages of Africa." The highest-ranking officer of the occupation, Leonard Wood, summarily disbanded and disarmed Liberation forces, creating a new national army with an all-white officer corps. Applicants of color to the rural and urban police forces were refused without explanation, while white Cubans from the middle and upper classes, many of whom had rushed to enlist in the separatist army after the explosion of the *Maine*, were elevated to positions of power. Many Spanish officials, with whom U.S. officials were more comfortable, were retained in their posts.[34]

Cubans' right to self-determination was left profoundly ambiguous when the military occupation ended in 1902. The popular press in the United States made clear why this had to be the case. In 1899, *The New York Herald* stated, "Cuba Libre signifies another Black Republic. We do not want something of that disposition so close. Haiti is already enough." Reaching back to white fears of "the horrors of Santo Domingo," and further back to the fear among Cuban elites that tinkering with the colonial status quo would expose them to race war, U.S. occupiers made sure property rights were firmly in the hands of elites, and that the rule of white law had been reasserted before they left the island.[35]

Leaders of the occupation like Secretary of War Elihu Root successfully imposed themselves on Cuba's first constitutional convention, ensuring that what would later be known as the Platt Amendment became Cuban law. The measure reserved to the United States the right to intervene militarily whenever necessary to preserve "a government adequate for the protection of life, property, and individual liberty"—in other words, no uprisings, no land reform, no debtor relief, and no socialism.[36]

The occupation's "securing" of private property, its decision to place white conservatives in power, and its scuttling of the 1896 land reform plan primed the island for what came next. The Platt Amendment gave a new breed of corporate plantation builders carte blanche to build and destroy anew, in ways not possible within the boundaries of the United States, nor in a fully independent nation. Republican Cuba was held in a shadow zone of empire, both a foreign territory and a domestic domain, a hybrid status tailor-made for rapacious planters.

CHAPTER 16

The White Whale

It was no small feat to repair Cuba's sugar industry after U.S. occupation officially ended in 1902. In the new global empire of sugar, mere proximity to the North American mainland was no guarantee of market share. Technical advances in oceangoing steamships had pushed global freight rates down by as much as 63 percent, bringing distant producers into direct competition with Caribbean planters. While the Reciprocity Act passed by the U.S. Congress in 1903 gave partial duty relief to Cuban sugar, the new American empire exerted direct control over Hawaii, Puerto Rico, and the Philippines. As legal appurtenances of the United States, they could sell their raw sugar to U.S. refiners without a tariff levy, while growers in Cuba still paid 80 percent of the full duty.[1]

Despite its disadvantages, Cuba supplied as much or more raw sugar to U.S. refiners than all "domestic" cane and beet producers combined between 1902 and 1926. By the eve of World War I, Cuban sugar had regained its global place of prominence, with about 20 percent of the world's total sugar and 30 percent of the world's cane sugar being made on the island.²

Such an achievement resulted from a new kind of plantation and a new breed of planter—not an individual, but a corporate board. American "trusts" with oligopoly power and a direct line of credit from National City Bank would control the postslavery Caribbean plantation. In 1888, the American refiner Theodore Havemeyer convinced his competitors on the East Coast to sacrifice their independent status in exchange for stock certificates in a new firm called the American Sugar Refining Company. As a group, they could exclude new entrants, limit production, and collude on prices. The organization pioneered new techniques of market manipulation like short selling, market cornering, and price slashing. Too well positioned to have to bother with committing outright crimes, Havemeyer boasted that he "used the stock exchange to bribe government officials and the commodities exchange to impose the prices that he wanted on the raw sugars of Cuba, Santo Domingo, and Puerto Rico."³

Between the 1870s and 1910, hundreds of small U.S. refiners were absorbed into the trust or bought out by bigger companies. In what is known as the "great merger movement" of late nineteenth-century American capitalism, the sugar industry was a leader. The ASRC—also known as the Sugar Trust—was the sixth-largest industrial firm in the country. Due to antitrust enforcement in the Progressive Era, the trust stopped short of establishing a monopoly, although they came close. The entire industry shrank to six firms by 1910, and the competition between them was often mitigated by a quasi-legal system of "interlocking directorates," in which the same individuals sat on the boards of directors of major banks and industrial firms. Two men, James Howell Post and Thomas Howell, sat on the boards of five of the six "independent" sugar companies organized under the trust. At the same time, they were board members of City Bank and First National Bank in New York. Post also served as chairman of the board of the Cuban American Sugar Company as well as the Guantánamo Sugar Company.⁴

In their structure and their strategy, the East Coast sugar companies represented the cutting edge of American capitalism: Neither commodity trader nor wholesaler nor manufacturer nor farmer, they took charge of every aspect of production from beginning to end, including distribution networks, sales, and advertising. Owing to the scale of investments they made in the long-distance, high-tech system of sugar making, the integrated firms sought absolute security for their supply of raw materials. While the Platt Amendment had put many of their concerns to rest, they nevertheless aggressively moved into eastern Cuba after the occupation because they thought it necessary to exercise direct control over their own sources of raw sugar. In other words, the U.S.-based, corporate-managed refining conglomerates became Cuba's dominant sugar planters in the early twentieth century.[5]

Just as steel trusts bought up iron, manganese, and nickel mines in Cuba, and the Tobacco Trust acquired cigar factories in Havana, the Cuba Cane Sugar Corporation bought up seventeen sugar mills in 1916, "making it the largest sugar company in Cuba and the largest permanent investment of North American capital in Cuba." J. P. Morgan partnered with other New York investors to form "Cuba Cane," and Hershey Chocolate and Hires Root Beer bought sugar plantations, mills, and railroads on the island.[6]

While Havemeyer had used the trust's market dominance to purchase cheap raw sugar from sellers in the Caribbean, firms like the Cuban American Sugar Cane Corporation, which controlled hundreds of thousands of acres in eastern Cuba, along with over half a dozen *centrales*, essentially purchased raw sugar from themselves. The legal fiction of the "administered price"—used when a vertically integrated firm purchases supplies from itself across national borders—put an end to the competitive dynamic between planter and merchant that had defined the history of the plantation up until the end of the nineteenth century. Sugar companies like United Fruit, with the help of New York banks like City, simply absorbed both roles.

When they adopted the Cuban model of the *central*, the new sugar companies distributed the risks of cane farming while reassuming control of the fields. They turned the *colono* of eastern Cuba—formerly a quasi-independent cane farmer who owned his own land and sold cane to area mills—into a glorified sharecropper. The *colono* contract reserved to the *central* the right to decision-making power over the details of cane planting, and obliged the *colono* to use expensive machines like cane loaders for field operation and to provide housing for the cane cutters and other laborers required for the harvest. The *central* manager could also make the *colono* pay in the event of a harvest failure or other problem in the fields. Many contracts imposed on the cane farmer a noncompete clause for the ensuing years, meaning they were contractually forbidden from selling any cane to competing *centrales*. Finally, any improvements made to the farm during the *colono*'s tenure reverted to the *central* upon his departure. Through the mechanism of the cane-supplying contract, then, sugar companies off-loaded the managerial costs and business risks of cane planting while applying pressure on tenant farmers to serve up endless quantities of low-cost, disease-free cane at the tempo the sugar mill demanded.[7]

The recovery of the plantation economy would ultimately depend upon a new mode of acquiring and controlling cheap labor, which was of particular importance amid the frontier conditions of eastern Cuba. While tractors and machine harvesters had reduced the manpower needs of other industrial crops like corn and wheat by 1920, the cane fields of Cuba were still harvested by people swinging machetes. Therefore, the larger, more intensively planted cane fields required workforces that were orders of magnitude larger than their pre-1900 predecessors. In the wake of a war that had severely depleted the rural population of the country, the planter's old fantasy of slave ships serving an unending supply of cheap labor beckoned. In the twentieth century, however, new levers would have to be pulled.

Because U.S. occupiers had forced Cuba to include Chinese exclusion in its laws, Chinese contract workers who had arrived under indenture contracts since the 1830s were soon replaced by the new streams of labor migrants. Poverty and political instability in Spain spurred a large wave of migration from the Iberian Peninsula, which helped stabilize cane farming after 1900. In the long run, however, sugar companies in eastern Cuba, with support from the Cuban state, brought in from other Caribbean islands what historian Matthew Casey has called "the first global generation of guestworkers." Between 1898 and 1948, 200,000 plantation workers arrived from Haiti, and another 140,000 from the British Caribbean islands, in hopes of a better wage than they could earn at home. They labored primarily as cane cutters and cart loaders. While the intense exploitation of these workers kept labor costs down, enabling more investment in *central* technology, they received a decidedly ambivalent welcome. On arrival, they were quarantined and examined for the diseases they were rumored to carry. Once on the island, they were subject to intense racist discrimination, accused of fomenting Black rebellion, and forced to return home until the next harvest season, when many would travel to Cuba once again.[8]

Like other members of the trust, the Cuban American Sugar Cane Corporation had a private port where it imported "thousands of migrant laborers beyond the purview of state officials." This mass of migrant labor, also now moving around the British Empire and beyond, was the workforce of the global postslavery plantation system. Presaged by the Middle Passage, their sojourns and their toil nevertheless represented a tectonic shift in the history of capitalism, as they affirmed and exceeded Ramón de la Sagra's hope that colonial power could rationalize the global distribution of nominally "free" labor without interrupting the growth pattern of the plantation.

The U.S.-owned *centrales* that had paid their passage were in some ways a world apart from Cuban society. By the 1890s, the typical eastern *central* was a company town. Churches, schools, and houses were all built and maintained by the *central*. The firms controlled the railroads, telegraph lines, and electrical grid in their sprawling remit. Although company scrip was outlawed by the Cuban state in 1909, the *centrales* made sure the wage they paid out found its way back to the firm's coffers.

Their private guards harassed itinerant merchants who might undersell the landowner. Security officers also patrolled the boundaries of the property, preventing cane workers from leaving in search of higher wages on a neighboring estate.[9]

The sugar refiners who took over eastern Cuba between 1900 and 1930 represented only one of the mammoth oligopolies in the new era of corporate capitalism in the United States. Oil, electricity, refrigeration, meatpacking, steel, and railroads had all undergone rapid processes of consolidation between 1890 and 1910. Putting to an end nearly three centuries of European control over Central America and the Caribbean, U.S. trusts forged a new postslavery plantation empire to supply everyday table items for the middle and working classes of the United States. Making available an unprecedented cornucopia of affordable coffee, grapes, and bananas, they created a new kind of informal corporate empire using massive amounts of chemical sprays, hybrid crops, systems of migrant labor, and political subjugation. They also felled forests with unprecedented rapacity.

Some in this new cohort of modern planter-corporations used practices reminiscent of antebellum cotton planters. Since bananas were so

A central surrounded by cane fields in Santa Clara province, Cuba, 1899.

genetically uniform, and importers considered just one or two varieties as salable to shoppers in the United States, United Fruit's Honduran plantations were vulnerable to crop diseases. After a few years of a single field being cultivated, diseases like sigatoka and Panama ran rampant. Every morning workers would soak banana leaves—and unknowingly coat their skin and lungs—with a variety of poison sprays to stay one step ahead of the crop-killing fungi. To no avail. Banana trees could only flourish on freshly cleared jungle lands.

In the never-ending search for lands that had not already been colonized by fungi and microbes, workers built massive dikes and levees to drain swampland for new plantations. United Fruit, along with a small number of other fruit companies, left behind faltering banana fields and took over new ones, by the tens of thousands of hectares. They let the railroads they had fought to build ten years earlier fall into disrepair. Such land-consuming practices are reminiscent of the "skimming husbandry" of antebellum cotton, but the ruins left behind by the new imperial plantations were worse—a toxic soup that made it difficult to use the land for other purposes. For banana and coffee companies in Central America, as well as for sugar firms in Cuba, the ability to monopolize land and labor in the hinterlands of American empire derived from the previous conquest of mass consumer markets at home. Their power was also premised on a new hierarchy of expertise, with their own agronomists, economists, engineers, and public health experts seated at the top.[10]

The 1898 U.S. intervention in Cuba centered around the claim that the "natives," incapable of self-government, were also doomed to mismanage their fertile island paradise. Private U.S. influence would remain after the military had departed from the island. While Caribbean plantations had long been the authoritative, "authentic" site of knowledge production on how to make sugar from cane, as the Cuban planter class declined, so too did their authority as "crop masters." By 1900, many were traveling to the United States to train at a new engineering college with a sugar program and a small-scale model set of machinery. This was the Audubon Sugar School, founded in 1897 at Louisiana State University in Baton Rouge. U.S. officials also set up provincial boards of agriculture, industry, and commerce in permanently occupied territories, which reflected the assumption about Caribbean farmers' ineptitude. Whereas most state governments in the United States oversaw their own agricultural extension agencies, for example, Puerto Rican officials had no such power. In Cuba, the country's many highly trained agronomists were treated like "junior partners" at the U.S.-run research stations.[11]

Agricultural experiment stations were a crucial tool for reshaping the global countryside. There were only 24 such institutions in the world in 1855. In 1900, there were 590. While the work of the experiment stations and the sugar companies' private labs solved certain problems in the fields, it also sped up what agronomists have called a "treadmill" of crop hybridization: When new hybrids were developed to resist a given fungus, mold, or insect, the old infestation would decline, leaving open an ecological niche for new pests to flourish. The new pest required a new hybrid variety, which opened the door to new infestations, and so on. The treadmill favored large-scale corporations, since only they had the capital, labor, and expertise to sustain the unending war of attrition against microorganisms. And even though it was often clean-field monoculture that allowed the diseases to take hold, once established they also spread to the fields of small farmers who had no resources to fight them.[12]

The gray zone of informal empire in which the United States held Cuba provided the new planter-conglomerates with unfettered access to land and labor while allowing the North American government to leave the onerous task of policing and regulating to the Cuban state. A key lever of informal power over Cuba was the differential tariff, which charged refined sugar a much higher rate than raw sugar. Scholars have often emphasized how the Cuban economy became focused ever more exclusively on raw sugar production, while the profits from making and selling a "finished" product accrued to North Americans. Yet things

The private railroad of the Central Victoria hauling cane from the fields to the mill, early twentieth century.

were not quite so simple. The differential incentivized importers to cheat the system.

The major refineries in New York and Boston were using similar vacuum pans, charcoal filtration, and centrifuges as the *centrales*. At the same time, members of the trust insisted, the *centrales* made "raw" sugar, and they, the trust, "refined" it. Just like Sagra's notion that brute Black laborers had no skills and no intelligence and belonged in the fields, the whole notion of Cuba being the site of brute raw materials production with little skill, and the United States being the rarefied site of high-tech industrial magic, was an illusion.

In theory, customs officials at U.S. ports were inspecting imported sugar with an optical instrument called a polarimeter, which measured what percentage of a given sample was sucrose—the chemical component of white sugar crystals. In practice, as they took over Cuban *centrales*, the U.S. conglomerates could avoid such inspections. As an industry journal wrote of the large refiners: "They have the immense advantage of receiving their cargoes at their own refineries [inside the United States], where, within 24 hours from the arrival of the vessel, the sugars [can] be dumped into the boiling vats, thus rendering all identification impossible."[13]

The big refineries do not seem to have been manufacturing sugar at all. They were laundering it, disguising the fraudulent importation of white sugar to dodge the tariff. This was cost effective because a major component of raw sugar is molasses, which is sucrose that has already been broken down and cannot be reconstituted. In other words, only a certain percentage of any shipment can be turned into higher-priced "white" sugar, while the rest of it has to be sold as cheap molasses. If a company imported refined sugar, it was able to sell all of it as white sugar.

Even though most of the sugar companies did not go this far, even in the twentieth century the refineries along the East Coast mostly just played with the Cuban product enough to justify not paying the import tariff. First, they took the "raw" material into the United States and melted it back down, reversing the careful evaporation process the *centrales* had accomplished. Then, with their filters, clarifiers, and centrifuges—all of which existed in the Cuban factories as well—they cleaned it up a bit more. Finally, they evaporated it again, to move the sugar from light brown crystals to white ones. With their private streams of unregulated migrant labor recruitment in Cuba and their private wharves in New York and Boston, these firms operated outside the purview of any state authority. The refineries were in essence dummy corporations. The whole hustle was made possible by the U.S. companies' adaptation of the preservative technologies of the older Cuban slave plantation that transformed a very perishable sweet juice into a sparkling repository of dry sweetness that would never decay.

If the North American refineries added any real value, it was not in sugar making, but in brand development: They had additional machinery that allowed them to bring the sugar to grains of different sizes, for confectioners' sugar, table sugar, sugar cubes, or different food additives. They also packed it into branded bags for retail sale. In other words, the

East Coast refiners were not so much manufacturers as they were innovators in packaging and branding. They used advancements in mechanized bagging and canning to operate at very low cost. And they sank a lot of their profits into advertising, especially with the Domino brand, established in 1906, which the members of the Sugar Trust shared.[14]

Their extra-refined product did make for an ideal item of market speculation. Unlike the slightly browner product the U.S. refiners insisted on importing from Cuba, their product was almost completely shelf stable. Sugar trading, formerly tied to real geographies of marketplace and warehouse and customs house, was by the early twentieth century conducted through rapidly circulating global streams of information along telegraph lines, stock indexes, and futures markets. The shelf stability of twice-refined, extra-white crystals enabled a futures market in sugar, since the commodity had to be in the same condition upon delivery to the futures purchaser as it had been when he made the order.[15]

Despite the industrial and legal complexities through which the trust tried to conceal its activities, the sugar complex that U.S. conglomerates and the state manufactured in the early twentieth-century Caribbean was still founded on the same dialectic that had defined the plantation from the start: cheap land and racialized labor brought into the service of consumers in wealthier countries—in particular, their bottomless longing for sweetness. The fantasy "blank slate" of free land and cheap labor that underpinned the New World plantation, however, would run into the resistance of free people who had sacrificed so much to forge independent lives for themselves.

Cuba's easternmost province of Oriente had long been a refuge for people of African descent fleeing the western plantation complex. Thousands had settled there after the official end of slavery in 1886. Such individuals had provided the majority of the troops to the Army of Liberation—they returned home to rebuild Oriente in 1899. Plantations were rare in the zone, and land was affordable. Eastern Cuba's old-growth forest was largely intact. Small farms accounted for 60 percent of Oriente's agricultural units. Forty-five percent of all farms were either owned or operated by people of African descent known as *sitieros*, in reference to their small, owner-operated farms, called *sitios*.¹⁶

With the most diversified agriculture in Cuba, along with iron, copper, and gold mines, as well as a vibrant fishing economy in coastal towns, Oriente seemed to have all the elements of a hard-won antiplantation: a racially diverse population of small cultivators living at a spatial remove from the capitalist center of the plantation, but more than willing to engage in market activity. By 1899, in fact, Afro Cubans' small farms were responsible for 48 percent of rice production in Oriente, as well as 59 percent of the coffee and 61 percent of the malanga, a tuber that was and is a ubiquitous staple of Cuban tables.¹⁷

As ex-slaves, Black *sitieros* were determined to realize José Martí's patriotic vision of racial equality through landownership, even though the venerated founding father had been felled in battle in 1895. "The Cuban Negro has a marked trait in the instinct of land ownership," observed Charles Pepper in 1899. "It is one of the standard complaints of the sugar planters that he clings to his cabin and his patch of ground to the detriment of successful cane-raising. He does not care to be swallowed up in the big plantation." Black cultivators often owned land through a colonial legal arrangement known as *hacienda comunera*—joint ownership divided into shares that guaranteed the purchaser the use of a certain plot of land. Unfortunately, even where official papers had been drawn up, thirty years of war and three handovers of power—from Spain, to the United States, to Republican Cuba—meant that the documentation attesting to ownership of these lands was often missing.¹⁸

Because the practice did not provide clear title, *hacienda comunera* would be vulnerable to legal challenge in new, Platt-era Cuban courts that had taken on U.S. notions of individual proprietorship. U.S. Military Order 62, which remained on the books because Cuban legislators were powerless to change laws that had been made during the occupation, existed to speed up the process of land alienation. Land tax laws put in place during the occupation—which, due to the Platt Amendment, Cuban policymakers were forbidden from changing—levied taxes not on assessed real estate values, but on active farm income. Much like with William Fitzhugh's legal innovations in colonial Virginia, this tax policy meant that U.S.-based real estate investors could purchase large tracts of land for purposes of speculation; as long as they did not build on them, their tax bill would remain low. In the meantime, U.S. investors were actively being recruited to buy up and develop these massive tracts by representatives of the military occupation.[19]

In his introduction to an English-language book of 1902 called *Opportunities in Cuba*, former governor general of the occupation Leonard Wood noted "the existing commercial opportunities in a practically undeveloped island like Cuba." He wrote, "The needs of Cuba today in the direction of foreign commercial assistance are many. . . . Especially is this true of agricultural pursuits." The book's main author was Perfecto Lacoste, who had fled the island during the war and gained U.S. citizenship. He became a close ally of the occupiers, who appointed him mayor of Havana in 1899, then soon after made him Cuba's secretary of agriculture. He was as much a booster for foreign investment as Wood. He noted that, in the wake of "the destructive war just terminated," in order to once again compete in world sugar markets, "all mechanical improvements" as well as agricultural advances will be necessary, but capital was lacking. Lacoste urged "the judicious investment of foreign capital" to help the island. "The investor," he concluded, would also achieve "increased wealth." U.S.-owned railroads were among the first to take up the invitation.[20]

The Cuba Company, under the aggressive leadership of William Van Horne, bent the law to buy up land during the occupation and build a transportation network. Once the trunk and branch lines of the Ferrocarril Central had been laid across the southeast, Americans more confidently invested in the construction of new sugar plantations. As early as 1902, the Cuba Company began to build its own sugar mills, both to take advantage of all the unused land it had accumulated, and to make the terrain appear safer for new entrants.[21]

An estimated thirteen thousand investors and corporations from the United States, both prominent firms and minor players with big dreams also flooded into the eastern half of the island. They were able to buy up a lot of the land held under *hacienda comunera*. Lawyers in the pay of the sugar companies descended on local courts, challenging peasant ownership. When they could not win on the merits of the case, lawyers had money to line the pockets of judges. Thus the "wild east," a land "unexplored, undescribed and unmapped" before the occupation, was conquered and turned over to the sugarcane. By 1905, 60 percent of rural properties across Cuba were owned by U.S. interests.[22]

As Van Horne rang in 1912 by doling out dividends of 6 percent to his happy shareholders in New York, the *sitieros* in Oriente had reached a crisis point. Between 1899 and 1905, the number of small farms in Oriente fell from 21,550 to 10,854, even though the province's population was growing rapidly. "In some municipalities [of Oriente]," writes historian Alejandro de la Fuente, "the process of land concentration was even more acute, with the number of independent farms declining 70–90 percent" in the three years after the official end of U.S. occupation. Those few *sitieros* who held on to their land saw a crash in the prices for their major cash crops of coffee and cacao. Both crops virtually disappeared from several of Oriente's major municipalities, as large plantations converted to sugar.[23]

Although *sitieros* and sugar workers continued to struggle with poverty and disfranchisement all over the island, the United States largely failed to make Cuba into a segregationist mirror of its Jim Crow self. The same Cuban Constitution that contained the Platt Amendment also enshrined Black men's suffrage, and white politicians competed for the votes of Black men throughout the history of the early Republic. And whereas the doctrine of white supremacy was openly avowed in the United States, in Cuba, at least the myth of a "colorblind democracy" created a certain security for Cubans of African descent that did not exist in the U.S. South.[24]

At the same time, urban men of color in Cuba were suffering from a different set of postindependence disappointments. Pushed out of officeholding, their service in the War of Independence minimized, they organized a political party called the Partido Independiente de Color to represent their own interests. In 1911, it was outlawed as "racist" by the Cuban president. Although the party mostly represented urban professionals seeking a place in the modern nation, when leaders of the party called for an armed rebellion to protest their suppression in 1912, widespread unrest came to Oriente.

U.S. consular officials sounded the alarm that American property might be in danger. Indeed, the thousands of *sitieros*, bandits, and other members of Cuba's wild east who joined the revolt focused their attacks on the foreign-owned sugar establishments. As in the 1791 uprising of the enslaved in Saint-Domingue, and in the 1895 war against capital organized by General Antonio Maceo and commander in chief Máximo Gómez, the rebels torched cane fields and sugar mills. They tore up railroad tracks, burned down *centrales*, and stole horses. Notably, they sacked several land registry offices. In El Caney, a town Maceo's forces had destroyed during the War of Independence, a local judge fled with the archives before the registry office was set aflame. The ten thousand or so participants in the 1912 rebellion, much like Maceo had taught them, avoided engaging the Cuban army, which was hunting them.

Reconcentration appeared again—this time in the free Republic of Cuba. Peasant villages suspected of offering protection to the rebels were cleared out. Thousands of individuals were relocated, and a true war seemed imminent. Responding to the emergency, U.S. Marines arrived to secure the property of American citizens, and a brutal counterinsurgency began. While American soldiers stood by, the Cuban military engaged in the summary mass execution of thousands of Black and brown peasants. The Cuban army was in no mood to discriminate, murdering dozens of migrant workers from Haiti who had the ill fortune of being dark-skinned and living in Oriente.[25]

Although the major grievances were economic, and the target of the rebels not white people but capitalist property, as well as the anti-Black discrimination that underpinned the plantations, Cuban elites predisposed to fear the eruption of Black genocidal savagery dubbed the uprising the Race War of 1912. In the wake of the repression, panic about African atavisms holding back Cuban progress led to the criminalizing of Black cultural associations and religious practices, and even the outlawing of African-derived hand drums.[26]

In its first overseas acts of conquest in 1898, the United States took up and transformed Spain's plantation system. While American interests built on an existing sugar infrastructure in Cuba, Puerto Rico's faltering plantation system was revitalized by American occupiers. The U.S. military ruled the Dominican Republic from 1916 to 1924, and it governed Nicaragua through a puppet government starting in 1912. In 1915, the military embarked on an occupation of Haiti that would continue for nineteen years. President Woodrow Wilson, a Southerner and Confederate apologist, appointed fellow Southern whites to take charge of the occupation of Haiti. Josephus Daniels, who had engineered the violent Wilmington Coup of 1898, was appointed lead officer. The Marines went about recreating the Black republic of Haiti in the mold of the Jim Crow South, designing a system of forced labor on road-building projects, closing down schools and replacing them with industrial education, segregating public facilities, and carrying out atrocities. After Louisianan John McIlhenny met with the Haitian minister of agriculture, he fantasized about selling him for "$1,500 at auction in New Orleans for stud purposes."[27]

Cuba was the first postemancipation location to occupy the cutting edge of agricultural investment, scale, and profitability in the late nineteenth century, outpacing plantations in the territorial United States. Seizing massive tracts of cheap subtropical forest and commanding cheap, racialized labor, American sugar conglomerates ushered in a profitable postslavery plantation. Cuba became much more dependent on plantation crops than it had ever been during slavery. Between 1860 and 1929, sugarcane acreage multiplied 3.5 times. In the 1910s and 1920s, recalled one author who grew up during that period, "the great, impenetrable forests were set aflame, whole jungles . . . were fired and razed to the ground to make way for sugar cane."[28]

U.S. investment in Cuba's sugar economy had reached $1.2 billion in 1929. Greater Cuba modeled what agrarian capitalism could be in a corporate, industrial world of mass consumption. For the moment, the epicenter of the American plantation resided in quasi-independent Cuba. In its antebellum heartland of Georgia and Alabama, the cotton plantation foundered, its recovery hampered by overfarmed soil and by Black resistance. Indeed, in these oldest parts of the cotton-farming system of the American South, descendants of the enslaved had fought planters to a stalemate by the early twentieth century.[29]

CHAPTER 17

Percy's Ode

In his 1941 memoir *Lanterns on the Levee*, the planter scion William Alexander Percy told readers that his Uncle George, a fabulously wealthy landowner in the Mississippi Delta, "was not deeply concerned with making a living, for in a mild way it made itself from those hundreds of acres." George worried much more "if the fish were biting." In 1906, Atlanta journalist Walter Paschall described the antebellum town of Lanier, Georgia, as "quite like a lovely dryad, who having ventured from her dwelling to dabble her toes in the river, became suddenly frightened by the whistle of a locomotive and scampered back, dissolving herself forever into a myrtle tree." While planters had abandoned the cotton boomtown in order to be closer to a new railroad line, Paschall concluded wistfully that Lanier was lucky "to have existed only at that most beautiful period when young men bowed bravely with tall hats at their breasts and young ladies curtsied sweetly from trailing fortresses!" Since no commodities were produced in these Jim Crow–era fairy tales, the labor on which cotton fortunes depended could fade into the myrtle tree at the back of planters' minds.[1]

This myth of the plantation as a pastoral idyll in which no work was performed goes back at least to the eighteenth century. In the 1750s, Virginia elite Richard Bland composed a fawning ode to tobacco planter Landon Carter. "At Sabine Hall, retir'd from public praise," Bland rhymed, "You'l spend in learned ease your future days. . . . Whilst you my friend! with pleasing joy survey / Your teeming flocks, as through the meads they stray / Whilst you, in Sylvian shades and pleasant groves / Hear Philomelas chanting to their Loves / Whilst you, secure from all domestic strife / Enjoy delightful scenes of rural life," and so on. Across nearly two centuries marked by radical historical transformation, the planters could still depend on their toadies to publish one-sided paeans to their way of life.[2]

Many Americans, and not just white Southerners, have clung tenaciously to the moonlight and magnolias myth of the antebellum South, using it to veil the brutal realities and ample fortunes of cotton slavery. However, the post-Reconstruction South has been obfuscated by a less obvious but equally pernicious myth: that the clawing back of antebellum power by the vanquished planters succeeded. That their victory was a flood tide that overwhelmed the entire South, burying it in awful subjugation until the great thaw of the Civil Rights movement of the 1960s. The truth is more complicated.

While northwestern Mississippi already produced large amounts of cotton in 1860, cultivation expanded after the war. It was not until the 1880s that planters wrestled the river and the swamps of the Delta into submission, making the state a world leader in cotton planting. By the early 1900s, large "business plantations" with hundreds of Black sharecropper families laboring under the supervision of a staff of white managers represented a new era for the plantation. But things proceeded along a different path in what had been the antebellum Cotton Belt, a zone called the Lower Piedmont, which arcs across the middles of Alabama and Georgia and reaches up into South Carolina. Here, planters' efforts to recapture wealth and power foundered on the twin shoals of economic weakness and Black resistance. Sherman's march across the places most thoroughly plantationized and cotton focused until the Civil War had set in motion a dissolution of the centrally managed plantation.

Across all cotton-growing areas of the South, the shift from antebellum slavery to post-Reconstruction sharecropping brought a profound spatial reorganization of the plantation. Free people's insistence on autonomy from planter oversight, combined with planters' inability to offer wages, meant that forms of tenancy like sharecropping became the norm. On the plantations, the closely packed slave quarters were split apart into forty-acre farm lots, each with its own small home, gardens, and outbuildings.

Rocked by the "betrayal" of their former slaves, planters abandoned the family manse and moved into town. Their on-site cotton gins and screw presses were likewise left to rot. These were replaced by two-story, steam-powered, gin-and-bale complexes in town that processed raw cotton much faster for a more demanding world market. Bustling new mill villages like Siloam, Georgia, under the rule of a few white families, typically had a cottonseed oil mill, a ginnery, a hotel, and a few stores where merchants "furnished" croppers with their year's supply of food, clothing, and fertilizer. Railroads tied the dispersed farms to the town, and the business district replaced the plantation as the center of everyday life in the Georgia Piedmont and Alabama Black Belt.[3]

Planters in the decaying post–Civil War Lower Piedmont grudgingly accepted the transformation of the world they had fought to defend. They had little choice in the matter. Slave property alone had accounted for over 45 percent of the total wealth possessed by all residents of the cotton states in 1860. The Emancipation Proclamation immediately extinguished all of it. The wealth and living standards of the free population of the South plummeted in relative terms to the North after 1865. The war itself was to blame for much of the decline, but recovery was also hobbled by a worldwide agricultural depression that lasted from the 1870s through the 1890s. Prices for most farm commodities remained low, especially relative to manufactured goods. But any Southern areas

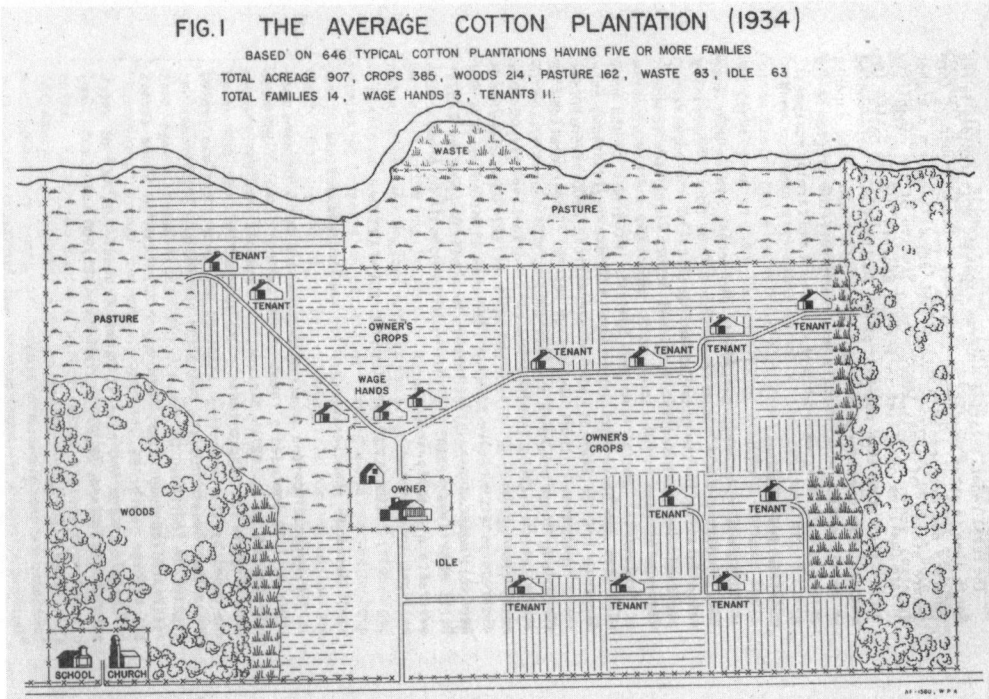

Typical layout of the sharecropped cotton plantation.

seeking to industrialize would have had to compete directly, with no tariff protections, against what was by then the most dynamic industrializing region in the world—that is, the North. Promoters of business in the South had to entice investment capital, skilled labor, and manufacturers' interest away from the Northern states, which had been spared the destruction of war. The depth of Southern whites' fall is hard to overstate. While in 1860, a place like Natchez, Mississippi, had more millionaires per capita than any other region in the nation, in 1900, per capita income in the former Confederacy was half the national average.[4]

The devastation of the region kept land and labor cheap. The inability of Southern state governments to promote economic diversification meant that semiprocessed goods like cotton and tobacco were still royalty: The two commodities made up 30 percent of total U.S. merchandise exports from 1861 to 1910. Yet planters benefited less than they once had. Industrialization in the Gilded Age Northeast meant that a greater proportion of Southern cotton was absorbed domestically than before the Civil War, giving New York bankers increased leverage and renewed interest in the cotton South. Having learned hard lessons during the "cotton famine" of the Civil War, these large, highly capitalized "aggregators" ensured a steady supply of cheap raw cotton to the world's multiplying factories. They were now competing with a large production of raw cotton in places that had been minor players before the Civil War, such as Brazil, Egypt, and India, which kept prices for their product low.[5]

Planters stuck with cotton not because they failed to imagine alternative paths for the South, but because they lacked options. In 1865, plantations were in ruins. Before emancipation, planters would have begun the rebuilding process by ordering the enslaved to clear new ground, but in the late 1860s they had no choice but to plant in long-planted crop fields. As historian Erin Mauldin writes, such a planter "needed fertilizers, and to get fertilizers, he had to plant cotton."[6]

The postwar cotton trap was made worse by Southern banking regulations—a legacy of the slave regime in which human property was used to secure loans—that did not allow the use of land for collateral. To get credit, planters had to commit their future cotton harvests as security. If they wanted to keep their properties, they had to dedicate all their land to growing cotton. Planters' defeat in the Civil War did not eradicate them, but they did not steer the national destiny as they once had. The reassertion of a cotton plantation order in the late nineteenth-century Piedmont was born not of continuing power. It was a symptom of weakness and poverty, carefully made over to look like power. That utter reversal of fortune for the region as a whole is essential to understanding the shifting place of the plantation in American life after 1865—not least why hundreds of millions of dollars were invested in Cuba in the early twentieth century.

In the years immediately following Reconstruction, the landlord-sharecropper relationship did not give planters the unchecked power they desired. Tenants often considered the cotton crop their own, expecting to farm what and how they chose. In fact, the promise of self-management at the family level was the main reason free people had accepted the arrangement in the first place. Gradually, however, the balance of power shifted back to ex-enslavers. William Alexander Percy celebrated the hegemony of his father's generation with surprising candor. As a wealthy planter and state politician in the 1870s, LeRoy "the Gray Eagle" Percy and his cohort had heroically beaten back "scalawaggery and Negro domination" in Mississippi. "[They] stole the ballot boxes, which, honestly counted, would have made every county official a Negro . . . And helped to shape the constitution of 1890, which, in effect and legally disfranchised the Negro." Similarly, in Georgia, planter-politicians under the leadership of the visceral racist Robert Toombs used the specter of financial panic and Black insurrection to call a new constitutional convention in 1877 that ensured the disfranchisement of Black voters, while empowering creditors to "dispossess smallholders and tenants of all they possessed save the clothes on their backs." In state after state, similar chicanery had enabled planters to retake political power after catastrophic defeat.[7]

Planters tried to monopolize local power as a recompense for weakness at the national level. After full disfranchisement of the Southern Black folk was accomplished, planters could again "throw as much expense on the labor as possible." As early as 1872, the Georgia Supreme Court codified sharecropping as "a mode of paying wages." The justices' decision made the cotton in the fields of the cropper the property of the landlord, from first seed to harvest. State governments supported planters' transfer of risk to the cropper through the legal mechanism of the crop lien.[8]

The cotton economy of the post-Reconstruction South was built around a three-person relationship: furnishing merchant, landlord, and cropper. Each year, the cropper went to the town store of the merchant and got allowances of food, clothing, tobacco, as well as seed and fertilizer. His—and on occasion, her—debits were marked off the account of the landlord. The family used these supplies to survive for the year and to grow cotton. At the end of each year, the cropper turned over his cotton bales to the landlord to sell on his behalf to the furnisher, who automatically deducted the cropper's existing debts from the proceeds of the sale of his cotton. The "crop lien" gave the landlord first crack at the money from the sale of the cropper's cotton. The furnishing merchant stood next in line, while, if prices were low or the bales were few, the cropper received nothing for his year of work but another load of high-interest debt.[9]

A maze of new state laws passed across the cotton states in the Jim Crow era further reduced the ability of sharecroppers to control their affairs. In 1904, a new vagrancy statute criminalized "Negro loafers" in Mississippi. Broadly interpreted, the statute made it a crime to be Black and not be working for a planter. Another Mississippi law, passed in 1906, imposed steep penalties for not fulfilling a contract if any advance had been accepted. Even if a cropper and his family were being abused, or found themselves farming worthless land, they broke the law if they left. "Anti-enticement" laws made it illegal for a cropper to leave one plantation for another where he was offered better conditions. Such laws kept all wages down by making it impossible for croppers to bargain in a competitive labor market.[10]

Especially in the Delta, the legal advantages granted to landlords enabled them to begin exerting direct supervision over croppers' daily activities, as they had in slavery. Many planters purchased the bales from their croppers on the plantation, then turned around and sold them in town for a good deal more per pound. A monopoly over information was key to their advantage, and they defended this monopoly fiercely. One planter who was said to have killed a tenant for trying to sell his cotton directly to cotton buyers in town was never even brought to trial; another landlord shot and killed an elderly cropper who dared to keep his own written account of the balance he owed. Whites' impunity before the law was a powerful incentive not to incur their displeasure.[11]

Even more humiliating for free people, planters refused to give advances in cash (they often had no cash to offer anyway). Instead, they provided the furnishing merchant with a list of goods individual tenants were "allowed" to purchase, including "the cheapest shoes and clothing available," along with a diet of salt pork, molasses, cornmeal, and canned beans. Sometimes even the decision whether the cropper and his family would receive new shoes or pants that year was made by an overseer. This was how the violent, grinding, hollowing-out of emancipation happened in the Delta. The planter, ever thirsty for a full complement of working hands, did what he could to keep workers dependent on his outlays.[12]

The "convict-lease" system underpinned the Jim Crow plantation. State governments short on tax revenue due to regional poverty as well as the "small government" mania of Southern Democrats "leased" convicts to planters for harvest-time labor rather than build penitentiaries to house offenders. The post-Reconstruction web of state and local regulations that criminalized nearly every form of noncompliance with the sharecropping regime—such as laws against loafing, restrictions on hunting and fishing, and the right to pursue other employment—fed as many as two hundred

Lange, Dorothea, photographer. Plantation overseer. Mississippi Delta, near Clarksdale, Mississippi. Mississippi United States Clarksdale Coahoma County, 1936. June. Photograph. Caption accompanies original photo.

thousand descendants of slaves into a labyrinthine system of criminal justice that convicted them on flimsy evidence and rented them out to mines, railroads, and factories, but also to planters and farmers in the vicinity of the county courthouse. In Georgia alone, lessees benefited from the labor of just under two thousand laborers per year, 90 percent of them Black men. Although lessees were legally responsible for feeding and housing prisoners, planters and other employers deprived them of basic needs and subjected them to gruesome punishments. Convict-lease was less a coherent system than an ad hoc web of laws, statutes, overzealous policing, nepotism, and corruption. The unpredictable nature of its rule is precisely what made it so hard to regulate and so terrifying to its victims.[13]

In 1931, a Black Coast Guardsman named Sam Edwards went on shore leave to visit his mother in Greenville, Mississippi. He was arrested in a small town for "trespassing without money," and taken to a "courtroom" in the back of a grocery store to be tried and sentenced. When it was discovered that he did in fact have cash on his person, he was convicted of "vagrancy" instead, and sentenced to a twenty-dollar fine, plus thirty days of hard labor on a nearby cotton plantation (which just so happened to belong to the father of the "judge" who convicted him). Alongside about sixteen fellow prisoners, Edwards served out his month-long sentence in the fields. He frantically but unsuccessfully tried to get word about his predicament to his commanding officer. He was beaten several times with a "seven pound strap," once for daring to drink more than the allowed one cup of water during a break in the fields. Even though his sentence was only thirty days, he was forced to sell his watch to one of the guards in order to be released.[14]

While new sharecropper laws put control in planters' hands, and the horrors of convict-lease made working for a white boss a life-preserving decision (white patrons often protected "their niggers" from the criminal justice system), whites had one final recourse when the legal system still did not work expeditiously enough for their taste. During the first three decades of the twentieth century, the Delta counties of northwestern Mississippi averaged a lynching every 5.5 months. Recalling the hideous 1903 mob execution of a Black man accused of assaulting a white woman, a Greenville resident named Harry Ball said that the crowd, dotted with members of the local elite, "was very orderly. There was not a shot, but much laughing and hilarious excitement. . . . It was quite a gala occasion, and as soon as the corpse was cut down, all the crowd betook themselves to the park to see a game of baseball." We are not told how the family and friends of the murdered man remembered the event, or of their powerlessness to intervene on his behalf. Delta elites like Percy laid the blame at the feet of the poor whites, even though there were far fewer lynchings in the North Mississippi hill country where the latter controlled things. Lynchings were most frequent where Black landownership and voting were rare—that is, in the Deep South Cotton Belt. Thus, extralegal terror combined with legal repression to enforce the supremacy of the post-Reconstruction plantation.[15]

The results of the planters' successful counterrevolution in the Delta could be seen in southeastern Arkansas. A local entrepreneur named Robert E. "Lee" Wilson had bought out distressed small farmers, both Black and white, in the early twentieth century, established a trust to evade taxes, and had a mostly Black workforce drain tens of thousands of acres of swamp to establish a cotton plantation. He also ran a lumber operation with "sawmills, box factories, and lumber distribution outlets in Memphis and St. Louis." The plantation was crisscrossed by internal railroads to carry cotton to his gins, as well as leftover seed to his cottonseed oil mills. Wilson employed 2,500 people in the 1920s to the 1950s. Some worked on their own plots as tenants or sharecroppers, but the majority of the cotton was grown by African American day laborers on the directly managed grounds of the company. As historian Jeannie Whayne reports, Wilson "employed twenty-nine white farm managers to oversee operations on his fourteen plantations and hired white riding bosses to supervise day laborers."[16]

Wilson's plantation had a network of company stores that kept croppers "ensnared in a web of debt," as well as housing and segregated schools for his white and Black tenants (the latter only getting an "industrial school," which was essentially job training for a life of low-paid work on Lee's plantation). While Wilson was the same as many Delta planters in using paternalism and the law to control their masses of workers, his unusually large firm also had "private armies of plantation thugs" to settle any conflicts in favor of the company.[17]

Then there was the Delta Pine and Land Company, the largest cotton planter in the world in the first half of the twentieth century. Founded in 1911 by a British investing conglomerate, Mississippi's DP&L had "a centralized office [that] made all major management decisions, determining hours of work, the amount and kind of fertilizer and such used, the maintenance and improvements required, tools, equipment and mules to be used, and the boll weevil poisoning to be applied. Supervisors or overseers directed the work and saw to it that the workers followed the routine set by the manager." Covering thirty-nine thousand acres, and broken up into fifteen distinct plantation divisions, the firm represented the full development of the postslavery cotton plantation system in the Delta. Here, the descendants of freedom seekers were reduced to a rural proletariat working in gangs under salaried overseers, with no agency over the work process. By the start of World War I, nearly nine out of every ten people who lived in the Delta were Black. And African Americans made up 95 percent of tenant farmers, while almost all landowners were white. So Blackness and landlessness, on the one hand, and whiteness and property ownership, on the other, went together in the Delta in striking fashion. In the Piedmont region of the southeast, where plantations had a longer history, the story was playing out differently.[18]

In spite of the obstacles, between the end of the Civil War and World War I, nearly a million Black farmers managed to rise into the ranks of independent landowners, controlling a total of sixteen million acres across the United States. For hundreds of thousands of Black families in the Old South, a plot of land meant stability, security, and independence. Yet the very ownership of land that held out the promise of liberation also exposed Black families to danger. In areas where Black farmers had been successful in moving into the ranks of landowners, and where

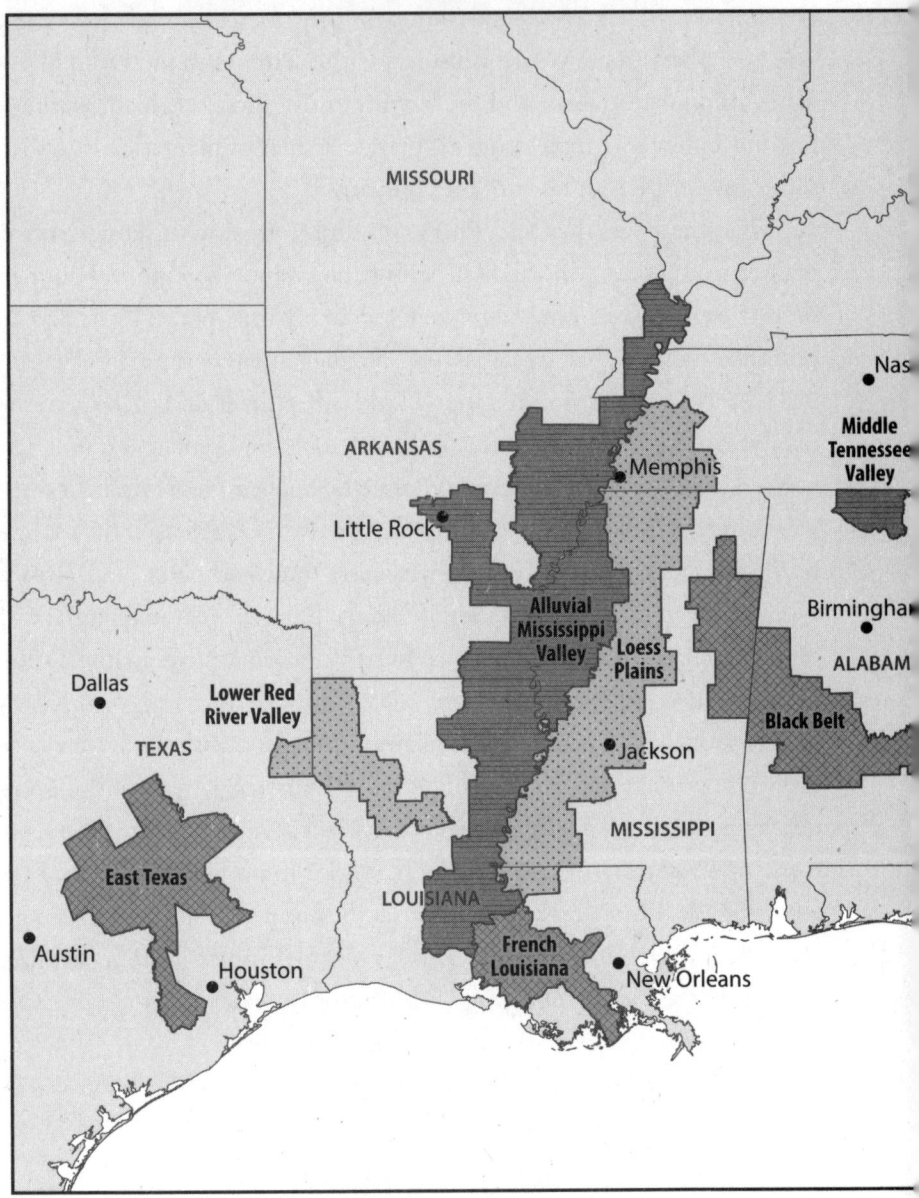

The Lower Piedmont Cotton Belt, stretching from northeast to southwest across the middles of South Carolina and Georgia, and continuing into the Alabama Black Belt, was the centerpiece of the cotton industry before the Civil War, along with the Lower Mississippi River Valley.

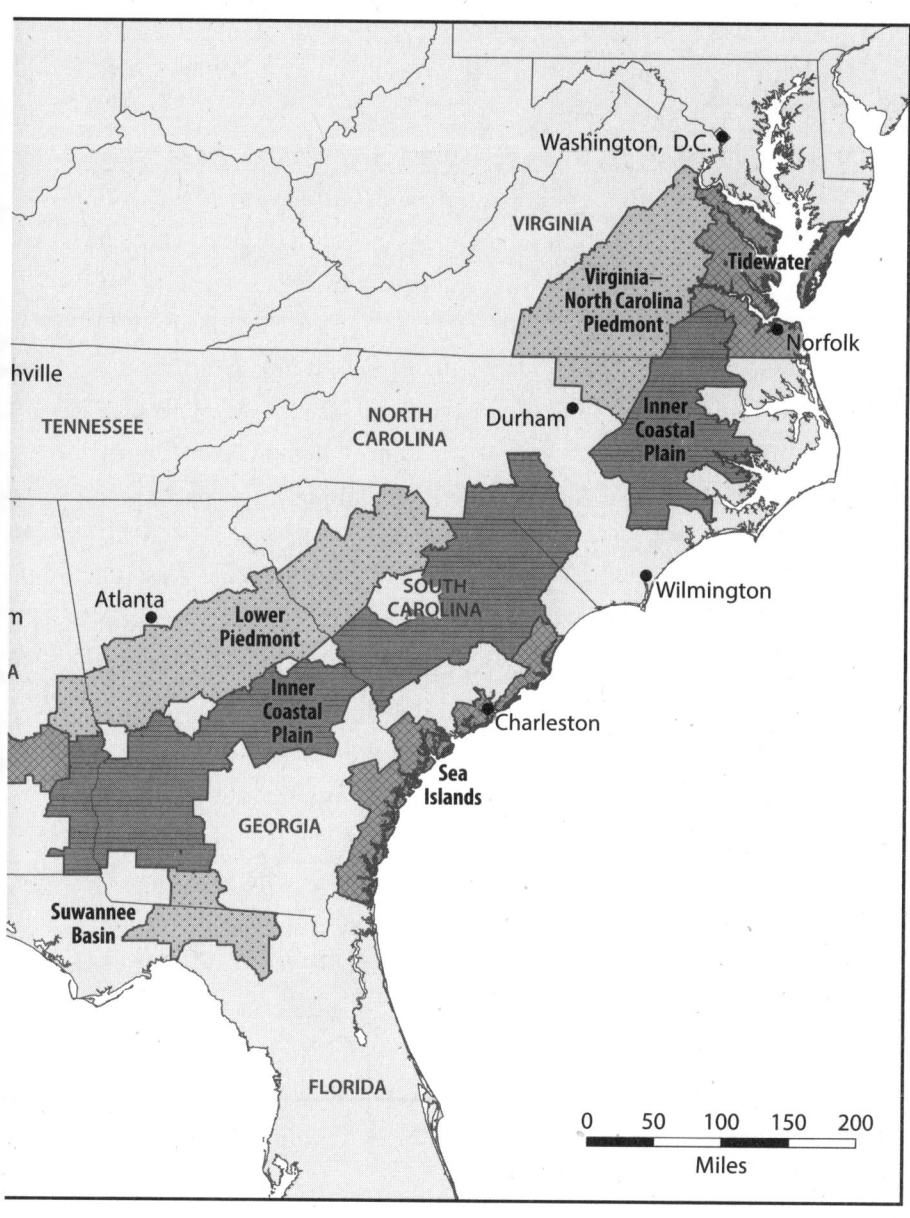

white tenancy was widespread, tensions ran high, with white croppers resenting both wealthy whites and Black people who were doing as well as or better than they were doing.[19]

Not only were Black landowners the most frequent targets of Klan violence across the South, but individuals and families often took on debt to buy property, sinking family resources into a single piece of often unfertile ground. Zora Neale Hurston recorded a Florida sharecropper's joke about being sold a piece of land that "was so poor they had to wire up to Jacksonville for ten sacks of [fertilizer] before dey could raise a tune" on it. Some observers put a racist spin on Black landownership. Whites in rural Georgia were believed to sell poor land to foolhardy Black farmers "with the expectation that they will not finish paying for it. The Negro, holding a bond for title, has to pay the taxes, and if he fails to make his payments the landowner has practically rented him the land and escaped taxes." Another white man "explained the increase of Negro farm ownership in his district by calling attention to the fact that the Negro, on account of his low standard of living, could make the first payment on attractive land more easily than a white tenant could."[20]

Black landowners were sometimes portrayed as paragons of a bootstrapping joylessness: One propertied couple in the Delta reportedly subsisted on "peas boiled without meat, and bread." The wife gave birth to their first child while at work in the fields. Even after the couple became quite wealthy, the farmer's frugality was the stuff of legend: "When there was a big hole in the top of his shoe," reported one descendant, "he just polished right over it so that the polish went onto his stocking and covered things up." The tale was told with pride, but also with a wink about the absurd depths of self-denial to which Black families were made to descend in order to own a farm.[21]

The patronizing idea that only obsequious Black men were able to purchase land was widespread. One New Deal official studying conditions in Georgia noted, "*The Prospective Owner Must Be Acceptable.* The Negro buys land only when some white man will sell it to *him*." Widely circulated tales of charitable bequeathals to loyal "Negroes" twisted

Black landowning into a case study in planter benevolence: "In Macon County," went one story from Georgia, "an elderly white owner without heirs said to his only tenant, a Negro: 'Now, Herbert, I have just a good one-horse farm here; I want you to work and be smart and save up some money, for when I die I want you to own it.' Not many years later the white man died and was buried in the nearby family cemetery. His grave, and those of his parents, are kept in order by Herbert Griffin who now owns the farm." Stories like these highlight the tension between Black landownership as subversive to and reaffirming of planter supremacy.[22]

Though planters dismissed Black landownership as fleeting and illusory, or as evidence of their own fitness to rule, there were other stories about Black landowning circulating. One sharecropper in the early twentieth-century Delta was a hard-enough worker that after every harvest the landlord "acquiesced" in his taking a fishing trip. After several years of this, the landlord lost patience and evicted the cropper. Instead of begging to be kept on, however, the cropper "smiled and said that was all right with him, as he was ready to move into his own place now. The landlord stared and asked what he meant. Then the story came out. The past six or seven years of fishing trips had been 'blinds' to give him time to go secretly to the land he had purchased some distance away. He had 240 acres.... And every year when he was supposed to be fishing, he had been clearing the land." Sometimes Black folk could turn the racist myth of their irresponsibility to their own ends. The land owned by this farmer stood not as the symbol of a white benefactor's charitable act, but of his outsmarting a white exploiter.[23]

Black landowners represented a stark contrast to sharecropper itinerancy. While sharecropping families moved to a new plantation an average of once every two to three years, in the Sandy Creek district of Clarke County, Georgia, researchers found that "one negro farmer had been in possession of his place 35 years, another 25, and a third 22 years." Their farms were smaller and more subsistence oriented than in other parts of the county. In a world where, as one of Zora Neale Hurston's characters puts it, "Colored folks is branches without roots," landownership promised some ground to grab hold of.[24]

Landownership mattered, but it was not everything. What free people wanted most was not their name on a deed but freedom from white bossing. Not only could outright landowning expose a farmer to unwanted attention as well as financial risk. It also meant going to the county courthouse to register a deed, which often required a reputable white patron speaking to the good character of the prospective buyer. The courthouse-planter-land-deed system was by the 1890s a largely white world. The intellectual equating of "possession" of a commodified piece of land with liberty was the central creed of that world. There were other ways to secure freedom in Georgia and Alabama.

We too often picture the Jim Crow South in all-or-nothing terms: either powerful landowner or powerless sharecropper. In truth, free people succeeded in obtaining all kinds of plots for themselves, under a welter of different arrangements that were hard for outsiders to understand, especially since they appeared quite similar, unless one looked closely. Any farm operator on land that they did not own outright fell into the broad category of tenancy. Sharecroppers occupied the bottom rung of cotton tenants. Croppers possessed nothing but their own labor power, so they committed a large share of their future harvest to the landlord in exchange for use of his land, mules, plows, and much else. Croppers submitted to the daily supervision of the landlord, as well as his patronizing efforts to control their spending habits. In the Lower Piedmont, however, croppers did not constitute the majority of farm operators.

In the counties of the lower Georgia Piedmont, while over nine out of ten Black farmers were in some sort of tenancy, sharecroppers represented only 38 percent of all farm tenants in 1920. "Standing renters," accounting for over half of all tenants, were far more common. This contrasts with counties in the Mississippi Delta, where sharecroppers dominated the population, representing 66 percent of all tenants. Only 0.5 percent of Delta farm tenants were "standing renters." Standing renters stood halfway between propertyless croppers and independent landowners. They possessed their own tools, animals, and other inputs, paying a fixed amount of cotton as rent on the land. They were "standing" because they had a year-over-year agreement with the landlord. They tended to stay in one place longer than sharecroppers, which encouraged longer-term stewardship of the land.[25]

While even share tenants and cash renters—who also owned their mules and farming implements—were governed by contracts instructing them to grow particular acreages of certain crops, as well as instructions on how to cultivate and fertilize and market their crops, standing renters received little instruction. And this was the most important thing. Renters interviewed by rural sociologist R. P. Brooks in 1912 told him that the landlord put them on worse land than his croppers. He also stiffed them on fertilizer. They did not care. They still preferred the autonomy of renting—they likely preferred it even over landownership because they did not have to go into debt to achieve it. As one Putnam County planter put it in 1912, "The Negro naturally seeks the position ... affording the most absence of white supervision and the privilege of personal independence."[26]

Standing renters' daily lives may have looked more like those of Black landowners, who, while they still had to grow cotton, could focus on many different lines of work. Since standing renters had agreed to a fixed quantity of their cotton and not a proportional share, they would have increased incentive to produce more bales because any surplus they produced was theirs to sell. They lived in quasi independence. They had discovered that they did not necessarily need capitalist property to exert independence over their daily lives.

Planters' power over the land where sharecropping prevailed shaped the physical space of plantations. Sharecropped plantations were often cultivated on a "through-and-through" basis, where all croppers would cooperate on plowing one big field, then planting and fertilizing the cotton as a crew. Only when the seedlings had begun to sprout was the field "laid off" into individual plots worked by single families. Even individual barns for storing harvested cotton were kept near the managers' residence, and wheeled out to fields during harvest time. The message to croppers was always the same: This land is not yours. You are not trusted. You own nothing but your physical capacity to work in the fields. As Brooks put it in 1912, "At the present time, an unsupervised 'cropper' . . . is almost never met with. The supervision of his operations is as close as the planter can make it." And Brooks emphasized that "the right of control [is] based on the fact that the owner furnishes all the capital necessary to make the crop."[27]

Where standing renters were prominent, the plantation landscape looked different. Their plots, which were larger than the thirty-five acres typically rented to each cropper, were not closely managed. They made the important decisions. They kept their mules, which they owned, in their own sheds and barns year round. The several structures a cotton farmer needed were not centralized near the manager's residence, as with croppers. In addition to their arable fields, each standing renter had his own fenced-off pasture of five to ten acres "for his work stock and the family cow." The pastures, which grew in proportion to the number of mules a renter had to support, "are dotted with widely spaced trees and occasional brush thickets." To protect their pastures, renters built a lot more fencing to clearly separate their home ground from the larger space of the plantation.[28]

Whether they owned their own land, or, far more often, climbed out of the ranks of the supervised sharecroppers and landless wage laborers to become standing renters, Black farmers' aspiration was not to create a dark mirror image of white plantations. It was not "integration" into a brutal system that they sought (though surely some did), but a different order altogether. They let the land rest. "The percentage of idle and waste land," geographer Merle Prunty noted in 1953, "appears to be highest on those of the tenant-renter type." In fact, the African-origin "swept yard" so typical of the rural South before the mid-century spread of suburban developments seemed slowly to be reconquering the plantation. The renters gradually expanded their yards at the expense of the landowner year after year, which "shocks owners when brought to their attention." Inheritors of the antiplantation ethos from the days of slavery, standing renters refused to accept the presumption that the plantation's doctrine of exhaustion was the only way to live with the land.[29]

As the head of agricultural programs at Tuskegee Institute, the Black agronomist George Washington Carver imparted a similar sensibility to his students (most of whom were the children of tenant farmers). He took them on nature walks to teach them about the native plants of the Alabama Black Belt. He sought to cultivate the young folks as though they were plants themselves: He started them off by "clustering" the "fundamental facts of agricultural science at the beginning of instruction and letting them radiate therefrom." Alumni, many of whom themselves became educators, wrote him warm letters addressed to "My Dear Dad," and "Prof Dady." Carver insisted on extending agricultural education to female students, in recognition of how central their work was in turning the products of the fields into food, clothing, and medicines for the community.[30]

In sharecropper families, women raised children, prepared meals over wood-burning stoves, and mended clothing, while engaging in home crafts like making dyes and concocting medicines from native plants. They also took in washing and other piecework for extra cash, all while working in the fields chopping and picking cotton for a lower wage than male counterparts. With boys' help considered indispensable in the fields, however, Black girls on average received more years of formal schooling. More likely to have basic literacy and numeracy than their husbands, then, Black women in Alabama often controlled household finances.[31]

On top of all the daily responsibilities, Black women often found themselves caring for people outside their immediate family. In two counties of Georgia's Lower Piedmont, Black landowners were three times more likely than white landowners to be caring for children other than their own. Even Black renters and croppers, many of them living on the margins of subsistence, undertook the same burden far more frequently than their white counterparts. This was happening in part because so many young adults were forced to migrate out of the area to make a living, leaving their children with older loved ones.[32]

Complementing the dedicated labors of his wife, Viola, Alabama farmer Ned Cobb countered the racialized notion of needlessness with insistent care, acknowledging not just children, but all the needful creatures of God's creation. "Well, Miss Hattie Lu, I feed anything that's around me," he told a white employer impressed by the appearance of his mules. "Any animal I tries to take care of it." His care for animals was not altruistic, or not merely so; it was part of his daily struggle for survival. He was not trying to squeeze the most out of the plants, animals, and people that surrounded him. He understood that they were helping him live. If a farmer lost a mule and had no work animals to help him get in the crop, he had little choice but to sign on with a local planter as a cropper, for he would need the mules and the plow of his new boss. Free people in the South knew that independence required a mule.[33]

Whereas only 5 percent of Black households in central Georgia owned a mule in 1870, by 1880, 20 percent of them did, even if they did not yet own their own farm. Merle Prunty suggested in 1953 that one of their main motives in ascending to the rank of standing renter was the possession of their own mule. On plantations dominated by croppers, plantation managers kept the mules in a barn for most of the year, doling them out to croppers only during cultivating season. "Control of the mules meant personal mobility," Prunty wrote, "the ability to go to town at will, to social gatherings, to church, to visit friends." Making sure the animals remained strong and healthy was sound practice.[34]

Mules were more expensive than most horses, largely because they plowed better. They could be trained not to trample seedlings, as horses tended to do. They also had more endurance in the traces, but their endurance had limits. In Hurston's *Their Eyes Were Watching God*, a local farmer known for his cheap ways is ridiculed for overworking and underfeeding his mule. When he shows up at the store in all-Black Eatonville, the men jokingly warn him: "De womenfolks got yo' mule. When Ah come round de lake 'bout noontime mah wife and some others had 'im flat on de ground usin' his sides fuh uh wash board." This joke, which kills in Eatonville, is also an act of community discipline that discourages any bystanders from mistreating their own animals in the future. And while some townspeople abuse the poorly treated mule in the street, the storekeeper Joe Starks eventually buys him. "Didn't buy 'im fuh no work," he growls at the mule's former owner. "Ah bought dat varmint to let 'im rest."[35]

Whereas Cobb reprimanded white men who mistreated their mules, referred to his draft animals as "babies," and even received lighthearted accusations of "worshipping" his mules instead of Jesus, novelist William Faulkner characterized the Southern mule as an implacable foe of the Southern farmer: "Outcast and pariah . . . [the mule] labors six days without reward for one creature whom he hates, bound with chains to another whom he despises. . . . Ugly, untiring and perverse, [the mule was] an object of general derision; unwept, unhonored and unsung." While Faulkner has earned endless plaudits for his supposed baring of the unsentimental truths of Southern history, nothing could be further from the experience of Cobb.[36]

While it is rarely acknowledged, the rural South had space for ways of relating to animals not limited to maximum use and careless abuse. A sense of reciprocal obligation and a fierce acknowledgment of the natural limits and feelings of an intelligent creature underpinned the relationship, a small challenge to the surplus-squeezing ethos of the plantation. This had been carried through from the days of slavery, where accepting the worldview of the planters would have amounted to accepting one's own status as a less-than-human drudge for making profit, as a being justifiably mined for energy. The antiplantation culture carried the formerly enslaved and their descendants into the rough but more promising terrain of freedom.

Tenants' subversive recognition of needfulness sometimes extended to the wounded land as well. Early in Faulkner's novel *The Mansion*, a murderous white sharecropper named Mink Snopes is engaged in a dispute with a wealthy planter. Asked to consider some evidence given by the planter's Black hireling, Snopes states his views on race relations succinctly: "I don't listen to niggers," he says. "I tell them." Although he had not yet ascended to the rank of planter, Snopes neatly articulated the large landowners' guiding philosophy. Soil, animals, and people are there for the planter's advantage; only a weak man lets them tell him what to do. Since the soil's own timescales do not conform to the itineraries of the railroad, or the maturation periods of bonds, it must be forced into line with guano, sodium nitrate, or ammonium made in a factory. Since a cotton plant's time is not synchronized to the unrelenting thwacks of a flying shuttle in a British textile mill, it must be wrestled into conformity through plant breeding and the spatial extension of cotton cultivation.[37]

As the nineteenth century came to an end, the newest thinking in soil chemistry decreed that the manifold biological processes in the furrow slice could be ignored. The soil was seen not so much a living thing, writes agricultural historian Paul Conkin, but as "a storage bin to receive nutrients from the outside." The mechanistic worldview coming out of land-grant universities and the USDA reduced crop health to three elements: nitrogen, phosphorus, and potassium. Different crops required different proportions of each, the reasoning went. If any of the three elements were found lacking in a farm's soil, the problem could be resolved by adding fertilizers "prepared in chemical manufactories, exactly as present medicines are given for fever."[38]

The simplification of the life of the soil to a three-part mechanical formula turned out to be an effective ideological catalyst for spreading the plantation after the end of chattel slavery. The extension of railroads in Georgia, for instance, made the shipment of fertilizer in, and cotton out, so cheap that cotton could be introduced onto acidic, worn soils.

Between 1874 and 1900, the decades in which cotton monoculture reasserted itself across much of the state, Georgia farmers' fertilizer purchases grew from 48,000 tons to 478,000 tons.[39]

New methods of measuring both the performance of individual cultivators and the agrarian economy as a whole reinforced the mechanistic view of plant nutrition. Beginning in the 1880s, programs in agronomic science and agricultural economics were established at land-grant universities throughout the United States. Faculty taught students to "quantify, rationalize, and standardize farm activity," consciously borrowing from the supposed efficiency and rationality of the American factory system. The federal government also reached deeper into the countryside. The Bureau of Agricultural Economics, founded in 1922, quickly became "one of the largest and most powerful agricultural agencies in the federal government." Through the rapid multiplication of its local offices and extension services following the Smith-Lever Act of 1914, the USDA spread a "standardizing language" of man-hours, mechanization, and annual productivity, which undercut regional diversity and long-term stability.[40]

The county extension services—in which a county agent disbursed educational material, advice, and help with the newest approaches to husbandry—were typically controlled by the better-off, who shaped the implementation of policies cooked up by academic agronomists and agricultural economists at land-grant colleges and the USDA. The favoring, at the national level, of large-scale monoculture was reinforced by state-level policies like that in Alabama, which had subsidized the use of commercial fertilizers, along with a focus on cotton, as far back as 1872. The Georgia Department of Agriculture was founded in 1874 not to understand and improve the soil fertility of the state, but to ensure the quality of commercial fertilizers. The idea that more surplus was always there for the taking underpinned the logic of chemical fertilizer: The land tells you no, and you say yes. The sharecropping system was the ideal host for a fertilizer-based system because the fields had been reduced as much as possible to cotton-growing petri dishes. Moreover, the constant movement of the cropper population ensured that the fact that fertilizers had negative impact on the long-term fertility of soils would go unnoticed.[41]

Living and teaching in the heart of fertilizer-centric cotton (mono) culture, George Washington Carver dissented from the predominant view among agricultural experts that synthetic chemicals provided the solution to the poverty of croppers. Phosphates, which provided a steroid-like infusion of short-lived fertility, only deepened croppers' indebtedness and masked the underlying soil crisis. Carver insisted on a lasting compost treatment of "pinetops, hay, bark, old cotton stocks, leaves etc. in fact, rubbish of any kind that would decay and ultimately make soil." While he did not shy away from laboratory-induced innovation, Carver's priority was making possible long-term residence on the land in Alabama.[42]

In a 1914 article titled "Being Kind to the Soil," Carver wrote that a farmer "whose soil produces less every year is unkind to it in some way; that is, he is not doing by it what he should." A dose of kindness, yoked to good, practical science, would allow even degraded lands "to yield abundantly." Stating that "plants were real, living things," Carver recognized, decades before the idea gained mainstream acceptance, that the topsoil was an open ecological complex, not a bounded chemical equation. It was complicated, and delicate. Plants had needs, he wrote, "just like animals." And the health of the soil was inseparable from the well-being of the people who worked in it. He saw the erosion gullies and washes that scarred the rolling hills of Macon County as extensions of farmers' exhausted bodies. Trying to convince landlords to allow tenants to grow fruits and vegetables, Carver pointed out that "a sick, worried, rest-broken person cannot do his best." The "broken doze" of slavery had not ceased, and the toll the work took on bodies as well as the economic health of the region made crop diversification "a worthwhile venture."[43]

However, any challenge to the fertilizer-cotton-debt cycle, especially one that insisted on the need for croppers to spend their energy growing things other than cotton, was intolerable from the perspective of both the landlords and the merchants who funded their operations. Having once narrowly escaped a lynching, Carver well knew this. Taking into account the economic constraints within which many Alabama farmers were operating, Carver sought to find readily marketable crops that were not soil killers.

Carver recognized that if croppers were to be expected to dedicate their scarce time and energy to a crop other than cotton, they would have to be able to make good money from it. He spent much of his working life in Tuskegee's laboratory developing new commercial uses for the peanut. Consumer demand for peanut-based products would guarantee Alabama's small farmers a good price for the nitrogen-replenishing legume, and help ensure the rebirth of the traditional African crop in the Old South. The many consumer products he invented—everything from peanut butter to peanut oil shampoo, to animal feed, to something called "mock cocoanut"—ensured that growing peanuts would be a real source of income for farmers and not an idealistic panacea.[44]

Carver paid close attention to the countryside around him, noting the factors that promoted long-term farm stability, like the plentiful acorns that coated the woodland floors of central Alabama that could be fed to livestock, or the swamp muck and rotting leaf litter from uncleared and difficult-to-farm grounds that could be used to fertilize the barren red clay of long-plowed fields. Such solutions, however, took time, while the plantation system worked at maximum speed. His ecological prescriptions mirrored his teaching philosophy at Tuskegee.

One taught a generation of young people minute by minute, hour after hour, day after day. Over the years, they internalized the lessons, went out into the world, applied them to the soil, and taught them to other Alabama farmers. The slow-and-steady, piecemeal, patient healing of lands and bodies would accrue over a long period of time— even Carver might not get to look upon the fruit of his labors. While his actual politics were accommodationist—he is often portrayed as a conservative foil to the more confrontational Civil Rights predecessor W. E. B. Du Bois—his insistence that the South deserved something better than land-killing, poverty-inducing cotton sharecropping offered a radical dissent from the rule of the plantation.

The stark reality of the Jim Crow South, where the smallest failure of attention to one's crop, or the most minor lapse in decorum on a planter's porch, could be punished by life-altering disasters or violence, did not make sense to Cobb, Carver, and many other workers of the Southern soil. These inheritors of the antiplantation tradition believed an ounce of grace, some extra feed, or a good long rest made life better for the land, for animals, and for people alike. Coming across a white man who had refused to rent him land when he was at a low point, and now looked enviously at his team of husky mules, Cobb thought to himself, "You see, I tried to get you to help me and you wouldn't do it. Somebody helped me and I made the best of their help." Needfulness not as a weakness, but as a guide to conduct and an encouragement to care: If one wanted to live a life in accord with that ethic, one had to do more than buy fertilizer or a plot of one's own.[45]

CHAPTER 18

Standing

In 1970, when Ned Cobb was in his eighties and leading a quiet life in the Lower Piedmont of rural Alabama, he received an unannounced visit from two Northern graduate students chasing the history of Black radical labor organizing in the Depression-era rural South. They asked him one question: "Why did you join the union?" and received an answer that was eight hours long. Over the next year, they visited him at his home again and again, eventually compiling hours of tape. They edited and compiled Cobb's narrative into a 550-page magisterial autobiography called *All God's Dangers*, which won a National Book Award in 1975. Historians of the South consider it one of the most invaluable sources for understanding daily life for the rural working class during the era of Jim Crow.

As Cobb's life history made clear, even when Black farmers carved out semi-independent lives as owners or standing renters, their neighborhoods—with all-white police forces and criminal justice systems, little support for education, and exploitative merchants and banks—were

Ned Cobb, his wife, Viola, and their first child in 1907.

still pitted against them. In response, they built a vibrant associational life through organizations like the Colored Farmers' Home Improvement Lodge, the Farmers' Improvement Societies, and the Agricultural Wheel. The Knights of Labor—a nationally prominent trade union—was particularly active in Louisiana, where thousands of sugar plantation workers, protesting stagnant wages, launched a series of wildcat strikes in 1887.

Planters in the region reacted as if the workers had declared war. They organized a counterinsurgent Peace and Order Committee that surrounded the town of Thibodeaux, where large numbers of striking workers had taken shelter with their families. Armed whites sacked the town and killed untold numbers of people. In spite of the lethal risks incurred, Black farmers elsewhere in the South continued founding new labor organizations.[1]

The Colored Farmers' Alliance (CFA) was designed to respond to the exploitative world in which all Black farmers, whether croppers, renters, or owners, had to operate. Established in East Texas in 1886, the CFA boasted a nationwide membership of around 1.2 million by 1890, with women comprising perhaps one quarter of members. The CFA aimed to promote landownership, the cooperative marketing of crops, and improved education. The organization turned political soon after its founding, because members realized that a political program to fight disfranchisement, to put a floor on wages, and to put an end to the convict-lease system would be a key part of their survival. Membership in the CFA was built by itinerant organizers who ranged carefully across the Southern countryside, speaking at church meetings and in private homes. They also got the word out through a number of Black newspapers, such as the *Alliance Advocate* in North Carolina.[2]

Not only did the papers carry news of CFA meetings and activities, but they also educated farmers on how the broader system of cotton farming and finance functioned to their disadvantage. The main enemies that farmers shared—whether they were Black or white, sharecroppers or landowners—were the railroads and warehouses that set usurious rates for transport. They also opposed "hard money" policies that kept borrowing costs high, while seeking alternatives to the local bankers on whom they depended for advances. The CFA organized its own system of stores and warehouses, along with cooperative purchasing mechanisms for fertilizer, and a cooperative to sell cotton and other goods.[3]

As with other Black-led efforts to craft alternatives to the exploitative system of landlords, agents, banks, and railroads, the CFA was met with violence. In the plantation boom region of the Mississippi Delta, Leflore County witnessed the most direct challenge to the white elite. In 1889, a local Black CFA leader by the name of Oliver Cromwell began to organize area farmers. He encouraged them to withdraw their patronage from local storekeepers and conduct their business with white Farmers' Alliance cooperative stores instead—while the Farmers' Alliance actively excluded Black members, the two groups still cooperated in certain areas.

Tarred as a "notoriously bad negro" by the local press, Cromwell was targeted for assassination, but he was able to call on the aid of "Three Thousand Armed Men" from the CFA. However, they were outnumbered and outgunned when the shooting started. Several leaders of the CFA were murdered by white mobs in Leflore, along with dozens of men, women, and children. Cromwell went on the run. He was pursued and shot to death, but not before gunning down five of his pursuers. Keen not to earn the enmity of the Delta power elite, the white chapter of the Farmers' Alliance in Leflore shut its one store in the county and ordered its members to break ties with the CFA.[4]

As the complicated relationship between white and Black farmers' organizations in Leflore County makes clear, there were overlapping struggles between poor white farmers and poor Black farmers in the post-Reconstruction South. At every point in the history of the plantation, there was a group of small landowning white farmers that was pushed aside to make way for more powerful actors. In the Jim Crow South, however, they were pulled directly into the exploitative world that advantaged planters, losing their lands but ending up as tenants under the thumb of large landowners. As tens of thousands of white farmers throughout the South fell from independence into cotton sharecropping in the decades after the Civil War (a process that will be detailed in chapter 21), their economic and legal superiority over Black farmers started to shrink.

The shared hardships of the depression-racked 1890s gave rise to a remarkable but ultimately limited interracial movement of farmers known as Populism. The small perks poor whites got from white supremacy overwhelmed the potential for sustained solidarity. The antidemocratic political structure of the South—one-party rule, the total disenfranchisement of Blacks, and the significant disenfranchisement of poor whites—doomed the Colored Farmers' Alliance, and the white Farmers' Alliance as well—not simply because of racist animus, but in large part because the racial difference between the two organizations overlapped with class distinctions.

Unlike the CFA, the white Farmers' Alliance was dominated by landowning farmers who depended on cheap Black labor during cotton-picking season. When the CFA organized a strike of cotton pickers in Arkansas and Mississippi in 1891, the white Farmers' Alliance not only did not support their fellows, they helped to brutally crush the strike. While the CFA never again had the same strength after 1891, its program lived on in third parties—the interracial People's Party in particular—at the state and national levels.

Given the risks of political violence across the South in the early twentieth century, Black people formed local cooperative ventures to pool money and purchase land instead of confronting the power structure directly. Judia Jackson Harris, a Black schoolteacher in Athens, Georgia, started a Mutual Benefit Society and assembled a group of Black tenants to buy contiguous land and develop "a healthy rural settlement," known by the simple name of Settlement. The organization started with ten members in 1900. Collectively, they laid out $350 to buy forty acres. The success of this first group quickly encouraged a second club of seven members, then a third club of seven members more. As of 1915, there were five of these land clubs in one area of Clarke County. They had purchased a total of 440 acres, at a value of $3,330. The collectively purchased property was then divided up to the satisfaction of families, who "erected neat homes" on their family plots. With the help of Northern philanthropists, a school was built, staffed, and maintained. Boasting a large library, as well as a music program, a Corn Club and a Land Club, it was said to be the best-equipped school for Black children in the county.[5]

Such gains could be made without angering the white elite—in fact, planters could look at a place like Settlement as evidence of their own benevolence. If only more of the Black people were what they often called "the better sort," all might succeed in the same way. Settlement's homeowners, however, clearly saw things in a different light. According to a sociologist's report from 1915, they "are adapting themselves readily to advanced ideas of cooperation.... They own a cooperative saw mill, a cotton gin and a threshing machine." Here was an autonomous, local, and less confrontational version of the CFA's program, one that had a chance of surviving the widespread white supremacist violence that beset the region in the late 1890s and again in the 1920s.⁶

Indeed, direct union organizing against the plantation continued to be met with massive violence. In 1919, Black farmers in Elaine, Arkansas, organized a tenants and sharecroppers' union. Their insistence on their right to merely hold meetings was sufficient cause for white residents of the area to perpetrate the deadliest single act of racist violence in American history. They murdered hundreds of Black Arkansans in a days-long frenzy. When a group of prominent white citizens—trying to contain the fallout from the massacre—conducted an investigation, they made the discovery that "some of the ringleaders [of the union] were . . . the oldest and most reliable negroes whom we have known for the past 15 years . . . [they] own mules, horses, cattle and automobiles and clear money every year on their crops." While we cannot be sure, they sound like standing renters. Sometimes such "reliable negroes" were viewed disparagingly as "trusties" enforcing a white man's unjust regime. However, given the history of "privileged" slaves, including the drivers and craftsmen who led Haiti's 1791 slave revolt, and the Virginia blacksmith Gabriel Prosser's revolt in 1800, perhaps it is no surprise that local Black landowners and renters led the charge to improve the conditions for all Black farmers in the Cotton Belt.⁷

High cotton prices between 1900 and 1920 had pulled farmers deeper into dependence on the crop, while masking many of the problems of the postslavery plantation. In what was the Roaring Twenties for the rest of the country, though, a new wave of troubles swept through the South. None was more devastating than the boll weevil, a crop pest that eviscerated harvests across the cotton-growing South in the years after World War I. But the weevil did not affect all cotton-growing areas in the same way. In fact, it highlighted the diverging fortunes of the Lower Piedmont and the newer cotton-growing regions.

In the Delta, the dystopia planters feared—they heard scientists threatening that the weevil plague would "break up the plantation system . . . and bring everything to the level of the small farm"—had not changed much since the secession debates of 1861. Yet, helped by the vastly superior fertility of Delta soils and the warmer climate, planters actually recovered from the ravages of the insect fairly quickly, continually expanding cotton acreage instead of moving to diversify their crops, as some government experts were advising.[8]

In the plantation boom counties of the Mississippi Delta, which were dominated by sprawling and profitable plantations managed by aggressive planter-entrepreneurs, 95 percent of all farmers were tenants of some sort, and over 65 percent of all tenants were sharecroppers. This elevated number of sharecroppers is significant, because it was the arrangement that gave planters the most say over the daily activities of tenants.[9]

Delta planters controlled the flow of information, and they successfully fought efforts to diversify, in spite of encouragement from the USDA to try other crops before the weevil arrived to devastate their cotton fields. When a group of USDA officials arrived in one Delta town in 1908 to spread the word about the coming infestation, they were met at the train station by leading planters, who told them to get right back on that train and leave town. Planters did nothing to fight the boll weevil but silence panic about its impact, so that laborers would not leave the region. Because of the earlier spring and the warm, humid weather, they could harvest earlier in the fall than other regions, and it was in fall that the weevils did most of their damage. As long as croppers kept working in the fertile, river-fed loams, landowners could plant their way out of the boll weevil crisis, committing ever more deeply to cotton monoculture, growing so much that they could accept some losses from the weevil without too much damage to their bottom line. Far from losing population, the Delta saw an influx of Black workers from more distressed areas of the South.[10]

In the post-Reconstruction Piedmont, on the other hand, the second-order land maintenance operations like ditching, fencing, manuring, and barn repair—essential for long-term profitability—ceased, especially as the land was subdivided among tenant farms. No individual tenant had reason to dedicate his own scarce labor to operations that would only help the plantation in later years, when he likely would have moved on already. For the west to east, county by county, farm by farm spread of the weevil population to be resisted effectively, central planning and organization would have been necessary. Planters are to blame for the absence of such coordination, because whenever Black farmers formed organizations, local whites violently suppressed them. The intentional decentralization of cotton culture in the Old South made the region vulnerable to a contagion like the boll weevil.[11]

In Lower Piedmont Georgia, where the semiautonomous standing renters represented the majority of tenants and cultivation was barely managed by absentee owners, the weevil's impact was devastating. Cotton production in Oglethorpe County, for example, fell from 33,760 bales in 1914 (the year before the weevil's arrival) to 2,492 bales in 1922. The impact of the rapacious weevil was as much a symptom as a cause of the decline of plantations. Facing their own deepening problems of erosion, and the resistance of the free people to the rebirth of the antebellum plantation system, Piedmont planters had bled tenants dry in every way they could. They assaulted the soil with a gambler's abandon, while they showered on their wealthy white neighbors hospitality that was "almost compulsive."[12]

In Georgia's Madison County, local notables fondly recalled the county seat as "a party town," where even in the dark days of Reconstruction "there seemed to be no end to parties and entertainments. . . . There were hops, soirees, masquerades, musicals, plays and a skating and terpsichorean festival." In the 1940s, one of the town's mansions hosted a *Gone with the Wind* costume party that lasted four days. To fund this lifestyle, planters marshaled every legal and political mechanism they could to make sure tenants grew only cotton. But the soil, having been cropped continuously since the 1830s, and lacking the replenishing floods of the Mississippi River, was already much worse than in the Delta. Planters in Georgia, for example, used far more fertilizer than their Mississippi counterparts and still suffered from lower yields of cotton per acre. The massive amounts of fertilizer they poured onto the rolling hills of red clay only exacerbated the underlying weakness of their system.[13]

Things got so bad because of the stalemate between planters and tenants. Delta planters, fully hegemonic, drew their society more deeply into cotton monoculture. Piedmont planters lacked the environmental advantages, the economic resources, and the power over tenants to do the same, but they had enough power to prevent tenants from diversifying away from cotton and developing the kind of land care that would have lessened the impact of the weevil invasion. It was the stalemate itself that doomed the rural Piedmont to worsening poverty and eventual depopulation.

While the weevil actually further embedded cotton monoculture in the Delta, places like Greene County, Georgia, never recovered. Both banks in the county closed in 1928. On the eve of the Great Depression, Greene County farmers, 65 percent of them Black, were already falling back into sharecropping or landlessness. The other option was to migrate out of the region. It was the standing renters who left the area, and they had been the backbone of the agricultural system. Between 1920 and 1930, the areas of Greene County characterized by large plantations lost 44 percent of their white population and 67.3 percent of their Black population. The vast majority of the five-thousand-odd virtual refugees fled to the easy-to-reach towns: Atlanta, Athens, and Augusta. Not all rural Black folk had Northern cities on their minds. Many, in the depths of the Depression, adopted new organizational strategies to retain their ties to the land, and to drive the taproot of a homeplace deeper in the Southern ground.[14]

Amid Alabama's economic collapse in 1932, a Tallapoosa County merchant-planter named W. S. Parker began refusing to advance any food supplies to his longtime customers. Since croppers were paid nothing until "settlement time" after the cotton harvest, and he would not let someone "transact with nobody else" if they were in debt to him, Parker's tenants and their families went hungry. One of his debtors was Ned Cobb, who had been mercilessly exploited by other merchants in the 1920s and fallen back into tenancy.

Yet federal efforts at economic relief had brought a transformative new player into the county for the first time since Reconstruction. Federal officials from out of state, sent by New Deal Democrats to stanch the flow of refugees out of the region, were now "furnishing" sharecroppers at far more reasonable rates of interest than local merchants and bankers. Most of Parker's tenants duly visited an office building in the county seat, underwent a brief interview, and were written checks for fertilizer, seed, and other needs. Thus, in a matter of weeks, they were farming independently of Parker. They would still owe him a share of their cotton as payment on existing debts. But otherwise, they were free and clear. Cobb made his crop that year without having to go into town to buy supplies on credit. In June, he got his cotton and corn laid by and took to the lumber-hauling operation he worked at whenever he could spare some time from the fields.[15]

As Cobb remembered, Parker did not plan to let "his niggers" go that easily. When Cobb got home from work at the sawmill one night, Viola had some disconcerting news. "Darling," she told him, "Mr. [Parker] come through here today. . . . He never did quit drivin, just drivin along slow and lookin every which way." Likely infuriated by the determination of his debtors to escape his clutches, Parker soon tried to lure them into new obligations. He left notes in their mailboxes inviting them to town "Saturday evenin to get em some beef." Cobb had his own meat, so he did not take the bait. After his carrot was refused, Parker started in with the stick. He began riding around the county telling everyone, Black and white, that "he goin to take all old Ned Cobb got this fall."[16]

Cobb and several others had reason to believe they could resist Parker's plans to keep them under his thumb. They had recently joined the Southern Tenant Farmers' Union, an organization affiliated with the Communist Party. The STFU had gotten started in Tallapoosa through the efforts of a young Black schoolteacher named Estelle Milner, who passed out party leaflets and newspapers in 1931. Soon after, a small group of the county's sharecroppers wrote a letter to the STFU, inviting organizers to the area. Union activists began to circulate through rural areas of the state, trying to keep a low profile while making their presence known to the poor. New chapters were formed, and members began holding meetings. White elites, attuned to any "communistic" threats to their authority, flew into rage and panic.[17]

Before Cobb joined up, Black union members at the other end of the county from his home had begun guarding their meetings with armed sentries because white vigilantes and local police kept breaking them up. In one of many violent episodes, local police fractured Estelle Milner's spine. An armed standoff resulted in the gruesome killing of a sharecropper and union leader named Ralph Gray. Fourteen union members were arrested and charged with intent to murder (Gray had shot the county sheriff in the stomach during a tense encounter), though all were eventually released by county officials fearful of national attention.[18]

Communist Party leadership left the area for a time, so local croppers began "carrying on the work on their own initiative." The ad hoc secretary for the croppers' union during this time of independence and regrowth was a nineteen-year-old Young Communist League leader named Eula Gray—the daughter of murdered cropper Ralph Gray.[19] As STFU members prepared for a new round of organizing efforts, they faced inevitable violence. Yet they went to the meetings anyway, and the union had almost six hundred members by the time Cobb joined.

Buoyed by the organization, the sharecropper members established a platform of demands that included the right to be furnished until harvest time, the right to sell one's own crop, and the right to be paid cash wages by the week instead of having to wait for "settlement" time once per year. Considering the depth of his anger over the lack of educational opportunities for his children, it is no surprise that the croppers' union platform when Cobb was a member included "a nine-month school year for Black children and free transportation to and from school." Seeing a chance to maintain land and improve his lot, Cobb became an active organizer for the union: "I recommended it thoroughly to particular ones I knowed," he said.[20]

Since his neighbor Clifford James was also a member of the STFU, when word got around that Parker had asked a deputy sheriff to impound James's livestock, "several other men of the organization" agreed to defend his property. Cobb walked over on Monday morning, lacking a specific plan. He encountered the kind of repossession scene that authorities dreaded. "Got there and good God I run into a crowd," Cobb remembered. At first, he posed as an uncommitted bystander, asking the deputy, "What's the matter here?" When he was told the police had come to "take all old [Clifford James] got," Cobb began with the politest appeal possible: "Mr. Logan, please sir, don't take what he got. He's got a wife and children and if you take all his stuff you leave his folks hungry."[21]

Cobb kept pleading, gently refusing to yield. Bit by bit, over the course of a late-morning conversation with police officers in a tenant's swept yard, Cobb's position firmed up. He grimly informed a white deputy, "I'll be damned if you don't take it over my dead body." When the deputy told one of the "superintending Negroes [who] didn't know no better" to go back in James's yard and start taking the mules out, Cobb called out, "Go ahead and catch him, if you that game. I'll be damned if you won't ever bring him out of that gate." By directly and publicly challenging the orders a white man had given to a Black trusty, Cobb had shattered an unwritten law of deference in the Jim Crow South. "You've done said enough already for me to done killed you," the deputy told him. Faced with a crowd of Black eviction resisters, however, the officer knew he was beaten, at least for the moment. As he pulled away in his vehicle, he swore to return with the sheriff.[22]

As the sun climbed to its highest point in the sky on that mid-December day, Cobb and his brothers in the union sat in James's cabin, thrilled by their momentary triumph but knowing that their lives were in danger. They discussed what they would do next. When the other men in the house heard a car coming down the road, they knew it was the sheriff and a posse. They ran out the back way and took cover in the swamps. Cobb was left to guard the house of Clifford James alone. As the sheriff and three other officers stepped out of the vehicle, Cobb walked out the front door to face them, wearing a white cowboy hat and knee-high Red Wing boots. His fists were stuffed into the deep pockets of his Big-8 overalls. In one hand he gripped a .32 pistol. When a policeman approached Cobb to place him in custody, grabbing his arm, Cobb, his limbs strong from years of slicing furrows and hauling oak, flung the officer to the ground.

Cobb then turned around to enter the house, when—"BOOM—Mr. Platt threwed his gun on me," spattering Cobb's lower body with buck shot. As his boots filled with blood, he wheeled around and fired through the front door, nearly hitting an officer who dove behind a tree. All four officers "outrun the devil away from there. . . . They hitched up to their ass-wagon and took off." Meanwhile, the group of armed sharecroppers who had taken cover in the swamp also exchanged fire with the police. Union member John McMullen was killed, while three other men, including Clifford James, were wounded. Escaping arrest, James walked seventeen miles to Tuskegee Institute. He received treatment that night, but was then turned in to county authorities. Along with another wounded STFU member named Milo Bentley, James was clapped in a cell at the Montgomery County Jail. The two men were forced to sleep on filthy blankets on the floor and denied medical care. James and Bentley died in custody two days after Christmas 1932.[23]

When Cobb fled the scene that night, he was picked up in a car by Viola, who took him to the hospital at Tuskegee. While university leaders did not turn him in as they had Clifford James, they did not let him stay overnight for fear of the violence his presence might bring to the doorstep of the HBCU in the rural Deep South. Cobb was in hiding at the house of a relative in a nearby county when a white posse aided county police in a campaign of violence against the Black community in Tallapoosa. "Riot crowd come to my home and shot all over my people," Cobb related. "One shot hit one of my little girls in the jaw—Leah Ann; it weren't no bad wound it didn't leave a mark. But it scared her and scared em all to death." His brother-in-law, Waldo, went to defend Cobb where he was recovering. Cobb tried to get Waldo to leave but he insisted on staying. When the deputies arrived at the house, Waldo dashed out the door, armed with a breech-loading rifle. He did not survive the encounter. Soon after, Cobb was taken into custody. Despite a national campaign and the efforts of STFU lawyers, an all-white jury convicted him of "intent to murder" and sentenced him to twelve to fifteen years.[24]

While such a prison sentence would be a gaping chasm in the life of most people, Cobb viewed his incarceration in the context of the longer history of his people. From slavery, through emancipation, the promises and disappointments of Reconstruction, and the contested rebirth of the cotton plantation, injustice, lack of care, and outright plunder had defined life in the South. Cobb understood his actions in Tallapoosa County as the only possible course, and the punishment he suffered in the penal system of Alabama all but inevitable.

Nevertheless, decades later, well after his release, Cobb still claimed Alabama, with all its faults, as his rightful inheritance. "Leaving never entered my mind," he said. It was a world he had made that had also made him. "I was born and raised here," he declared, "and I have sowed my labor into the Earth and lived to reap only a part of it, not all that was mine by human right." "I stays on if it gives em satisfaction for me to leave," he concluded. "And I stays on because it's mine." He was not in the majority though. In the years of Cobb's confinement—from 1932 to 1945—the federal government's New Deal policies prompted many more Black farmers to leave the Old South.[25]

To win needed support for his ambitious economic plans, President Franklin Delano Roosevelt courted the Southern wing of the Democratic Party, appointing people like Oscar Johnston and Mississippi Senator Theodore Bilbo to high-level positions within the Agricultural Adjustment Administration, founded in 1933. Johnston owned one of the largest cotton plantations in the Mississippi Delta. Bilbo, a proud member of the Klan and an ardent segregationist, spent half his time in Congress advocating a genuine economic populism, and the other half sputtering about "Catholics [and] rabbis trying to bring about racial equality for niggers."[26]

The planters Bilbo represented betrayed a deep fear of organized labor, which they rightly suspected could not be disentangled from civil rights for Black people. Their hesitance led to the scuttling of prolabor and profarmer agencies such as the Resettlement Administration, which fought to keep small farmers on the land. The AAA thus crafted a more planter-friendly approach to economic relief: It paid farmers for reducing the acreage they planted in cotton, seeking to help all cotton growers by lifting prices.

Not surprisingly, the payments were delivered to landlords, who were supposed to share the proceeds with everyone who worked their land. Instead, most planters evicted croppers and invested the money in tractors to cut down on the need for manual labor. It was the rapid adoption of tractors beginning in the New Deal that put the final nail in the coffin of the world of "mule and hoe" farming that Ned Cobb had tried to turn into a version of freedom on the land. Intended to help desperate farmers, the AAA thus initiated what historian Pete Daniel calls a new era of "Southern enclosure."

In addition, the 1999 Supreme Court case *Pigford v. Glickman* revealed that Black farmers had been victims of decades of racial discrimination at the hands of the USDA—discrimination that made it more difficult to stay on the land. Operating through the land-grant institutions like the University of Georgia, the USDA's Federal Extension Service consistently favored large-scale, mechanized, and chemicalized agriculture at the expense of small farmers' hard-won knowledge. And since most Black farmers were small, they were unduly impacted.

John Vachon, photographer. Parkin vicinity, Arkansas. The families of evicted sharecroppers of the Dibble plantation. They were legally evicted ... plantation having charged that by membership in the Southern Tenant Farmers' Union they were engaging in a conspiracy to retain their homes; this contention granted by the court, the eviction, though at the point of a gun, was quite legal. The pictures were taken just after the evictions before they were moved into the tent colony they later enjoyed. Mississippi United States Parkin Cross County, 1936. Jan.?. Photograph. Reproduced from the Collections of the Library of Congress. Caption accompanies original photo.

More explicit racism worsened the situation. In Georgia, the extension agencies were segregated. Like the sharecroppers they were supposed to serve, Black extension agents had little power to shape aid programs. White superiors failed to notify them of important meetings. They were assigned substandard offices and were paid salaries far lower than less qualified white agents.[27]

Alongside the ravages of the boll weevil and the arrival of expensive new machines like tractors, and, in the 1950s, the mechanical cotton picker, government policy helped propel Black people out of the Old South, after seventy years of marginally successful class struggle on miserly land. From a high of a million Black farm owners in 1920, by 1969, only eighty-seven thousand remained.[28]

Starting in the 1870s, a new pattern emerged in global agriculture. From French colonial Vietnam, to modernizing Egypt, to the Brazilian Mato Grosso, millions of formerly independent subsistence cultivators, or formerly enslaved people, were pulled into the global market economy by new forms of state and colonial taxation, as well as military levies. Those struggling to survive on the land had no choice but to pump out more and more staple goods like rice, cotton, sugar, and coffee, which had the perverse effect of pushing wholesale prices ever lower, meaning the primary producers fell ever further into a debt trap. This was the situation the formerly enslaved of the American South were ushered into after slavery. Considering the fact that they were trying to make themselves a new farmer-landowner class in a highly unfavorable economic environment, their ability to get ahold of family plots throughout the South is all the more impressive. But it was an uphill plow in both directions.[29]

At times tenants cursed their lot. Because of the penury, the lack of opportunity, the underlying danger, and the petty humiliations, 3.5 million Black people left the South between 1910 and 1950, 1.5 million in the 1940s alone. The migrants to Cleveland, Chicago, Harlem, and other cities left indelible marks on American music, art, and literature. There would have been no American Modernist city without them. Their exodus also transformed American politics. Black migrants left a region where they could not vote for one where they could, adding to Black political clout within the Democratic Party and encouraging a more pro–civil rights stance at the national level, which boomeranged back to the rural South, where voting rights efforts and civil rights law put the nails in the coffin of one-party authoritarian rule in half the country, arguably turning the United States into a fully functioning democracy for the first time in its two-hundred-year history.[30]

While the "Great Migration" of refugees from a broken plantation system transformed the nation for the better, we too often forget that this northward flow of poor people was the result of the shattered dream of an interracial landed democracy. It should have gone differently. The farms should have been larger, the soil not so poor, the educational system better supported, financial and agricultural advice not so stingily given out. If Black farmers had been permitted to build their many regional associations, to cooperatively purchase fertilizer, and to diversify their crops, the boll weevil would not have had the devastating impact it did. When they left the region, many of them with no other choice but to end up dead like Clifford James, or in jail like Ned Cobb, a whole world was left to wither on the vine.

Especially in the South—where the air is warmer than in the Northeast and moister than in the American West—when a farm is left without care for even a year, sedge grows on the fallow fields and raccoons move into the barn; precocious mulberry saplings set roots with surprising speed; and the fences sit moldering in a slough of grass. Such abandonments happened hundreds of thousands of times in the middle decades of the twentieth century all throughout the South, on small farms and large plantations. Even in 2025, on state routes in central Georgia, a decaying sharecropper's shack—its planks and shingles stained a deep, mottled gray by decades of rain, mold, and fungus—can be spotted, reminding us of how long the descendants of slaves toiled, of how little chance they were given, and of the world they were forced to give up. The Great Migration, while worthy of celebration in many ways, also marks the decisive uprooting of African Americans from the American ground. It was never a world of affluence, ease, or security, and few who grew up on the land remembered it with unalloyed fondness. Yet we ignore the loss, remarkably recent as it was, at our peril.

The lives of Cobb, Carver, and many others complicate the common understanding of life in the rural South as one of unremitting deprivation and oppression. Building on the antiplantation traditions of their forebears, they crafted a rural subculture not weighed down by utopianism or nostalgia. But a dissenting view can be heard in the stories told by farmers as clear, full, and unhurried as a barred owl in the pines.

When the young child of a white Georgia tenant farmer was stricken by a mysterious six-month paralysis in the 1920s, his caretaker was a former slave called Auntie, who lived with her children and grandchildren on a neighboring plot. She sat by the boy's bedside through his long, sleepless nights of pain and terror, rubbing his contorted limbs with liniment, enthralling him with her understanding of the dangers and the promise of all God's created beings. Auntie lived in the kind of world where birds tried to "spit in ur mouf" and take over your body; and where a snake with the head of your former master might catch you on the roadside, force you to share your vittles with him, and make your body waste away, until some real root-work freed you of his hold. Auntie's home of Bacon County, Georgia, teemed with spirits, poisons, plots, and betrayals. It also bore hidden in its furrows and hollows the knowledge that might keep loved ones free from the manifold afflictions associated with malnutrition and industrial food.[31]

While Southern whites concocted a lunatic pseudo-history of the plantation as a lovely garden staffed by loyal "negro" attendants, the Black poet Thomas Jefferson Flanagan, a native of Stewart County, Georgia, crafted a more ambivalent appreciation. In a poem called "The Erosion March," he allowed that "a strangeness of beauty and tragedy blends [in] the boneyard of the farmer and his farm." Auntie would have agreed that the Georgia landscape had little of innocence or romance. Shot through with danger and deprivation, it was a lifeworld nonetheless, with its share of beauty built upon an immense amount of knowledge and tactile skills.[32]

Instead of being encouraged to build upon that foundation, croppers, renters, and small landowners in the mid-twentieth century were told they were right to hate it, even when their feelings toward it were more complicated. They were told that if they did not farm monoculturally, and at large scale, they were not real farmers. That their lives would always be backward and isolated. That the American Dream was happening somewhere else. While farmers of all races left the countryside in these decades, no one was pushed off the land with greater force than Black Americans.

In the 2020s, a book on African American birders, or an Instagram account maintained by a young Black man who rides horses, is a delightful surprise to many urbanites and suburbanites because it violates the expectation that Black people have no relationship to rural life. That surprise is enabled by a romance of innocence on the part of white people, an erasure of the fact that no group carried more knowledge of farming, hunting, woodworking, and gardening than Black people, and no group of Americans was torn more violently and suddenly from the world they had made at such great cost. And while hundreds of thousands of Black people, given extremely compelling reasons to leave, did so, and created lives in Northern cities they considered better, many rural Black Southerners never entertained leaving.

There is no reason to idealize the lives they carved out. The soil was terrible. Erosion gullies ran as deep as croppers' debts. Acts of racist violence were common. Yet the steadfast refusal of the free people to resubmit to the rule of their daily lives, to the daily invasion of their dwellings, hobbled the recovery of a plantation order in the Old South, even as the plantation flourished in the Mississippi Delta.

The standing renters descended from enslaved ancestors articulated a powerful dissent to the plantation way of mining the soil and the people. As slaves they had experienced on their bodies the violence of the property relation. Many did not aspire to extend that violence to the land. By fashioning various modes of autonomy that stopped short of fee-simple landowning, these carriers-on of the antiplantation tradition also disconnected the powerful link between property ownership and liberty that planters had insisted upon since the revolutionary era.

A key part of that enslavers' violence was the ruse of the Black surplus. Less could always be given to, and more could always be demanded of, the enslavable race. Planters extended the canard of Black needlessness—which lies at the heart of the longer history of the plantation—to the entire world around them: the plants, the animals, and the soil. Black farmers like Ned Cobb saw no path to salvation in perpetuating the myth that people and animals do not have needs or limits; that with a monopoly on political power and the wonders of modern technology, one needed no longer to listen. Though I am sure he had his faults, the Cobb we come to know through his narrative continually attended to the needs of his animals, of the soil, and of his people. The needfulness at the root of his relationship with the land was a standing riposte to the planters' values. That tradition, lost beneath the dominant narratives of twentieth-century progress, requires reclaiming.

Part Five

PLANTATION FUTURES

The spindle picker in operation. Tulare County, California.

CHAPTER 19

The Slave Empires of History

California is going the way of the slave empires of history.

—UPTON SINCLAIR, 1934

Charles Ramsdell's presidential address at the 1929 meeting of the Mississippi Valley Historical Association was called "The Natural Limits of Slavery Expansion." In it, the eminent Southern historian reminded his audience that the western frontier had been a principal cause of the Civil War. White Northerners were so convinced that wealthy Southerners intended to monopolize western lands with their plantation-dominated society, he argued, that they started a war to prevent it. But Ramsdell considered that fear overblown. Since "soil, climate, and native labor [formed] a perpetual bar to slavery" west of Texas, he averred, the South's age of expansion was already over in 1860. In truth, "those who wished [plantation slavery] destroyed had only to wait a little while—perhaps a generation, probably less." It would have died of natural causes if simply left alone. As evidence for his thesis, Ramsdell looked farther to the west. He noted that only "small quantities" of cotton were being produced in California in the 1920s—thus it could never have become the new dominion of a continent-spanning master class.[1]

Had Colonel James G. Boswell attended Ramsdell's lecture, he would have arched an eyebrow at this last claim. A wealthy cotton planter from Greene County, Georgia, and the grandson of an enslaver, Boswell had elected to move to California at the start of the 1920s. In the ensuing years he helped spark a full-scale cotton boom in the San Joaquin Valley, a 230-mile stretch of arid, sun-drenched lowlands running down the spine of the state. Whereas only 9,000 California acres were planted in cotton in 1923, by 1929 this number had grown to 247,000, a twenty-five-fold increase. One California journalist sang out the steps like an emcee at a hoedown: "Men are picking cotton, hauling cotton, ginning cotton, thinking cotton, breathing cotton, dreaming cotton." By the year of Ramsdell's speech, California was already growing more "white gold" than Georgia, and Boswell was running the largest cotton operation in the state. His empire included massive fields, precision gins, and seed-oil mills. Boswell did not rule alone. Already in 1929, nearly a third of the large-scale cotton farms in the United States were located in California.[2]

Despite Ramsdell's confidence in its self-destructive tendencies and spatial limits, the cotton plantation did in fact lay deep roots in the Golden West. Yet even modern scholars have been reluctant to acknowledge this fact. While geographers and historians talk freely of the "neoplantations" and "portfolio plantations" of Cold War Texas and Arkansas, the mammoth cotton monocultures of California are labeled "agribusinesses," and their owners "growers," or even cotton "ranchers." California's cotton workers knew better. Santiago Delgado toiled for Boswell's rival Fred Salyer for three decades. He told a journalist in 1985 that Salyer and his ilk "brought the plantation to Corcoran. Except they never called it the plantation. They called it 'the Company.'" When Delgado used the word "plantation," he meant racialized management, low wages, and soil mining husbandry for an export product that was not incorporated into local economies. If euphemisms have covered over the reality of plantation and planter in California, that is merely evidence of the success of the state's ideologists in crafting and disseminating the idea of California as a libertarian paradise unsullied by history.[3]

While there was no Big House on the cotton plantations of California, and successful planters typically lived in the upscale neighborhoods of San José and Los Angeles, Boswell and other transplants from the Piedmont South cleaved to planter ways. By the 1960s, a time when many Americans thought of the West Coast as the cradle of the counterculture, the birth scars of Big Agriculture in California still had not faded. Journalist Mark Arax, who grew up in the San Joaquin Valley in the 1960s, "felt for the first time the strange and mannered presence of the South" as a teenager, when his lower-middle-class parents moved to a tony northwest Fresno suburb called Fig Garden.[4]

After being invited to the home of a new friend from school, Arax found himself at the "Georgian mansion with white columns" of Berson Frye. Frye was from New Orleans, his wife hailed from Memphis, and Frye was the California purchasing agent for a Louisiana-based cotton company. Mrs. Frye paid a Japanese gardener to maintain the grounds, while a Black woman in full maid's regalia entered and left through the back door. Playing billiards with Mr. Frye one afternoon, Arax was regaled with tales of "cotton and slaves and plantations pillaged and a government that had stolen a way of life from the people." Still brimming with resentment from a century before, Frye and his wife had traveled the world in the service of a cotton economy their kind still controlled. He showed Arax pictures and postcards from India, Egypt, and other distant, cotton-growing locales.[5]

California was never a monocultural state in the way Mississippi was. It exported, and still exports, hundreds of different agricultural products. From the 1950s until the end of the twentieth century, California produced more agricultural value than any other state, beating out Iowa and Texas. Despite all the fruits, vegetables, nuts, oils, and wines California was churning out in the middle decades of the twentieth century, though, cotton was the most valuable crop of all. During the decades following World War II, at the height of American prosperity, California was the leading cotton-producing state in the nation, with the exception of Texas. More workers were employed in cotton than in any other agricultural sector in the state.[6]

Why not focus on perhaps a more obvious story, that of the corn and wheat sectors of the Great Plains? Because, while extremely large and monocultural, and creating a product tied up in global markets, grain farms in a state like Iowa are an "edge case" in histories of the plantation. They grew out of Euro-American family farms that mechanized and chemicalized so they could grow bigger and more efficient without ever needing to recruit masses of labor. Though Iowa farms have their roots—as much as Southern plantations—in the widespread theft of Indian land, they were never directly connected to the history of the Black surplus and the Atlantic slave trade. Through the late decades of the twentieth century, most farms in Iowa were still family owned and often family worked, with small numbers of migrant workers to mind the machines.

The cotton-producing units of central California, on the other hand, grew directly out of Piedmont Georgia. Planter exiles from the Deep South relocated to central California, where they fell back on the tried-and-true practices of their planter forebears. California—and thus the system of modern industrial agriculture more broadly—was directly transformed by the arrival, the flourishing, and then the decline of a cotton plantation system. Indeed, California's identity was more Southern than many of the state's boosters were willing to admit.

A Kentucky enslaver named Robert Baylor Semple was one of the leaders of the 1846 Bear Flag Revolt that resulted in California's independence from Mexico. A few years later, the Gold Rush drew legions of young Southern white men to the state, many of whom brought enslaved people to assist them in their search for fortune. By 1850, 36 percent of U.S.-born residents of California had come from slave states. They tended to be wealthier and more politically powerful than the average white. One California abolitionist bemoaned the "exceedingly strong . . . Southern element" in Sacramento, which made any abolitionist "practically an outcast" in the legislature.[7]

Even though the state constitution of 1850 outlawed slavery, Southern-aligned leaders in the state's Congress and Supreme Court enshrined new forms of racialized labor exploitation. Black Californians who had been declared free after statehood were often forced into exploitative labor contracts that amounted to indentured servitude. Chinese and South American migrants were brought in under indenture contracts, while Chinese women were sex trafficked. "Guardianship" arrangements legalized the buying and selling of Native Americans as "domestic servants." Bucking the trend of other "Free-Soil" states, California passed its own fugitive slave law, which allowed for the arrest and reenslavement of Black people who had successfully escaped from the South.[8]

While California remained loyal to the Union during the Civil War, military officials had enough reason to fear a pro-Confederate uprising in the region that they maintained a troop presence among the scrub oak woodlands and tule marshes of the far west. Mark Arax writes that Southern sympathizers in the San Joaquin Valley "stole hundreds of horses from local ranchers and dispatched them to the Confederate Army," although full-scale guerrilla war never materialized.[9]

The influence of white Southerners continued with little interruption into the Reconstruction period. Isaac Friedlander, the "Wheat King" of San Francisco, was raised in antebellum Charleston, where he imbibed the mores of a "plantation gentleman" before pursuing a fortune in the Gold Rush, moving west in 1849. He never prospered himself. Instead, he went into trade, buying up flour on San Francisco's docks and selling it to miners, often in exchange for land claims. Friedlander thereby cobbled together an empire of a million acres in Fresno and surrounding counties. By the end of the 1860s, he was one of a small number of oligarchs who dominated landholding in what was supposed to be the last promised land of the yeoman farmer.[10]

Friedlander sold some of these lands to wealthy ex-Confederate enslavers fleeing the nightmare of Black equality after the Civil War. Seeking what one contemporary called "a happy retreat from the degradation and tyranny of 'former residences,'" a dozen or so arrived from Alabama, Mississippi, and Georgia, buying a large plot of land together. They keenly hoped that "the lovely plantations of former days were to be renewed." While one of the founders of this expat community had been keen to christen their new home with the name of his plantation back in the Old South, it came to be known informally as "the Alabama Settlement."[11]

Mississippi planter scion Harry St. John Dixon and others, swollen with indignation and wounded pride, attempted to turn themselves into successful farmers during the state's "wheat bonanza" of the 1860s, '70s, and '80s. In the absence of the labor and expertise of enslaved workers, however, they failed. As one neighbor of theirs tactfully put it, "The hard struggle for bread [is not] conducive to that honor of the gentleman which had been the proudest boast of the colonists." Even though they had sometimes referred to themselves as "farmers," when it came time to plan, plow, plant, weed, and harvest with their own hands, they lacked the skills, the know-how, or the simple physical endurance to do so.[12]

Giving up the agrarian dream after a few penurious years in the countryside, Dixon decamped for Sacramento, entered Democratic politics, and dedicated his working years to solidifying a one-party state and securing a democracy for white men. California was one of the first Union states during Reconstruction to lose its Republican majority, and Dixon was a key player. As the "unreconstructed clerk of Fresno County," he won plaudits for refusing to enforce the Fifteenth Amendment, which had guaranteed to all male citizens the right to vote without regard to race or former condition of servitude. A former master himself, Dixon considered himself qualified to pronounce Black men "stupid fools" not worthy of the vote. In spite of its reputation as the cutting edge of American progress, California was the only nonslave state that failed to ratify the Fourteenth and Fifteenth Amendments in the years after the Civil War (California did not do so until 1959 and 1962!). At the same time, a genocide was transforming the demographics of the state.[13]

Scholars now agree that anti-Indian violence was as pervasive in early California as anywhere in the history of the American frontier. During and after the Civil War, the young state refused to recognize previous treaties and forbade Indians from testifying against whites in court, which made it difficult to bring white squatters and murderers to justice. Government officials eventually earmarked over $1.5 million to support punitive campaigns of extermination against Native Americans resisting the theft of their lands. White vigilantes, often backed up by regular soldiers of the U.S. Army, received reimbursements for killing Indians, and California's Indian policy achieved exactly what it was meant to: In 1846, 150,000 Indians lived in California. In 1880, only 16,277 remained. Colonial conquest and ethnic cleansing wrenched open massive amounts of fertile, flat, and frost-free terrain, making postgenocide California a prime setting for the next phase of the plantation.[14]

Along the route of the new Southern Pacific Railroad, the plowing up of the vast San Joaquin Valley of central California began in the 1870s. The railroad eagerly recruited white settlers who would grow wheat the firm could ship east. Farmers used new implements to reshape the hydrology of the state to meet the needs of large-scale agriculture. A five-foot-wide iron blade known as the Fresno scraper, pulled across the land by teams of mules, "reconfigured the land field by field, leveling knolls and hog wallows and filling in gulches." Tulare Lake, once the largest freshwater lake west of the Mississippi, was dammed, drained, and flattened to make way for grain.[15]

New technologies suited to the vastness of the landscape arose one after another among the fields of grain. Machinists in California built the first steam-powered tractor in 1868. They also developed massive compound plows with eight shares to slice simultaneous furrows in the arid soil. Every summer, monster combines pulled by dozens of horses vacuumed up uninterrupted fields of golden grain. Tulare's lakebed soils were incredibly fertile, helping the state yield nearly twice as many bushels per acre as the national average. By the end of Reconstruction, even as a global trade in Midwestern wheat began to transform international capitalism, "the counties in the Sacramento and San Joaquin Valleys numbered among the world's leading grain-producing districts."[16]

The head of Miller & Lux, a mammoth ranching and grain conglomerate, described the Valley as "wheat, wheat wheat and nothing but wheat" in all directions. By 1905, the *San Francisco Chronicle* reported that the diverse wetlands ecosystem once carefully managed by Yokut tribes had gone "so dry that a mosquito cannot find in its bed enough water wherewith to moisten its parched bill." In the decades of the wheat boom, hundreds of plant species once nurtured and utilized by Native groups like the Cahuilla were eradicated. Tens of millions of migrating geese, now lacking watery resting spots, disappeared from the skies. Jackrabbits, elk, condor, antelope, and mink were likewise exterminated by settlers. The uniform landscape, ironed flat and made machine-ready for the energies of speculative capitalism, looked like a more perfect representation of the planter's dream than any other place in the history of the plantation. And in quasi plantation fashion, the wheat boom ended as quickly as it began: Drought and overpumping for irrigation brought subsoil salts to the root zone. Planters had also farmed too intensively without rotating or fertilizing, draining key nutrients from the soil. In spite of the downsides of modern, mechanized agriculture made clear by the end of the Tulare wheat boom, its initial success set the pattern for what central California would become in the mid-twentieth century.[17]

In 1917, a South Carolinian agronomist named Wofford Camp was sent west on an important military mission: to develop a reliable domestic supply of high-quality, long-staple cotton for military uses during World War I. Camp successfully bred a hybrid strain with many of the same qualities as the Egyptian Pima that war industries were no longer able to obtain, thanks to German U-boats blowing up U.S.-bound freighters. After the war, Camp's new Acala variety turned out to answer commercial demands as well, consistently receiving better inspection grades than preexisting varieties of cotton, which allowed planters to sell it for higher prices. It also produced more lint per plant than southern breeds, and was easier to gin and spin.[18]

Before arriving in California, Camp had witnessed uncontrolled cross-pollination in the Old South. Agronomists working in Georgia had been shocked to discover over three hundred localized varieties across the state. He knew more than laboratory breeding would be required for a modern cotton industry to take shape. In 1924, Camp convinced the state legislature to pass a law forcing all California planters to grow nothing but Acala. To strengthen the law, the USDA's Cotton Research Center in Riverside County prevented commercial seed companies from selling in the state. California was thus the first state to boast homogeneous, genetically controlled cotton. Such "one-variety communities" soon developed all over the country, but only in California was it state law. So much for the libertarian paradise. The California standard allowed cotton planters like Boswell to sell their product at higher prices than planters elsewhere. Gins would get a uniform product, which made deseeding a simpler operation. It was the creation of homogeneous, machine-suited cotton lint that underlay the state's cotton boom of the 1920s.[19]

In the meantime, cheap land free from frost, erosion, and pests like the boll weevil had begun to draw more and more Southern cotton planters into the state. Given the immense scale of agriculture in California, capital was essential. Particularly important was the Bank of Italy, which had begun in 1904 with the efforts of a San Francisco fruit merchant named Amadeo Giannini to organize and scale up the fruit-growing industry in the Valley. When it began to broaden its portfolio beyond the produce economy of San Francisco, Giannini merged his firm with a Los Angeles bank and took the institution's name to elide his own firm's ethnic roots. The newly christened Bank of America—which was the largest financial institution in the world by 1949—was key for the rise of cotton in the San Joaquin Valley. Lending $10 million per year to California planters, Giannini's bank accounted for about half of total investment in the state's cotton industry. The growing financial institution was joined by private electric utilities and bond buyers to create the irrigation infrastructure western cotton needed.[20]

After his work on the Acala variety of cotton was complete, Wofford Camp served as the head of agricultural appraisal for Bank of America in California from 1928 to 1933. In that job, he would visit farms and review paperwork for mortgage loan applications. The development of banking institutions within the state, and of linkages with East Coast banks, were instrumental in bringing high interest rates down and thus forging agricultural capitalism on the West Coast.[21]

While they now had plenty of capital, California cotton planters still needed workers, especially at harvest time. Cotton was probably the most labor-intensive crop in California. The unusually strong anti-immigrant sentiment in the United States in the 1920s, as well as the widespread sense in California that its agricultural utopia had to be white, complicated the project of recruiting a plantation workforce. Nonwhite farmers—particularly Sikh and Japanese immigrants who began working as tenant farmers on the properties of white landowners in the late nineteenth century—had been responsible for making California's deserts bloom with melons, lettuce, and other vegetables. In spite of their important role in the history of the state's agriculture, Japanese were excluded from the right to own or rent farms by the Alien Land Laws of 1913 and 1920, while Sikh Americans, lumped in as "Hindus," were declared ineligible for both citizenship and landownership in 1923. In spite of the discriminatory measures, some Japanese agriculturists hung on to their farms until World War II, when mass internment made their lands vulnerable to a wholesale property transfer to white citizens.[22]

Exploiting anti-immigrant animus to push potential competitors for land out of the way, planters also capitalized on racist ideas to realize the plantation dream of a laboring class that was both flexible and captive. In league with fruit growers, cotton planters formed the California

Farm Bureau Federation. The group helped tailor policies on immigration, making sure that the immigration acts of both 1917 and 1924 were not applied to Mexico. This enabled them to get the number of workers they wanted. It also made the place of these workers in the United States precarious enough that they could be easily deported if they engaged in labor organizing. In the initial decade of the cotton boom, central California's agricultural workforce transitioned from primarily South Asian, Chinese, Pilipino, and African American to majority Mexican. Planters helped design a differential pattern of exclusion and recruitment that gave them the laborers they needed while reinforcing the image of "real" California citizens as white.[23]

With a pool of legally vulnerable, economically desperate workers in place, in 1926, G. W. Guiberson and his fellow cotton planters established the Agricultural Labor Bureau of the San Joaquin Valley. The ALB employed Spanish-speaking labor contractors to hang flyers "in pool rooms, mutual aid societies, and neighborhood halls" in Latino areas of Los Angeles and San Francisco. Once contracted, families loaded up their cars and headed for the cotton fields, where they were housed in makeshift labor camps and paid a uniform, nonnegotiable wage. The former Georgia planter James G. Boswell alone housed 180 families on his California plantation in 1927. Workers were paid around one dollar for picking one hundred pounds of cotton. Picking totals were unlikely to exceed four hundred pounds per day. At that level, daily pay would have been four dollars, 20 percent lower than the daily wage drawing workers from across the country to Henry Ford's Detroit assembly lines, which was a highly competitive working-class wage at the time.[24]

However, there was no pretense of equal treatment in California's cotton bowl. The labor contractors who recruited plantation employees managed them throughout the season. Since workers were not welcome in town, often facing abuse from white police officers, shopping anywhere other than the planter's "company store" was not an option. They often found themselves working mainly to pay off debts they owed to their employer, as well as to the labor contractors who had recruited them and who oversaw their gang labor. Even though California planters rarely referred to their properties as plantations, they had no problem acknowledging the many continuities with past labor systems. "Southerners didn't think [of] a Mexican or Nigger as anything but a slave," admitted one.[25]

Planters tried mightily to create a completely pliable workforce, but the people they recruited brought their own traditions of workplace resistance. Many migrant pickers from Mexico had already experienced capitalist agriculture with the growth of coffee and sugar plantations, as well as cattle ranches, in the late nineteenth century. Their own peasant villages had been thrown into disarray as a result. A man named Elias Garza, for example, had lost his tenancy on a hacienda in the state of Michoacán. He then found work in a sugar mill in a nearby city before crossing the border to work on the railroads in Kansas. Finally, he made

Dorothea Lange, photographer. Company housing for cotton workers near Corcoran, California. King County United States, 1936. Nov. Photograph. Reproduced from the Collections of the Library of Congress. Caption accompanies original photo.

a new home in Los Angeles, where he combined work as a cotton picker with jobs in a packinghouse and a stone quarry. Some of the San Joaquin Valley's workforce had even been cotton pickers in Mexico prior to migrating.[26]

Many others were veterans of military conflict and labor organizing. Cotton worker Refugio Hernández told an interviewer that his grandfather had fought for Mexico's liberation from French rule in 1863, while his father had been a comrade-in-arms of both Pancho Villa and Emiliano Zapata during the Mexican Revolution. Before ever leaving Mexico, tens of thousands of miners, farmworkers, and sharecroppers had experienced variants of anarchism, communism, and trade unionism. While the lack of gainful employment opportunities and access to land in Mexico forced them to search for work in California, those same experiences of capitalist agriculture and political activism made them formidable opponents for a planter class seeking to maintain profits amid the Depression.

When planters drastically cut wages and work hours after cotton prices took a nosedive in 1932, workers "organized locals in tents, and hovels, and in holes in the wall," as one union organizer recalled. "The strike cry began to ring through the valley. . . . 'Not a pound for less than one dollars a hundred.'" In September 1933, just when the harvest was to begin, over eighteen thousand cotton pickers in the San Joaquin Valley left the fields. Labor historian Devra Weber calls it "the largest, longest, and most bitter agricultural conflict" in California up to that point. Over three-quarters of the strikers were Mexican, and they formed the backbone of the newly organized Cannery and Agricultural Workers' Industrial Union. Boswell simply loaded his resident workers' possessions onto a truck and dumped them on the highway, locking the gates of his plantation.[27]

Left with no other choice, strikers set up makeshift camps in the cotton towns of Tulare, McFarland, and Porterville. The largest camp, however, was created in the Boswell-run town of Corcoran, with 3,500 workers gathering on the land of a sympathetic small farmer. The encampment took up more acreage than the town itself, and strikers began using it as a base for further organizing and mutual aid. A labor economist from the University of California, Berkeley, named Paul Taylor was asked to observe the strike by the California Department of Industrial Relations. While the state agency was preoccupied with labor strife and communist agitation, Taylor sympathized with the plight of the workers. He visited their encampments, where he saw makeshift tents consisting of a tarp stretched between the roof of the family car and two poles in the ground. Their shelter, he wrote, "in addition to the family car, cooking utensils, bedding and the ever-present dog, represented the total possessions of the evicted strikers—with perhaps a goat or several chickens for the more fortunate."[28]

The union members repurposed the nearest irrigation ditch as a "collective washtub and bathtub for the children." They even rigged up a system of pipes to commandeer the planter's irrigation water, which flowed out through several spigots across the camp. Strikers idled from work progged the surrounding countryside, trapping rabbits, foraging edible plants, and bringing down small game. Sympathetic local teachers opened a small school, and several women operated a community kitchen. There was even El Circo Azteca, a Mexican circus that "provided nightly entertainment, as did guitar players and singers among the strikers." Each day a "mobile caravan" of strikers would affix pro-union signs to their automobiles and head out into the Cotton Belt, urging other field workers to join the work stoppage. When they encountered a farm where cotton picking was still in process, the caravan would stop and form a picket outside the gates, blowing bugles and chanting, "*Huelga pizcadores!*"[29]

Aware of the violent propensities of California planters with roots in the cotton South, members of the Corcoran encampment built a barbed-wire fence around the perimeter. Veterans of the Mexican Revolution like Manuel Mireles and Manuel Garcia took charge of camp security, with round-the-clock sentries wielding firearms and crowbars. Keen to break the strike, cotton planters took action under the leadership of none

Caravan of striking cotton pickers south of Tulare, California. California United States Tulare Tulare County, 1933. Oct. Photograph. Reproduced from the Collections of the Library of Congress. Caption accompanies original photo.

other than Wofford Camp. A planter in his own right, as well as an unabashed white supremacist, Camp served as president and treasurer of the infamous Associated Farmers of California, which recruited groups of scabs, thugs, and right-wing vigilantes to break strikes. Camp would later organize public burnings of John Steinbeck's *The Grapes of Wrath* in Bakersfield in support of his fellow planters who so loathed the book's depiction of large landowners.[30]

· Although they despised Steinbeck for representing them unfairly, the Pulitzer Prize–winning author was undeniably right about one thing. Camp and the planters had the police on their side. A local under-sheriff made no attempt to present an image of neutrality: "We protect our farmers here in Kern County," he declared. "They are our best people ... we serve them. But the Mexicans are trash. ... We herd them like pigs." Purchasing machine guns and swearing in scores of new "deputies" among the planters and ranch managers, the county sheriff's department assembled a paramilitary force to defend the interests of the cotton planters.

A month into the strike, a fleet of ten vehicles pulled up in front of the CAWIU union hall in Pixley, where a meeting was getting started. As wary workers hurried into the hall, dozens of shotgun-toting planters climbed out of their cars and trucks. One worker, Dolores Hernández, trying to push a planter's weapon out of his face, was shoved to the ground by a member of the mob. He was then shot to death as he lay in the street. The planters opened fire on the crowd, killing two more people and wounding eight. Later investigations into the leadership of the Pixley assault pointed to a man named F. G. Kruger. Kruger was the manager of Wofford Camp's plantation and a newly minted deputy of Kern County.[31]

In multiple sites across the California Cotton Belt on the same day as the Pixley assault, strikers were attacked by deputized mobs of planters and their enforcers. Planters typically operated with impunity, but when a man named Delfino D'Avila turned up dead, it became clear that the planters had overplayed their hand. D'Avila had close ties to the Mexican Consulate, whose leadership, normally eager to cooperate with the Americans, protested publicly. At a time of heightened class consciousness, much of the nation was now focused on the cotton plantations of the San Joaquin Valley. The extent of collusion between planters and local law enforcement (who had, at best, stood by doing nothing during the violent episodes) just made things look worse. Officials from the National Recovery Administration in Washington, D.C., stepped in to mediate the strike and forced the planters to the bargaining table. The strike, together with the beginnings of federal support to planters and the quick recovery of cotton prices in 1934, led to higher wages for workers, so in one sense the strikes were a success. The 1933 strike, however, marked the high point of federal intervention on behalf of California farmworkers.[32]

Founded earlier that year and focused on enforcement and deportation of destitute immigrants during the Depression, the Immigration and Naturalization Service hounded migrant workers in California and elsewhere. Further discouraged by the lack of employment opportunities just as they were welcomed back by the leftist Mexican President Lázaro Cárdenas in the midst of land reform, at least 355,000 people left the United States for Mexico in the 1930s, a large proportion of them from California. Forty percent of those who left were U.S. citizens, mostly children leaving with noncitizen parents. The most conservative estimates suggest over 35,000 people were forcibly deported in official federal proceedings. Luckily for planters, however, desperate white sharecroppers who had been driven out of Oklahoma and Texas by the boll weevil, drought, and economic depression, flooded the state. In just five years, 400,000 "Okies" entered California in search of work, becoming the predominant workforce in the cotton industry by the end of the decade.[33]

Chambers of Commerce in Oklahoma's cotton counties planted stories in local newspapers that boasted of high wages and glorious weather to the west. The son of one sharecropper remembered the sense of hope as his father saved up enough to leave their "rundown mortgaged Oklahoma farm." "California was his dream," the Bakersfield singer-songwriter Merle Haggard sang of his father in 1969, "for he had seen pictures in magazines that told him so." He was quickly disillusioned. Instead of working profitable farms under a gentle sun, thousands of men like Haggard's father found themselves settled in "labor camps . . . filled with worried men with broken dreams." Haggard focused on the continuity between old Cotton Belt and new, singing that the only change he saw in his father was his hair going gray from worry. But if anything, the migrants from Oklahoma found themselves in a world more like that of the classic plantation than they had ever experienced.[34]

Instead of working their own plots under sharecropping agreements, as they had back home, these men now worked "on large ranches in labor crews, chopping and picking mile-long rows of seemingly endless cotton," as historian Devra Weber puts it. They were brought on to centrally managed plantations as temporary hands for chopping and picking season. They had no claims to a homeplace on the property, so if they came on to the land at other times of year, they were treated as trespassers. In Oklahoma, they had planted and cultivated the cotton crop from seed to boll, worrying seedlings into growth, tracking the weather in the sky as they followed their mule down the rows of cotton. No longer did most of them have the chance to apply their hard-won knowledge of plants, animals, and the weather. In counties like Kern and Fresno, workers had a distant relationship to the crop itself, and no pride to take in the harvest.[35]

As the travails of Okie migrants reveal, during the New Deal, California planters continued to draw on the historical patterns set by the Deep South plantation system. They benefited from its economic and ecological weaknesses as well as from its continued political power. On the one hand, the economic decline of the Deep South Cotton Belt produced a cohort of desperate white sharecroppers that became the core of the new workforce in California cotton fields after 1933. On the other hand, they drew strength from the Southern plantation belt's Democratic senators and congressmen, whose votes made the difference between the success and failure of Roosevelt's major policy initiatives in the 1930s.

Southern lawmakers committed to maintaining the plantation's low-wage, white-supremacist system insisted that the new rights and protections accorded to American workers at the federal level exclude agricultural and domestic laborers. Not surprisingly, these were the two branches of employment in which the vast majority of Black Southerners toiled, a legacy of the antebellum cotton field and the Great House, respectively. California's planters benefited directly from this exemption, because it also protected their own plantations from the threat of federally supported unionization, arbitration, and a minimum wage.

West Coast planters also found allies in the Southern-dominated Agricultural Adjustment Administration, with Wofford Camp serving as head agricultural economist for the cotton industry nationwide in the mid-1930s. In an act of self-dealing extreme even for California agricultural magnates, Camp's cotton plantation was paid over $30,000 of relief money by his own agency (planters received compensatory payments from the AAA for voluntarily reducing the acreage of cotton they planted, which was far less of a sacrifice in California, because they got so much more cotton out of each acre than in the Southern Piedmont). Boswell beat him out, getting $53,000, while small cotton farmers received little payout from the AAA, and laborers received none. With the Southern-inflected version of the New Deal operating in their favor, California cotton planters supported other parts of the New Deal's agenda, especially when it came to the water they needed to nourish their sprawling fields.[36]

CHAPTER 20

Sinking

The Central Valley's arid climate meant that planters from the Old South were now free from the pests and fungi that had long vexed their efforts to maximize cotton harvests. The same climate made them dependent on a reliable supply of piped water. By 1920, 60 percent of California's agricultural units already depended on the federal government's $200 million worth of irrigation works. Large planters had also commandeered the region's rivers by building canals on an individual basis, but by the early twentieth century plans were afoot to engineer a far more ambitious and centralized system of water control across the entire state. The first iteration of a master plan was seen in 1919. It would bring together what geographers Theo Claire and Kevin Surprise describe as "hundreds of disparate irrigation projects in a unified system of water resource management" that involved dams, aqueducts, canals, and pumping stations. In preparation, the state engineer of California carried out a detailed hydrological survey of over two hundred thousand acres of land to ensure "the maximum conservation, control, storage, distribution, and application of all the waters of the state."[1]

Discussed for decades, such gargantuan projects became possible under the expanded infrastructural state of the New Deal. In what eventually became known as the Central Valley Project, engineers and laborers rearranged the water flow of the entire western region in the 1930s. The CVP encompassed land from some of the highest points in the continental United States (the fourteen-thousand-foot peak of Mount Shasta) all the way to the Pacific Ocean. The project's centerpiece was a network of canals, river improvements, and pumping stations that stretched half the length of the state. As Mark Arax writes, "Scientists would one day record California's irrigated miracle as the greatest human alteration of a physical environment in history," nearly all of it to slake the thirst of commodity crops.[2]

While the hulking Shasta and Hoover dams immediately became incorporated into America's iconography of engineering feats, huge

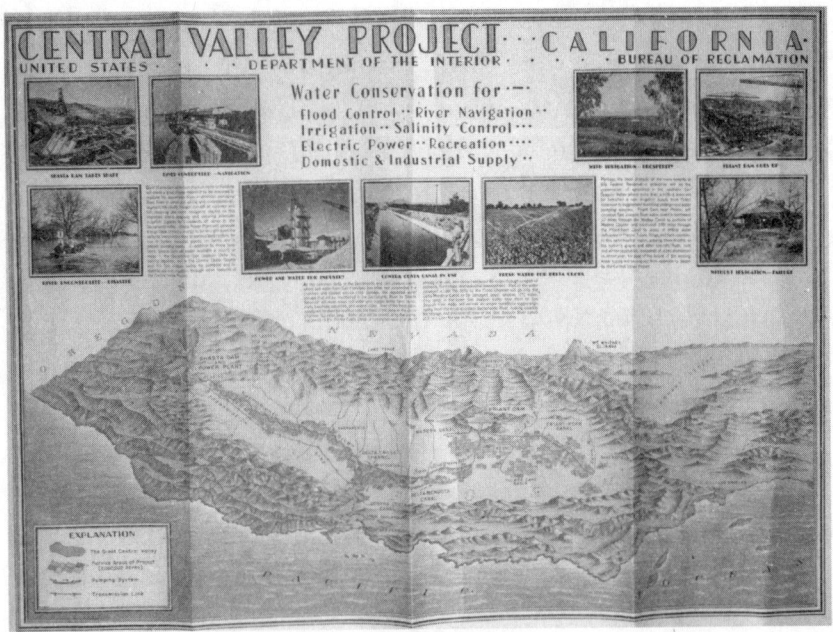

Central Valley Project water conservation map, ca. 1930–1940.

waterworks like the 150-mile long Friant-Kern Canal received less notice. Just one of the four major canals that made up the CVP, it bathed the cotton plantations and other agribusiness units of the arid Tulare Basin in millions of acre-feet of water per year. The replumbing of North America's far western watershed was largely complete by the early 1940s. Piped water became a "second nature," reported on in daily newspapers as if it were a facet of the weather: "San Joaquin River inflow 519 second-feet; Friant Dam storage 247,945 acre-feet; dam release 50 second-feet," read a typical column.[3]

Water became so cheap that by 1960 agronomists at the U.S. Cotton Field Station in Shafter were advising the region's cotton planters to stop overirrigating their plants. The state's provision of abundant water gave planters like James G. Boswell an actually existing monocultural landscape they could only have dreamed of back in Georgia. Instead of having to look at the skies and hope for rain, California planters could rely on a flattened, drained, ditched, dammed, and watered environment tailor-made for centralized management and large-scale monocrop agriculture.[4]

Just as the Fresno scraper had flattened the hills and dales of central California, the CVP smoothed out the peaks and troughs of nature's seasons. Given the balmy temperatures in the Valley, irrigated water made an array of crops available to consumers year-round. Cotton could now provide a bridge between spring and fall. "Five and six years ago," wrote one breathless booster, "the summer was a dead season here in the [Imperial] Valley. It was a time when many fields lay fallow, when nothing was being produced or marketed from a large portion of our lands. Unlimited production of cotton changed all that. People stayed in the Valley, worked hard, made money. As a result, business improved, air-conditioning became a necessity, people began to keep up their houses and yards and the whole Imperial Valley community made great progressive strides. We owe a great deal to King Cotton."[5]

Although large-scale monocrop agriculture and large-scale hydraulic engineering had been conjoined ever since the California wheat craze of the 1880s, a third factor now entered the picture: petroleum. As early as 1903, California led the nation in barrels of crude oil produced. The state boosted production throughout the 1920s, ranking near the top of oil-producing states for the rest of the century. An "epicenter of petrochemical R&D," California pioneered new applications to make sure its endless gush of oil stayed profitable. When Shell Oil Company's new Los Angeles factory commenced operations in 1929, it became the first facility in the United States to manufacture synthetic nitrate fertilizer from the by-products of oil extraction. The state soon operated as many such factories as the rest of the nation combined. Not surprisingly, California's planters and growers also led the nation in the adoption of petroleum-dependent farming. In spite of the native fertility of much of the soil, which had only been intensively cultivated for a few decades, use of synthetic fertilizer in the state increased by twenty times between 1940 and 1980.[6]

While cheap water allowed for year-round productivity, new kinds of petroleum-based soil "preparations" seemed to make real another long-held dream of the plantation's ruling classes: intensified monoculture on the same fields, year after year. The impossibility of farming the same fields in the nineteenth century had created in many cotton planters a fever for territorial acquisition that helped cause the Civil War. If one instead wanted to farm the same ground over decades, costly and labor-intensive crop rotations and "green manuring" were needed to fight the insects, aphids, and fungal pathogens that build up in soil. No longer. New synthetic pesticides and fungicides, made in and for California in the age of cheap oil, enabled what geographer Adam Romero calls "monocultures of time."[7]

In order to be plantable year after year, for example, strawberry fields were treated with methyl bromide. Subsoil fumigators injected the root zone of the freshly plowed rows with a toxic steam treatment that included chloropicrin, the active ingredient in tear gas. The field was then covered in plastic (another new use for petroleum), and the young strawberry plants pushed through holes in the tarp. Methyl bromide is now classified by the EPA as an "acute toxin" and a "Class 1 ozone-depleting substance." It is extremely toxic, causing "central nervous system and respiratory system failures" in people exposed to even small doses. In large doses, it can cause a lingering death, with ataxia, muscle spasms, and a coma lasting a couple of weeks. In the 1980s, nearly twenty people died due to exposure to trace amounts of the chemical through its use as a household fumigant. In the soils of the Central Valley, few microorganisms survived repeated methyl bromide treatment, so while there were no productivity-sapping pests, any fertility had to be added artificially to the field—with the petroleum by-product of synthetic nitrogen fertilizer.[8]

Methyl bromide was far from the only such substance to find wide application. California companies like Pacific R&H Chemical Corporation, founded in the 1930s, developed new variants of borax, chlorine, and even cyanide gas, which was used to fumigate citrus groves. Farm machinery companies invented new tools for applying insecticides, moving from handheld pumps to engine-powered spray rigs. Planters added crop-dusting helicopters and airplanes to their antipest arsenal in the 1950s. Millions of pounds of these substances were dropped, sprayed, pumped, poured, steamed, and injected into the state's environment every year. Effective in producing monocultures, but requiring planters to use more of the chemicals each cycle, these technologies then spread to the rest of the country.[9]

In the middle decades of the twentieth century, "fossil capitalism," a "hydraulic state," and the monocultural plantation together pushed California to the top of the national heap in agricultural productivity. Between 1930 and 1997, California was always in the top three farm states by value of output. From the 1950s until the end of the twentieth century, California was always first. The abundant gushes of water and oil in the new Eden of the American West sometimes led to delusions of grandeur and a forgetting of nature's limits. One scientist even blushed that soil fumigation could "restore [the] virginity" of cropland. Perhaps, such optimists wondered, plantation capitalism's cycle of booms and busts was over.[10]

Yet the yoking of water and oil to the plantation created unprecedented dangers. Throughout the history of agriculture, yield-killing microorganisms had provided an important guardrail, forcing farmers to strike a balance between growth and constraint. The planter's heedless desire for "making everything work" now found no counterweight. At least not in the short term. While the conjuncture of petroleum engineering, piped water, and California sun was celebrated as a revolutionary unshackling of productive power, this hitherto unimaginable plenty soon became an existential risk in itself.

In the 1860s, Karl Marx described the unemployed masses in any capitalist society as a "reserve army of labor" standing behind the actively employed working class. No accident in the normal functioning of markets, a two-tiered proletariat was essential to how capitalism worked. Every time the economy expanded, firms employed more workers. Yet that same expansion spurred technical advancements in factory production that ejected an even larger number of manual laborers into the ranks of the unemployed. Industrial capitalism exhaled a mass of people so desperate for work that their very existence held down wages for everyone else, lowering costs for capitalists. Although capitalism continually created this labor surplus, Marx observed, capitalists still took extra measures to increase the numbers of desperate poor at their disposal. Land enclosures, vagrancy laws, and the criminalization of noncapitalist livelihoods shunted ever more people into the ranks of the "reserve army."

Over the decades of its agricultural supremacy in the mid-twentieth century, the State of California would create a new kind of reserve army: a cross-border flow of noncitizen workers lacking political rights who found themselves in a position of physical deprivation, and who were defined by a disparaged racial identity that made their very lives cheap. Union organizer Ernesto Galarza described planters' ideal workforce as "a completely elastic farm labor pool which could be marshaled on a few hours' notice." Cotton planter G. W. Guiberson admitted, "The class of labor we want is the kind we can send home when we get through with them." As the labor pool of Okie migrants dried up, planters turned back to the southern border as the source of the majority of their workers.[11]

Between 1942 and 1964, a bilateral agreement between the United States and Mexico known as the Bracero Program brought 4.75 million Mexican citizens—an average of 200,000 per year—on short-term contracts to labor in American agriculture. The public sector even assumed many of the costs of allocation: Growers were allowed to take over the large government labor camps constructed with taxpayer money during the Great Depression. The government negotiated and administered the Bracero Program, doling out workers to different employers. While it was originally designed to help farmers deal with wartime labor shortages, the program continued for another two decades after the end of World War II.[12]

Unsatisfied with the numbers of workers thus made available to them, big planters and growers would combine the Bracero Program with the employment of undocumented workers to keep wages low and workers unorganized. Their goal was to maximize the number of needy seekers of work, which made individual workers readily replaceable and thus unlikely to demand higher wages or an improvement in conditions. One Border Patrol officer who had participated in immigration raids in the 1940s stated that the planter who used undocumented workers "has a conscience similar to that of the pre–Civil War slave owner. He is an overlord of all that he surveys and considers his right to the peon labor as practically a divine one."[13]

Planters took this philosophy so far that in 1948, Mexico temporarily suspended the program because U.S. planters had continued to recruit unilaterally across the border, against the terms of the agreement. As a record cotton crop ripened in the fields, the INS had "opened the border wide at El Paso . . . to allow the entrance of some four thousand undocumented workers," which would lower the wages of the braceros and others already employed.[14]

Immigration hawks in U.S. policymaking circles were displeased with such "open borders" shenanigans, even if California's ruling class deemed them a necessary evil to keep agricultural profits robust and cheap products flowing to U.S. consumers. Among the opponents of undocumented immigration was Harlon Carter, the Border Patrol chief under President Eisenhower. Carter was a troubling choice for the post. Hailing from Laredo, Texas, he had shot and killed a Mexican American teenager named Ramon Casiano for the sin of hanging out in front of Carter's home. A jury convicted him, but he was let off on a technicality. In 1954, he spearheaded "Operation Wetback," which he described as an "all-out war to hurl ... Mexican wetbacks back into Mexico." Indeed, Border Patrol set up a maze of new checkpoints and conducted raids on workplaces in California as well as other Southwestern states. Before the program went into effect, Carter met with agricultural employers, promising to loosen the requirements that the Bracero Program imposed on employers in return for them giving up their dependence on the undocumented.[15]

After 1954, Carter's changes allowed planters and growers to reduce braceros' wages and let their housing deteriorate. Even the limited provisions that still existed were rarely enforced. Many planters felt the contract was "just a piece of paper," and they could pay the wages and provide the housing that they chose. More and more, the immigration agencies of federal, state, and local governments excluded organized labor and the Mexican Consulate from policymaking decisions. Planters and growers who had once loathed the restrictions of the Bracero Program as "socialistic" now advocated for its expansion.[16]

The creation of a permanent labor surplus in the San Joaquin Valley made the cotton counties of California more plantationized than contemporary cotton zones in the rural Piedmont of Georgia and Alabama, where the descendants of enslaved people formed a majority of the population in the early twentieth century. Heirs of the struggles of Reconstruction, Black tenants and landowners in the Old South exercised historical claims to the land, however tenuous. And they continued to insist on controlling their own work, however grueling it was.

In California, by contrast, planters won the labor arrangement they had been clamoring for since 1865: a racialized workforce, toiling in gangs, for cash wages, under the supervision of bosses. These workers had no property claims to the land or to the crop. With few legal protections and no citizens' rights, the braceros were forced to leave each season. Lacking full-time residences or legal status, they struggled to unionize or to exert influence through local politicians, churches, or community groups.

The collusion between California agribusiness and the federal government reached its most absurd point in 1954, when the U.S. Department of Labor created the Regional Foreign Labor Operations Advisory Committee. RFLOAC was, in essence, an official avenue for big cotton planters, as well as large produce growers, to advise the Department of Labor on immigration policy. The committee included no representatives of the workers, and none from the Mexican government. So scandalous was the one-sidedness of the organization that its existence was kept secret. The moment journalists sniffed it out, RFLOAC's heads resigned and discontinued the program. If they had had to face public scrutiny, the truth would likely have become undeniable: In running a peacetime Bracero Program for two crucial decades in the history of California agriculture, the U.S. Department of Labor, along with the INS and Border Patrol, had with little controversy relegalized an international traffic in unfree labor 150 years after the legal end of the Atlantic slave trade.

This dependence on rightless, racialized laborers, transferred across national boundaries by the hundreds of thousands per year to work on centrally managed, large-scale commodity crop agricultural units marks the California cotton fields as plantations. And the United States, supposedly the leader of the free world and an arsenal of democracy, had been acting as a disciplinary arm of capital, working on behalf of planters to maintain a reserve army of plantation labor. Still, the continuing risk of strikes drove California's cotton planters to empty the fields of human labor almost entirely in the 1950s.[17]

In 1949, disturbing reports surfaced about conditions in the workers' camps of the Central Valley. In the cotton counties of Tulare and Kings alone, twenty-eight infants were certified to have died from malnutrition and poor sanitary conditions that year. Protesting the widespread suffering, woefully inadequate wages, and inconsistent employment, cotton pickers rocked Tulare and Kings counties with a massive strike that year. Organized under the umbrella of the National Farm Labor Union, an offshoot of the STFU, which Ned Cobb had joined in Georgia in 1932, the interracial strike even included a young Cesar Chavez. Southern planters like Boswell, Salyer, and Camp suffered the most walkouts. Desperate to recommence the harvest, they urged local law enforcement to pass new laws curtailing free speech. Many strikers were arrested for the crime of "parading." The NFLU's Mexican, Okie, and Black members let themselves be arrested, vowing to "fill jails" in defense of their strike for better pay. Yet this time the big planters were foiled by a group of smaller landowners who broke ranks, signing a separate agreement with the union that included higher wages.[18]

Facing the reality of increased labor costs, planters now made good on their mid-strike threat to "use all available picking machines." Two years after the strike, 50 percent of the state's cotton was picked without human hands. "With the hum of mechanical planters, choppers and pickers growing louder in California's fields," *The Madera Tribune* reported sunnily in 1952, "growers are predicting that the Golden State will overtake Texas, claim highest place in King Cotton's courts." Chopping and picking had been done with the same techniques of hand and hoe since the colonial era; the conquest of America's cotton fields by gas-powered machinery after World War II was incredibly rapid, and nowhere more so than in California. Of six thousand mechanical pickers in use across the country in 1951, about half were operated in the San Joaquin Valley alone.[19]

As much as higher wages, the anxiety over falling prices sat at the root of the race to mechanize. "Through it all ran the fear of surpluses," noted one observer from the USDA of planters' interest in ridding the fields of working people.[20] The threat posed by synthetic cloth like nylon—a laboratory-made by-product of surplus petroleum—had become clear to planters even before the strike. As early as 1946, the American Cotton Council's California branch was warning planters that if they wanted to compete "with such fibers as rayon, nylon, etc... cotton growers must... do everything possible to reduce their costs." Most planters seemed to agree "that this could most effectively be done by complete mechanization." One influential cotton magnate noted that because "one machine can replace 35 to 40 cotton pickers," mechanization had become an urgent necessity. In the context of infinitely expanding cheap products made from surplus commodities like petroleum and pine, even the existence of a permanent labor surplus in California did not cut enough costs on its own. The cotton bowl was pushed by global competitors into a productivity revolution that changed the face of the San Joaquin Valley. The strike wave of 1949 simply made their decision easier.[21]

To develop a better harvesting machine, planter-led groups including the Cotton Council and the Delta Council had teamed up with USDA agricultural experiment stations and International Harvester under the aegis of the federally funded Cotton Mechanization Project in 1946. Their collective task: not simply to manufacture the right kind of machine, but to reengineer the entire system of cotton production around an automatic harvester. First, new varieties of cotton had to be developed. Since mechanical pickers vacuumed up plants, twigs, and dirt indiscriminately, cotton experts sought to breed varieties where the bolls would set higher on the stalk. Wofford Camp's one-variety community, established in 1924 to fight grade degeneration and thus maintain sale prices, turned out to be a boon for mechanization in the fields as well. A monoculture in higher stalk bolls allowed easier adoption of machinery.[22]

The cheap, fast, though imprecise work of the mechanical picker sealed the fate of the Piedmont cotton regions of Georgia and Alabama, solidifying the status of the flat, open plains of the Mississippi Delta, central Texas, and the San Joaquin Valley as the national cotton bowls. The large number of localized cotton varieties in the Southeastern states slowed the adoption of a functioning mechanical harvester. Moreover, picking machines were so expensive that they did not pay on any but the largest fields, and California's fields were on average far larger than their competitors in the Lower Piedmont. Equally important were the ways in which renters had forced on the planters a subdivided landscape. Planters in the southeast would have had to break the power of the renters, tear down all the fences, and move all their structures away to cultivate a single large field as they had during slavery. While some planters did this, most did not see the use. Because California averaged twice the yields of cotton per acre as competing states, the cash laid out in buying the machine was recouped at a much faster rate than in the rest of the country. And because the picking season was so much longer in Central California, and the rain-related delays in picking so infrequent, harvesting machinery could be used for four times as many working hours as in the Southeast.[23]

Planters pursued mechanization out of a fear of falling prices due to excessive supply—workers' predominant experience was being made surplus themselves. Mechanization and chemicalization lifted labor productivity ceaselessly upward, pushing more and more workers out of the cotton sector. In the 1950s, the rapid mechanization of California's cotton sector eliminated more than one of every ten jobs in the state's agricultural workforce. Thus, while the number of workers required for the cotton harvest shrank rapidly, so did the number of individual farms growing the white fiber. There were three hundred thousand independent operators growing cotton in the United States in 1950; in 1974, just eighty thousand remained.[24]

The attempts of the USDA to restrict cotton acreage in order to stem the falling prices only worsened the problem. Hemmed-in planters further mechanized and chemicalized their operations in the race to grow more pounds of cotton on a reduced number of acres. They were quite successful: Yields of California cotton increased from around five hundred pounds per acre in the mid-1930s to a thousand pounds per acre in 1964. As the productive capacity of the plantation system grew, the government's attempts to rein in surpluses became a lid rattling atop a simmering volcano.[25]

Again, oil was crucial. And no place in America embodied that fact better than Kern County, California, which was both one of the leading cotton counties and one of the leading oil counties in the nation. The delaborization of cotton through mechanization itself required new petrochemicals. When a field was harvested by hand, pickers could work around invasive grasses, but machines would simply gather them in with the cotton. Thus, the machine picker called for better preemergent herbicides. Chemical defoliants were used to strip the leaves off the plants just before harvest for the same reason. Cotton petroplanters used so much defoliant that they made their own weather in the Valley. Every fall, when harvest began and the crop dusters dropped thousands of gallons of "Ginstar" defoliant from the sky, an unusual number of town dwellers would come down with a flu-like respiratory sickness they dubbed "defoliant cold."[26]

The prodigious use of fertilizer, herbicides, and defoliants created unforeseen consequences that could only be dealt with via the application of still more petroleum products. Cropfield weeds, for example, feed on nitrates as promiscuously as crops do. Fields that had been soaked in fertilizers thus suffered from weed problems, calling for preemergent herbicides, most of which were fossil fuel–based. Crops nursed on generous amounts of cheap water and fertilizer also grew broad, moist leaves that attracted expanded populations of worms, grubs, mollusks, and other yield killers. Petrofertilizer husbandry thus beckoned petroinsecticides to the fields. Much like herbicides, insecticides also forced farmers onto a "treadmill." If an insect species could withstand an initial round of broad-spectrum poisoning, it would find itself with no predators. Local birds, bats, and other insectivores were all killed. The surviving pest would reproduce prodigiously, meaning that ever-intensifying rounds of spraying were needed.[27]

Clearly, the mechanization of cotton was a boon for the oil industry. After the 1930s, Shell Oil, often in collaboration with the faculty in the University of California system and the USDA, began to explore ways of capturing waste gas from the petroleum industry and transforming it into marketable materials. The results, heralded as a brilliant success of modern chemistry, included the toxic soil fumigant DDT, along with thousands of other novel petrochemical products.

California was the undisputed leader in the use of these generalized poisons, absorbing into its soils, waterways, and air "more pesticides than anywhere else on earth" by the 1960s, according to historian Doug Sackman. And no sector of the state's agriculture used more pesticides per acre than cotton. Workers faced exposure to these chemicals on a daily basis in the fields, and even on their journey from Mexico: Thousands of braceros were forced to disrobe in government "delousing sheds" at the southern border, where they were sprayed with copious amounts of DDT. The manifold new uses for petroleum, which were often doctored up to resolve problems of overproduction and falling prices, augured a new approach to the government regulation of capitalism in the post–World War II era.[28]

During the New Deal, policymakers had dealt with the issue of low prices for farm goods by restricting production. The most noteworthy example is the great cotton plow-up of 1933, when the federal government offered payments to farmers who would agree to have one-third of their cotton crop, already in the ground, destroyed. However, a new era in state-sponsored agro-industrial science began in 1946 when Congress passed the Research and Marketing Act, which earmarked research dollars to attack the scourge of overproduction with research into new applications for surplus goods. Ceaseless expansion, not rational limits, was the only appropriate response to problems in the economy. Too much cotton? Invent new uses and sell new needs to the public. Too much oil? Engineer countless novel products to absorb the supply, especially products that will engender the need for still more petroleum goods. While California's environment was one crucial sink for petrochemical surpluses that enabled continual expansion of drilling and refining, an even more pivotal discovery was that the body of the consumer could be a dumping ground for petro-agricultural surpluses.

As Michael Pollan has written, the salient fact of modern agriculture is that you can't make money from growing things in fields. Profit comes from processing those things into a huge variety of slightly different goods that come in shiny packages, are easy to ship, never rot, and contain habit-forming levels of sodium and sugar. The industrial science of dealing with surpluses by coming up with new consumer products emerged around 1900, and its practitioners called it "chemurgy." Like cool water flowing out of the Sierra snowpack every spring, the chemurgical urge required a sink. And the "old" cotton plantation led the way.[29]

David Wesson's laboratory at the Cottonseed Oil Company in Savannah, Georgia, in the 1890s had first resolved the problem of how to neutralize the stink from cottonseed oil to make it seem more like a food product. The old plantation bale became the main ingredient in Wesson's Vegetable Oil. However, cotton did not fully make the leap to industrial food product until the development—first broadly applied amid the agricultural recession of the 1920s—of a new hydrogenation process that allowed seed oils to be used in solid spreads like margarine and mayonnaise. Hydrogenation may have helped counteract the decline in prices for raw cotton by turning the cottonseeds—now a waste item because California's "one-variety" law forced planters to buy seed on an annual basis from breeders—into countless different salad dressings, or an unending cascade of slivers of fried potato. Most importantly, California cottonseed began to be processed into cheap cattle feed that helped the city of Dallas "turn a billion steers / into buildings made of mirrors," as David Berman of the band Silver Jews once crooned about the profits ranchers used to build a glimmering skyline in Texas. In 1948, the American Cotton Council boasted that 99 percent of cottonseed oil went into edible products.[30]

While other commodity producers lagged behind cotton at first, the chemurgical urge soon spread to all products of California's high-powered agricultural sector, which were increasingly threatened by the specter of profit-killing surpluses. America's modern food system is in many ways the result of the "fear of surpluses" that transformed the mindsets of planters, growers, agronomists, and policymakers in the twentieth century. No other state has contributed as much in terms of acreage, dollar value, or technology to America's processed food industry, and no state played as pioneering a role in its emergence as California. The surplus dump par excellence was the modern supermarket—that was created in California as well.

Safeway started as a statewide chain of small grocery stores in the 1920s, but pioneered the giant "supermarket" model in the 1940s. Averaging six thousand items for sale by 1960 (over half of these products had not even existed in 1945, and "high-value added prepared foods" predominated among these), the novel consumer space was tailor-made for profitable dumping of excess agricultural products. Safeway supermarket, along with other chains that followed its lead in exponentially expanding offerings, coevolved with car culture. Because so many of the purchases were refrigerated or frozen and had to be taken home fast, big parking lots coated with blacktop made from petroleum hosted big cars guzzling cheap oil in front of the supermarket. Fossil capitalism had been responsible for bringing product and customer to their meeting point at the gleaming, frosty displays of orange juice concentrate and homogenized milk.[31]

In the decades after World War II, self-service shopping, intense lighting, high ceilings, broad aisles, and open displays of blemish-free produce replaced the more ethnically specific mom-and-pop grocery stores. Safeway was the biggest grocery chain in America by the 1970s. However, certain parts of the country had populations with so little disposable income that they could not sustain a supermarket, creating food deserts in regions that exported food products to the rest of the nation, and indeed, the world. Nothing is more plantation-like than that. One of those places was the origin point of the California plantation: James G. Boswell's old stomping ground of Corcoran, where the only Safeway market shut down in the late twentieth century due to the dwindling buying power of the folks living in town.[32]

In 1985, Corcoran cotton magnate—and longtime Boswell family rival—Fred Salyer defaulted on a Bank of America loan. Eager to cut costs, Salyer hatched a plan to outsource plantation jobs to independent contractors whose laborers would earn far less than company employees. When the UFW responded by going on strike, an article in the elite-run *Corcoran Journal* reminded workers that cotton jobs were on the decline, and "the community isn't the same as it was 15 or 20 years ago." Indeed, the 1970s had not been kind to California's cotton bowl.[33]

In 1973, the Organization of Petroleum Exporting Countries established a cartel and launched its first oil embargo (along with a much more damaging restriction of oil production in 1979), putting an end to the post-Depression period of high-growth capitalism based on fossil fuels. Cotton plantations had propped themselves up on the tripod of cheap oil, cheap water, and government subsidy, but now one of the legs was taken away. Then, as runaway inflation was already bringing down agricultural wages and planters' profits, severe drought hit California in 1976 and 1977. State water regulators severely restricted the flows of water through the canals of the CVP. That pulled away a second leg of support.[34]

Ceaseless groundwater pumping was agricultural firms' solution to the new limits on state water. Massive wells dug by planters like Boswell and Salyer soon brought selenium salts to the surface. At the same time, state geologists noticed that, while the state's ecology was being used as a "sink" for excess petroleum, and the bodies of its citizens as a "sink" for surplus food, the land of the Central Valley itself was sinking. Overpumping of groundwater made the areas around Corcoran "subside" into the earth as much as five feet a decade. The environmental blowback of the reengineered Central Valley was becoming undeniable. All the selenium that farmers were drawing to the surface salinated their lands, so they pumped the chemical in unheard-of concentrations into hundreds of acres of ponds they kept for the purpose. Those ponds, however, surrounded the Kesterton National Wildlife Refuge and looked inviting to hundreds of thousands of migrating birds. Moreover, in 1983, a cotton planter named Russell Giffen had suffered leakage into the refuge, killing thousands of ducks. A wildlife biologist working for the federal government found "beaks twisted into corkscrews. Gullets half-formed. Brains spilling out from skulls. Eyes missing. Wings that could not flap," writes Mark Arax.[35]

The problems continued to mount. A strong dollar in the 1980s made it difficult for California's producers to compete on world markets. Cotton producers in China, Russia, and Brazil cut into California's share of the world market, and synthetics continued to take customers away. By the 1980s, much of the cotton land in Tulare and Kings counties had been left fallow. Planters found they could make millions of dollars a year simply by selling their surface water allowances to growing metropolitan areas like Los Angeles. However, there was hope. Just before the 1985 strike, the Kings County Board of Supervisors had unanimously approved a plan "to ask the [California Department of Corrections] to site a prison near Corcoran in order to aid the town's flagging economy." "Corcoran needs another anchor," a local cotton planter noted, and a prison would be just that. The state purchased a plot of abandoned land outside of town, likely once planted in cotton.[36]

Atop the drained, scraped bed of Tulare Lake, where first wheat farmers and then cotton planters had engineered cash crop booms in the nineteenth and twentieth centuries, the construction of Corcoran State Prison began the same year as the cotton strike. The prison went into operation in 1988. It was just one of the correctional facilities built in the Central Valley. The region would be the site of what Ruth Gilmore has described as "the biggest prison-building project in the history of the world." By the 1990s, the cotton valley had become "Prison Alley." Corcoran's prison architects foregrounded the connection between plantations and corrections by featuring a cotton field on the institution's coat of arms, which new inmates could see as they were bused in. Converting spent, polluted, and exhausted plantation ground into prison ground for young people of color makes sense from the perspective of the planters who still wielded outsize power over the town. For four centuries, the plantation has been prisonlike for those who have been made to work inside it.[37]

The surpassing of the very idea of limits had created a deadly feedback loop in California. Surplus money from the USDA and cheap water from the state kept the system of overfarming a rational approach from the perspective of planters and growers. Surplus fertility through petrochemicals fed algae and weeds, and surplus labor fed the prison system. Far from having escaped the burden of the past, people living in and around the California cotton bowl seemed to be coughing, sinking, and drowning in the history of the plantation.

CHAPTER 21

In Cotton's Wake

Driving west from Athens, one passes through Gainesville, Georgia. Nowadays a commuter college exurb of Atlanta, the town is also known as "the Poultry Capital of the World." There is even a Chicken Monument at the center of town, a twenty-foot granite column with a rooster at the top. Most of the major private-sector employers are chicken processors like Pilgrim's Pride. Another giant is Koch Foods, one of the 125 biggest privately owned companies in the United States. Supplying packaged meat to Kroger and Walmart, as well as fast-food chains like Burger King, the Illinois-based company sites all of its major poultry processing plants in the former Cotton Belt of the South, employing fourteen thousand workers in Alabama, Mississippi, Tennessee, and Georgia. Why might this be so? The answer to this question, as to so many others in this book, lies in the history of the plantation, which first colonized this upcountry belt of northern Georgia in the decades after the Civil War, preparing it to become ground zero for the development of the industrial poultry system—and cheap fast food more broadly—in the United States.[1]

Although the Confederacy was created to save plantation slavery, regions that lay outside the Cotton Belt suffered much of the destruction during the Civil War. Consider "Upcountry" Georgia—the region in which Gainesville is located. A belt of hill counties running west to east across the state, it is sandwiched between the Lower Piedmont on its southern edge and the "mountain South" on its northern edge. After the expulsion of Cherokee landowners in the 1830s, smallholding white settlers had grown a broad mix of crops in the Upcountry, most of them for home use. While some owned a small number of slaves, most farmers did not. They pursued independence more than a fortune.

At twelve hundred feet above sea level, the rolling hills of the Upcountry saw cold come sooner in the fall and stay longer in the spring than in the Piedmont region to its south. The region was not well suited to clean-field agriculture, much less cotton husbandry. In all of Hall County, for example, there were only two plantations in 1860, while a typical Lower Piedmont county like Wilkes had ninety-eight. Though the non-slave-owning white yeomen who formed the vast majority of the Upcountry population were lukewarm on the matter of secession, when war came, they joined the fight in large numbers.[2]

Among the legions of farmers' sons that one typical Upcountry county provided to the Confederacy, the death toll may have exceeded 40 percent. When survivors returned home, they encountered scenes of profound neglect and devastation. Sherman's northern flank had come through Franklin and Hart counties, and the soldiers "just tore up everything as they came along. . . . They took all the cows, horses, and mules. They killed the hogs in the pens and carried them off for their own food." A Freedmen's Bureau agent dispatched to Carroll County in 1867 was shocked by "the extreme destitute poor of this poor poverty-stricken and godforsaken country." "Nothing plentiful here except pine trees flint rocks and reconstructionists," he joked. To make matters worse, veterans returned home to drought conditions, which played a role in reducing per capita grain production to 60 percent of its prewar level.³

While Upcountry farmers had not been wealthy in 1860, most of them had been independent. By 1870, they were searching desperately for a way to recover that independence. "I was glad that my life had been spared with whole bones," said one ex-Confederate soldier, "but I was in a tight place." Farmers' fences had been torn down by troops from both armies. The fields were overrun with weeds. Farmers needed to pay for repairs, draft animals, labor, and new machinery to get their farms back in order, but the sudden evaporation of millions of dollars in slave property had destroyed the South's banking system, making credit scarce. The diversified farming long practiced by Upcountry yeomen was not well suited to generating the short-term infusions of cash they now needed.⁴

The high price and cheap haulage of cotton made it the only crop that would pay. Upcountry farmers started contracting loans to buy cottonseed and fertilizer. *The Carroll County Times* reported in 1872 "that a considerable revolution has taken place in the last year or two.... Cotton, formerly cultivated on a very limited extent, has increased rapidly." Since credit could only be obtained in exchange for cotton, other aspects of a formerly mixed farming economy received less attention. As much as 40 percent of all Southern livestock had been destroyed during the war. For the rest of the century, livestock populations remained well below prewar levels. Basic food production likewise declined, and white farmers desperate to make ends meet plowed more and more of their domains, leaving little in forest. In effect, postwar hardship forced them to cannibalize the resources meant for the future to survive the present.⁵

Many white farmers had been drawn into cotton farming by abnormally high prices in 1865 and 1866. When cotton prices dipped in the 1870s, those who had gone into debt in the immediate postwar years lost their land to foreclosure, while their sons never had a chance to become landowners at all. By the 1880s, the majority of formerly independent yeomen in the Upcountry had fallen into the ranks of the landless. As with the evolving system of sharecropping within the Black-majority Piedmont of Georgia and Alabama, largely white farmers in the Upcountry had little choice but to enter tenancy arrangements with wealthy landowners. They soon found themselves losing control over the mix of crops that should be planted on the fields they rented. A typical 1870 contract stipulated that cropper Moses Moreland plant "30 acres in cotton and the balance in corn." He would owe half of each to the landowner. Food, clothing, and other farm inputs were increasingly purchased from the store, as landlords wanted croppers spending as much time as possible working their cotton crop. "This letting hands have [garden] patches ... is not a good plan and don't work well," groused Upcountry planter John Dent in 1876.[6]

A white working class sucked into the maw of the plantation system was something new. Now that the plantation was emancipating itself from slavery, it could bring in and exploit the kinds of workers it used to use as overseers or simply push out of the way. The global market forces of the post–Civil War world spread the cotton plantation across much wider parts of the American South than it had ever occupied before 1861. In the United States as a whole, "King Cotton" in 1860 had covered about nine million harvested acres. Expanding steadily from 1866, the total harvested acreage was thirty-five million in 1914.[7]

With the help of imported guano and newly laid railroads, cotton production surged out of its antebellum heartland to flood the Upcountry after the Civil War. In the 1870s, cotton production grew by 950 percent along the route of the new Southern Railway in Georgia, much of which traveled through a climatic area not well suited to the crop. No matter: New phosphate fertilizers allowed the cotton to be harvested before the first cold snap. By 1900, nearly half the state's total farm acreage was planted in cotton. One observer described the Upcountry landscape in the early twentieth century as having "no grain, no hay, no poultry, no vegetable gardens, no orchards." This is not a farming society. This is a zone given over entirely to producing cheap raw materials for global industry. Upcountry sharecroppers were not former slaves like their fel-

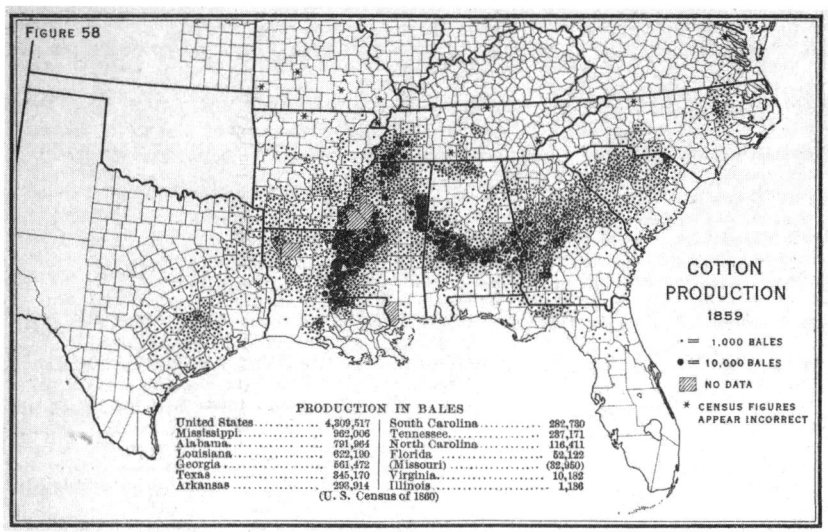

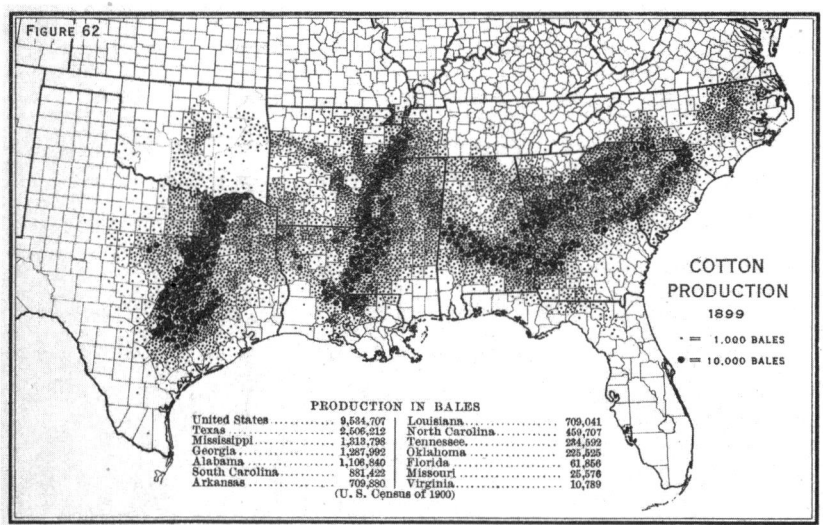

Cotton colonizes the South after Reconstruction.

low tenants in the Lower Piedmont. They had not risen up to their status from enslavement, but had descended into it from landownership. Otherwise, they had a lot in common.[8]

As the sharecropped, centrally managed plantation took over parts of the South that had not been plantationized previously, the rural working class both Black and white experienced a nutrition crisis. Deprived of healthy foods as well as medical care, one white sharecropper family kept close watch for "the worms that would rise out of their children's stomachs and nest in their throats so they had to be pulled out by hand to keep the children from choking." While poor Southerners of all races were saddled with many disease threats in the late nineteenth century, pellagra may have been the most relentless. With lesions, blisters, and thick peach fuzz on the face, along with severe diarrhea, the lethargic "pellagrin" would eventually succumb to dementia and death.[9]

The disease was a physical manifestation of the market pressure toward efficient monoculture. Conducting wide surveys throughout the South, researchers found that "hardly any sufferer had a garden." The vast majority of people diagnosed with the illness grew only cotton or tobacco, buying their supplies at a plantation commissary or company store. Most days, "fatback" pork from Midwestern packing firms was served with corn bread and molasses, livened up, in the good times, with hot coffee and sugar or "an occasional can of salmon." The prototypical "Southern" biscuit, although often assumed to be a "traditional" rural food in the South, was a twentieth-century addition to the tables of poor people, having been made affordable by an influx of cheap Midwestern wheat flour, usually bleached, and shorn of nutritional content by modern technology. When other niacin-rich foods like peas or greens were missing, such a diet led almost inevitably to pellagra and other plantation diseases.[10]

When asked to explain widespread ill health, planters often blamed their tenants for being lazy, dirty, and irresponsible. Lack, however, was not the lot of the irresponsible few. It was the bedrock of the plantation economy, and it impacted white sharecroppers caught up in the spread of the plantation system beyond its antebellum heartland. By 1920, cotton dominated the Upcountry. In Hall County, where 90 percent of all farm operators were white, over half of them were in some form of tenancy. Thus, outside the historic Cotton Belt, where the working class of the new cotton plantation was majority white, exploitation, indebtedness, and deprivation became their story as well. The plantation boom that beset the region in the latter half of the nineteenth century would lay the groundwork for America's industrial poultry system in the first half of the twentieth.[11]

In the years before the Great Depression, Upcountry croppers in Hall County hitched up their mules and made an annual trip to the county seat of Gainesville with loads of cotton for the gin. While in town, many of them stopped at the store of a feed, seed, and fertilizer dealer named Jesse Dickson Jewell to deliver their yearly cotton crop and pick up supplies for the next harvest. However, when cotton prices fell from over 18 cents per pound in 1929 to 6 cents per pound in 1932, the federal government, along with state governments, began to incentivize farmers and planters to grow less cotton. Between 1935 and 1940, one out of every four tenants in Cherokee, Forsyth, Hall, and Jackson counties dropped out of farming or became agricultural wage laborers. The plantation era of the Upcountry South had lasted about fifty years—enough time for about three generations of a family to live their lives serving the cotton plant.[12]

Jewell's client base thus dwindled. Amid the misery and upheaval, however, he saw opportunity. While cotton farmers were looking desperately for a new source of income, national feed manufacturers like Ralston Purina, suffering from the Depression's lack of consumer demand, had loads of surplus wheat and corn in their silos. He brought the two sides together in a fateful new combination. He began to advance baby chicks along with cheap feed to his former cotton croppers, telling them that raising hens was a sure replacement for their old line of work.

As cotton production died, the new occupation of "broiler-raising" spread among Upcountry landowners like Tom and Velva Blackstock. The couple had used their Agricultural Adjustment Administration check to repurpose their small cotton plantation for chick raising. In the transition, they evicted four tenant families, tore down a tenant house, and built their first poultry barn. This story repeated itself thousands of times in the Upcountry during the 1930s. As a local journalist declared in 1939, "The fuzzy down of the baby chick has all but ousted the fleecy lock of the cotton boll from its pedestal as chief money crop of Hall County." The sharecropped plantation's end was sped along by the draw of this new business opportunity—mainly for white farmers.[13]

At first, it was a great deal for Upcountry whites, especially considering the lack of alternatives. Most families already knew how to raise chickens, and doing so on a larger scale did not require expensive purchases. Even before Jewell got involved, rural women were capitalizing on the increased demand in towns and cities for the chickens and eggs they had long raised. After she began to raise chickens for herself in 1930, Mrs. O. H. Cooper remarked on "the joy and happiness of being the means of saving our home which we surely would have lost without my help, and my family having a decent living in the meantime, pays for all the discouragement." They could even sell their chickens to new grocery chains like A&P and Piggly Wiggly, which liked to advertise their meat and vegetables as "country produce" purchased from area farmers. Farm women familiarized themselves with breeding science and the newest feeds while navigating expanding and professionalized markets in meat and egg sales.[14]

The transition from cotton to poultry in the Upcountry accelerated during World War II, when hundreds of thousands of young people were drawn out of the Southern countryside by military service or by wage work in booming wartime factories. These mass migrations made rehabilitating the cotton industry difficult, especially because the rolling hills of the Upcountry didn't allow for easy adoption of automatic harvesters. The military, moreover, began to buy massive numbers of ready-to-cook chickens. Jewell took advantage, buying a processing plant in Gainesville and expanding it.[15]

By 1950, he was well on his way to cobbling together the country's first vertically integrated poultry industry. His company hatched chicks, outsourced them to area farmers, collected the grown hens, slaughtered them, packaged them, and sold them. Georgia produced only half a million chickens in 1935; the figure was sixty-three million in 1950. While Gainesville's surrounding area of Hall County was still cotton country during the Depression, poultry accounted for 86 percent of all of its agricultural sales by mid-century. As the business became more centralized and high volume in the postwar years, local farm women lost the ability to compete; the poultry industry became dominated by white capitalists like Jewell.[16]

With millions of people across the United States no longer growing crops and meat for themselves, and instead working for wages, a new kind of industrial food system took shape. The poultry industry emerged in tandem with the new institutions of the chain restaurant, and especially the national grocery chain. Previously, growers of chickens and eggs had clustered around cities. However, a new system of federally funded interstate highways, refrigerated trucks, and cheap diesel fuel made it possible to ruralize the poultry industry. Cheap land and cheap labor were served up by the predictable pattern of plantation booms and busts. For the chicken industry grew directly out of the plantation, in more ways than one.[17]

The relationship between the company J. D. Jewell, Inc., and the white ex-cotton farmer Arthur Flemming started when Flemming signed a "feed conversion contract." Soon after, one of Jewell's trucks rumbled down the lane to drop off a load of baby chicks, along with feed, medicine, chicken houses, heat lamps, and other means of production. Using Jewell's supplies, Flemming raised the birds to broiler size over several weeks. A truck from Jewell's company would then show up at the farm to transport the hens to the processing plant. The costs of all the supplies would be deducted from Flemming's share of the sale. Since he was operating on his own land, Flemming was on the hook for the water and electricity bills. The animal waste was also his responsibility. The farmer did not sell the grown birds in a competitive marketplace—anything he raised to maturity had been promised in advance to Jewell. The arrangement was "a formalized form of sharecropping" with the cropper taking on the risk but being kept blind to the conditions of the market within which his own produce was sold.[18]

Every five to ten years, the poultry company, known as an "integrator" because of its control over all the stages of production, would "modernize" its broiler-raising equipment in the name of quality control. The feed conversion contracts obligated farmers to purchase new henhouses and new feeding systems, as well as other equipment demanded by the companies. The seller of all the costly equipment? The very processing company demanding they be purchased. One of Jewell's contractors might step in at this moment and offer high-interest financing to help the farmer pay the poultry company.

This is the secret to why integrators like Jewell never raised broilers and fryers themselves. While they were selling cheaper and cheaper meat to grocery stores, restaurants, and schools, it was the *chicken farmers* who were always their main customers. Desperate ex–cotton farmers were a captive market, made vulnerable by previous rounds of plantation underdevelopment. Ironically, poultry farmers' ownership of the land, and their embedded ideology of landed independence, was used by the poultry firms to off-load costs of production, forgoing costly investments in land and machinery. Property ownership was transformed from an unusual freedom into a burden for the chicken farmers of the postcotton Upcountry. As historian Monica Gisolfi writes, Flemming and others like him gradually figured out "they had replaced one form of one-crop agriculture with another, and one form of debt for another."[19]

Early integrators did not just capitalize on the poverty of the post–cotton boom Upcountry region. They even repurposed the cotton landlords' exploitative crop lien system for poultry. Just as the Georgia Supreme Court had defined the sharecropping arrangement as a wage relation in the 1870s, in the 1950s the USDA declared the feed conversion contract as "close to a wage contract," codifying the subservient status of the poultry farmer. Although he was technically an independent owner-operator on his own land, Flemming felt more like an alienated factory worker. "You don't touch it," he said of the feed delivered to the flock.

In the new mechanized feeding system, "[The feed] goes from the truck into the bin, from the bin into the feeder in the chicken house and from that feeder in the chicken house, distributes itself automatically through the chicken house." Although Flemming was able to keep ownership of his land, what happened on it was increasingly out of his power. He was visited weekly by supervisors from the company who instructed him how to raise the birds. He tried hard to do what they said, because if he lost their favor, or refused to purchase new equipment required in the feed conversion contract, "you got to hunt you up somebody else," and there were fewer and fewer competitors in the market. Too often, the basic arrangement ended badly for farmers.[20]

Putting pressure on the chicken growers to cut costs, new national poultry giants took shape amid a wave of consolidation in the 1960s: established grain millers like Ralston Purina and Perdue Farms bought the first generation of integrators—Jewell's Gainesville processing mill was absorbed by Pillsbury. Poultry firms discovered chickens could be raised more cheaply in high concentrations, so they stopped signing deals with small farmers altogether. As the farmer B. A. Tatum put it in 1965, "The big boys has got all the chickens [and] they ain't going to turn any of it loose."[21]

The change in Hall County was astounding. While over 1,100 farms were involved in poultry raising in 1954, by 1969 only 308 remained. Early integrators like Jewell had promised poor cotton farmers that the new poultry-raising game would save their way of life, but it ended up accelerating the outmigration of white people from the Southern countryside. In the 1940s, over a million whites left the South; in the 1950s, nearly one and a half million whites did. Even those hanging on to their land through poultry farming had increasing reason to quit.[22]

After 1950, writes Jack Temple Kirby, "Gross profits and production increased, but net profits to poultry farmers shrank." In northern Alabama, chicken growers' net earnings added up to negative thirty-six cents an hour in 1969. Although most of these growers were white, there was little that could be done to remedy their situation. Pro-planter exemptions to New Deal labor protections simply excluded *all* agricultural workers from the rights to a minimum wage and to organize unions. This arrangement was a very effective mechanism for white supremacy in the Mississippi Delta, where 95 percent of farmworkers were Black. But in the Upcountry, where over three quarters of farm tenants were white, the planter-influenced New Deal order primarily exposed white folk to poverty and dependence.[23]

By 1970, 70 percent of chicken farmers in Upcountry Georgia held a second job. Flemming worked the night shift at a hosiery plant in Gainesville, caring for his chickens by day. Having spent his life working outdoors, he found the confined space of the factory disconcerting. "I never had been fastened up in a building before," he remarked. "I had a space about four foot wide and about twenty-one feet that I walked eight and ten hours a day." Flemming's life had started to resemble that of the chickens he kept penned in similarly airless, artificially lit confines on his farm. In Dawson County, poultry was the only game in town, accounting for 95 percent of farm income when a farmer named Tatum lost his home and his farm because of debts he fell into working as a broiler raiser. An unequal partnership between big feed companies and poultry growers raising fifty thousand or more birds at a time was pushing some of the last independent farmers in the state of Georgia off the land.[24]

Even in the depths of Jim Crow, many Black farmers had been able to use poultry raising to maintain autonomy, as well as a more diversified, healthier diet than that provided by the system of cotton sharecropping. In 1915, Black landowners in one area of Upcountry Georgia owned an average of less than one hog per family, but around thirty chickens. Chickens can flourish in gardens and on smaller plots. They are hearty consumers of garden pests like snails and caterpillars. Black farmers in this region kept enough birds to provide daily eggs and occasional meat for the family.

Poultry products were not just consumed at home. They provided

The waiter-carriers of Gordonsville, Virginia, in 1875.

one way that Black landowners could increase their income while gaining autonomy from a white-controlled system of food supply. Food historian Psyche Williams-Forson tells the story of a group of Black women entrepreneurs in Gordonsville, Virginia, known as "waiter-carriers." They prepared packaged fried-chicken meals at home and sold them at the train depot, exchanging boxed lunches for cash through the open windows of passenger cars waiting to leave the station. Interviewed in the local paper in 1970, the daughter of one waiter-carrier proudly surveyed her house, concluding, "My mother paid for this place with chicken legs." Another of the waiter-carriers, Hattie Edwards, used the proceeds from her trackside chicken business to open Hattie's Inn, making herself into one of the leading entrepreneurs in the "Negro section of Gordonsville." It "meant something" to make money independently of husbands, fathers, or white employers, especially because the waiter-carriers also fed "many a hungry mouth among the neighborhood children."[25]

Yet as the sharecropping world was drained of its population and deprived of its ways of life in the middle decades of the twentieth century, such forms of economic autonomy and community building through the ownership of and distribution of chickens came under increasing pressure across the South. The arrival of the boll weevil–fueled crisis after World War I coincided with an organized effort by the Ku Klux Klan to carry out an ethnic cleansing in the Upcountry. In Forsyth County, white residents responded to the rape and murder of a white woman by unleashing a campaign of terror upon the Black population, burning down churches, attacking families in their homes, and forbidding them to return to the county. One Black survivor of the expulsion recalled that groups of night riders told Black residents, "Nigger, you got to move—Niggers now out of Forsyth. Take everything you got or don't take anything but move."[26]

The Black and mixed-race population of Forsyth County, over a thousand in 1910, had shrunk to a mere thirty people by 1920. Unlike in the Cotton Belt, where planters' need for Black laborers insulated them from expulsion, in Forsyth County they competed with poor whites over access to land and to wage work. Hence repression took the form of expulsion. In 1921, reports reached the governor that Black farmers were being driven out of Hall County by the KKK. After sacking homes and churches, the terrorists left a note reading, "Get out you damned nigger. We give you ten days to get south of the Chattahoochee or have your house blown up."[27] Thus, while Upcountry Black folk already were beset by many of the same challenges of their white neighbors, racist terror was added to their difficulties.

While the U.S. armed forces and the USDA, as well as county governments and county extension agents in the Upcountry, provided training, equipment, and research findings to aid white cotton farmers in the transition to poultry raising, Black farmers were offered no such lifeline, especially sharecroppers caught up in cotton contracts. There was only one Negro Home Demonstration Agent for all of Georgia, a woman named Camilla Weems. She noted that the farm women with whom she worked lacked access to "proper poultry houses, poultry feed and good breeds of poultry, and the proper knowledge of how to make poultry raising commercially profitable." A white-dominated extension service and mercantile system would never satisfy any of these needs. As a result, Black farmers in the Upcountry were actively excluded from the process of transforming cotton farms into chicken farms. Since this was one of the major strategies governments used to help ex-cotton farmers stay on the land, Black farmers in the Upcountry left in even larger proportion than white.[28]

In chapter 7, we met the enslaved fowl-keeper Sukey, who managed Landon Carter's considerable flock of ducks, geese, and chickens on his Virginia tobacco plantation in the 1760s. Indeed, from the beginning of slavery, Black women had used their skills in bird raising to create zones of dignity and autonomy. In order to rationalize white supremacy, however, purveyors of "humorous" racist imagery obsessively reworked such symbols of Black autonomy into pernicious emblems of Black lasciviousness and criminality. Watermelon, an African crop frequently grown in the provision grounds of enslaved people throughout the antebellum South, and in the garden patches of freed people during Reconstruction, is the most obvious example. Cartoons portraying a watermelon-gulping stereotype encouraged readers of popular magazines to see Southern Black folk not as self-sustaining horticulturalists but as drooling thieves, simultaneously comical, pathetic, and dangerous. Put to similar political purposes, stereotypes about Black people and chicken eating seem to have emerged in the years after Reconstruction. Currier & Ives published the racist *Dark Town* series in the 1880s, a collection of eighty cheap prints ridiculing all manner of supposed Black behaviors, including watermelon eating and chicken stealing.[29]

Makers of American print media like magazines and postcards tirelessly recycled the trope that Black men and boys were so completely enslaved by their own hunger for chicken and watermelon that they could not help but pilfer them from unsuspecting white farmers. In one postcard collected by Williams-Forson, an elderly Black man in tattered clothing reaches into a henhouse to grab a bird. The caption reads, "I'se bound' to hab a Christmas Dinna!" Other similar images often show a suspicious white farmer, armed with a shotgun, pursuing the miscreant. Assumptions about who owned land, buildings, and fowl, and who had neither, underpinned these ubiquitous jokes.[30]

As a white-controlled chicken industry robbed Black Southerners of a key ingredient of their cultural and economic power, such racist imagery was adopted into modern marketing schemes. New chain restaurants, perched at the side of government-funded highways, used the plantation stereotype of chicken-loving "Negroes" to sell meals to a white clientele. The Coon Chicken Inn, a regional chain in Seattle, Portland, and Salt Lake City, operated from the 1920s until after World War II. At the front of each restaurant, readily visible from the highway, was a humongous, cartoonish minstrel face, his sideways-tilted bellman's cap reaching twice as high into the sky as the rest of the structure. To enter the establishment, diners walked through "a doorway of thick red open lips."[31]

Inside the restaurants, white diners encountered cartoonish black faces on the menus, the walls, even the silverware and the toothpicks. In this case, the minstrel character served up was not the hen-snatching, overalls-wearing field negro of plantation legend, but his mythical counterpart: an obliging, polished footman of the plantation Great House. A longtime headwaiter at the restaurant, a Black man named Roy Hawkins, noted the nostalgic marketing ploy played on the common notion that "coons steal chickens." Early versions of "fast food" along Cold War–era highways marketed access to plantation slowness, Black service, and even the opportunity for all whites to call somebody, "*Hey boy.*" (Hawkins would politely correct them, saying, "You almost got it right. It's Roy.") While the fryers and broilers such restaurants used had been raised largely by white ex–cotton farmers, when the big poultry integrators trucked the grown birds back to their processing plants, it was often Black women who worked the "kill line" to ready the meat for sale.[32]

Governed as a white-supremacist, one-party region from the 1890s through the 1950s, the Jim Crow South was well suited to drive the cheapening of meat in America. The region's fixation on preventing sharecroppers and landless agricultural workers from having any alternatives to growing cotton or tobacco was so powerful that even when Progressive reforms came to the South in the early twentieth century, no changes were permitted in the area of labor relations. The same "over my dead body" attitude of Deep South politicians when it came to wages, labor, and racial equality was embodied by the self-proclaimed probusiness groups of the 1950s, who had delegated to themselves the responsibility of "selling the South" to potential industrial developers. It is little surprise, then, that groups like the Arkansas Free Enterprise Association and the Louisiana Right to Work Councils had overlapping memberships with that of the white supremacist Citizens Councils.[33]

Responding to the incentives long associated with plantation busts—cheap land, permissive regulatory regimes, and poverty wages—the J-M Poultry Packing Company opened in El Dorado, Arkansas, in 1956. Town booster organizations had explicitly enticed them with the promise of cheap, obedient, and plentiful labor from across the state line in Bernice, Louisiana. During the 1950s, the number of Black farm operators in Louisiana had dropped by 56 percent. Many Black people, including women—who were eager to escape the long hours and social control of waged domestic work in the houses of white people—found jobs in poultry. Black women like Vivian West took low-paid jobs along the kill line at J-M.

With three daughters to support, West became an "eviscerator," pulling the innards out of carcasses as they slid by on a conveyor belt. The room was hot, loud, and had an indescribable smell. "It was hard," she concluded of the job, "but I did it." Over the following decade, J-M would follow the vertical integration model pioneered by Jewell, buying a hatchery and building a feed mill. The company assembled a labor force of over a thousand people, strictly segmented by race and gender: as on the plantations out of whose failure this industry grew, the vast majority of the foremen and managers were white men, and the line workers were almost exclusively Black women.[34]

Throughout the history of the plantation, Black women were forced to work in occupations that supposedly robbed them of the feminine qualities that were the preserve of elite white women. In the growing system of American fast food, old ideas of Black needlessness were repurposed. Line worker Trinity Mays said of plant owners, "They act like [white women] wouldn't be able to stand it, but if they can't stand it, how can we? It tells you what they think of us." Managers betrayed their attitudes in other ways as well. The owner of Sanderson Farms habitually called Black workers "my people." Worker Gloria Jordan rightly pointed out that this was a "plantation phrase." Ultimately, the growth of the industry of cheap meat depended on the bringing together of cheap (subsidized) feed, distressed white ex–cotton farmers on their own land, and low-wage, Black ex–cotton farmers in the processing plants.

The consolidated poultry firms that emerged in the 1950s and 1960s had a simple business model: pursuing the never-ending cheapening of meat to increase the numbers of Americans who consumed it multiple times per day. Every microphase of the production process was examined for ways to cut costs. With profit margins sitting at only two or three cents per pound, the poultry industry was only profitable at scale. Assembly-line technology was imposed on kill-line workers. North Carolina poultry worker Rose Harrell summed up the change: "They started bringing in machines, and everything got faster."[35]

Yet wages remained at the same level. Integrators leveraged the desperation of the dying plantation South to increase the output per worker while holding wages down. Indeed, reports historian LaGuana Gray, "whereas output per worker nearly tripled between 1960 and 1987, wages rose only half as quickly as chicken prices." Line workers earned the same wage whether they processed three thousand or five thousand chickens per day. They had to keep up with the mechanized pace of the conveyor belts, however, so they had little ability to slow down the pace of work as a form of protest against the stagnant wage levels. If they failed to keep up, they would be fired, and the "right to work" legal system of states like Arkansas meant that few of them had unions to come to their aid.[36]

The imperative to constantly accelerate the pace of killing, cleaning, and packing left its imprint on workers like Vivian West. Carpal tunnel and other repetitive motion disorders were ubiquitous, as eviscerators made up to forty thousand precision knife cuts per day. West's condition grew so serious she required hand surgery. Neysha Mallory, who worked on the deboning line at J-M, noted that "people start being took off the line 'cause they can no longer use knives and scissors and stuff because that's just how badly their hands have been damaged." Workers were also systematically deprived of bathroom breaks. Nor were they allowed to leave work to care for sick children. A poultry plant worker named Sylvia Martin remembered a time when her young son had accidentally ingested some seizure medication while she was at work. "My supervisor let me work all day till it was time to go home," she recalled bitterly, "[then] tell me my baby was in the emergency room and couldn't wake up. The *whole* shift." When Martin was asked by her interviewer about the dehumanizing imperatives of kill-line speed, she said: "I done seen the place blow up. Keep on working. The whole building shook. And we did not stop working that day. They cleaned up out back. We kept working. By-product blew up . . . Keep working. We have had ammonia leaks . . . so bad where you can't even hardly get through the front door . . . Keep working." As in a seventeenth-century Barbadian sugar mill, "they never stopped the line."

And just like in the sugar mills, a stop in one part of the kill line would shut down the whole operation. A crowd of squawking birds at the front. Live chickens pinned upside down, electrocuted into obeisance, waiting to have their throats slit. Half-eviscerated chickens splayed on cones farther down the line. Plucked, cooled, and cleaned carcasses, ready for packing, their temperatures climbing into the danger zone for contamination. Even in moments of human death, the flow of dead chickens would not stop. Sylvia and Lydia Martin saw a man "fall down dead" of a heart attack. "The chickens just falling all over the man," they recalled, "the man lying on the floor dead. Laying on the floor in a puddle of bloody water, chickens everywhere. Saddest thing I've seen.... They opened the back door and rolled him out like a pile of trash.... Everybody better keep on working or you're going to personnel," the foremen told them. "You *better* keep on working."[37]

The combined exploitation of white ex–cotton farmers like Arthur Flemming and the descendants of enslaved cotton workers like Vivian West helped make chicken a staple in American homes. The inflation-adjusted price of store-bought chicken products dropped by more than half between the 1950s and the 1980s. The yearly chicken consumption of the average American rose from 23 pounds in 1960 to nearly 50 pounds in 1982. That figure has continued to rise: While red meat consumption peaked in 1972 at 105 grams per day, then dropped to 85 grams per day in 2007, poultry consumption doubled over that same time period, from 25 to 55 grams per day.[38]

Many poultry line workers somehow found ways to make the kill line more humane for themselves. Even in the hell of the line, with the noise, the danger, the aching wrists and fingers, and the damp feet, they built community. Deena Shine remembered that in the early 1980s, she and her fellow kill-line workers held holiday dinners in the break room, even bringing decorations from home. They held baby showers as well. Neysha Mallory fondly recalled the camaraderie on the line: "If you done been there for a minute, then you pretty much done got your group that's on your side, and y'all gonna work together as a team.... Y'all laughing and talking and making the day go by... you ... got people that can sing and we have church on the line." Increasingly, solidarity along the line grew into union drives. Alongside the ever-present imperative to grow, kill, and sell chickens, Black people's unionization efforts, as well as the pull into better work opportunities, led the poultry industry to search for new forms of cheap, disenfranchised labor—and to ransack the ruins of the plantation beyond the boundaries of the United States.[39]

Kill-line workers on the job in Forest, Mississippi, 1974. Around the time this photo was taken, the Mississippi Poultry Workers Union held a strike that lasted six weeks.

CHAPTER 22

From Killing Fields to Kill Lines

In 1989, Case Farms of Morganton, North Carolina, hired the first wave of Guatemalan asylum seekers to work in the poultry sector. It housed new arrivals in a trailer park as well as a shut-down hotel it had repurposed, distributing bicycles to the new workers. Recruited from an Indigenous village in the Guatemalan highlands called Aguacatán, the workers had been allowed into the country with temporary work permits under the Refugee Act of 1980, which gave relief to victims of civil wars in Central America that had been exacerbated by U.S. foreign policy. Company management found the situation cost-effective, because the new pool of workers was captive in a new way. As one plant manager pointed out, "Guatemalans can't go home. . . . If they go back home, they get shot. So they stayed on with us, and we went from running 50 percent production and in six weeks, I had it fully staffed and running at 100 percent production."[1]

Much like previous waves of poultry workers, the supply of cheap labor from Aguacatán had a longer history that intersects with that of the plantation. Starting in the 1870s, Guatemalan elites committed the country to export-oriented agriculture, forsaking internal economic development. The privatization of Indigenous landholdings in the lowlands allowed new coffee planters to dispossess the Maya majority, and increasing revenue from coffee exports paid for a state-supported system of coercing labor from other Indigenous groups living in the highlands to work on the new coffee plantations. In 1876, President Justo Rufino Barrios instructed highland governors to make sure the "Indian towns of your jurisdiction provide to the owners of fincas . . . the number of workers that they need" through a government-controlled system of forced labor called the *mandamiento*. To avoid the state-sponsored labor draft, in which wages were the lowest and conditions the worst, most highland Maya signed on as *colonos*.[2]

Colonos were voluntary permanent workers who would accept advances from an employer and travel to the lowland to work off their debt among the coffee trees over three to four years before returning home. They were subject to overwork and physical abuse on the plantations. In spite of the illusion that they were "free" workers, they could not leave the premises without the owner's permission. They were not allowed to contract debts with another planter, nor to return home until they had paid off their debt. While the advance payments helped *colonos* contribute to independent village life, the constant drain of labor from highland communities had long-term effects, making it difficult to keep up the production of corn and beans in Indigenous villages far from the plantations.[3]

Following the trail blazed by foreign investors in Guatemala's coffee economy, in the early twentieth century, American firms like the United Fruit Company established export plantations for bananas. United Fruit built its own railroad lines and private port facilities, exploiting migrant labor in *colono*-like arrangements from around the Caribbean. The company practiced a large-scale form of shifting cultivation described in chapter 15. United Fruit and other foreign fruit companies thus gobbled up more and more land in Central America.[4]

By the end of the 1930s, United Fruit was the largest landholder in Guatemala. It was also the top employer in the nation. "Controlling the country's only Atlantic port, almost every mile of the railroads, and the nation's sole telephone and telegraph facilities," journalist and author Jonathan Blitzer adds, the company's managers had come to exercise control over the government. In 1952, as United Fruit was dealing with its own business difficulties in the United States, Guatemala's citizens elected a progressive president named Jacobo Arbenz. While not a Communist, Arbenz had run on a platform of economic nationalism, promising to squeeze a better deal out of American corporations operating on Guatemalan soil. New labor regulations were also on the horizon. Watching in dread as the government embarked on a major land reform, United Fruit's American investors, including members of the United States Senate, sounded the alarm that Arbenz was a Communist dictator in disguise. Journalists picked up the refrain, and the CIA began to assist United Fruit executives in putting together a "liberation" force comprised of conservative Guatemalan military officers to rescue the country.[5]

Primarily to safeguard America's plantation empire in Central America, Arbenz was overthrown and forced into exile in 1954. The dictatorship that replaced the democratically elected leader reversed the land reform. Civil war and repression began almost immediately. While political violence subsided in the seventies, pressure from agribusiness on peasant communities only intensified. Coffee, cotton, and banana plantations continued to encroach on their land and to exploit their labor. Military officers, running the Guatemalan state without opposition or oversight, had taken to enriching themselves by stealing peasants' communal land. In 1978, a group of fifty Maya land activists staged a peaceful public demonstration with the Guatemalan Labor Party to protest the theft of their land. Soldiers showed up with machine guns and sprayed the crowd with bullets, killing several dozen.[6] This was but a sign of the horror to come to the Guatemalan highlands.

Filled with staunch Cold Warriors, the Reagan administration, which took power in 1981, embraced any means necessary to fight communism abroad. Although leftist guerrilla groups and Indigenous movements were in fact winning victories against the military government in Guatemala, the U.S. definition of "subversion" embraced nearly any form of protest against the dictatorship. When four American nuns visiting Guatemala to aid the poor were raped and murdered on the orders of the military government in 1982, Reagan's foreign policy adviser Jeane Kirkpatrick responded with a sneer. Instead of condemning the murder of American citizens, she said, "The nuns were clearly not just nuns. The nuns were also political activists." Such language was a clear sign to the far right in Central America: No level of brutality would cross the line.[7]

When a newly installed military dictator named Efraín Ríos Montt—who had received training at the United States Army School of the Americas in the Panama Canal Zone—tried to stomp out the just-established Guatemalan Revolutionary National Unity Party, his counterinsurgent campaigns descended into what one allied general described as "blindness and madness." In the Indigenous-dominated rural highlands, "the military killed, tortured, and raped as many Maya as it could." While Ríos Montt was attempting to wipe out the Ixil Maya ethnic group in 1982, Reagan protected him with praise, calling the dictator "a man of great personal integrity and commitment [who] wants to improve the quality of life for all Guatemalans and to promote social justice." Convinced that communists had infiltrated peasant communities—some indeed had joined the guerrilla struggle against the dictatorship—the army conducted a scorched-earth campaign that soon engulfed Aguacatán.[8]

A schoolteacher named Emiliano Rodríguez Castro recalled that soldiers "burned farms, corn, clothes, everything. The people filed down from the mountain villages—women, men, children, dogs, hens, all the animals, fleeing from there to here. I had an aunt, they massacred her whole family. . . . It was a difficult time for Aguacatán." The human cost of the war was staggering: a UN-sponsored truth commission later estimated that there had been two hundred thousand casualties during the civil war. In the first half of the 1980s, the U.S.-sponsored counterinsurgency campaigns had displaced one million Maya, about one out of every four Maya in the entire country.[9]

The Guatemalan peace accord ending the civil war was signed in 1986, but the World Bank—led at the time by the American banker A. W. Clausen—forced the new, democratically elected government to pay off the debts piled up by the pro-American military dictatorship. In such circumstances, the economic recovery of highland peasant villages was low on the new government's list of priorities. In fact, the imposition of structural adjustment policies, such as the removal of trade barriers, made recovery for highlanders impossible. Cheap imports of garlic from China and onions from Mexico flooded the Guatemalan market for precisely the crops Maya highlanders had formerly sold to maintain the independence of their villages.

First World demands to lower trade barriers also led to the massive dumping of cheap corn, rice, and wheat from subsidized Midwestern megafarms beginning in 1996, which accelerated after the signing of the Central American Free Trade Agreement with the George W. Bush administration in 2005. This gave rise to "the first neoliberal purge of the Guatemalan countryside... [in which] hundreds of thousands of farmers fled to Guatemala City and the United States." Refugees from the successive crises of civil war and free trade made up the first waves of Indigenous Guatemalan people who would work in the expanding U.S. poultry industry.[10]

At first, they picked produce all over the South, from Florida to Arizona. But word quickly spread of year-round work in the poultry plants of North Carolina. "Soon there was an almost constant van service ferrying Guatemalan workers to Morganton," historian Leon Fink writes. In this way, U.S. policy originally instituted to preserve a plantation empire in Central America cheapened labor for the poultry industry, serving up refugees without citizenship. By the early 1990s, Latinos represented one-quarter of poultry line workers in the United States. The Latino population of North Carolina increased by 600 percent between 1990 and 2005, and the Latino population of Georgia by 480 percent.[11]

Just as the flow of workers to the booming poultry industry of the American South was the result of plantation busts in the United States and Central America, worker resistance in the industry was also informed by that history. In May 1993, during a lunch break at Case Farms in Morganton, around one hundred workers stood up in the cafeteria and announced they would not return to work until management dealt with a series of alleged issues. Most of them were the same issues that had confronted African American women poultry workers in Arkansas: insufficient bathroom breaks, unpaid hours, and having the cost of safety gear deducted from their paychecks. In response to the work stoppage, Case Farms plant managers called the police. Fifty-two workers, most of them Guatemalan, were arrested for trespassing. Eventually the company dropped the charges. Nothing came of the workers' complaints, however, and nearby labor unions failed to get involved in organizing the workers, although clearly the plant was ripe for unionization.[12]

One of those involved in the work protest at Case Farms was a forty-eight-year-old Aguacatán farmer named Paulino López Castro. When he explained his participation in the labor actions at the poultry plant, his community's historical experiences with coffee plantations were central. He had been raised hearing stories of how ancestors had outsmarted abusive coffee planters.[13] "In the [coffee] plantations," he explained, "the owners always tried to mistreat the workers, and thus the [villagers] learned to defend themselves by stopping work.... In the case of a work protest the people would call for the [government] inspector, always he helped the workers." As López said, "This tradition existed in Aguacatán, it is remembered in Morganton even after two decades of military regimes. Yes, the people always kept in their minds that they must activate their human rights, that's just what happened here in Morganton with Case Farms."[14]

López and his coworkers applied the tools forged over a century of struggles against coffee planters to contend with poultry plant speedups in North Carolina. In fact, he emphasized that, even under a dictatorship, Indigenous workers in Guatemala had *more* recourse to the rule of law than they did in the United States, because in the protest at Case Farms, there was no neutral state official to intervene on the workers' behalf. Toiling in the American South, on "cotton graveyards" in most cases, the new generation of poultry workers would confront the ghosts of planter power in their own struggles to shape a better life for themselves in the 1990s and beyond.

In the early twenty-first century, thanks to the massive rollback of the New Deal's regulatory order, truly dominant mercantile corporations have arisen for the first time since the peak of mercantile capitalism that aided the birth of the plantation in the seventeenth century. Walmart and Amazon, together with a small number of national grocery chains like Kroger and Albertson, wield unprecedented control over retail food sales in the United States. Their unusual market power allows them to exert pressure on a global network of suppliers, demanding extremely cheap products on a highly flexible schedule.[15]

The consolidated poultry companies like Perdue and Pilgrim's Pride are quite powerful, but they answer to yet larger firms like Walmart, who push them to consolidate, cut costs, accelerate production, and slash wages in a trickle-down process that makes it impossible for all but the most streamlined, scaled-up, and low-wage firms to stay in business. A century ago, the country's poultry production was in the hands of perhaps hundreds of thousands of independent farmers, sharecroppers, and rural homeowners. Today, precisely five poultry companies remain in the country. While this momentous transformation has provided the nation's consumers with cheap meat and eggs, as the ongoing bird flu epidemic reveals, the arrangement is quite precarious in several ways. They have been indifferent to the welfare of workers as well as that of the animals they raise and slaughter.[16]

Pushed to provide cheap meat on demand by mega retailers like

Walmart and Kroger, the modern poultry integrators constantly speed up their kill lines and keep animals immobile in cages so that they reach kill weight with less feed and in less time. They breed them for maximum weight gain in the breasts, and they maintain the hens in an artificially lit and heated world so they eat twenty-four hours a day and lay eggs year-round. Companies have also pressed down on wages in a union-wary South. "As the biggest companies expanded their control," notes journalist Isaac Arnsdorf, "they raised farmers' average pay by a mere 2.5 cents a pound from 1988 to 2016, while the wholesale price of chicken rose by 17.4 cents a pound."[17]

While many U.S.-based manufacturers responded to the new demands of consolidation by searching out low-wage, lax-regulation environments in the Global South in the 1990s and early 2000s, poultry companies have found it useful to remain where they began, in the graveyards of cotton busts in the American South. Theoretically, poultry could be raised and slaughtered nearly anywhere. There is nothing in the climate or topography of the American South that makes it better suited than anyplace else to raising and slaughtering chickens. Its historical location is far more important than its geographic location. In 2000, Alabama, Arkansas, Georgia, and North Carolina were home to nearly half of all poultry processing capacity in the United States.[18]

The Illinois firm Koch Foods keeps a low profile in the Southern towns where it operates—often selling its poultry under the brand names of processors it has acquired—but it entered the public eye when its Mississippi plants were raided by Immigration and Customs Enforcement in 2019 and 680 people were taken off the lines in a few hours. The raids coincided with the first day of school in the state. Local officials were inundated with phone calls because so many kids were never picked up from school. Eventually, around half of the workers taken into custody were removed from the country.

One of them was a man of forty-seven named Edgar López. He had lived and worked in Carthage, Mississippi, for a quarter century. He was a prayer leader and a youth minister at his church. An Indigenous Maya, he had grown up in the same Guatemalan highland town as many of his undocumented coworkers. When deported from Carthage, he was forced to leave behind his wife, his children, his grandchildren, and his tight-knit community of Guatemalan poultry workers.

Determined to return home to Mississippi after his deportation to Guatemala, López traveled to Mexico's northern border in January 2021, paying a smuggler to sneak him back into the United States. Along with eighteen fellow migrants, López was loaded into the back of a truck. Somewhere near the border crossing, the truck was stopped by an elite unit of the Mexican state police. No one knows exactly what happened next, but the following day the charred remains of López and sixteen others were found in the back of the truck, which was riddled with 113 bullet holes. Later, a Mexican court convicted eleven police officers of murder. At least two of them had participated in a police training program offered by the U.S. State Department. The elite police unit appeared to be tied up in cartel rivalries over the smuggling of drugs and of humans across the border.

The most serious charge leveled against the Carthage poultry plants raided by ICE was probation for three of the managers found guilty of "harboring illegal aliens." As of early 2025, the majority of the undocumented workers arrested in the 2019 raid either still await a hearing, or have returned to Carthage. They found it easy to get rehired at Koch and other poultry plants.[19]

While it has escaped the deadly sort of consequences its plant workers have faced, Koch has also preyed on the chicken farmers it contracts with, seeming to exert a planter's sense of ownership, privilege, and power over areas of the rural South the plantation had already rendered poor and vulnerable. When a retired Black sheriff's deputy named John Ingrum put his savings into buying a small farm east of Jackson, Mississippi, in 2002, he had no plans to use the old chicken houses sitting on his property. That was until a contractor from Koch Foods knocked on his door, offering a feed conversion contract. The man showed Ingrum projections of a steady income from a small amount of work. Ingrum

ICE immigration enforcement raid at poultry plant in Jackson, Mississippi, 2019.

was not told that he would have to modernize the chicken houses and buy other equipment from the company, so he signed on.

Soon after, he began to receive instructions to engage in costly improvements. He spent $50,000 in 2009 alone on things like feed bins, compost sheds, and lights. In some deliveries of chicks, 35 percent would be dead on arrival. Even if they had shown up sick, he would be punished for not raising them to weight. The company shorted him on feed, then docked his pay when he delivered underweight hens. On one occasion, the feed delivered by Koch was so inadequate that the young chickens began to eat one another. When he complained about these issues, Ingrum started getting fewer deliveries of chicks, although he was still on the hook for the equipment he had financed. A company representative spread a rumor that Ingrum's farm had been foreclosed. He began to fall into debt. Just like his predecessor Arthur Flemming, Ingrum complained, "I had no control over the feed they delivered me."

In 2010, when he learned that the USDA was holding hearings in Alabama to collect testimony about farmers' experiences with the consolidated agribusiness industry, he decided to go, even though it was three hundred miles miles from his farm. When he got home from his trip, he found a note in his mailbox. Koch Foods had terminated his contract. Heavily indebted, and saddled with now-useless chicken-raising infrastructure, Ingrum had no income. His power was cut off. A few months later, he received an eviction notice. He was escorted from the premises by officers of the Sheriff's Department where he had once worked. He moved in with family and got a job at a car dealership. Of the experience with Koch Foods, Ingrum said, "It just ruined me." Several other Black farmers had similar experiences with the company. But the flood of cheap chicken to American grocery stores continues.[20]

The story of industrial poultry in the United States suggests that what happens in the wake of the plantation is as important as what happened on the plantation. As we will see in the final chapter, however, problems caused by one plantation bust are still being solved by launching another plantation boom in a new place.

CHAPTER 23

Caindo na Cana

In 1961, a film crew for ABC went to northeastern Brazil to shoot a documentary called *The Troubled Land*. In it, the narrator drew repeated connections between "the twenty million" landless peasants clamoring for better lives in the impoverished region and the successful revolutions in China and Cuba. "The only answer to Communist promises," he warned, "is results." Unless "the twenty million" were given access to their own land and better wages, they would be "wooed" by Communist operatives, and Brazil would become another Cuba, only one that was far more populous.

Home to Brazil's sugar plantations since the 1500s, the country's northeast was a hotbed of rural labor radicalism at the time the film was made. Low sugar prices in the post–World War II era had led traditional planters—who struggled to find profitable alternatives to sugar—simply to plant more cane at the expense of subsistence crops. Peasants were caught in a vise of rising food costs and falling wages. A nationally known peasant leader named Francisco Julião vowed that the land-poor cultivators of rural Brazil would gain their own farms "by law or by force." He is portrayed as a podium-pounding demagogue in the film.

Julião's foil was a sugar planter named Constâncio Maranhão. A former state governor and Chief of the Legislature, his family had held sway in the region as slaveholders and sugar masters for nearly four hundred years. He owned thousands of cattle, as well as tens of thousands of acres. A self-described "simple man," Maranhão nonetheless sported "a fifteen-karat diamond ring." Asked about the plight of the poor while standing in front of his ample plantation home, Maranhão answered with an impish smile: "All of my peasants are happy, rich, and fat, don't you see?" One hears echoes of the Mississippian Walker Percy's description of the tenants at his plantation as "limber-jointed, oily-black, well fed, decently clothed peasants." Just in case he was wrong about the contentment of his tenants, Maranhão went about his daily business with a revolver at his waist.

In the middle of the interview, while a bodyguard in mirrored sunglasses grinned approvingly, Maranhão unholstered his weapon. He looked into the camera and spoke. "This is my gun. It is the law here. It decides everything. Not any police, or any law, but my gun. It is of the best made in the United States." He pointed the revolver at the ground and pulled the trigger several times, spooking a few cattle who had wandered into the yard. Seeming to make it up as he went along, Maranhão then fired a few shots into the air. After pausing to reload, the planter began to shoot wildly around the feet of two cameramen, laughing and taunting them. He finished the unsettling interview by vowing to kill anyone who tried to come on his land and organize his "lazy" peasants.[1]

Despite the danger presented by influential men like Maranhão, the administration of President João Goulart that would come into office later that year announced a plan to redistribute some land to the poor. Having been caught flat-footed by the 1959 Communist takeover in Cuba, United States officials were immediately suspicious. Ambassador Lincoln Gordon, with enthusiastic support from USAID, the CIA, and even the ad firm McCann Erickson, helped conservative leaders in

Brazil undermine Goulart's presidency. In a pattern they had already established in supporting Guatemala's 1954 coup, they aided a takeover by right-wing Brazilian military officers, many of whom had received political and counterinsurgent training in the United States. A cohort of generals forced Goulart into exile and seized power in 1964.[2]

When *The Troubled Land* finally aired in the United States, it functioned to justify the military coup its producers had once hoped could be avoided. The new message was clear: Keeping Communism at bay required the suspension of democratic processes and the support of a reactionary planter class, not conceding to landless people's demands. In fact, the generals justified their coup by sowing panic about rural upheaval in the sugar-growing northeast. While the dictatorship sought agricultural modernization as keenly as the left-leaning reformers they overthrew, theirs would be a "conservative agricultural revolution" that did not threaten planters' monopoly on land and wealth in the countryside.[3]

The U.S. government's plan to help the Brazilian generals restore order, which they dubbed Operation Brother Sam, reflected an increasing interest in Latin America. After the devastation of the Second World War, the Marshall Plan and other forms of aid and trade had rebuilt Western Europe and Japan so well that their industries had begun to pinch U.S. profit rates. The business community of the 1960s was finding American capitalism, with its powerful labor unions and broad electoral franchise, increasingly constraining. Thus, it looked southward for new avenues of direct investment, as well as for new export markets. Between 1960 and 1969, U.S. investment in Latin America grew from $6 billion to $12 billion. By the late sixties, "20% of total U.S. foreign investment was tied up in Latin America, and U.S. firms had 5,436 subsidiaries in the region." It seemed Latin America had an important role to play in the future growth of U.S. capitalism, although North American companies new to the southern continent found constraints they had not expected.[4]

Even though economic development in the decades following the Great Depression had been impressive across Latin America, much of it had happened under the direction of populists including Lázaro

Cárdenas of Mexico, Juan Perón of Argentina, and Getúlio Vargas of Brazil. They redistributed land, nationalized important sectors like oil, erected tariff walls to protect new industries, and courted domestic labor unions in both city and countryside. Aiming to achieve self-sufficient national economies with broad-based consumption and a balance between agriculture and industry, the populist regimes of post-Depression Latin America would not constitute a sufficient consumer base for U.S. exports. To bring economies like these into the sphere of U.S. industry, a different sort of modernization would have to be imposed. But first, a new problem would have to be identified.

An influential American agronomist named Norman Borlaug diagnosed the region, as well as much of the rest of humanity, with a single malady. "It goes without saying," he noted in a 1967 interview, "[that] in all traditional agricultures throughout the world . . . there is a deficiency of nitrogen" in the soil. Blaming inefficient peasant farmers in the developing world while ignoring geographic and ecological differences across regions, Borlaug's reductive diagnosis of nitrogen deficiency nevertheless became orthodoxy among U.S. advisers after he won the Nobel Peace Prize in 1970.[5]

His nitrogen fixation found a partner in the "calorie." A notion first developed in the late nineteenth century, the calorie allowed economists to quantify levels of economic development in the decolonizing world with a standard unit of measure. Armed with the idea of the human body as a machine absorbing interchangeable units of heat energy, Cold War economists discovered an "overabundance of calories" in the United States and an "underabundance" in Latin America. Borlaug held that if countries in the Global South had enough "nitrogen" (shorthand for modern commercial agriculture), they could pump out sufficient calories from rice, corn, and wheat to keep poor people well fed and quiescent, thus guaranteeing the victory of the free world over Communism without ever having to confront political questions.[6]

An apolitical program of rural transformation known as the Green Revolution would solve rural poverty with a modernizing package of hybrid seeds, synthetic fertilizer, efficient irrigation, and agricultural machines, as well as plentiful credit. The idea was that large, mechanized farms with lots of high-tech inputs would produce adequate calories for the masses while shedding rural workers to cities and towns. Growing urban working classes would then purchase imports from the United States. In a world-spanning project of aid and forced advice in the 1960s and 1970s, U.S. government agencies spread the Green Revolution, producing impressive-sounding increases in total agricultural yield and calorie production per capita. The Green Revolution sought to solve problems of land inequality by committing more deeply to land inequality, while betting that the overall increase in calorie production would forestall agrarian discontent.[7]

While American bureaucrats and advisers played a critical role in the spread of Green Revolution ideas, in Brazil, the right-wing dictatorship wanted to raise a corps of homegrown experts who had a "business obsession" and an "American mentality" to put such sweeping rural transformations into place. To spread the Green Revolution gospel, land-grant colleges like Iowa State and University of California, Davis, trained scores of Brazilian students. One of the more notable was Alfonso Wisniewski, who spent a "particularly impactful" time in the Central Valley of California in 1969. Certainly, he was familiar with the United Farmworkers strikes rocking the state at the time. Nevertheless, he admired the achievements of the cotton and orange magnates in the U.S. West and thought they could be replicated in Brazil. Agronomists like Wisniewski were not the only Brazilian professionals traveling north to imbibe new ideologies. Running from 1957 to 1970, the Ford Foundation–funded Chile Project brought in hundreds of economics students from Chile, Argentina, Brazil, and Mexico to absorb free-market purism at the knee of Milton Friedman of the University of Chicago.[8]

Despite faith in the incontestable wonders of scale, science, and free enterprise, the dictatorship's reversal of Goulart's land reform, along with other unpopular policies, generated resistance from peasants and urban protesters alike. The regime responded by unleashing a wave of unprecedented terrorism against its own population in the years after 1968, subjecting approximately twenty thousand Brazilians to interrogation and torture. While some victims were eventually released, most of them were "disappeared" forever.

Much like its agronomists and economists, Brazil's military and police received training from American advisers. To learn how to break opposition effectively, Brazilian officers received training in interrogation techniques at the School of the Americas in Fort Benning, Georgia, as well as other secret sites. CIA officers also visited various South American countries to educate rapt right-wing officers in the finer points of effective interrogation, while providing them with better equipment to fight Communists, like electrical generators for administering shocks and super-fine electrical needles that could be placed deep inside an ear cavity, or even be lodged between a subject's teeth. U.S. police trainers instilled in their pupils a modernized, efficient approach to torture, counseling "the precise pain in the precise place, in the precise amount" to break, humiliate, or confuse their captives. Such policies helped bring the seeds of the Green Revolution to fruit in Brazilian soil, but its plantation past would be a central part of authoritarian modernization.[9]

Cold War geopolitics helped considerably. When Fidel Castro's guerrillas overthrew the U.S.-supported dictatorship of Fulgencio Batista in 1959, Castro took the provocative step of nationalizing large plantations, many of them American-owned. In protest, the United States transferred Cuba's sugar quota to Brazil in 1962. Brazil capitalized on this opportunity to modernize the country's traditional sugar sector, which had been in continuous operation since the late 1500s. Brazil's right-wing agricultural renaissance focused on reviving what the dictatorship's minister of energy imagined as its "colonial glory as the world's biggest sugar exporter." Indeed, total sugar cultivation in Brazil grew by 422 percent from 1960 to 1985. While the opportunity to serve the growing American sugar market was an important spur, the politics of oil played an even larger role.[10]

The glorious colonial past of the plantation would push Brazil forward into the energy future as the world's first modern industrial economy powered by biofuels. Hoping to reduce the nation's dependence on imported oil, and to prop up expensive new sugar factories reeling from the global crisis of 1973—when OPEC's new restrictions raised oil prices and pushed down on consumer demand across the capitalist world— the dictatorship established one of the world's first large-scale alternative fuel initiatives. Thanks to the Proálcool program promulgated by the Brazilian government in 1975, millions of Brazilian cars came off assembly lines with ethanol-ready engines in the ensuing years. Ethanol cars, trucks, and buses provided a booming domestic market for ethanol distilleries, which used sugarcane as their raw material. With the Proálcool program subsidizing the expansion of cane plantations, biofuel production in Brazil grew by 450 percent between 1975 and 1978.[11]

Ironically, it would not be the traditional class of sugar lords like Constâncio Maranhão in the Brazilian northeast who would capitalize on these opportunities. Instead, a new class of planters in São Paulo state used government funding to follow the costly recipe of the Green Revolution, using more machinery and chemicals. Fertilizer consumption in the state grew by a factor of twenty-five between 1948 and 1972, with most of that growth happening after 1965. Even though Proálcool was supposed to mitigate Brazil's dependency on foreign oil, the new plantations were such great consumers of America's surplus petroleum that U.S. chemical firm Union Carbide built a plant in São Paulo to turn cheap petroleum into synthetic fertilizer.[12]

To aid in the replantationization of central-southern Brazil after decades of decline in the region's coffee economy, the dictatorship removed laws that protected small farmers, including the mandate that sugar mills purchase a certain amount of their cane from minor producers. Refiners grew more and more of their own cane, pushing out cane sharecroppers and coffee farmers. Those who lost their land were thrown onto the market as "*boias frias*"—cold lunches, or temporary farmworkers. Now lacking access to subsistence plots and wild resources, the new rural working class of Brazil, millions strong, "fell into the temporary, shifting, informal work of modern agriculture." The "twenty millions" who received a few minutes of attention in *The Troubled Land* had grown in number since 1961. By 1979, a third of the country's total population was classified as "migrants in the country."[13]

In one of the São Paulo municipalities particularly dedicated to sugar, temporary workers fulfilled nearly two-thirds of labor needs. Removed from their old tenancies, they settled in small towns that functioned as recruitment centers for casual labor. Before dawn, people would gather in the town plaza, hoping to be recruited for a day's work. As one resident remembered the scene, "Children of twelve years or less leave to cut cane. Many children are mutilated during the work, cuts on the hands, fingers chopped off. And there's nothing they can do in the courts because children of less than thirteen years aren't allowed to work!" Planters also preferred to hire women because of the prevailing notion that "women work hard, don't demand registration, don't take complaints to the courts, don't need to work the full year, and earn about 80 percent of what a man earns." And while the total calories produced in the country had increased thanks to the improvements of the Green Revolution, given the low wages and inconsistent work, a healthy diet was still out of reach for the rural poor.[14]

Beans, or *feijao*, had long been the protein staple of the Brazilian people. "If you don't throw beans in the lunch, it seems like you didn't eat at all," explained one worker in 1976. But as the population boomed and people moved to cities, yields of beans lagged badly. Looking at thin profit margins, large agribusinesses stayed away from legumes, leaving the feeding of the nation to small farmers. And with little credit, capital, or research money lavished on the bean sector, machine manufacturers ignored it as well. Even though the total cultivated acreage in Brazil nearly doubled between 1960 and 1980, food production as a percentage of national population dropped by 25 percent. In São Paulo state alone, sugarcane had directly displaced three hundred thousand acres of pasture, one hundred thousand of rice, ninety thousand of corn, and eighty thousand of peanuts. Shockingly, Brazil was forced to import beans starting the next year—just as it had during its coffee boom of the mid-nineteenth century.[15]

Taking the measure of how the government-sponsored ethanol boom reduced food availability, one union organizer in São Paulo observed, "There will come a day when people will have to adapt an alcohol motor in place of their stomach." Maybe that day had not quite arrived, but the dictatorship's Green Revolution had moved the sugar industry back to the center of the Brazilian economy, bringing with it the predictable fallout of the plantation: the uprooting of small farmers, intensified labor exploitation, increasing inequality, and increasing dependence on imported food. In the process, the moribund sugar estates of the northeast were displaced by dynamic sugar mills in the reborn plantation districts of São Paulo state. The world of Constâncio Maranhão, with his fat, happy peasants living on plantations under long-term arrangements, living in row houses and working in the fields of the *patrón*, faded away, even though he got the regime change he wanted.[16]

Proálcool ended in the 1980s, as its debt mounted and government-backed economic development became politically controversial. But a new, privately funded sugar boom beginning in the 1990s drove Brazilian sugar to new heights. The same year that Bill Clinton declared that "the age of big government is over," the U.S. Farm Bill of 1996 ended a long-standing policy of maintaining emergency grain reserves. Those stockpiles existed not only for emergency situations, but to keep prices for American consumers below a certain ceiling. With those stockpiles gone, any change in food availability, due to weather events or a dockworkers strike, now provided tantalizing opportunities in food arbitrage for institutional investors.[17]

In 1999, Congress repealed the Glass-Steagall Act, a New Deal–era law that had created a firewall between financial and savings banks. Then, Congress passed the Commodity Futures Modernization Act of 2000, which allowed more non-food-related financial entities to take big positions in commodity futures. Unleashed from long-standing restrictions on their activities, and eager for new sources of profitable investment after the dot-com bust of 2000, investment banks quickly organized Commodity Index Funds, which sped up the exchanges of agro-commodity futures. The "financialization of food" was under way. People's diets in the Global South were now captive to the whims of hedge fund whiz kids in the United States.[18]

The entry of high finance into the life-and-death realm of basic food happened at an auspicious time in history. Decades of Green Revolution "depeasantization," exacerbated by the massive dumping of subsidized U.S. grain on world markets, had contributed to making humanity a predominantly city-dwelling species for the first time. In the early twenty-first century, global cities like Cairo, Mombasa, São Paulo, and Chongqing—lacking basic services and formal employment, never mind safe, affordable food—exploded. High-risk traders were profiting directly from the volatility of food prices on which the world's urban masses, separated from agriculture more than ever before, now depended.[19]

After two decades of rock-bottom food prices brought on by advances in crop breeding and mechanization, as well as trade liberalization, U.S. grain subsidies, and cheap oil, world food prices rose 130 percent between 2000 and 2012. The soaring price of oil, along with the emergence of China, Russia, and India as food importers, were partly to blame for the surge. Nevertheless, the central promise of post–Cold War triumphalism—that America's spectacular buffet of endless consumption could spread across the planet if markets were allowed to function without regulation—was looking increasingly unrealistic. People rioted in several countries in the Global South as prices peaked in 2008; according to many scholars, issues around food affordability set the stage for the Arab Spring. While food prices came down in 2010, they surged to new highs in 2012, and broke records again in 2022.[20]

The food price rise since 2000, while imposing new hardships on the world's poor, also created big opportunities for food-exporting nations like Brazil. With the influx of credit from global institutional investors,

Brazil became an agro-export giant: Between 2005 and 2012, Brazil's exports grew from $118 billion to $256 billion. It sold more beef, chicken, oranges, sugar, and soybeans than any other country in the world. However, small farmers did not benefit.[21]

When voters chose Workers' Party leader Luiz Inácio Lula da Silva to lead the country in 2002, they put a left-populist government in power for the first time since 1961. Lula, who hoped to pay off massive international debts while delivering grand social programs to the poor, capitalized on the food price rise not by supporting the commercialization of small farms, but by promoting agro-export giants. While Workers' Party policies lifted millions out of poverty, rural income equality, which was already more pronounced than in any country on the planet save Namibia, only deepened. Although, to its credit, Lula's administration deployed cadres of investigators to make sure employers were following new laws against child labor, debt peonage, and third-party contracting, high prices during the commodity boom made Brazil open for business as never before.[22]

Energy was quickly added to the list of Brazil's agro-export successes. Cane sugar is still the world's number one industrial food sweetener today, while also serving as the world's most popular biofuel—a promising nonpetroleum energy source that many investors and environmentalists hope will slow the pace of climate change. The 2002 Kyoto Protocol, along with climate-conscious regulations put in place by the European Union, have sparked new plantations to life around the world, nowhere more so than in Brazil, which produces nearly one-fourth of the world's ethanol. More importantly, skyrocketing costs for petroleum intensified the search for alternative fuels. In part because the U.S.-led Coalition Provisional Authority in Iraq struggled to reorganize production, oil prices increased sixfold between 2005 and 2008—this price rise was triple the one that had occurred in the oil shocks of the 1970s. Finally, in 2008, Al Gore's maudlin blockbuster *An Inconvenient Truth* hit theaters, and the Intergovernmental Panel on Climate Change released its bleakest report to date.

In 2009, the European Union signaled a strong commitment to a future driven by biofuels with its Renewable Energy Directive. Thereafter, major investment banks like Deutsche Bank established "global-warming themed mutual funds." They did so quietly, without voicing an opinion on the scientific reality of climate change, presumably so they could keep investing in climate-warming industries while "hedging" with their new mutual funds so they could still profit from worst-case climate scenarios. Overall, alternative fuels came to seem a promising avenue for investment for the first time.[23]

While First World climate concerns have led to the development of "alternative fuels," in the absence of a deep reconsideration of the massive energy needs of expanding capitalism, this simply means unleashing more forms of energy—none of which can be used without environmental costs. Because alternative fuels have emerged within a capitalist energy regime, moreover, their production has replicated the traditionally exploitative dynamic of plantations. "We run, we cut, we sweat," noted a cane cutter working on the plantation of Nova Era Bioenergia. It was the height of the sugarcane harvest in São Paulo state, Brazil, in July of 2022, and his pay was so low that he had no choice but to keep working until he could at least afford passage home. The daily routine of this man, who declined to give his name to government observers, included avoiding "spider, scorpion, or snake bites" in the closely planted fields. Paid according to the number of kilos of cane he cut each day, he had seen fellow workers experience the "kangaroo attack," in which "the neck, ribs, spine or thighs become paralyzed, and the hands stiffen with cramps, like the legs of a kangaroo." At the end of each grueling day, he returned to "makeshift dwellings," confronting a "repulsive stench" from waste collecting at the door. He and his seventeen mates threw their aching bodies upon tattered mattresses strewn around the floor, settling in for a broken doze.

The workers had been recruited by labor contractors from an impoverished northeastern state a thousand miles away. Enticed by the promise of high wages that never materialized, they had in essence been turned into involuntary laborers. Poverty in their place of birth had forced them to do this before. When rural women and men like them found themselves once again swinging machetes in endless fields of cane far from home, they plaintively referred to their condition as *"caindo na cana"*: falling back into cane.[24]

Brazil has indeed fallen back into cane. For the first time since the early 1600s, the country is the dominant global producer of refined sugar, accounting for nearly half of world exports. The single megafirm Copersucar operates forty-eight refineries that process tens of millions of tons of cane annually. Another publicly traded company, São Martinho, currently boasts "the largest sugarcane processing facility in the world, with a crushing capacity of 10 million tons/year." In Barbados during slavery, early capitalists had first brought agricultural and manufacturing phases of production together. In a far larger and more technically sophisticated version of colonial enslavers' "integrated" plantation, São Martinho features machine-harvested cane fields, crushing mills, ethanol distilleries, and a sugar refinery, worked by five thousand employees. The company grows cane on 350,000 hectares, an area two-thirds the size of Delaware and larger than even the most sprawling corn farms in Iowa.[25]

Along with sugar conglomerates like Copersucar, oil majors such as Royal Dutch Shell have invested heavily in cane-based alternative fuels. British Petroleum now operates eleven sugar mills across five Brazilian states. The company signed a deal in August 2024 to expand its crushing capacity—the quantity of sugarcane a mill can process in a year—in the state of Tocantins to 3.4 million tons of sugarcane for ethanol. Thus, the same firms that have spent decades furthering global warming while denying the troubling findings of their own scientists are now tasked with saving the world from climate disaster. And they are doing so through a return to the sugar plantation. Scholars call the phenomenon CEPA, which stands for corporate-led, external input-dependent, plantation agriculture. Despite its promise to be a key player in the "transition" away from fossil fuels, the CEPA sector is one of the biggest emitters of methane and other greenhouse gases in the world.[26]

Between 2005 and 2008, sugarcane cultivation in Brazil grew by 69 percent, or four million hectares. In 2013, Brazil planted more acres in cane than the next top four producers (India, China, Thailand, and Pakistan) put together. With the estimated price tag of building a modern sugar mill approaching half a billion dollars, deep-pocketed multinational corporations gained control of a third of the industry. U.S. conglomerates invested heavily in reborn "energy plantations." Indeed, American multinationals are propping up the new plantation economy in Brazil.[27]

In 2012, Copersucar was taken over by a company called Cargill. A privately owned, U.S.-based firm primarily focused on grain (it currently controls more than 25 percent of the global grain trade), Cargill has expanded into numerous global commodity lines since the deregulatory measures of the late 1990s. Its massive investment in Brazil's sugar plantations solidified Copersucar's dominant global position: The Cargill-Copersucar partnership in Brazil produced 11 percent of world sugar exports in 2014. Not to be outdone, also in 2012 Royal Dutch Shell merged with Brazilian sugar conglomerate Cosan to create the world's largest ethanol producer, Raízen. While each new sugar-ethanol partnership has its own pipelines and port facilities in Brazil, the transnational megaproducers also run a shared transport infrastructure through a joint venture called Logum Logistica. Begun in 2011 with a $1 billion loan from the Brazilian government, the firm built an ethanol pipeline 830 miles long.[28]

The growth of Brazil's "energy plantations," now under the control of commodity giants like Cargill and Shell, has required vast amounts of land. The sugar boom has formed an important part of what legal scholars call the "global land grab" of the early twenty-first century, often carried out in Global South countries already rendered vulnerable by civil war and famine. International investors speculating in land depend on local intermediaries. Poor communities in the northeastern state of Maranhão had lived in the area for generations before plantation-builders set their eyes on it.

Many lived on public land and had never had their possessions clearly titled. In the 1990s, a "shadowy business figure" named Euclides de Carli first became known as a "grileiro," or cricketer, because of how he forges land titles. De Carli is repeatedly alleged to have registered deeds for those lands in the names of nonexistent people, or random people who had never been to Maranhão. Then he would "buy" it from them, bribing local officials to go along with the ruse. He would then hire crews of men to lay fences on the territory he had appropriated. Before submitting bogus documents to the proper officials, he places the papers in boxes filled with grasshoppers, which after a period leave the papers looking gently aged. If the communities thus cheated out of their land refused to clear out, de Carli had other means of securing their farms: In 2018, a prominent Brazilian legislator publicly accused him of responsibility for the murder of two people.

While he perfected these strategies in the 1990s, de Carli's unique skill set would become much more important in the twentieth century commodity boom, which raised the value of land in the Global South. Between 2004 and 2009, foreign investors came to control 2.5 million hectares of Brazil's agricultural land in deals that involved around $100 billion. One of the most influential investors was TIAA-CREF, a retirement fund for teachers and higher-education retirees in the United States. TIAA-CREF skirted Brazilian laws against foreign land monopolies by signing a partnership with the sugar conglomerate Cosan in 2008. Together, they created a specialized fund known as RADAR, which partnered with de Carli to "acquire properties in Brazil, convert them into plantations of sugarcane and other commodity crops, and then sell them at a profit within a few years," as *The New York Times* put it in an investigative piece from 2015. By that time, TIAA-CREF owned 633,391 acres of land in Brazil, largely in the frontier zones of the Cerrado bordering the Amazon, in depressed states like de Carli's home turf of Maranhão. In the twenty-first century, then, global pension funds and other institutional investors have become a new class of plantation builders.[29]

Once known for staid but steady growth, pension funds like TIAA-CREF now guarantee the hard-earned retirement dreams of underpaid teachers and higher-education workers in the Global North by grabbing the land of the poor and disempowered in the Global South, often to transform them into cane plantations for ethanol. Ranking itself as the "largest global agricultural investor" in the world in 2017, TIAA-CREF has trained special attention on places already softened up by the blows of plantation capitalism. The poultry industry is not alone in erecting new models of profit generation on the boneyard of plantation busts.[30]

TIAA-CREF has also bought up lands in Mississippi that had been taken from Black farm owners over the course of the twentieth century. As journalist Vann Newkirk noted in a seminal 2019 piece, "The foundation of these portfolios was a system of plantations whose owners absorbed thousands of small black-owned farms into ever larger white-owned farms. America has its own *grileiros*, and they stand on land that was once someone else's." The plantation builders of the twenty-first century are massive institutional investors partnering with globally dominant energy companies. We have come a long way from the Portuguese in sixteenth-century São Tomé, though the core of the plantation—securing racialized labor and cheap land for the production of export commodities—has remained consistent.[31]

However distant that early modern world may seem, today we find that we have come full circle, back to the fantasy of endless free wealth. In the twenty-first century, what is being mined is different, but the aspirations are similarly infinite.

We are told that ours is the age of artificial intelligence: a time when human thought itself can be mined by the thinking machines we have built. While their techno-utopian designers promise a "postbiological" future for humanity, currently those technologies require immense amounts of energy. AI is bringing a flood of new investment into old coal-fired, natural gas, and nuclear power plants. To drive its large language models and other AI systems, Microsoft now wants its own source of nuclear power. In 2024, the firm signed a deal with an energy company to restart one of the reactors on Three Mile Island in Middletown, Pennsylvania—the facility that came perilously close to melting down, Chernobyl-style, in 1979. This deal is one of many to signal a major expansion in demands on the national power grid, due to the data centers' AI-fueled energy demands, as well as increased manufacturing, and the charging needs of electric vehicles. In this world of new energy demands, sugar plantations are likely to become more pivotal.[32]

Mega-planters like BP and Copersucar, as well as policymakers and "socially responsible investors," are falling back on the plantation's tempting and often impressive powers to solve climate change without considering its built-in downsides. In spite of the effusiveness of ethanol's promoters, as early as 2008 some discouraging research was starting to emerge. The expansion of ethanol "feedstocks" like sugarcane, corn, and palm oil can, under certain circumstances, mitigate environmental damage, because ethanol puts half as much carbon dioxide into the air as an equivalent volume of gasoline. However, the amount of new acreage that must be cleared to plant all the feedstock reduces forested area globally, taking away an important carbon sink and directly putting carbon dioxide and methane into the air.[33]

Taking into account both direct pressure upon "undisturbed ecosystems" when planters clear land for cultivation, and "indirect pressure" when landowners pushed out of already cultivated zones by ethanol producers settle in the Amazon to establish new farms and cattle ranches, scholars found that biofuels actually pump somewhere between 17 and 420 times "more carbon dioxide than the annual greenhouse gas reductions that these biofuels would provide." Thus, plowing up rainforests, peat bogs, savannas, and grasslands worldwide so that there is enough ethanol to power lots of industry and transport may actually be worse for the climate than simply sticking with fossil fuels. Nevertheless, the entry of globally dominant firms like Cargill, Royal Dutch Shell, and BP has deepened our economic system's commitment to Brazilian ethanol, which reached 33 billion liters in 2023—about ten times its peak during Proálcool.[34]

Moreover, the World Bank has estimated that as much as 75 percent of the food price rise between 2000 and 2008 was attributable to biofuels' competition with food crops. This problem continues to be ignored. Five days before the presidential election of 2024, Joe Biden announced a new initiative to provide more ethanol for American consumers, but dedicating vast amounts of corn and sugar to making fuel instead of food made another serious problem—high food prices—threaten to grow worse. While the Trump administration will try to return the power grid to fossil fuel dependency, that approach is unlikely to last, and even less likely to spread to the rest of the world. The more we use AI to entertain us and keep us company, as well as to solve social and economic crises, the more energy intensive our economy will become. And the more energy intensive our lives become, the deeper the plantation will embed itself in them.[35]

CODA

Burying Ground

In the summer of 1865, a formerly enslaved reverend in the United States named Richard Edwards addressed his recently liberated congregants. "So long ez de shadder ob de great house falls acrost you," he told them, "you ain't gwine ter feel lak no free man, an' you ain't gwine ter feel lack no free 'oman. You mus' all move." To get away from former masters; to avoid domestic servitude; to foil the planters' plans to entangle the freed people in new forms of subjection; this is what Edwards meant. But his warning still rings true. The struggle for the future still centers on challenging the rule of the plantation. But as the last chapter showed, extricating ourselves from it continues to be difficult.[1]

As Americans, we are forced and seduced into carrying with us the values, the self-serving tales, and even the physical remnants of the plantation. Its history, its legacy, and its persistence must be faced, because the plantation can't be forgotten or wished away. It cannot even be buried, because slavery's dead refuse to remain hidden.

In 2015, the University of Georgia, where I am employed, undertook an expansion of Baldwin Hall, a building I can see from my office window. During the excavation phase of the project, workers accidentally disturbed a large burial ground of over one hundred bodies. Initially the university claimed they were "of European descent," but members of the Black community in Athens insisted that the site was a burial ground of enslaved ancestors, and that the university had callously built over it in the mid-twentieth century. DNA analysis subsequently carried out, under community pressure, by the university affirmed the claims of Black Athenians, but the initial response of UGA's administration only hinted at a deeper reticence to confront the institution's historical entanglements with slavery.

Efforts to bury and silence the enslaved people of Athens had failed in the past. In 1937, the initial construction project for Baldwin Hall uncovered what one report described as "120 wooden boxes of remains." Construction crews quickly reburied them. An official report sent to the university noted with a flourish of racist humor that "numerous tibias, vertebrae and grinning skulls of colored brothers were unearthed and thrown 'over the dump.'" The story of a tragic desecration is translated into the dismissive language of minstrelsy by way of the "Black grin." These wounds were reopened in 2016, when the university hurriedly reburied the remains—behind locked gates—in a mass grave during spring break. They did so without reaching out to potential descendants of the folks being unceremoniously reinterred.[2]

They keep burying the history, and they keep acting surprised when it resurfaces. In their stubborn efforts to consign the legacy of the plantation to oblivion, the university's leaders tried to silence the voices echoing up through the linoleum floors of Baldwin Hall, saying: You must continue to reckon with us. The episode makes clear how the self-serving, toxic myths of the planters still ripple through our lives; the plantation's cruel realities refuse to let us go. To move out of its shadow, as Reverend Evans advised in 1865, requires an honest and full recounting of its history, not endlessly repeated reburial. I hope this book serves as a step in that direction.[3]

Acknowledgments

As I was racing through the final edits for this book one recent afternoon, my seven-year-old walked over to my desk, wrote a few words on a sticky note, and pressed it onto the bottom corner of the computer screen. The note reads, "there's a lot more to a book than writing." It was an observation he had made a few weeks before, and now, seeing his tired dad combing through endnotes and reordering images, he must have thought I needed a reminder. He might also have reminded me that there is a lot more to a book than its writer.

Writing a book that spans four centuries, while traversing several academic specialties, I have often waded into worlds about which other scholars know more. During the revision process I leaned heavily on the expertise of several people who read individual chapters and offered crucial input. Most of these kind readers are colleagues of mine at the University of Georgia. Deepest thanks to Jim Cobb, Claudio Saunt, Reinaldo Román, Tracey Johnson, Pablo Lapegna, Joshua Barkan, Benjamin Roy, Steve Krug, Andrew Craig, and Ben Prostine. As teaching assistants in my History of Southern Food class, Jared Asser and Devin Jerome helped me think through key issues. David Singerman of the University of Virginia and Camillia Cowling of the University of Warwick in the

UK also helped me refine important arguments. To the students in my History of Southern Food and History of the Atlantic World classes, many of whom promised to read this book: Know that your queries, and more than a few of your observations, have made their way into its pages. For your patience with a professor exploring sometimes unfamiliar territory, I am forever grateful.

My editor, Dan Gerstle, first suggested this project to me on the advice of Walter Johnson. I thank both of them for trusting in me. Dan has read more drafts of this book than I can count. He has had a strong hand in shaping whatever is good about it. At the start of the project, Tanya McKinnon, literary agent extraordinaire, agreed to take me on as a client. From our first conversation, she has encouraged me to remember one thing: When one writes about bygone people—especially those whose experiences have been silenced or distorted—one incurs a moral obligation to represent their full humanity. Together, Dan and Tanya shepherded me out of the fold of academic writing and into the wider pastures of creative nonfiction. They helped me to expand and clarify my thinking, to give myself permission to tell stories, and to remember that nuanced arguments are best expressed in compelling narratives. I am also grateful for the editorial labors of Zeba Arora and the production team at W. W. Norton, as well as Julie Tesser and Jane Cavolina, who transformed a swollen Word document into the elegant book you hold in your hands. Finally, it has been a deep pleasure to grow into a different kind of writer and teacher at mid-career. I could not have done it without the careful listening, intellectual enthusiasm, and steadfast friendship of Ashley Beresch, Brock Cutler, and Miki Johnson.

Notes

Prologue: The False King of São Tomé

1 John Thornton, *Africa and Africans in the Making of the Atlantic World* (Cambridge University Press, 1998), 170.
2 Unless otherwise cited, my account of Amador's Revolt is based on "Relatório dos factos ocorridos em S. Tomé," 1595, *Monumenta Missionaria Africana*, vol. 3 (Agencia Geral do Ultramar, 1964), 522–24.
3 The phrase is from W. E. B. Du Bois, *Black Reconstruction in America, 1860–1880* (Touchstone, 1995), 727.
4 Luiz Felipe de Alencastro, *The Trade in the Living: The Formation of Brazil in the South Atlantic, Sixteenth to Seventeenth Centuries* (State University of New York Press, 2018), 61.
5 Arturo Teodoro de Matos, coordinator, *Nova História da Expansão Portuguesa a Colonizacão Atlantica*, vol. 3 (Editorial Estampa, 2005), 278.
6 Alencastro, *The Trade in the Living*, 61.
7 "Relatório dos factos ocorridos em S. Tomé."
8 Eddy Stols, "The Expansion of the Sugar Market in Western Europe," in *Tropical Babylons: Sugar and the Making of the Atlantic World, 1450–1680*, ed. Stuart B. Schwartz (University of North Carolina Press, 2004), 251; David Wheat, *Atlantic Africa and the Spanish Caribbean, 1570–1640* (University of North Carolina Press, 2017), 76.
9 Alencastro, *The Trade in the Living*, 72.
10 Alencastro, *The Trade in the Living*, 211, 219; Linda M. Heywood and John

K. Thornton, *Central Africans, Atlantic Creoles, and the Foundations of the Americas, 1585–1660* (Cambridge University Press, 2007), 151–53.
11 Geoffrey Parker, *Global Crisis: War, Climate Change, and Catastrophe in the Seventeenth Century* (Yale University Press, 2017), 341.

Introduction: This Grand Consumer

1 Philip Curtin, *The Rise and Fall of the Plantation Complex* (Cambridge University Press, 1990).
2 Ian Kumamoto, "People Are Renting Out Actual Slave Cabins on Airbnb," Mic.com, July 29, 2022. Airbnb has since taken down the links.
3 Frederick Douglass, *My Bondage and My Freedom* (Norton Critical Editions, 2021), 177.
4 The Trans-Atlantic Slave Trade Database estimates about 388,000 captives were trafficked through the Middle Passage to British North America and the United States between 1600 and 1866.
5 If a unit of agricultural production has some but not all of the following characteristics, I do not count it as a plantation. For example, Midwestern grain farms are an edge case because they grew out of family farms that mechanized and chemicalized so they could raise grain far more cheaply without ever needing masses of labor.
6 Russell R. Menard, *Sweet Negotiations: Sugar, Slavery, and Plantation Agriculture in Early Barbados* (University of Virginia Press, 2006), 98.

Chapter 1: The Great Gulph

1 Evidence given by William Bennett in *Kidermister & Jefferyes v. Berenger*, October 4 and 9, 1663, Court of Delegates, Public Records Office. Quoted in P. F. Campbell, *Some Early Barbadian History* (Barbados: n.p., 1993), 121–24.
2 Campbell, *Some Early Barbadian History*, 121–24.
3 M. Alston Read, "Notes on Some Colonial Governors of South Carolina and Their Families," *South Carolina Historical and Genealogical Magazine* 11, no. 2 (1910): 109.
4 Alan Taylor, *American Colonies: The Settling of North America* (Penguin Books, 2002), 223.
5 Richard S. Dunn, *Sugar and Slaves: The Rise of the Planter Class in the English West Indies, 1624–1713* (University of North Carolina Press, 2000), 96–97; Dan Richter, *Before the Revolution: America's Ancient Pasts* (Harvard University Press, 2011), 245–46.
6 Dunn, *Sugar and Slaves*, 85; Hilary McD. Beckles, *Natural Rebels: A Social History of Enslaved Black Women in Barbados* (Rutgers University Press, 1989), 10; Simon Newman, *A New World of Labor: The Development of*

Plantation Slavery in the British Atlantic (University of Pennsylvania Press, 2013), 214.
7 Russell R. Menard, *Sweet Negotiations: Sugar, Slavery, and Plantation Agriculture in Early Barbados* (University of Virginia Press, 2006), 69, 81; Dunn, *Sugar and Slaves*, 85, 267.
8 Justin Roberts, "Surrendering Surinam: The Barbadian Diaspora and the Expansion of the English Sugar Frontier, 1650–75," *William and Mary Quarterly* 73, no. 2 (2016): 232.
9 J. Hector St. John de Crèvecoeur, *More Letters from the American Farmer* (University of Georgia Press, 1995), 107.
10 Vincent Harlow, *A History of Barbados, 1625–1685* (1926; repr.: Negro Universities Press, 1969), 272.
11 John J. McCusker and Russell R. Menard, *The Economy of British America, 1607–1789* (University of North Carolina Press, 1985), 96–97.
12 McCusker and Menard, *The Economy of British America*, 108; Harlow, *A History of Barbados*, 285.
13 "Robt. Quarry. 2½ pp. *Endorsed*, Recd. Read, 22 Sept., 1697" [*America and West Indies*, 599, No. 32.], America and West Indies: September 1697, 17–30, in *Calendar of State Papers Colonial, America and West Indies: Volume 15, 1696–1697*, ed. J. W. Fortescue (London, 1904), 611–26.
14 Seth Rockman, *Plantation Goods: A Material History of American Slavery* (University of Chicago Press, 2024), 7; Nuala Zahedieh, *The Capital and the Colonies: London and the Atlantic Economy, 1660–1700* (Cambridge University Press, 2010), 189.
15 Linford D. Fisher, "'Dangerous Designes': The 1676 Barbados Act to Prohibit New England Indian Slave Importation," *William and Mary Quarterly* 71, no. 1 (2014): 99–124; Taylor, *American Colonies*, 230–31.
16 James Merrell, *The Indians' New World: Catawbas and Their Neighbors from European Contact Through the Era of Removal* (University of North Carolina Press, 1989), 52.
17 Robbie Ethridge, *From Chicaza to Chickasaw: The European Invasion and the Transformation of the Mississippian World* (University of North Carolina Press, 2010); William L. Ramsey, "'Something Cloudy in Their Looks': The Origins of the Yamasee War Reconsidered," *Journal of American History* 90, no. 1 (2003): 44–75; Taylor, *American Colonies*, 233–35; Paul M. Pressly, *On the Rim of the Caribbean: Colonial Georgia and the British Atlantic World* (University of Georgia Press, 2013), 19–20; D. Andrew Johnson, "Displacing Captives in Colonial South Carolina: Native American Enslavement and the Rise of the Colonial State After the Yamasee War," *Journal of Early American History* 7, no. 2 (2017): 115–40.

Chapter 2: Broken Rice

1. P. F. Campbell, *Some Early Barbadian History* (Barbados: n.p., 1993), 125; Will of Sir John Yeamans, transcribed in M. Alston Read, "Notes on Some Colonial Governors of South Carolina and Their Families," *South Carolina Historical and Genealogical Magazine* 11, no. 2 (1910): 111–16; Gregory E. O'Malley, "Beyond the Middle Passage: Slave Migration from the Caribbean to North America, 1619–1807," *William and Mary Quarterly* 66, no. 1 (2009): 136–37, 140, 165.
2. S. Max Edelson, *Plantation Enterprise in Colonial South Carolina* (Harvard University Press, 2011), 59, 67.
3. Ras Michael Brown, *African-Atlantic Cultures and the South Carolina Lowcountry* (Cambridge University Press, 2012), 151.
4. Judith Ann Carney and Richard Nicholas Rosomoff, *In the Shadow of Slavery: Africa's Botanical Legacy in the Atlantic World* (University of California Press, 2010), 125, 149; Lorena S. Walsh, *From Calabar to Carter's Grove: A History of a Virginia Slave Community* (University of Virginia Press, 1997), 60, quoted in Paul S. Sutter, *Let Us Now Praise Famous Gullies: Providence Canyon and the Soils of the South* (University of Georgia Press, 2015), 148.
5. David Eltis, Philip Morgan, and David Richardson, "Agency and Diaspora in Atlantic History: Reassessing the African Contribution to Rice Cultivation in the Americas," *American Historical Review* 112, no. 5 (2007), 1356–57; Walter Hawthorne, *Planting Rice and Harvesting Slaves: Transformations Along the Guinea-Bissau Coast, 1400–1900* (Heinemann, 2003).
6. Edelson, *Plantation Enterprise*, 78; Walter Hawthorne, "From 'Black Rice' to 'Brown': Rethinking the History of Risiculture in the Seventeenth- and Eighteenth-Century Atlantic," *American Historical Review* 115, no. 1 (2010), 157.
7. Edelson, *Plantation Enterprise*, 71; Jessica B. Harris, *High on the Hog: A Culinary Journey from Africa to America* (Bloomsbury, 2011), 106, 71.
8. Edward Ball, *Slaves in the Family* (Farrar, Straus and Giroux, 2017), 190, 153, 180.
9. Paul M. Pressly, *On the Rim of the Caribbean: Colonial Georgia and the British Atlantic World* (University of Georgia Press, 2013), 97.
10. Ball, *Slaves in the Family*, 52, ix, 96.
11. Richard Drayton, *A View of South Carolina as Respects Her Natural and Civil Concerns* (W. P. Young, 1802), 120; Marc Egnal, *New World Economies: The Growth of the Thirteen Colonies and Early Canada* (Oxford University Press, 1998), 104–6; Edelson, *Plantation Enterprise*, 211.
12. Drayton, *A View of South Carolina*, 119, 115; Joyce E. Chaplin, "Tidal Rice

Cultivation and the Problem of Slavery in South Carolina and Georgia, 1760–1815," *William and Mary Quarterly* 49, no. 1 (1992): 35–36, 56.
13 Chaplin, "Tidal Rice Cultivation," 30.
14 Ryan Quintana, *Making a Slave State: Political Development in Early South Carolina* (University of North Carolina Press, 2018).
15 Chaplin, "Tidal Rice Cultivation," 59.
16 Peter A. Coclanis, *The Shadow of a Dream: Economic Life and Death in the South Carolina Low Country, 1670–1920* (Oxford University Press, 1989), 102–3, 106.
17 Coclanis, *The Shadow of a Dream*, 104; Alex Borucki, David Eltis, and David Wheat, "Atlantic History and the Slave Trade to Spanish America," *American Historical Review* 120, no. 2 (2015): 439, n. 16.
18 Edelson, *Plantation Enterprise*, 94; Egnal, *New World Economies*, 102; Kenneth Morgan, "The Organization of the Colonial American Rice Trade," *William and Mary Quarterly* 52, no. 3 (1995): 433; E. L. Fields-Black, *Deep Roots: Rice Farmers in West Africa and the African Diaspora* (Indiana University Press, 2014), 182.
19 McCusker and Menard, *Economy of British North America*, 174; Morgan, "The Organization of the Colonial American Rice Trade," 434, 436; Egnal, *New World Economies*, 101, 99; Drew Swanson, *Remaking Wormsloe Plantation: The Environmental History of a Lowcountry Landscape* (University of Georgia Press, 2014), 46.
20 Francesca Bray, "Introduction," in *Rice: Global Networks and New Histories*, eds. Francesca Bray, Peter A. Coclanis, Edda L. Fields-Black, and Dagmar Schäfer (Cambridge University Press, 2015).
21 Quintana, *Making a Slave State*, 19; Coclanis, *The Shadow of a Dream*, 98; Egnal, *New World Economies*, 104–6; Drayton, *A View of South Carolina*, 115.
22 Edelson, *Plantation Enterprise*, 152–55.
23 Barbara Spence Orsolits, "The Draytons Of Drayton Hall: Land, Kinship Ties and the British Atlantic World," (PhD diss., Georgia State University, 2019); Amber Satterthwaite, "Carolina—An Enslaved Mason," *Drayton Hall* (blog), 2023.
24 William Bartram, *The Travels of William Bartram, Francis Harper's Naturalist Edition* (University of Georgia Press, 1998), 297.
25 Bartram, *The Travels of William Bartram*, 298–99.
26 Edelson, *Plantation Enterprise*, 119, 117.
27 Edelson, *Plantation Enterprise*, 161–62.
28 Henry Laurens to Richard Oswald, April 27, 1768, in *The Papers of Henry*

Laurens, vol. 5, eds. George C. Rogers, David R. Chesnutt, and Peggy J. Clark (University of South Carolina Press, 1968), 667–68.
29 Edelson, *Plantation Enterprise*, 114; Charles Ball, *Slavery in the United States* (John S. Taylor, 1837), 14.
30 Ball, *Slaves in the Family*, 30; Coclanis, *The Shadow of a Dream*, 26; Taylor, *American Colonies*, 224–25.
31 Drayton, *A View of South Carolina*, 116.
32 Coclanis, *The Shadow of a Dream*, 90.
33 Chaplin, "Tidal Rice Cultivation," 38, 43.

Chapter 3: People That Can Go in the Ditch

1 Johann Martin Bolzius, "Reliable Answer to Some Submitted Questions Concerning the Land Carolina" (1751), reprinted in *William and Mary Quarterly* 14, no. 2 (1957): 234; Alan Taylor, *American Colonies: The Settling of North America* (Penguin Books, 2002), 238.
2 Kenneth Morgan, "The Organization of the Colonial American Rice Trade," *William and Mary Quarterly* 52, no. 3 (1995): 393.
3 Charles Ball, *Slavery in the United States* (John S. Taylor, 1837), 74–75.
4 Bolzius, "Reliable Answer to Some Submitted Questions," 234; Laura Sandy and Gervase Phillips, "'Known to Be Equal to Management': The Modernising Planter and the Enslaved Overseer," *Journal of Global Slavery* 6, no. 1 (2021): 164–65.
5 Samuel Massey to Henry Laurens, June 12, 1780, in *The Papers of Henry Laurens*, vol. 14, eds. C. James Taylor, George C. Rogers, and Peggy J. Clark (University of South Carolina Press, 1994), 305–7.
6 S. Max Edelson, *Plantation Enterprise in Colonial South Carolina* (Harvard University Press, 2011), 79; Philip D. Morgan, *Slave Counterpoint: Black Culture in the Eighteenth-Century Chesapeake and Lowcountry* (University of North Carolina Press, 1998), 184–85.
7 Mart Stewart, "Islands, Edges, Globe: Environmental History of the Georgia Coast," in *Coastal Nature, Coastal Culture: Environmental Histories of the Georgia Coast*, eds. Paul S. Sutter and Paul M. Pressly (University of Georgia Press, 2018), 42.
8 "Memoirs of the Life of Boston King, a Black Preacher. Written by Himself, during his Residence at Kingswood-School" (London, 1798), in *Unchained Voices: An Anthology of Black Authors in the English-Speaking World of the Eighteenth Century*, ed. Vincent Carretta (University Press of Kentucky, 2003), 351; Joyce E. Chaplin, *Anxious Pursuit: Agricultural Innovation and Modernity in the Lower South, 1730–1815* (University of North Carolina Press, 1993), 123; Robert L. Paquette, "The Drivers Shall Lead

Them: Image and Reality in Slave Resistance," in *Slavery, Secession, and Southern History*, eds. Robert Louis Paquette and Louis Ferleger (University Press of Virginia, 2000), 32; John Brown, *Slave Life in Georgia* (Beehive, 1972), 155.

9. Morgan, *Slave Counterpoint*, 223.
10. Paquette, "The Drivers Shall Lead Them," 53, 41.
11. Mart A. Stewart, *What Nature Suffers to Groe: Life, Labor, and Landscape on the Georgia Coast, 1680–1920* (University of Georgia Press, 2002), 176.
12. Betty Wood, *Women's Work, Men's Work: The Informal Slave Economies of Lowcountry Georgia* (University of Georgia Press, 1995), 18; Hayden R. Smith, "Reserving Water: Environmental and Technological Relationships with Colonial South Carolina Inland Rice Plantations," in *Rice: Global Networks and New Histories*, eds. Francesca Bray, Peter A. Coclanis, Edda L. Fields-Black, and Dagmar Schafer (Cambridge University Press, 2015).
13. Brown, *Slave Life in Georgia*, 156; Morgan, *Slave Counterpoint*, 149.
14. Brown, *Slave Life in Georgia*, 156; Ball, *Slavery in the United States*, 83.
15. Brown, *Slave Life in Georgia*, 157.
16. Wood, *Women's Work, Men's Work*, 21; Peter A. Coclanis, *The Shadow of a Dream: Economic Life and Death in the South Carolina Low Country, 1670–1920* (Oxford University Press, 1989); 42, Morgan, *Slave Counterpoint*, 153, 156.
17. Joyce E. Chaplin, "Tidal Rice Cultivation and the Problem of Slavery in South Carolina and Georgia, 1760–1815," *William and Mary Quarterly* 49, no. 1 (1992): 33.
18. Edelson, *Plantation Enterprise*, 83–85, 157; Brown, *Slave Life in Georgia*, 160; Wood, *Women's Work, Men's Work*, 26.
19. Brown, *Slave Life in Georgia*, 157.
20. Maxine Hong Kingston, *Tripmaster Monkey: His Fake Book* (Vintage International, 1990), 49.
21. Ball, *Slavery in the United States*, 36; Jessica B. Harris, *High on the Hog: A Culinary Journey from Africa to America* (Bloomsbury, 2011), 99; Richard Drayton, *A View of South Carolina as Respects her Natural and Civil Concerns* (W. P. Young, 1802), 113.
22. Wood, *Women's Work, Men's Work*, 40, 43.
23. Ball, *Slavery in the United States*, 166–67.
24. Wood, *Women's Work, Men's Work*, 43.
25. Morgan, *Slave Counterpoint*, 138–39, 56.
26. Wood, *Women's Work, Men's Work*, 33.
27. Morgan, *Slave Counterpoint*, 33, 101; Smith, "Reserving Water," 208–9; Drayton, *View of South Carolina*, 33.

28 Andrea Wulf, *Founding Gardeners: The Revolutionary Generation, Nature, and the Shaping of the American Nation* (Vintage, 2012); Ras Michael Brown, *African Atlantic Cultures and the South Carolina Lowcountry* (Cambridge University Press, 2012), 148; Morgan, *Slave Counterpoint*, 141.
29 Ray Berry, "The Real Reason for Sweeping Yards Is Snakes," *New York Times*, August 22, 1993.
30 Wood, *Women's Work, Men's Work*, 25; "Memoirs of the Life of Boston King," 351; Sharla M. Fett, *Working Cures: Healing, Health, and Power on Southern Slave Plantations* (University of North Carolina Press, 2002); Morgan, *Slave Counterpoint*, 249.
31 Wood, *Women's Work, Men's Work*, 86, 82.
32 Bolzius, "Reliable Answer to Some Submitted Questions," 227, 242; Linford D. Fisher, "'Dangerous Designes': The 1676 Barbados Act to Prohibit New England Indian Slave Importation," *William and Mary Quarterly* 71, no. 1 (2014): 111; Wood, *Women's Work, Men's Work*, 54.
33 Wood, *Women's Work, Men's Work*, 62–63.
34 Chaplin, *Anxious Pursuit*, 108; Ryan Quintana, *Making a Slave State: Political Development in Early South Carolina* (University of North Carolina Press, 2018), 117; Vincent Brown, *Reaper's Garden: Death and Power in the World of Atlantic Slavery* (Harvard University Press, 2008), 249; Brown, *African-Atlantic Cultures and the South Carolina Lowcountry*, 143.
35 Isabel Wilkerson, *The Warmth of Other Suns: The Epic Story of America's Great Migration* (Vintage Books, 2010), 239; Wood, *Women's Work, Men's Work*, 71, 29.
36 Brown, *Slave Life in Georgia*, 159; Morgan, *Slave Counterpoint*, 143.
37 Morgan, *Slave Counterpoint*, 450–51; Jane Landers, *Black Society in Spanish Florida* (University of Illinois Press, 1999), 29–30.
38 Quoted in Morgan, *Slave Counterpoint*, 450.
39 Taylor, *American Colonies*, 239–40; Edward B. Rugemer, *Slave Law and the Politics of Resistance in the Early Atlantic World* (Harvard University Press, 2018), 113–15; Edward Ball, *Slaves in the Family* (Farrar, Straus and Giroux, 2017), 187; Morgan, *Slave Counterpoint*, 373–75.
40 Gregory O'Malley, "Beyond the Middle Passage: Slave Migration from the Caribbean to North America, 1619–1807," *William and Mary Quarterly* 66, no. 9 (2009): 144; Ball, *Slaves in the Family*, 146.

Chapter 4: The Apotheosis of Johann Bolzius

1 Phinizy Spalding, *Oglethorpe in America* (University of Chicago Press, 1977), 3; Phinizy Spalding, "James Edward Oglethorpe's Quest for an American Zion," in *Forty Years of Diversity: Essays on Colonial Georgia*, eds.

Harvey H. Jackson and Phinizy Spalding (University of Georgia Press, 1984); Noeleen McIlvenna, *The Short Life of Free Georgia: Class and Slavery in the Colonial South* (University of North Carolina Press, 2015).
2 "Letter from Bolzius to Oglethorpe, 13 Mar 1739," reprinted in *The Clamorous Malcontents: Criticisms & Defenses of the Colony of Georgia, 1741–1743*, ed. Trevor R. Reese (Beehive Press, 1973), 251.
3 Betty Wood, "A Note on the Georgia Malcontents," *Georgia Historical Quarterly* 63 (1979): 266–72.
4 Patrick Tailfer, "A True and Historical Narrative of the Colony of Georgia in America (1741)," reprinted in Reese, *The Clamorous Malcontents*, 24, 28.
5 Tailfer, "A True and Historical Narrative," 55, 54.
6 Samuel Eveleigh to Oglethorpe, October 19, 1734, quoted in Spalding, *Oglethorpe in America*, 62.
7 Tailfer, "A True and Historical Narrative," 57.
8 Drew Swanson, *Remaking Wormsloe Plantation: The Environmental History of a Lowcountry Landscape* (University of Georgia Press, 2014), 31–32; Peter A. Coclanis, *The Shadow of a Dream: Economic Life and Death in the South Carolina Low Country, 1670–1920* (Oxford University Press, 1989), 42–45.
9 Paul M. Pressly, *On the Rim of the Caribbean: Colonial Georgia and the British Atlantic World* (University of Georgia Press, 2013), 29–30, 32.
10 Betty Wood, *Women's Work, Men's Work: The Informal Slave Economies of Lowcountry Georgia* (University of Georgia Press, 1995), 4–5; Kenneth Coleman, "The Southern Frontier: Georgia's Founding and the Expansion of South Carolina," *Georgia Historical Quarterly* 56 (1972): 163–74.
11 Pressly, *Rim of the Caribbean*, 9, 215; Henry Laurens to John Tucker, November 21, 1767, in *The Papers of Henry Laurens*, vol. 4, eds. George C. Rogers, David R. Chesnutt, and Peggy J. Clark (University of South Carolina Press, 1968), 466.
12 Pressly, *Rim of the Caribbean*, 100, 7.
13 Klaus G. Loewald et al., "Johann Martin Bolzius Answers a Questionnaire on Carolina and Georgia: Part II," *William and Mary Quarterly* 15, no. 2 (1958): 237, 241.
14 Johann Martin Bolzius, "Reliable Answer to Some Submitted Questions Concerning the Land Carolina" (1751), reprinted in *William and Mary Quarterly* 14, no. 2 (1957): 233, 245; Francesca Bray, "Introduction," in *Rice: Global Networks and New Histories*, eds. Francesca Bray, Peter A. Coclanis, Edda L. Fields-Black and Dagmar Schäfer (Cambridge University Press, 2015), 31; Peter Coclanis, "Distant Thunder: The Creation of a World Market in Rice and the Transformations It Wrought," *American Historical Review* (October 1993): 1050–78; Loewald et al., "Johann Martin Bolzius Answers a Questionnaire," 243.

15 Charles Ball, *Slavery in the United States* (John S. Taylor, 1837), 192–93.
16 Loewald et al., "Johann Martin Bolzius Answers a Questionnaire," 250.

Chapter 5: Counterblaste

1 *The Secret Diary of William Byrd of Westover, 1709–1712*, Louis B. Wright and Marion Tinling, eds. (Dietz Press, 1941), 410.
2 *Thomas Branagan, the Penitential Tyrant; or, Slave Trader Reformed* (New York, 1807), 271.
3 Betty's story is drawn from Wright and Tinling, *The Secret Diary of William Byrd*, 195–99, 202, 205, 206, 216, 254, 257.
4 Alan Taylor, *The Internal Enemy: Slavery and War in Virginia, 1772–1832* (W. W. Norton, 2014), 8; Christopher Iannini, *Fatal Revolutions: Natural History, West Indian Slavery, and the Routes of American Literature* (University of North Carolina Press, 2012), 248–49.
5 John Huxtable Elliott, *Empires of the Atlantic World: Britain and Spain in America, 1492–1830* (Yale University Press, 2006), 7–10.
6 William Simmonds, *The Proceedings of the English Colonie in Virginia Since Their First Beginning from England in the Yeare of Our Lord, 1606, till This Present 1612, with All Their Accidents That Befell Them in the Journies and Discoveries* (Oxford, 1612), in *The Old Dominion in the Seventeenth Century: A Documentary History of Virginia, 1606–1700*, ed. Warren M. Billings (University of North Carolina Press, 2012), 32; Camilla Townsend, *Pocahontas and the Powhatan Dilemma* (Hill & Wang, 2004), 27; Daniel K. Richter, *Before the Revolution: America's Ancient Pasts* (Harvard University Press, 2011), 100–101.
7 Townsend, *Pocahontas and the Powhatan Dilemma*, 59.
8 Townsend, *Pocahontas and the Powhatan Dilemma*, 80–81; *Works of Captain John Smith*, II, 232–33, in Billings, *The Old Dominion*, 34.
9 Townsend, *Pocahontas and the Powhatan Dilemma*, 84; Lisa Raffensperger, "Starving Jamestown Colonists Engaged in Cannibalism," *Discover*, May 2013.
10 James Horn, *A Land as God Had Made It: Jamestown and the Forging of American Democracy* (Basic Books, 2005), 233, 243, 246; Nuala Zahedieh, *The Capital and the Colonies: London and the Atlantic Economy, 1660–1700* (Cambridge University Press, 2010), 198–99.
11 Darrett B. Rutman and Anita H. Rutman, *A Place in Time: Middlesex County, Virginia, 1650–1750* (W. W. Norton, 1986), 38–39.
12 John J. McCusker and Russell R. Menard, *The Economy of British America, 1607–1789* (University of North Carolina Press, 1985), 121; Anthony S. Parent, *Foul Means: The Formation of a Slave Society in Virginia, 1660–1740* (University of North Carolina Press, 2003), 16; Alison Games, *The Web of*

Empire: English Cosmopolitans in an Age of Expansion, 1550–1660 (Oxford University Press, 2009), 137.
13. "George Percy's Account of the Voyage to Virginia and the Colony's First Days," 1625, in Billings, *The Old Dominion*, 27–29.
14. Parent, *Foul Means*, 17.
15. "Sir Francis Wyatt, Report to the Virginia Company," 1622, in Billings, *The Old Dominion*, 274.
16. Lorena S. Walsh, *Motives of Honor, Pleasure, and Profit: Plantation Management in the Colonial Chesapeake, 1607–1763* (University of North Carolina Press, 2012), 87; Games, *The Web of Empire*, 143.
17. Richter, *Before the Revolution*, 117; Elliott, *Empires of the Atlantic World*, 42; "John Martin's Scheme for Defeating the Indians," 1622, in Billings, *The Old Dominion*, 275–77.
18. Rutman and Rutman, *A Place in Time*, 42; McCusker and Menard, *Economy of British America*, 121; Charles City County Order Book, 1655–1665, in Billings, *The Old Dominion*, 119.
19. Rutman and Rutman, *A Place in Time*, 40–41.
20. Walsh, *Motives of Honor, Pleasure, and Profit*, 143; Ira Berlin, "From Creole to African: Atlantic Creoles and the Origins of African-American Society in Mainland North America," *William and Mary Quarterly* 53, no. 2 (1996): 277.
21. Walsh, *Motives of Honor, Pleasure, and Profit*, 101; Zahedieh, *The Capital and the Colonies*, 207.
22. James Rice, *Tales from a Revolution: Bacon's Rebellion and the Transformation of Early America* (Oxford University Press, 2012), 26–28.
23. Rice, *Tales from a Revolution*, 79.
24. Rice, *Tales from a Revolution*, 44.
25. Rice, *Tales from a Revolution*, 98.
26. Parent, *Foul Means*, 24.

Chapter 6: To Dye in Smoke

1. Fitzhugh to John Cooper Mercht. in London, May 6, 1689, in Richard Beale Davis, *William Fitzhugh and His Chesapeake World* (University of North Carolina Press, 1963), 256.
2. Fitzhugh to Nicholas Hayward, April 1, 1689, in Davis, *William Fitzhugh and His Chesapeake World*, 250; Davis, *William Fitzhugh and His Chesapeake World*, 38, 31.
3. Fitzhugh to Nicholas Spencer, n.d., 1689, in Davis, *William Fitzhugh and His Chesapeake World*, 252.
4. Virginia. General Assembly. House of Burgesses, H. R. (Henry Read) McIlwaine, and Virginia State Library. *Journals of the House of Burgesses*

of Virginia, 1695–1696, 1696–1697, 1698, 1699, 1700–1702 (Colonial Press, E. Waddey, 1913), 28.

5 Jordan Goodman, *Tobacco in History: The Cultures of Dependence* (Routledge, 1994), 57; Anthony S. Parent, *Foul Means: The Formation of a Slave Society in Virginia, 1660–1740* (University of North Carolina Press, 2003), 60; Lorena S. Walsh, "Boom-and-Bust Cycles in Chesapeake History," *William and Mary Quarterly* 68, no. 3 (July 2011): 387–92; David Eltis, Philip Morgan, and David Richardson, "Agency and Diaspora in Atlantic History: Reassessing the African Contribution to Rice Cultivation in the Americas," *American Historical Review* 112, no. 5 (2007): 1339.

6 Parent, *Foul Means*, 69; Fitzhugh to Ralph Wormeley, June 19, 1681, in Davis, *William Fitzhugh and His Chesapeake World*, 93; Joseph Miller, "The Transatlantic Slave Trade and the Middle Passage," Encyclopedia Virginia.org.

7 Ira Berlin, "From Creole to African: Atlantic Creoles and the Origins of African-American Society in Mainland North America," *William and Mary Quarterly* 53, no. 2 (1996): 278–79.

8 Parent, *Foul Means*, 126–28.

9 Kathleen Brown, *Good Wives, Nasty Wenches, and Anxious Patriarchs: Gender, Race, and Power in Colonial Virginia* (University of North Carolina Press, 1996), 118; Fitzhugh to Nicholas Hayward, January 30, 1687, in Beale, *William Fitzhugh and His Chesapeake World*, 205.

10 Lisa Wilson, *A History of Stepfamilies in Early America* (University of North Carolina Press, 2014); Allan Kulikoff, *Tobacco and Slaves: The Development of Southern Cultures in the Chesapeake, 1680–1800* (University of North Carolina Press, 1988), 51; Parent, *Foul Means*, 214–16; Rutman and Rutman, *A Place in Time*, 52–53.

11 Parent, *Foul Means*, 31; Holly Brewer, "Entailing Aristocracy in Colonial Virginia: 'Ancient Feudal Restraints' and Revolutionary Reform," *William and Mary Quarterly* 54, no. 2 (1997): 337–38.

12 Hunter Dickinson Farish, ed., *Journal and Letters of Philip Vickers Fithian, 1773–1774: A Plantation Tutor of the Old Dominion* (Colonial Williamsburg, 1943), 126, 107.

13 Brown, *Good Wives, Nasty Wenches*, 269; Hunter Dickinson Farish, ed., *Journal and Letters of Philip Vickers Fithian*, 202.

14 Vincent Brown, *Reaper's Garden: Death and Power in the World of Atlantic Slavery* (Harvard University Press, 2008), 17; Richard S. Dunn, *Sugar and Slaves: The Rise of the Planter Class in the English West Indies, 1624–1713* (University of North Carolina Press, 2000), 77.

15 Farish, *Journal and Letters of Philip Vickers Fithian*, 59.

16 Farish, *Journal and Letters of Philip Vickers Fithian*, 56; Louis B. Wright and

Marion Tinling, eds., *The Secret Diary of William Byrd of Westover, 1709–1712* (Dietz Press, 1941), 165.

17 Brown, *Good Wives, Nasty Wenches*, 250.
18 Author's tour of Drayton Hall, June 2024.
19 Wright and Tinling, *The Secret Diary of William Byrd*, 414, 413. This Captain Jefferson was a significant planter and was also Thomas Jefferson's grandfather.
20 John J. McCusker and Russell R. Menard, *The Economy of British America, 1607–1789* (University of North Carolina Press, 1985), 136.

Chapter 7: Crop Masters

1 Darrett B. Rutman and Anita H. Rutman, *A Place in Time: Middlesex County, Virginia, 1650–1750* (W. W. Norton, 1986), 41–42.
2 William Fitzhugh to Nicholas Hayward, May 20, 1691 in Richard Beale Davis, *William Fitzhugh and His Chesapeake World* (University of North Carolina Press, 1963), 291.
3 Hunter Dickinson Farish, ed., *Journal and Letters of Philip Vickers Fithian, 1773–1774: A Plantation Tutor of the Old Dominion* (University Press of Virginia, 1978), 243.
4 Lorena S. Walsh, *Motives of Honor, Pleasure, and Profit: Plantation Management in the Colonial Chesapeake, 1607–1763* (University of North Carolina Press, 2012), 361, n69.
5 Timothy Hall Breen, *Tobacco Culture: The Mentality of the Great Tidewater Planters on the Eve of Revolution* (Princeton University Press, 2001), 65–67.
6 Louis B. Wright and Marion Tinling, eds., *The Secret Diary of William Byrd of Westover, 1709–1712* (Dietz Press, 1941), 202, 232, 274, 285, 333.
7 Allan Greer, "Commons and Enclosure in the Colonization of North America," *American Historical Review* 117, no. 2 (2012): 365–86; Virginia DeJohn Anderson, *Creatures of Empire: How Domestic Animals Transformed Early America* (Oxford University Press, 2004), 210–11.
8 Rutman and Rutman, *A Place in Time*, 144.
9 Wright and Tinling, *The Secret Diary of William Byrd*, 72, 43, 507.
10 Allan Kulikoff, *Tobacco and Slaves: The Development of Southern Cultures in the Chesapeake, 1680–1800* (University of North Carolina Press, 1988), 220.
11 Wright and Tinling, *The Secret Diary of William Byrd*, 528, 306, 344, 411, 413.
12 Frederick C. Knight, *Working the Diaspora: The Impact of African Labor on the Anglo-American World, 1650–1850* (New York University Press, 2010), 67; Jack P. Greene, ed., *The Diary of Colonel Landon Carter of Sabine Hall, 1752–1778*, 2 vols. (University Press of Virginia, 1965), 1:455.

13 Greene, *The Diary of Colonel Landon Carter*, 2:267; Walsh, *Motives of Honor, Pleasure, and Profit*, 360.
14 Rhys Isaac, *Landon Carter's Uneasy Kingdom: Revolution and Rebellion on a Virginia Plantation* (Oxford University Press, 2005), 23, 20.
15 Isaac, *Landon Carter's Uneasy Kingdom*, 26, 206.
16 Greene, *The Diary of Colonel Landon Carter*, 1:299, 301, 303, 357. On the weight of hogsheads in Virginia at this time, see *Report from Committees of the House of Commons*, vol. 1 (1715), 622.
17 Greene, *The Diary of Colonel Landon Carter*, 2:840; Greene, *The Diary of Colonel Landon Carter*, 1:574–575.
18 Farish, *Journal and Letters of Philip Vickers Fithian*, 57; Greene, *The Diary of Colonel Landon Carter*, 2:840, 834; Isaac, *Landon Carter's Uneasy Kingdom*, 190–92.
19 Walsh, *Motives of Honor, Pleasure, and Profit*, 402; Holly Brewer, "Entailing Aristocracy in Colonial Virginia: 'Ancient Feudal Restraints' and Revolutionary Reform," *William and Mary Quarterly* 54, no. 2 (1997): 339, 323.
20 Rutman and Rutman, *A Place in Time*, 181–83.
21 Davis, *William Fitzhugh and His Chesapeake World*, 11.
22 Davis, *William Fitzhugh and His Chesapeake World*, 176.
23 Fitzhugh's will is included in Davis, *William Fitzhugh and His Chesapeake World*.
24 Wright and Tinling, *The Secret Diary of William Byrd*, xi; Marion Tinling, ed., *Correspondence of the Three William Byrds of Westover, Virginia, 1684–1776*, 2 vols. (University Press of Virginia, 1977), 1:282, note 1.
25 Nuala Zahedieh, *The Capital and the Colonies: London and the Atlantic Economy, 1660–1700* (Cambridge University Press, 2010), 93.
26 Wright and Tinling, *The Secret Diary of William Byrd*, xi; Tinling, *Correspondence of the Three William Byrds*, 2:613.
27 Gordon Wood, *American Revolution: A History* (Modern Library, 2003), 13.
28 John J. McCusker and Russell R. Menard, *The Economy of British America, 1607–1789* (University of North Carolina Press, 1985), 132, 177; Walsh, *Motives of Honor, Pleasure, and Profit*, 407, 409.
29 Joyce Chaplin, *An Anxious Pursuit: Agricultural Innovation and Modernity in the Lower South, 1730–1815* (University of North Carolina Press, 1993), 8; McCusker and Menard, *The Economy of British America*, 61, 40, 132, 160, 174.
30 Corinne Fowler, *The Countryside: Ten Rural Walks Through Britain and Its Hidden History of Empire* (Scribner, 2024), 260–63; Eric Williams, *Capitalism and Slavery* (University of North Carolina Press, 2021), 91.
31 Walsh, *Motives of Honor, Pleasure, and Profit*, 17; Rutman and Rutman, *A Place in Time*, 188.

32 David Jaffee, *A New Nation of Goods: The Material Culture of Early America* (University of Pennsylvania Press, 2011), 14–16; Washington to Cary, August 1770, in *Plantation and Frontier Documents: 1649–1863*, ed. Ulrich Bonnell Philips (A. H. Clark, 1909), 301–4.
33 Walsh, *Motives of Honor, Pleasure, and Profit*, 458–59; Christopher French, "Productivity in the Atlantic Shipping Industry: A Quantitative Study," in *The Atlantic Staple Trade: The Economics of Trade*, ed. Susan Socolow (Routledge, 1996), 559–84; Rutman and Rutman, *A Place in Time*, 226–27; Zahedieh, *The Capital and the Colonies*, 201–2, 206–7, 209–10, 57.
34 Walsh, *Motives of Honor, Pleasure, and Profit*, 476.
35 Walsh, *Motives of Honor, Pleasure, and Profit*, 398–99.

Chapter 8: The Chiefest of My Estates

1 Quote in Timothy Hall Breen, *Tobacco Culture: The Mentality of the Great Tidewater Planters on the Eve of Revolution* (Princeton University Press, 2001), 145.
2 Breen, *Tobacco Culture*, 138.
3 Breen, *Tobacco Culture*, 190–92.
4 Edward Countryman, *The American Revolution* (Macmillan, 2003), 46.
5 Breen, *Tobacco Culture*, 36; Alan Taylor, *American Revolutions: A Continental History, 1750–1804* (W. W. Norton, 2016), 76–77; Holly Brewer, "Entailing Aristocracy in Colonial Virginia: 'Ancient Feudal Restraints' and Revolutionary Reform," *William and Mary Quarterly* 54, no. 2 (1997): 322; Adam Rothman, *Slave Country: American Expansion and the Origins of the Deep South* (Harvard University Press, 2007), 24.
6 Robert Beverley, *The History and Present State of Virginia*, quoted in *The Literary South*, ed. Louis D. Rubin Jr. (Louisiana State University Press, 2016), 25.
7 John J. McCusker and Russell R. Menard, *The Economy of British America, 1607–1789* (University of North Carolina Press, 1985), 130.
8 Hunter Dickinson Farish, ed., *Journal and Letters of Philip Vickers Fithian, 1773–1774: A Plantation Tutor of the Old Dominion* (University of Virginia Press, 1978), 99; McCusker and Menard, *The Economy of British America*, 132.
9 Countryman, *The American Revolution*, 21–22.
10 Countryman, *The American Revolution*, 73–75.
11 Michael A. McDonnell, "Class War? Class Struggles During the American Revolution in Virginia," *William and Mary Quarterly* 63, no. 2 (2006): 335.
12 Taylor, *American Revolutions*, 257–63.
13 Sylvia R. Frey, *Water from the Rock: Black Resistance in a Revolutionary Age* (Princeton University Press, 1991), 149.
14 Frey, *Water from the Rock*, 153–55, 164–65.

15 Frey, *Water from the Rock*, 156–57.
16 Frey, *Water from the Rock*, 158–59, 167.
17 Frey, *Water from the Rock*, 169.
18 Trevor Burnard and John Garrigus, *The Plantation Machine: Atlantic Capitalism in French Saint-Domingue and British Jamaica* (University of Pennsylvania Press, 2016), 20, 212–13.
19 Frey, *Water from the Rock*, 170–71.
20 James Sidbury, *Ploughshares into Swords: Race, Rebellion, and Identity in Gabriel's Virginia, 1730–1810* (Cambridge University Press, 1997).
21 Lynn A. Nelson, *Pharsalia: An Environmental Biography of a Southern Plantation, 1780–1880* (University of Georgia Press, 2009), 38–39; Alan Taylor, *The Internal Enemy: Slavery and War in Virginia, 1772–1832* (W. W. Norton, 2014), 6.
22 Countryman, *The American Revolution*, 192.
23 Robin L. Einhorn, "Patrick Henry's Case Against the Constitution: The Structural Problem with Slavery," *Journal of the Early Republic* 22, no. 4 (2002): 549–73; David Waldstreicher, *Slavery's Constitution: From Revolution to Ratification* (Hill and Wang, 2009), 142–45.
24 Eric Nelson, *The Royalist Revolution: Monarchy and the American Founding* (Harvard University Press, 2014), 218; Einhorn, "Patrick Henry's Case Against the Constitution," 554.
25 Lorena S. Walsh, *Motives of Honor, Pleasure, and Profit: Plantation Management in the Colonial Chesapeake, 1607–1763* (University of North Carolina Press, 2012), 635–37. The phrase comes from Dylan Penningroth, *The Claims of Kinfolk: African American Property and Community in the Nineteenth-Century South* (University of North Carolina Press, 2003).

Chapter 9: The Colonians

1 Quobna Ottobah Cugoano, "Thoughts and Sentiments on the Evil and Wicked Traffic of the Slavery and Commerce of the Human Species" (London, 1787), abridged in *Unchained Voices: An Anthology of Black Authors in the English-Speaking World of the Eighteenth Century*, ed. Vincent Carretta (University Press of Kentucky, 1996), 163, 165.
2 Gordon A. Wood, *Empire of Liberty* (Oxford University Press, 2009), 367.
3 Trevor Burnard and John Garrigus, *The Plantation Machine: Atlantic Capitalism in French Saint-Domingue and British Jamaica* (University of Pennsylvania Press, 2016), 22.
4 Paul Cheney, *Cul de Sac: Patrimony, Capitalism, and Slavery in French Saint-Domingue* (University of Chicago Press, 2019), 7–8, 27; Laurent Dubois, *Avengers of the New World: The Story of the Haitian Revolution* (Harvard University Press, 2004), 91.

5 Burnard and Garrigus, *The Plantation Machine*, 247–48.
6 Burnard and Garrigus, *The Plantation Machine*, 42; Daniel Rood, *The Reinvention of Atlantic Slavery: Race, Labor, Technology, and Capitalism in the Greater Caribbean* (Oxford University Press, 2017), 52–53.
7 Burnard and Garrigus, *The Plantation Machine*, 196.
8 Burnard and Garrigus, *The Plantation Machine*, 250–51; Johnhenry Gonzalez, *Maroon Nation: A History of Revolutionary Haiti* (Yale University Press, 2019), 51.
9 Manuel Covo, *Entrepôt of Revolutions: Saint-Domingue, Commercial Sovereignty, and the French-American Alliance* (Oxford University Press, 2022), 56; Timothy Pitkin, *A Statistical View of the Commerce of the United States of America* (n.p., 1816), 214; Thomas Jefferson to James Monroe, June 17, 1785, https://founders.archives.gov/documents/Jefferson/01-08-02-174.
10 Jean Casimir, *The Haitians: A Decolonial History* (University of North Carolina Press, 2020), 269; Dubois, *Avengers of the New World*, 130–31.
11 Dubois, *Avengers of the New World*, 94.
12 Carolyn E. Fick, *The Making of Haiti: The Saint Domingue Revolution from Below* (University of Tennessee Press, 1990), 97.
13 Fick, *The Making of Haiti*, 110–111; Dubois, *Avengers of the New World*, 102.
14 Dubois, *Avengers of the New World*, 102.
15 Dubois, *Avengers of the New World*, 96–97.
16 Fick, *The Making of Haiti*, 56.
17 Casimir, *The Haitians*, 279.
18 Gonzalez, *Maroon Nation*, 77.
19 Gonzalez, *Maroon Nation*, 66–68.
20 Gonzalez, *Maroon Nation*, 142, 86; Casimir, *The Haitians*.
21 Gonzalez, *Maroon Nation*, 45, 4.
22 Njoroge M. Njoroge, *Chocolate Surrealism: Music, Movement, Memory, and History in the Circum-Caribbean* (University Press of Mississippi, 2016); Gonzalez, *Maroon Nation*, 148–50.
23 Gonzalez, *Maroon Nation*, 8, 46.
24 Ada Ferrer, "Haiti, Free Soil, and Antislavery in the Revolutionary Atlantic," *American Historical Review* 117, no. 1 (2012): 40; Gonzalez, *Maroon Nation*, 19, 184.

Chapter 10: Vlangbengdeng

1 Ada Ferrer, *Freedom's Mirror: Cuba and Haiti in the Age of Revolutions* (Cambridge University Press, 2014), 23–25.
2 Ferrer, *Freedom's Mirror*, 33–34.
3 Ferrer, *Freedom's Mirror*, 34–35.

4 Victor Bulmer-Thomas, *The Economic History of the Caribbean Since the Napoleonic Wars* (Cambridge University Press, 2012), 170; Timothy Pitkin, *A Statistical View of the Commerce of the United States of America* (n.p., 1816), 214; Manuel Moreno Fraginals, *El ingenio: Complejo económico social cubano del azúcar*, vol. 1 (Editorial de Ciencias Sociales, 1978), 76.

5 Ferrer, *Freedom's Mirror*, 36; Leví Marrero, *Cuba: Economía y sociedad: Azúcar, ilustración y conciencia (1763–1868)*, vol. 10 (Editorial Playor, 1984), 80–81; Fraginals, *El ingenio*, 67.

6 Marrero, *Cuba*, vol. 12, 105–7; Pitkin, *A Statistical View of the Commerce of the United States of America*, 214.

7 Marrero, *Cuba*, vol. 12, 26–28, 105–7.

8 Manuel Covo, *Entrepôt of Revolutions: Saint-Domingue, Commercial Sovereignty, and the French-American Alliance* (Oxford University Press, 2022), 9.

9 Christopher Iannini, *Fatal Revolutions: Natural History, West Indian Slavery, and the Routes of American Literature* (University of North Carolina Press, 2012), 221, 248.

10 Alan Taylor, *American Revolutions* (W. W. Norton, 2016), 422; Gordon Wood, *Empire of Liberty* (Oxford University Press, 2009), 533–34.

11 Adam Rothman, *Slave Country: American Expansion and the Origins of the Deep South* (Harvard University Press, 2007), 29–30.

12 Susan Scott Parrish, *American Curiosity: Cultures of Natural History in the Colonial British Atlantic World* (University of North Carolina Press, 2006); Iannini, *Fatal Revolutions*, 236.

13 This included white and Black populations, but excluded Indigenous people. See Michael Haines, "The Population of the United States, 1790–1920," in *The Cambridge Economic History of the United States*, vol. 2, ed. Stanley Engerman and Robert Gallman (Cambridge University Press, 2000), 156; Robert E. Lipsey, "U.S. Foreign Trade and the Balance of Payments, 1800–1913," in Engerman and Gallman, *The Cambridge Economic History of the United States*, 690.

Chapter 11: The Comprehensive Jaws of America

1 Charles Dickens, *American Notes* (Modern Library, 1996), 177; Steven Deyle, *Carry Me Back: The Domestic Slave Trade in American Life* (Oxford University Press, 2005), 148; Charles Dickens, "To the Editors of the Morning Chronicle," July 25, 1842, in *The Selected Letters of Charles Dickens*, ed. Jenny Hartley (Oxford University Press, 2012), 107.

2 Frederick Douglass, *My Bondage and My Freedom* (Norton Critical Editions, 2021), 177.

3 Dickens, *American Notes*, 178.

4 Percy Wells Bidwell and John I. Falconer, *History of Agriculture in the Northern United States, 1620–1860* (Carnegie Institution of Washington, 1925), 323; Daniel Rood, "Bogs of Death: Slavery, the Brazilian Flour Trade, and the Mystery of the Vanishing Millpond in Antebellum Virginia," *Journal of American History* 101, no. 1 (2014): 22.

5 Michelle Craig McDonald and Steven Topik, "Americanizing Coffee: The Refashioning of a Consumer Culture," in *Food and Globalization: Consumption, Markets and Politics in the Nineteenth and Twentieth Centuries*, ed. Alexander Nutzenadel and Frank Trentmann (Berg, 2008), 121.

6 Alan dos Santos Ribeiro, "The Leading Commission-House of Rio de Janeiro": Os negócios da Maxwell, Wright & Co. (c. 1827–c. 1850)," *Tiempo & Economía* 8, no. 2 (2021), 56; Michael Haines, "The Population of the United States, 1790–1920," in *The Cambridge Economic History of the United States*, vol. 2, ed. Stanley Engerman and Robert Gallman (Cambridge University Press, 2000), 156; Steven Topik, "The World Coffee Market in the Eighteenth and Nineteenth Centuries, from Colonial to National Regimes," London School of Economics, Working Paper no. 04/04 (May 2004), 24.

7 Topik, "The World Coffee Market in the Eighteenth and Nineteenth Centuries," 19–20; Rafael de Bivar Marquese, "As desventuras de um conceito: capitalismo histórico e a historiografia sobre a escravidão brasileira," *Revista de História São Paulo* 169 (July–December 2013): 241–42.

8 Trans-Atlantic Slave Trade Database, Slave Voyages, https://www.slavevoyages.org/voyage/database#tables; Leonardo Marques, *The United States and the Transatlantic Slave Trade to the Americas, 1776–1867* (Yale University Press, 2016), 143; Camillia Cowling, *Conceiving Freedom: Women of Color, Gender, and the Abolition of Slavery in Havana and Rio de Janeiro* (University of North Carolina Press, 2013), 35; McDonald and Topik, "Americanizing Coffee," 121.

9 Daniel Kidder, *Brazil and the Brazilians, Portrayed in Historical and Geographic Sketches* (Philadelphia, 1857), 238–39; Topik, "The World Coffee Market in the Eighteenth and Nineteenth Centuries," 26.

10 Daniel Rood, *The Reinvention of Atlantic Slavery: Race, Labor, Technology, and Capitalism in the Greater Caribbean* (Oxford University Press, 2017), 136; Eulalia Maria Lahmeyer Lobo, *História do Rio de Janeiro: Do capital comercial ao capital industrial e financeiro*, vol. 2 (Instituto Brasileiro de Mercado de Capitais, 1978), 164–65.

11 Rood, *The Reinvention of Atlantic Slavery*, 133.

12 Rood, *The Reinvention of Atlantic Slavery*, 131.

13 Rood, *The Reinvention of Atlantic Slavery*, 134.

14 Rood, *The Reinvention of Atlantic Slavery*, 134.

15 Rood, "Bogs of Death," 22; Rood, *The Reinvention of Atlantic Slavery*, 148.
16 Rood, "Bogs of Death," 26.
17 Thomas Berry, "The Rise of Flour Milling in Richmond," *Virginia Magazine of History and Biography* 78, no. 4 (1970): 406.
18 Rood, "Bogs of Death," 26.
19 Rood, "Bogs of Death," 27.
20 Rood, "Bogs of Death," 39; Jack Temple Kirby, *Poquosin: A Study of Rural Landscape and Society* (University of North Carolina Press, 2014), 50; Lynn A. Nelson, *Pharsalia: An Environmental Biography of a Southern Plantation, 1780–1880* (University of Georgia Press, 2009), 53; Lorena Walsh, "Land Use, Settlement Patterns, and the Impact of European Agriculture, 1620–1820," in *Discovering the Chesapeake*, eds. Philip D. Curtin, Grace S. Brush, and George W. Fisher (Johns Hopkins University Press, 2001), 241, 242.

Chapter 12: The Mother of Slavery

1 David Landes, *The Unbound Prometheus: Technological Change and Industrial Development in Western Europe from 1750 to the Present* (Cambridge University Press, 1969), 83; Sven Beckert, *Empire of Cotton: A Global History* (Knopf, 2014), 33.
2 Marcus Rediker, *The Slave Ship: A Human History* (Penguin, 2007), 5.
3 Beckert, *Empire of Cotton*, 52; Jeremy Prestholdt, "On the Global Repercussions of East African Consumerism," *American Historical Review* 109, no. 3 (June 2004): 755–81; Alfred P. Wadsworth and Julia De Lacy Mann, *The Cotton Trade and Industrial Lancashire, 1600–1780* (Manchester University Press, 1931), 150–53; Joseph Inikori, *Africans and the Industrial Revolution in England: A Study in International Trade and Economic Development* (Cambridge University Press, 2002), 405.
4 Alka Raman, "From Hand to Machine: How Indian Cloth Quality Shaped British Cotton Spinning Technology," *Technology and Culture* 64, no. 3 (2023): 707–36; Beckert, *Empire of Cotton*, 66–67; Landes, *The Unbound Prometheus*, 81.
5 Inikori, *Africans and the Industrial Revolution*, 428.
6 Beckert, *Empire of Cotton*, 73.
7 Andreas Malm, *Fossil Capital: The Rise of Steam Power and the Roots of Global Warming* (Verso, 2016), 251–52; Barbara Freese, *Coal: A Human History* (Basic Books, 2016), 77–78, 82; P. E. H. Hair, "Mortality from Violence in British Coal-Mines, 1800–50," *Economic History Review* 21 (1968): 545–61; John Hodgson, *The Funeral Sermon of the Felling Colliery Sufferers: To which are Prefixed, a Description and Plan of that Colliery; An Account of the*

Late Accident There; of the Fund Raised for the Widows; and Suggestions for Founding a Collier's Hospital (Edward Walker, 1815), 13–15.

8 Beckert, *Empire of Cotton*, 67, 94, 96, 85.
9 Joyce Chaplin, "Creating a Cotton South in Georgia and South Carolina, 1760–1815," *Journal of Southern History* 57, no. 2 (May 1991): 187–89.
10 Angela Lakwete, *Inventing the Cotton Gin: Machine and Myth in Antebellum America* (Johns Hopkins University Press, 2003).
11 Brian D. Schoen, *The Fragile Fabric of Union: Cotton, Federal Politics, and the Global Origins of the Civil War* (Johns Hopkins University Press, 2009), 47.
12 Edward Baptist, *The Half Has Never Been Told: Slavery and the Making of American Capitalism* (Basic Books, 2015), 20, 33.
13 Adam Rothman, *Slave Country: American Expansion and the Origins of the Deep South* (Harvard University Press, 2007), 44–45.
14 Rothman, *Slave Country*, 45.
15 Claudio Saunt, *Unworthy Republic: The Dispossession of Native Americans and the Road to Indian Territory* (W. W. Norton, 2020), 48; Rothman, *Slave Country*, 135.
16 Rothman, *Slave Country*, 138–39.
17 Saunt, *Unworthy Republic*, 32–33, 36.
18 Saunt, *Unworthy Republic*, 308–10.
19 Steven Deyle, *Carry Me Back: The Domestic Slave Trade in American Life* (Oxford University Press, 2006), 296, 146–48.
20 Deyle, *Carry Me Back*, 105–6; John Hebron Moore, *The Emergence of the Cotton Kingdom in the Old Southwest: Mississippi, 1770–1860* (Louisiana State University Press, 1988), 118; William Warren Rogers, Robert David Ward, Leah Rawls Atkins, and Wayne Flynt, *Alabama: The History of a Deep South State* (University of Alabama Press, 2018), 103; Bureau of the Census, by Classified Population of the States and Territories, by Counties, on the First Day of June, 1860: State of Alabama" (1864), 8.
21 Deyle, *Carry Me Back*, 248, 249.
22 Deyle, *Carry Me Back*, 246.
23 Joshua D. Rothman, *Flush Times and Fever Dreams: A Story of Capitalism and Slavery in the Age of Jackson* (University of Georgia Press, 2014); Joseph P. Reidy, *From Slavery to Agrarian Capitalism in the Cotton Plantation South* (University of North Carolina Press, 1995), 31, 38–39.
24 Anthony Kaye, *Joining Places: Slave Neighborhoods in the Old South* (University of North Carolina Press, 2007), 98–99.
25 Paul S. Sutter, *Let Us Now Praise Famous Gullies: Providence Canyon and the Soils of the South* (University of Georgia Press, 2015), 140; William K.

Hutchinson and Samuel H. Williamson, "The Self-Sufficiency of the Antebellum South: Estimates of the Food Supply," *Journal of Economic History* 31, no. 3 (1971): 591–612; Robert Gallman, "Self-Sufficiency in the Cotton Economy of the Antebellum South," *Agricultural History* 44, no. 1 (1970): 5–23.

26 Alan L. Olmstead and Paul W. Rhode, "Biological Innovation and Productivity Growth in the Antebellum Cotton Economy," *Journal of Economic History* 68, no. 4 (2008), 1123–71, 35–36; Alan L. Olmstead and Paul W. Rhode, *Creating Abundance: Biological Innovation and American Agricultural Development* (Cambridge University Press, 2008), 100.

27 *Colonial Records of the State of Georgia*, vol. 20 (University of Georgia Press, 2021), 164.

28 Olmstead and Rhode, *Creating Abundance*, 100, 102, 107; Walter Johnson, *River of Dark Dreams: Slavery and Empire in the Cotton Kingdom* (Harvard University Press, 2017), 249.

29 Olmstead and Rhode, *Creating Abundance*, 102, 104.

30 Olmstead and Rhode, *Creating Abundance*, 108–10, 114; *Vicksburg Sentinel*, July 7, 1847.

31 Dale W. Tomich, Rafael de Bivar Marquese, Reinaldo Funes Monzote, and Carlos Venegas Fornias, *Reconstructing the Landscapes of Slavery: A Visual Hisgtory of the Plantation in the Nineteenth-Century Atlantic World* (University of North Carolina Press, 2021), 28–31.

32 Kaye, *Joining Places*, 97, 101; Olmstead and Rhode, "Biological Innovation," 36.

33 Tomich et al., *Reconstructing the Landscapes of Slavery*, 35.

34 Erin Stewart Mauldin, *Unredeemed Land: An Environmental History of Civil War and Emancipation in the Cotton South* (Oxford University Press, 2018), 34–35.

35 Sutter, *Let Us Now Praise Famous Gullies*, 133–34; Mauldin, *Unredeemed Land*, 34–35.

36 John Majewski and Viken Tchakerian, "Industry and Agriculture in the Antebellum South and Midwest," in *Global Perspectives on Industrial Transformation in the American South*, eds. Susanna Delfino and Michele Gillespie (University of Missouri Press, 2005), 150; Mauldin, *Unredeemed Land*, 30–31; Sutter, *Let Us Now Praise Famous Gullies*, 129.

37 Mauldin, *Unredeemed Land*, 6.

38 Thomas Huertas, "Damnifying Growth in the Antebellum South," *Journal of Economic History* 39, no. 1 (1979): 89; Scott Reynolds Nelson, *Oceans of Grain: How American Wheat Remade the World* (Basic Books, 2022).

39 Robert E. Lipsey, "U.S. Foreign Trade and the Balance of Payments, 1800–1913," in *The Cambridge Economic History of the United States*, vol. 2, eds.

Stanley Engerman and Robert Gallman (Cambridge University Press, 2000), 701; Olmstead and Rhode, "Biological Innovation," 35.
40 Mauldin, *Unredeemed Land*, 38.
41 Brian DeLay, *War of a Thousand Deserts: Indian Raids and the US-Mexican War* (Yale University Press, 2008); Daniel Walker Howe, *What God Hath Wrought: The Transformation of America, 1815–1848* (Oxford University Press, 2009), 659, 665, 667.
42 Howe, *What God Hath Wrought*, 671.

Chapter 13: Bottom Rail on Top This Time

1 Charles B. Dew, *Apostles of Disunion: Southern Secession Commissioners and the Causes of the Civil War* (University of Virginia Press, 2002), 54–55, 62, 67.
2 James McPherson, *Battle Cry of Freedom: The Civil War Era* (Oxford University Press, 2003), 862; U.S. Work Projects Administration, *Slave Narratives: A Folk History of Slavery in the United States* (Federal Writers' Project, 1941), 148.
3 Document 129A: South Carolina Planter to the Commander of the Subdistrict of Coosawhatchie. Hammock, Beaufort District, SC, September 8, 1865, in *Freedom: A Documentary History of Emancipation, 1861–1867*, series 3, vol. 1: *Land and Labor 1865*, eds. Leslie S. Rowland, Steven F. Miller, Steven Hahn, and Susan E. O'Donovan (University of North Carolina Press, 2008), 538–39.
4 James McPherson, *War on the Waters: The Union and Confederate Navies, 1861–1865* (University of North Carolina Press, 2012), 37.
5 McPherson, *War on the Waters*, 136–37.
6 Emory Johnson, T. W. Van Metre, G.G. Heubner, and D.S. Hanchett, *History of Domestic and Foreign Commerce of the United States*, vol. 2, *Contributions to American Economic History* (Carnegie Institute, 1915), 47–49.
7 Johnson et al., *History of Domestic and Foreign Commerce of the United States*, vol. 2, 47–49.
8 Matthew Karp, *This Vast Southern Empire: Slaveholders at the Helm of American Foreign Policy* (Harvard University Press, 2016); William Gregg, "Southern Patronage to Southern Imports and Domestic Industry," *De Bow's Review* 30, no. 1 (January–June 1861): 102–4.
9 George Fitzhugh, "Cuba—The March of Empire and the Course of Trade," *De Bow's Review* 30, no. 1 (January–June 1861): 30–42.
10 William B. Freehling, *The South vs. the South: How Anti-Confederate Southerners Shaped the Course of the Civil War* (Oxford University Press, 2002), 4; McPherson, *Battle Cry of Freedom*, 318–19, 276.

11 Freehling, *The South vs. the South*, 61.
12 Mary W. Milling, Mill View, Fairfield District, SC, February 16, 1864, to David Milling, Milling Papers, Personal Correspondence, 1861–1864: Electronic Edition, https://docsouth.unc.edu/imls/milling/milling.html.
13 John Majewski, *A House Dividing: Economic Development in Pennsylvania and Virginia Before the Civil War* (Cambridge University Press, 2000), 168–71; William Thomas, *The Iron Way: Railroads, the Civil War, and the Making of Modern America* (Yale University Press, 2011); Aaron W. Marrs, *Railroads in the South: Pursuing Progress in a Slave Society* (Johns Hopkins University Press, 2009).
14 Joseph T. Glatthaar, *General Lee's Army: From Victory to Collapse* (Free Press, 2008), 216; Andrew Smith, "Did Hunger Defeat the Confederacy?," *North and South* 13, no. 1 (May 2011), 41; McPherson, *Battle Cry of Freedom*, 319.
15 Earl Hess, *The Rifle Musket in Civil War Combat: Reality and Myth* (University Press of Kansas, 2016), 58–60; Joseph T. Glatthaar, *The March to the Sea and Beyond: Sherman's Troops in the Savannah and Carolinas Campaigns* (New York University Press, 1985), 152.
16 Joan E. Cashin, "Hungry People in the Wartime South: Civilians, Armies, and the Food Supply," in *Weirding the War: Stories from the Civil War's Ragged Edges*, ed. Stephen Berry (University of Georgia Press, 2011), 168.
17 Chandra Manning, *What This Cruel War Was Over: Soldiers, Slavery, and the Civil War* (Vintage, 2007), 62; William Tecumseh Sherman, *Memoirs of General W. T. Sherman* (Penguin, 2000), 608–9.
18 WPA, *Slave Narratives*, 63.
19 Glatthaar, *March to the Sea*, 139.
20 William G. Thomas, *The Iron Way: Railroads, the Civil War, and the Making of Modern America* (Yale University Press, 2013), 159; Brian Melton, "'The Town That Sherman Wouldn't Burn': Sherman's March and Madison, Georgia, in History, Memory, and Legend," *Georgia Historical Quarterly* 86, no. 2 (Summer 2002): 203; 1860 U.S. Census Slave Schedules for Putnam County, Georgia (NARA microfilm series M653, Roll 150), transcribed by Tom Blake, March 2003; Joseph P. Reidy, *From Slavery to Agrarian Capitalism in the Cotton Plantation South: Central Georgia, 1800–1880* (University of North Carolina Press, 1995), 62, 108.
21 Sherman, *Memoirs*, 549.
22 Glatthaar, *March to the Sea*, 106.
23 Mark Grimsley, *The Hard Hand of War: Union Military Policy Toward Southern Civilians, 1861–1865* (Cambridge University Press, 1997), 196; Glatthaar, *March to the Sea*, 141–42.
24 Glatthaar, *March to the Sea*, 130.

25 Thavolia Glymph, *Out of the House of Bondage: The Transformation of the Plantation Household* (Cambridge University Press, 2008), 107.
26 Glatthaar, *General Lee's Army*, 217, 447, 451.
27 Donald Stoker, *The Grand Design: Strategy and the U.S. Civil War* (Oxford University Press, 2012), 389.
28 Gary Gallagher, *The Confederate War: How Popular Will, Nationalism, and Military Strategy Could Not Stave Off Defeat* (Harvard University Press, 1999), 28–29.
29 Laura Edwards, quoted in Stephanie M. H. Camp, *Closer to Freedom: Enslaved Women and Everyday Resistance in the Plantation South* (University of North Carolina Press, 2004), 119, 133; Glymph, *Out of the House of Bondage*, 115, 137.
30 WPA, *Slave Narratives*, 103; Glymph, *Out of the House of Bondage*, 115, 120.
31 Carole Emberton, *Beyond Redemption: Race, Violence, and the American South After the Civil War* (University of Chicago Press, 2013), 187.
32 Glymph, *Out of the House of Bondage*, 133, 138.
33 Camp, *Closer to Freedom*, 121; Document 146: Affidavit of a Georgia Freedwoman, Columbia County, Georgia, November 9, 1865, in Rowland et al., *Freedom: A Documentary History of Emancipation*, series 3, vol. 1, 580–81.
34 Angela Davis, *Blues Legacies and Black Feminism* (Vintage, 1999); Document 183: Georgia Freedman to an Unidentified Military Official, Savannah, Georgia, June 16, 1865, in Rowland et al., *Freedom: A Documentary History of Emancipation*, series 3, vol 1, 697–98.

Chapter 14: Sherman's Reserve

1 Eric Foner, *Reconstruction: America's Unfinished Revolution* (Harper Perennial, 2014), 70–71, 162.
2 Eric Foner, *The Fiery Trial: Abraham Lincoln and American Slavery* (W. W. Norton, 2011), 321; Leslie S. Rowland, Steven F. Miller, Steven Hahn, and Susan E. O'Donovan, eds., *Freedom: A Documentary History of Emancipation, 1861–1867*, series 3, vol. 1: *Land and Labor 1865* (University of North Carolina Press, 2008), 396.
3 Document 131A: South Carolina Planter to the Commander of the Subdistrict of Coosawhatchie, Matthews Bluff, SC, September 14, 1865, in Rowland et al., *Freedom: A Documentary History of Emancipation*, series 3, vol 1, 546.
4 Steven Hahn, *A Nation Under Our Feet: Black Political Struggles in the Rural South from Slavery to the Great Migration* (Harvard University Press, 2004), 96.
5 Document 152: South Carolina Planter to the Commander of the Department of South Carolina, Old Turkey Hill Plantation, 9 miles above

Grahamville, SC, December 1865, in Rowland et al., *Freedom: A Documentary History of Emancipation*, series 3, vol 1, 590.

6. Paul A. Cimbala, "The Freedmen's Bureau, the Freedmen, and Sherman's Grant in Reconstruction Georgia, 1865–1867," *Journal of Southern History* 55, no. 4 (1989): 622–23, emphasis in original.

7. Document 142: Georgia Planter to the Freedmen's Bureau Commissioner, Scriven County, Georgia, November 7, 1865, in Rowland et al., *Freedom: A Documentary History of Emancipation*, series 3, vol 1, 571.

8. "The Suicide of Ruffin," *New York Times*, June 22, 1865.

9. Jack Temple Kirby, *Mockingbird Song: Ecological Landscapes of the South* (University of North Carolina Press, 2006), 123.

10. Frederick Cooper, Thomas C. Holt, and Rebecca J. Scott, *Beyond Slavery: Explorations of Race, Labor, and Citizenship in Postemancipation Societies* (University of North Carolina Press, 2000).

11. Amy Dru Stanley, *From Bondage to Contract: Wage Labor, Marriage, and the Market in the Age of Slave Emancipation* (Cambridge University Press, 1998).

12. Headquarters, Ass't Commissioner, Bureau Refugees, Freedmen, and Abandoned Lands, South Carolina, Georgia, and Florida, Beaufort, South Carolina, August 16, 1865. Reproduced in U.S. Congress, *Report of the Joint Committee on Reconstruction* (Washington, 1866), pt. 2, 230–31.

13. Paul A. Cimbala, "The 'Talisman Power': Davis Tillson, the Freedmen's Bureau, and Free Labor in Reconstruction Georgia, 1865–1866," *Civil War History* 28, no. 2 (1982): 153–71; Foner, *Reconstruction*, 157.

14. Document 143: Commander of the 4th Subdistrict of the Military District of Charleston to the District Headquarters. Georgetown, SC, November 7, 1865, in Rowland et al., *Freedom: A Documentary History of Emancipation*, series 3, vol 1, 573–75.

15. Document 147: Circular by the Freedmen's Bureau Acting Subassistant Commissioner of the 4th Subdistrict of the Military District of Charleston. Georgetown, SC, November 10, 1865, in Rowland et al., *Freedom: A Documentary History of Emancipation*, series 3, vol 1, 581–83.

16. Erin Stewart Mauldin, *Unredeemed Land: An Environmental History of Civil War and Emancipation in the Cotton South* (Oxford University Press, 2018), 74, 89, 90, 93.

17. Russell Duncan, *Freedom's Shore: Tunis Campbell and the Georgia Freedmen* (University of Georgia Press, 1986); Allison Dorsey, "'The Great Cry of Our People Is Land!' Black Settlement and Community Development on Ossabaw Island, Georgia, 1865–1900," in *African American Life in the Georgia Lowcountry: The Atlantic World and the Gullah Geechee*, ed. Philip Mor-

gan (University of Georgia Press, 2010), 226–28; Cimbala, "The Freedmen's Bureau, the Freedmen, and Sherman's Grant," 619.
18 Cimbala, "The Freedmen's Bureau, the Freedmen, and Sherman's Grant," 621.
19 U.S. Congress, *Report of the Joint Committee on Reconstruction* (Washington, 1866), pt. 2, 216–31.
20 Evan Kuntzler, *Ossabaw Island: A Sense of Place* (Mercer University Press, 2016).
21 Karen B. Bell, "'The Ogeechee Troubles': Federal Land Restoration and the 'Lived Realities' of Temporary Proprietors, 1865–1868," *Georgia Historical Quarterly* 85, no. 3 (2001): 386, 391.
22 William Tecumseh Sherman, *Home Letters of General Sherman*, ed. M. A. De Wolfe Howe (C. Scribner's Sons, 1909), 346.
23 Sherman, *Home Letters of General Sherman*, 346.
24 Sherman, *Home Letters of General Sherman*, 353; Glatthaar, *March to the Sea*, 177.
25 Carole Emberton, *Beyond Redemption: Race, Violence, and the American South After the Civil War* (University of Chicago Press, 2013); Matthew Carr, *Sherman's Ghosts: Soldiers, Civilians, and the American Way of War* (New Press, 2015), 139.
26 Hannah Rosen, *Terror in the Heart of Freedom: Citizenship, Sexual Violence, and the Meaning of Race in the Postemancipation South* (University of North Carolina Press, 2009), 179–80.
27 Rosen, *Terror in the Heart of Freedom*, 216–17.
28 Carr, *Sherman's Ghosts*, 139.
29 Gavin Wright, *Old South, New South: Revolutions in the Southern Economy Since the Civil War* (Louisiana State University Press, 1997), 89; U.S. Work Projects Administration, *Slave Narratives: A Folk History of Slavery in the United States* (Federal Writers' Project, 1941), 28.
30 James C. Cobb, *The Most Southern Place on Earth: The Mississippi Delta and the Roots of Regional Identity* (Oxford University Press, 1994), 71.

Chapter 15: The Bronze Titan

1 Rebecca F. Scott, "Reclaiming Gregoria's Mule: The Meanings of Freedom in the Arimao and Caunao Valleys, Cienfuegos, Cuba, 1880–1899," *Past & Present* 170, no. 1 (February 2001): 199, 201–02.
2 Louis A. Pérez Jr., *Cuba: Between Reform and Revolution* (Oxford University Press, 1995), 124.
3 Alan Dye, *Cuban Sugar in the Age of Mass Production* (Stanford University Press, 1998), 26.

4. Michael Zeuske, "Out of the Americas: Slave Traders and the Hidden Atlantic in the Nineteenth Century," *Atlantic Studies* 15, no. 1 (2018): 103–35; María del Carmen Barcia Zequeira, "Caracterizando la trata ilegal en Cuba: Espacios, redes y actores," *Ayer: Revista de Historia Contemporánea* 128, no. 4 (2022): 71–102; Dye, *Cuban Sugar in the Age of Mass Production*, 27; Richard S. Dunn, "The Barbados Census of 1680: Profile of the Richest Colony in English America," *William and Mary Quarterly* 26 (1969): 5; Leví Marrero, *Cuba: Economía y Sociedad*, vol. 10 (Editorial Playor, 1984), 135.

5. Justo Germán Cantero, *Los ingenios: Colección de vistas de los principales ingenios de azúcar de la Isla de Cuba* (Havana, 1857); eds. Luis Miguel García Mora and Antonio Santamaría García (Madrid: Editorial CSIC, 2005), 191; Antonio Santamaria Garcia and Alejandro Garcia Alvarez, *Economía y colonia: La economía cubana y la relación con España, 1765–1902* (Consejo Superior de Investigaciones, 2004), 198; Marrero, *Cuba: Economía y Sociedad*, vol. 10, 32, 198.

6. Marrero, *Cuba: Economía y Sociedad*, vol. 11, 159; Camillia Cowling, "'The People of All Kinds Who Walk Along the Lines': The Precarious Mobilities of Unfree Workers on Cuba's Early Railroads," *Slavery & Abolition* 44, no. 3 (2023): 457; Daniel Rood, *The Reinvention of Atlantic Slavery: Race, Labor, Technology, and Capitalism in the Greater Caribbean* (Oxford University Press, 2017), 64–65; Marrero, *Cuba: Economía y Sociedad*, vol. 10, 31.

7. Herman Merivale, *Lectures on Colonization and Colonies* (Longman, Green, Longman and Roberts, 1861), 91.

8. Evelyn Hu-Dehart, "Chinese Coolie Labour in Cuba in the Nineteenth Century: Free Labour or Neo-slavery?," *Slavery and Abolition* 14, no. 1 (1993): 67–86; Benjamin Narváez, "Abolition, Chinese Indentured Labor, and the State: Cuba, Peru, and the United States During the Mid-Nineteenth Century," *The Americas* 76, no. 1 (2019): 5–40.

9. Ramón de la Sagra, *Cuba en 1860, ó sea cuadro de sus adelantos en la poblacion, la agricultura, el comercio y las rentas publicas. Suplemento a la primera parte de "La Historia Politica y Natural de la Isla de Cuba" por D. Ramon de la Sagra* (Paris, 1862), 57.

10. Lisa Yun and Ricardo Rene Laremont, "Chinese Coolies and African Slaves in Cuba, 1847–74," *Journal of Asian American Studies* 4, no. 2 (2001): 112, 116.

11. Sagra, *Cuba en 1860*, 56.

12. Manuel Moreno Fraginals, *Cuba/España, España/Cuba: Historia común* (Crítica, 1995), 90.

13. Dye, *Cuban Sugar in the Age of Mass Production*, 71–72, 12.

14 Fe Iglesias García, "The Development of Capitalism in Cuban Sugar Production, 1860–1900," in *Between Slavery and Free Labor: The Spanish-Speaking Caribbean in the Nineteenth Century*, eds. Manuel Moreno Fragiinals, Frank Moya Pons, and Stanley Engerman (Johns Hopkins University Press, 1985), 67, 69, 59.

15 Louis A. Pérez Jr., *Cuba and the United States: Ties of Singular Intimacy* (University of Georgia Press, 1990), 18–21.

16 David Murray, *Odious Commerce: Britain, Spain, and the Abolition of the Cuban Slave Trade* (Cambridge University Press, 1980), 208–10; "Exports of Produce from Havana and Matanzas," *Hunt's Merchant Magazine* 22 (1850): 430–32; *Letter of the Secretary of State, Transmitting a Report of the Commercial Relations of the United States with Foreign Nations, for the Year Ending September 30, 1861* (U.S. Government Printing Office, 1862), 167–68.

17 Inés Roldán de Montaud, "Baring Brothers and the Cuban Plantation Economy," in *The Caribbean and the Atlantic World Economy*, eds., A. B. Leonard and David Pretel (Palgrave Macmillan, 2015), 256; César Ayala, *American Sugar Kingdom: The Plantation Economy of the Spanish Caribbean, 1898–1934* (University of North Carolina Press, 1999), 57, 61.

18 Ayala, *American Sugar Kingdom*, 30; April Merleaux, *Sugar and Civilization: American Empire and the Cultural Politics of Sweetness* (University of North Carolina Press, 2015), 60–61; Roldán de Montaud, "Baring Brothers and the Cuban Plantation Economy," 256.

19 Bartow J. Elmore, *Citizen Coke: The Making of Coca-Cola Capitalism* (W. W. Norton, 2014), 77, 88.

20 Scott, "Reclaiming Gregoria's Mule," 199.

21 Scott, "Reclaiming Gregoria's Mule," 193–95.

22 Perez, *Cuba: Between Reform and Revolution*, 147–48.

23 John Lawrence Tone, *War and Genocide in Cuba, 1895–1898* (University of North Carolina Press, 2006), 64; Ada Ferrer, *Insurgent Cuba: Race, Nation, and Revolution, 1868–1898* (University of North Carolina Press, 1999), 148; Perez, *Cuba: Between Reform and Revolution*, 160.

24 Perez, *Cuba: Between Reform and Revolution*, 162–64.

25 Perez, *Cuba: Between Reform and Revolution*, 166.

26 Perez, *Cuba: Between Reform and Revolution*, 167.

27 Perez, *Cuba: Between Reform and Revolution*, 175.

28 Glenda Elizabeth Gilmore, *Gender and Jim Crow: Women and the Politics of White Supremacy in North Carolina, 1896–1920* (University of North Carolina Press, 1996), 92–93, 111–12.

29 Edward Rugemer, "Jamaica's Morant Bay Rebellion and the Making of Radical Reconstruction," in *United States Reconstruction Across the Americas*,

ed. William A. Link (University Press of Florida, 2019), 102; Ferrer, *Insurgent Cuba*, 189–91.

30 Richard D. Starnes, "Forever Faithful: The Southern Historical Society and Confederate Historical Memory," *Southern Cultures* 2, no. 2 (1996): 177–94; Edward Longacre, "Fitzhugh Lee (1835–1905)," Encyclopedia Virginia.

31 Fitzhugh Lee, Joseph Wheeler, and Teddy Roosevelt, *Cuba's Struggle Against Spain: With the Causes for American Intervention and a Full Account of the Spanish-American War, Including Final Peace Negotiations* (American Historical Press, 1899), 39.

32 Lee et al., *Cuba's Struggle Against Spain*, 617.

33 Perez, *Cuba: Between Reform and Revolution*, 177.

34 Ferrer, *Insurgent Cuba*, 219; David Sartorius, *Ever Faithful: Race, Loyalty, and the Ends of Empire in Spanish Cuba* (Duke University Press, 2014), 221, 223.

35 Sartorius, *Ever Faithful*, 218, 220.

36 Perez, *Cuba: Between Reform and Revolution*, 186.

Chapter 16: The White Whale

1 Manuel Moreno Fraginals, "Plantations in the Caribbean: Cuba, Puerto Rico, and the Dominican Republic in the Late Nineteenth Century," in *Between Slavery and Free Labor: The Spanish-Speaking Caribbean in the Nineteenth-Century*, ed. Manuel Moreno Fraginals, Frank Moya Pons, and Stanley Engerman (Johns Hopkins University Press, 1985), 9; Leida Fernández Prieto, *Cuba Agrícola: Mito y Tradición, 1878–1920* (CSIC, 2005), 117; April Merleaux, *Sugar and Civilization: American Empire and the Politics of Sweetness* (University of North Carolina Press, 2015), 38–41.

2 César Ayala, *American Sugar Kingdom: The Plantation Economy of the Spanish Caribbean, 1898–1934* (University of North Carolina Press, 1999), 67; Manuel Moreno Fraginals, *El ingenio: Complejo económico social cubano del azúcar*, vol. 3 (Editorial de Ciencias Sociales, 1978), 39.

3 Moreno Fraginals, "Plantations in the Caribbean," 13.

4 Merleaux, *Sugar and Civilization*, 17; Ayala, *American Sugar Empire*, 82.

5 Alfred D. Chandler Jr., *The Visible Hand: The Managerial Revolution in American Business* (Belknap Press of Harvard University Press, 1993), 329; Oscar Zanetti and Alejandro García, *Sugar and Railroads: A Cuban History, 1837–1959* (University of North Carolina Press, 1998), 196, 211.

6 Alan Dye, *Cuban Sugar in the Age of Mass Production* (Stanford University Press, 1998), 60–61.

7 Dye, *Cuban Sugar in the Age of Mass Production*, 196.

8 Matthew Casey, *Empire's Guestworkers: Haitian Migrants in Cuba During the Age of US Occupation* (Cambridge University Press, 2017), 3.

9. Moreno Fraginals, "Plantations in the Caribbean," 7; Jorge Giovanetti-Torres, *Black British Migrants in Cuba: Race, Labor, and Empire in the Twentieth-Century Caribbean, 1898–1948* (Cambridge University Press, 2018), 59–60; Casey, *Empire's Guestworkers*, 136, 7, 123.
10. John Soluri, *Banana Cultures: Agriculture, Consumption, and Environmental Change in Honduras and the United States* (University of Texas Press, 2005); Steven Topik and Allen Wells, eds., *The Second Conquest of Latin America: Coffee, Henequen, and Oil During the Export Boom* (University of Texas Press, 1998).
11. Prieto, *Cuba Agrícola*; David Singerman, "Sugar Machines and the Fragile Infrastructure of Commodities in the Nineteenth Century," *Osiris* 33 (2018): 63–84; Stuart McCook, *States of Nature: Science, Agriculture, and Environment in the Spanish Caribbean, 1760–1940* (University of Texas Press, 2002), 66, 62.
12. McCook, *States of Nature*, 81, 79, 100, 102, 89.
13. Alfred S. Eichner, *The Emergence of Oligopoly: Sugar Refining as a Case Study* (Johns Hopkins University Press, 1969), 54.
14. Alfred D. Chandler Jr., *Scale and Scope: The Dynamics of Industrial Capitalism* (Harvard University Press, 1990), 152.
15. Dye, *Cuban Sugar in the Age of Mass Production*, 84; Moreno Fraginals, "Plantations in the Caribbean," 12–13.
16. Robert B. Hoernel, "Sugar and Social Change in Oriente, Cuba, 1898–1946," *Journal of Latin American Studies* 8, no. 2 (1976): 222–23.
17. Hoernel, "Sugar and Social Change in Oriente, Cuba," 220; Alejandro de la Fuente, *A Nation for All: Race, Inequality, and Politics in Twentieth-Century Cuba* (University of North Carolina Press, 2001), 106.
18. Shannon Lee Dawdy, "La Comida Mambisa: Food, Farming, and Cuban Identity, 1839–1999," *New West Indian Guide* 76, nos. 1 and 2 (2002); Lou Perez, "Politics, Peasants, and People of Color: The 1912 'Race War' in Cuba Reconsidered," *Hispanic American Historical Review* 66, no. 3 (1986): 517–18.
19. Hoernel, "Sugar and Social Change in Oriente, Cuba," 226.
20. Perfecto Lacoste, *Opportunities in Cuba* (Lewis, Scribner, 1902), 154–56.
21. Zanetti and García, *Sugar and Railroads*, 226–27, 229–30.
22. De la Fuente, *A Nation for All*, 105.
23. Zanetti and García, *Sugar and Railroads*, 232; De la Fuente, *A Nation for All*, 105.
24. De la Fuente, *A Nation for All*.
25. The above account is drawn from Perez, "Politics, Peasants, and People of Color."

26 Aisha Finch and Fannie Rushing, eds., *Breaking the Chains, Forging the Nation: The Afro-Cuban Fight for Freedom and Equality, 1812–1912* (Louisiana State University, 2019), 217.
27 Glenda Elizabeth Gilmore, *Defying Dixie: The Radical Roots of Civil Rights, 1919–1950* (W. W. Norton, 2009), 22–25.
28 Dye, *Cuban Sugar in the Age of Mass Production*, 9; Hoernel, "Sugar and Social Change in Oriente, Cuba," 233–34.
29 Dye, *Cuban Sugar in the Age of Mass Production*, 57.

Chapter 17: Percy's Ode

1 William Alexander Percy, *Lanterns on the Levee: Recollections of a Planter's Son* (Knopf, 1941), 273; Arthur Raper, *Preface to Peasantry: A Tale of Two Black Belt Counties* (University of North Carolina Press, 1936), 16.
2 Richard Bland, "An Epistle to Landon Carter, Esqu., upon Hearing That He Does Not Intend to Stand a Candidate at the Next Election of Burgesses," quoted in *The Literary South*, ed. Louis D. Rubin Jr. (Louisiana State University Press, 2016), 52.
3 Charles Aiken, *The Cotton Plantation South Since the Civil War* (Johns Hopkins University Press, 1998), 46.
4 Roger Ransom and Richard Sutch, "The Impact of the Civil War and of Emancipation on Southern Agriculture," *Explorations in Economic History* 12, no. 1 (1975): 12; James Cobb, "Beyond Planters and Industrialists: A New Perspective on the New South," *Journal of Southern History* 54, no. 1 (1988): 53–54.
5 Peter Coclanis, "The Southern Economy in the Long Twentieth Century," in *A New History of the American South*, ed. W. Fitzhugh Brundage (University of North Carolina Press, 2023), 476–78; Sven Beckert, *Empire of Cotton: A Global History* (Knopf, 2014), 318.
6 Erin Stewart Mauldin, *Unredeemed Land: An Environmental History of Civil War and Emancipation in the Cotton South* (Oxford University Press, 2018), 112, 96.
7 Percy, *Lanterns on the Levee*, 68–69: Joseph Reidy, *From Slavery to Agrarian Capitalism in the Cotton Plantation South: Central Georgia, 1800–1880* (University of North Carolina Press, 1992), 233–35.
8 Gavin Wright, *Old South, New South: Revolutions in the Southern Economy Since the Civil War* (Louisiana State University Press, 1997), 102.
9 Wright, *Old South, New South*, 102–3.
10 James C. Cobb, *The Most Southern Place on Earth: The Mississippi Delta and the Roots of Regional Identity* (Oxford University Press, 1994), 103–4.
11 Cobb, *The Most Southern Place on Earth*, 117. Ned Cobb's dictated autobiog-

raphy was published under the following title: Theodore Rosengarten, *All God's Dangers: The Life of Nate Shaw* (Knopf, 1974).

12 Cobb, *The Most Southern Place on Earth*, 102.
13 Douglas A. Blackmon, *Slavery by Another Name: The Re-Enslavement of Black Americans from the Civil War to World War II* (Anchor, 2008); Talitha L. LeFlouria, *Chained in Silence: Black Women and Convict Labor in the New South* (University of North Carolina Press, 2015), 10–11.
14 Cobb, *The Most Southern Place on Earth*, 121.
15 Cobb, *The Most Southern Place on Earth*, 113.
16 Jeannie Whayne, *Delta Empire: Lee Wilson and the Transformation of Agriculture in the New South* (Louisiana State University Press, 2016), 94–95.
17 Whayne, *Delta Empire*, 125, 114, 53.
18 Cobb, *The Most Southern Place on Earth*, 101, quoting Harold Woodman; Whayne, *Delta Empire*, 88; Merle Prunty, "The Renaissance of the Southern Plantation," *Geographical Review* 45, no. 4 (1953): 461; James C. Giesen, "'The Truth About the Boll Weevil': The Nature of Planter Power in the Mississippi Delta," *Environmental History* 14, no. 4 (2009): 688.
19 Pete Daniel, *Dispossession: Discrimination Against African American Farmers in the Age of Civil Rights* (University of North Carolina Press, 2013), 6; Adrienne Petty, *Standing Their Ground: Small Farmers in North Carolina Since the Civil War* (University of North Carolina Press, 2013); Mark Ellis, "Racial Unrest and White Liberalism in Rural Georgia: Barrow and Oconee Counties in the Early 1920s," *Georgia Historical Quarterly* 97, no. 1 (Spring 2013).
20 Zora Neale Hurston, *Mules and Men* (Harper Perennial, 1990), 102; Walter Barnard Hill, "Rural Survey of Clarke County, Georgia, with Special Reference to the Negroes," *Bulletin of the University of Georgia* 15, no. 3 (1915): 21.
21 Hortense Powdermaker, *After Freedom: A Cultural Study in the Deep South* (Viking, 1939), 100.
22 Cobb, *All God's Dangers*, 337; Raper, *Preface to Peasantry*, 122–23.
23 Powdermaker, *After Freedom*, 106.
24 Hill, "Rural Survey," 21–22; Zora Neale Hurston, *Their Eyes Were Watching God* (Harper Perennial, 1990), 14.
25 Numbers compiled from the following census reports (contact author for details): Bureau of the Census, *Fourteenth Census of the United States: 1920 Bulletin Agriculture: Georgia*, 84–97; Bureau of the Census, *Fourteenth Census of the United States: 1920 Bulletin Agriculture: Mississippi*, 62–69.
26 W. Fitzhugh Brundage, "A Portrait of Southern Sharecropping: The 1911–1912 Georgia Plantation Survey of Robert Preston Brooks," *Georgia Historical Quarterly* 77, no. 2 (1993): 374–76.

27 Robert P. Brooks, *The Agrarian Revolution in Georgia* (PhD diss., University of Wisconsin, Madison, 1914), 440.
28 Prunty, "The Renaissance of the Southern Plantation," 475, 481.
29 Prunty, "The Renaissance of the Southern Plantation," 479.
30 Mark D. Hersey, *My Work Is That of Conservation: An Environmental Biography of George Washington Carver* (University of Georgia Press, 2011), 100, 104, 107.
31 Robin D. G. Kelley, *Hammer and Hoe: Alabama Communists During the Great Depression* (University of North Carolina Press, 1990), 36.
32 Raper, *Preface to Peasantry*, 73–74.
33 Cobb, *All God's Dangers*, 122.
34 Reidy, *From Slavery to Agrarian Capitalism*, 235; Prunty, "The Renaissance of the Southern Plantation," 471, 475.
35 Hurston, *Their Eyes Were Watching God*, 53–55.
36 William Faulkner, *Sartoris*, quoted in George Ellenberg, *Mule South to Tractor South: Mules, Machines, and the Transformation of the Cotton South* (University of Alabama Press, 2007).
37 William Faulkner, *The Mansion: A Novel of the Snopes Family* (Vintage International, 2011, orig. 1955), 16.
38 Paul K. Conkin, *A Revolution Down on the Farm: The Transformation of American Agriculture Since 1929* (University Press of Kentucky, 2008), 112; Ed Melillo, "The First Green Revolution: Debt Peonage and the Making of the Nitrogen Fertilizer Trade, 1840–1930," *American Historical Review* 117, no. 4 (October 2012): 1037.
39 Timothy H. Johnson, "Growth Industry: The Political Economy of Fertilizer in America, 1865–1947" (PhD diss., University of Georgia, 2016); Paul S. Sutter, *Let Us Now Praise Famous Gullies: Providence Canyon and the Soils of the South* (University of Georgia Press, 2015), 153.
40 Deborah Fitzgerald, *Every Farm a Factory: The Industrial Ideal in American Agriculture* (Yale University Press, 2003), 33–35.
41 Sutter, *Let Us Now Praise Famous Gullies*, 26.
42 Hersey, *My Work Is That of Conservation*, 126; Monica White, *Freedom Farmers: Agricultural Resistance and the Black Freedom Movement* (University of North Carolina Press, 2018), 46–48.
43 George Washington Carver, "Being Kind to the Soil," *Negro Farmer* 31 (1914), quoted in Hersey, *My Work Is That of Conservation*, 142, and 128, 130.
44 Hersey, *My Work Is That of Conservation*, 167.
45 Cobb, *All God's Dangers*, 127.

Chapter 18: Standing

1. Rebecca J. Scott, *Degrees of Freedom: Louisiana and Cuba After Slavery* (Harvard University Press, 2008), 84–85.
2. Omar Ali, "Black Populism: Agrarian Politics from the Colored Alliance to the People's Party," in *Beyond Forty Acres and a Mule: African American Landowning Families Since Reconstruction*, eds. Debra Reid and Evan Bennett (University Press of Florida, 2012), 11–12.
3. Ali, "Black Populism," 113–14, 119.
4. Ali, "Black Populism," 119.
5. Walter Barnard Hill, "Rural Survey of Clarke County, Georgia, with Special Reference to the Negroes," *Bulletin of the University of Georgia* 15, no. 3 (1915): 56–57; Sarah Thurmond, "A Comparison of the Intelligence and Achievement of 12-Year-Old Negro Children in the Rural Schools of Clarke County, Georgia," *University of Georgia Bulletin* 33, no. 11C (1933): 6.
6. Hill, "Rural Survey," 56–57.
7. Jeannie Whayne, *Delta Empire: Lee Wilson and the Transformation of Agriculture in the New South* (Louisiana State University Press, 2011), 121–22; A. F. Hickmott, "'Brothers Come North': The Rural South and the Political Imaginary of New Negro Radicalism," *Intellectual History Review* 21, no. 4 (2011): 405.
8. James C. Giesen, "'The Truth About the Boll Weevil': The Nature of Planter Power in the Mississippi Delta," *Environmental History* 14, no. 4 (2009): 683–704.
9. Bureau of the Census, *Fourteenth Census of the United States: 1920 Bulletin Agriculture: Mississippi*, 62–69.
10. Giesen, "The Truth About the Boll Weevil," 697–98.
11. Erin Stewart Mauldin, *Unredeemed Land: An Environmental History of Civil War and Emancipation in the Cotton South* (Oxford University Press, 2018), 101.
12. Charles Aiken, *The Cotton Plantation South Since the Civil War* (Johns Hopkins University Press, 1998), 78–81; Trevor Burnard and John Garrigus, *The Plantation Machine: Atlantic Capitalism in French Saint-Domingue and British Jamaica* (University of Pennsylvania Press, 2016), 169.
13. Louise McHenry Hicky, *Rambles Through Morgan County: Her History, Century Old Houses and Churches, and Tales to Remember* (Morgan County Historical Society, 1971), 38, 52.
14. Arthur Raper, *Preface to Peasantry: A Tale of Two Black Belt Counties* (University of North Carolina Press, 1936), 190–91, 195.

15 Ned Cobb, *All God's Dangers: The Life of Nate Shaw* (Knopf, 1974), 288, 290, 291.
16 Cobb, *All God's Dangers*, 292, 295; Lawrence Powell, "The Prussians Are Coming," *Georgia History Quarterly* 71, no. 4 (1987).
17 Robin D. G. Kelley, *Hammer and Hoe: Alabama Communists During the Great Depression* (University of North Carolina Press, 1990), 39.
18 Kelley, *Hammer and Hoe*, 41–42.
19 Kelley, *Hammer and Hoe*, 44.
20 Kelley, *Hammer and Hoe*, 40; Cobb, *All God's Dangers*, 305.
21 Cobb, *All God's Dangers*, 306.
22 Cobb, *All God's Dangers*, 307.
23 Kelley, *Hammer and Hoe*, 49–51.
24 Cobb, *All God's Dangers*, 314–15.
25 Cobb, *All God's Dangers*, 500.
26 Ira Katznelson, *Fear Itself: The New Deal and the Origin of Our Times* (W. W. Norton, 2013), 87.
27 Pete Daniel, *Dispossession: Discrimination Against African-American Farmers in the Age of Civil Rights* (University of North Carolina Press, 2013), 164–65.
28 Daniel, *Dispossession*, 6.
29 Sven Beckert, *Empire of Cotton: A Global History* (Knopf, 2014), 343.
30 Gavin Wright, *Old South, New South: Revolutions in the Southern Economy Since the Civil War* (Louisiana State University Press, 1986), 201.
31 Harry Crews, *A Childhood: The Biography of a Place* (University of Georgia Press, 1978), 88.
32 From Thomas Jefferson Flanagan, "The Erosion March," quoted in Paul S. Sutter, *Let Us Now Praise Famous Gullies: Providence Canyon and the Soils of the South* (University of Georgia Press, 2015), 79.

Chapter 19: The Slave Empires of History

1 Charles W. Ramsdell, "The Natural Limits of Slavery Expansion," *Mississippi Valley Historical Review* (1929): 160–71.
2 Paul S. Sutter, *Let Us Now Praise Famous Gullies: Providence Canyon and the Soils of the South* (University of Georgia Press, 2015), 203; Mark Arax and Rick Wartzman, *The King of California: J. G. Boswell and the Making of a Secret American Empire* (PublicAffairs, 2003), 6; Devra Weber, *Dark Sweat, White Gold: California Farm Workers, Cotton, and the New Deal* (University of California Press, 1994), 21, 23.
3 For the terminology of cotton "ranches," see Weber, *Dark Sweat, White Gold*; Arax and Wartzman, *The King of California*, 415.

4 Mark Arax, *The Dreamt Land: Chasing Water and Dust Across California* (Knopf, 2019), 415.
5 Arax, *The Dreamt Land*, 415–16, 459.
6 Richard A. Walker, *The Conquest of Bread: 150 Years of Agribusiness in California* (New Press, 2004), 3, 58; Weber, *Dark Sweat, White Gold*, 7.
7 Stacey Smith, *Freedom's Frontier: California and the Struggle over Unfree Labor, Emancipation, and Reconstruction* (University of North Carolina Press, 2013), 15, 8, 126.
8 Smith, *Freedom's Frontier*, 9, 76, 234.
9 Arax, *Dreamt Land*, 186.
10 Arax, *Dreamt Land*, 179–80, 182–83.
11 *History of Fresno County, California, with Illustrations* (San Francisco, 1882), 118–19.
12 *History of Fresno County, California, with Illustrations* (San Francisco, 1882), 118–19.
13 David C. Parker, "Rebels in Sentiment: Harry St. John Dixon, White Masculinity, Slavery, and Politics in Antebellum Mississippi and Reconstruction California" (MA diss., University of Georgia, 2021).
14 Benjamin Madley, *An American Genocide: The United States and the California Indian Catastrophe* (Yale University Press, 2016), 3, 14.
15 Richard White, *Railroaded: The Transcontinentals and the Making of Modern America* (W. W. Norton, 2011), 167, 206; Edna Monch Parker, "The Southern Pacific Railroad and Settlement in Southern California," *Pacific Historical Review* 6, no. 2 (1937): 103–19; Arax and Wartzman, *The King of California*, 77, 79.
16 Walker, *Conquest of Bread*, 25, 165; Alan L. Olmstead and Paul W. Rhode, *Creating Abundance: Biological Innovation and American Agricultural Development* (Cambridge University Press, 2008), 224; Jessica B. Teisch, *Engineering Nature: Water, Development, and the Global Spread of American Environmental Expertise* (University of North Carolina Press, 2011), 21.
17 Arax and Wartzman, *The King of California*, 81–82.
18 Arax and Wartzman, *The King of California*, 36–37, 117.
19 Moses Musoke and Alan Olmstead, "The Rise of the Cotton Industry in California: A Comparative Perspective," *Journal of Economic History* 42, no. 2 (1982): 386–87, 389–90; Olmstead and Rhode, *Creating Abundance*, 166–67, 181.
20 Walker, *Conquest of Bread*, 260, 265; Weber, *Dark Sweat, White Gold*, 33; "Bank of America: The Humble Beginnings of a Large Bank," Office of the Comptroller of the Currency.

21. Malcolm Harris, *Palo Alto: A History of California, Capitalism, and the World* (Back Bay Books, 2023), 164.
22. Douglas Cazaux Sackman, *Orange Empire: California and the Fruits of Eden* (University of California Press, 2005), 198–200; Don Mitchell, *They Saved the Crops: Labor, Landscape, and the Struggle over Industrial Farming in Bracero-Era California* (University of Georgia Press, 2012), 175–76.
23. Joon K. Kim, "California's Agribusiness and the Farm Labor Question: The Transition from Asian to Mexican Labor, 1919–1939," *Aztlán: A Journal of Chicano Studies* 37, no. 2 (2012): 43–72.
24. Walker, *Conquest of Bread*, 138; Weber, *Dark Sweat, White Gold*, 41, 63, 43; Alan L. Olmstead and Paul W. Rhode, "Biological Innovation and Productivity Growth in the Antebellum South," NBER Working Paper 14142, June 2008, 28.
25. Weber, *Dark Sweat, White Gold*, 69, 45.
26. Weber, *Dark Sweat, White Gold*, 53.
27. Weber, *Dark Sweat, White Gold*, 85, 79–81.
28. Richard Street, "The Economist as Humanist: The Career of Paul S. Taylor," *California History* 58, no. 4 (1979): 350–61; Weber, *Dark Sweat, White Gold*, 90.
29. Weber, *Dark Sweat, White Gold*, 90, 95.
30. Weber, *Dark Sweat, White Gold*, 84–86, 93; Harris, *Palo Alto*, 163–64, 172, 177; Arax and Wartzman, *King of California*, 173.
31. Weber, *Dark Sweat, White Gold*, 100.
32. Weber, *Dark Sweat, White Gold*, 100–101.
33. Brian Gratton and Emily Merchant, "Immigration, Repatriation, and Deportation: The Mexican-Origin Population in the United States, 1920–1950," *International Migration Review* 47, no. 4 (2013): 944–75; Weber, *Dark Sweat, White Gold*, 77; Benny J. Andrés, "Invisible Borders: Repatriation and Colonization of Mexican Migrant Workers Along the California Borderlands During the 1930s," *California History* 88, no. 4 (2011): 5–65.
34. "California Cottonfields," Dallas Frazier and Earl Montgomery, 1969, first released by Merle Haggard and the Strangers, 1971.
35. Weber, *Dark Sweat, White Gold*, 143.
36. Weber, *Dark Sweat, White Gold*, 117.

Chapter 20: Sinking

1. Mark Arax, *The Dreamt Land: Chasing Water and Dust Across California* (Knopf, 2019), 224; Theo Claire and Kevin Surprise, "Moving the Rain: Settler Colonialism, the Capitalist State, and the Hydrologic Rift in California's Central Valley," *Antipode* 54, no. 1 (2022): 162–63.

2   Arax, *The Dreamt Land*, 189.
3   "Friant Water," *Madera Tribune*, February 10, 1961.
4   "ACALA 4–42 Many Cotton Growers Probably Over-Irrigating," *Madera Tribune*, June 10, 1960.
5   "Salute to Cotton," *Calexico Chronicle*, May 21, 1957.
6   "The History of Oil Production in the United States," Boston University, VisualizingEnergy.org; Adam M. Romero, *Economic Poisoning: Industrial Waste and the Chemicalization of American Agriculture* (University of California Press, 2022), 124, 129; Timothy Mitchell, *Carbon Democracy: Political Power in the Age of Oil* (Verso, 2023), 205; Richard A. Walker, *The Conquest of Bread: 150 Years of Agribusiness in California* (New Press, 2004), 183.
7   Romero, *Economic Poisoning*, 137.
8   "Methyl Bromide Poisoning," EWG.org; "Methyl Bromide," EPA. In spite of its toxic effects on workers at the site, as well as on the atmosphere, the product was not phased out until 2005.
9   Douglas Cazaux Sackman, *Orange Empire: California and the Fruits of Eden* (University of California Press, 2005), 76–77; Alan L. Olmstead and Paul W. Rhode, *Creating Abundance: Biological Innovation and American Agricultural Development* (Cambridge University Press, 2008), 259.
10 Walker, *Conquest of Bread*, 1–3; Romero, *Economic Poisoning*, 123, 132.
11 Don Mitchell, *They Saved the Crops: Labor, Landscape, and the Struggle over Industrial Farming in Bracero-Era California* (University of Georgia Press, 2012), 152, 15.
12 Mitchell, *They Saved the Crops*, 1–2, 95.
13 Kelly Lytle Hernandez, *Migra! A History of the U.S. Border Patrol* (University of California Press, 2010), 178.
14 Mitchell, *They Saved the Crops*, 118.
15 Hernandez, *Migra!*, 68–69, 182; Greg Grandin, *The End of the Myth: From the Frontier to the Border Wall in the Mind of America* (Macmillan, 2019), 166.
16 Hernandez, *Migra!*, 178.
17 Mitchell, *They Saved the Crops*, 264–66, 281–82.
18 Mitchell, *They Saved the Crops*, 129–30, 127–28.
19 Mitchell, *They Saved the Crops*, 127–28; Gilbert Fite, "Mechanization of Cotton Production Since World War II," *Agricultural History* 54, no. 1 (January 1980): 203; "New Records Made in County Cotton Output," *Madera Tribune*, May 15, 1952; Craig Heinicke and Wayne Grove, "'Machinery Has Completely Taken Over': The Diffusion of the Mechanical Cotton Picker, 1949–1964," *Journal of Interdisciplinary History* 39, no. 1 (2008): 70.
20 Douglas E. Bowers, "The Research and Marketing Act of 1946 and Its Effects on Agricultural Marketing Research," *Agricultural History* 56, no. 1 (1982): 253.

21 "Mechanization Is Urged for Cotton Grower," *Madera Tribune*, February 1, 1946; "See End of Hand Cotton Picking Here," *Madera Tribune*, December 20, 1948; Bowers, "The Research and Marketing Act of 1946 and Its Effects on Agricultural Marketing Research," 251.

22 Devin Jerome, "'Lay Down the Shovel and the Hoe': The Delta Council and Cotton Mechanization in the Yazoo-Mississippi Delta, 1942–1955" (MA diss., University of Georgia, 2020); Fite, "Mechanization of Cotton Production Since World War II," 191.

23 Walker, *Conquest of Bread*, 142; Paul K. Conkin, *A Revolution Down on the Farm: The Transformation of American Agriculture Since 1929* (University Press of Kentucky, 2008), 105; Fite, "Mechanization of Cotton Production Since World War II," 201.

24 Conkin, *A Revolution Down on the Farm*, 106; Fite, "Mechanization of Cotton Production Since World War II," 207; Mitchell, *They Saved the Crops*, 304; Alan Olmstead and Paul Rhode, "A History of California Agriculture," Giannini Foundation of Agricultural Economics, University of California (December 2017), 3.

25 Walker, *Conquest of Bread*, 143.

26 Mark Arax and Rick Wartzman, *The King of California: J. G. Boswell and the Making of a Secret Empire* (PublicAffairs, 2003), 411.

27 Walker, *Conquest of Bread*, 186–88; Sackman, *Orange Empire*, 77.

28 Louis Warren, "Paths Towards Home: Landmarks of the Field in Environmental History," in *A Companion to American Environmental History*, ed. Douglas Cazaux Sackman (Wiley, 2010), 26.

29 Michael Pollan, *The Omnivore's Dilemma: A Natural History of Four Meals* (Penguin Books, 2006).

30 Gerry Strey, "The 'Oleo Wars': Wisconsin's Fight over the Demon Spread," *Wisconsin Magazine of History* 85, no. 1 (2001): 2–15; David S. Shields, "Prospecting for Oil," in *The Larder: Food Studies Methods from the American South*, eds. John Edge, Elizabeth Engelhardt, and Ted Ownby (University of Georgia Press, 2013), 71; David Berman, "Dallas," first released on Silver Jews, "The Natural Bridge," Drag City LP; "Cotton Talks," *Calexico Chronicle*, March 4, 1948.

31 Walker, *Conquest of Bread*, 247, 230–32, 243, 249.

32 Walker, *Conquest of Bread*, 230; Arax and Wartzman, *The King of California*, 420.

33 Ruth Wilson Gilmore, *Golden Gulag: Prisons, Surplus, Crisis, and Opposition in Globalizing California* (University of California Press, 2007), 105.

34 Jason W. Moore, "Cheap Food & Bad Money: Food, Frontiers, and Financialization in the Rise and Demise of Neoliberalism," *Review (Fernand*

Braudel Center) 33, nos. 2/3 (2010): 225–61; Arax and Wartzman, *The King of California*, 382.

35 Arax, *The Dreamt Land*, 451.
36 Gilmore, *Golden Gulag*, 105.
37 Gilmore, *Golden Gulag*, 38; Arax and Wartzman, *The King of California*, 418.

Chapter 21: In Cotton's Wake

1 Koch Foods, Wikipedia.
2 Charles Aiken, *The Cotton Plantation South Since the Civil War* (Johns Hopkins University Press, 1998), 57. Plantations are defined here as a farm of over five hundred acres.
3 Steven Hahn, *The Roots of Southern Populism: Yeoman Farmers and the Transformation of the Georgia Upcountry, 1850–1890* (Oxford University Press, 1983), 132, 138, 141.
4 Erin Stewart Mauldin, *Unredeemed Land: An Environmental History of Civil War and Emancipation in the Cotton South* (Oxford University Press, 2018), 72–74.
5 Hahn, *The Roots of Southern Populism*, 141.
6 Hahn, *The Roots of Southern Populism*, 157–60, 163.
7 Hahn, *The Roots of Southern Populism*, 164; Gavin Wright, *Old South, New South: Revolutions in the Southern Economy Since the Civil War* (Louisiana State University Press, 1986), 58.
8 Scott Nelson, "The Bourbon South," in *A New History of the American South*, ed. Fitzhugh Brundage (University of North Carolina Press, 2023), 355; Monica Gisolfi, *The Takeover: Chicken Farming and the Roots of American Agribusiness* (University of Georgia Press, 2017), 5.
9 Harry Crews, *A Childhood: The Biography of a Place* (Penguin Books, 1978), 11.
10 Jack Temple Kirby, *Mockingbird Song: Ecological Landscapes of the South* (University of North Carolina Press, 2006), 205; Hortense Powdermaker, *After Freedom: A Cultural Study in the Deep South* (Viking, 1939), 79; Marcie Cohen Ferris, *The Edible South: The Power of Food and the Making of an American Region* (University of North Carolina Press, 2014), 128.
11 Bureau of the Census, *Fourteenth Census of the United States: 1920 Census Bulletins, Agriculture Statistics: Georgia*, 18; Arthur Raper, *Preface to Peasantry: A Tale of Two Black Belt Counties* (University of North Carolina Press, 1936), 157.
12 Gisolfi, *The Takeover*, 13.
13 Gisolfi, *The Takeover*, 14, 21.
14 Gisolfi, *The Takeover*, 16; Rebecca Sharpless, "'She Ought to Have Taken

Those Cakes': Southern Women and Rural Food Supplies," *Southern Cultures* 18, no. 2 (2012): 49–50.
15 Gisolfi, *The Takeover*, 29–31.
16 Gisolfi, *The Takeover*, 21; LaGuana Gray, *We Just Keep Running the Line: Black Southern Women and the Poultry Processing Industry* (Louisiana State University Press, 2014), 27.
17 Katie Rawson, "'America's Place for Inclusion': Stories of Food, Labor, and Equality at the Waffle House," in *The Larder: Food Studies Methods from the American South*, ed. John Edge, Elizabeth Engelhardt, and Ted Ownby (University of Georgia Press, 2013), 220; Shane Hamilton, *Trucking Country: The Road to America's Wal-Mart Economy* (Princeton University Press, 2008), 5, 137.
18 Gisolfi, *The Takeover*, 45; Douglas H. Constance, "The Southern Model of Broiler Production and Its Global Implications," *Culture & Agriculture* 30, no. 1–2 (2008): 27.
19 Gisolfi, *The Takeover*, 39–41, 46–47, 37, 3.
20 Gisolfi, *The Takeover*, 42, 53, 55.
21 Gisolfi, *The Takeover*, 51; Jack Temple Kirby, *Rural Worlds Lost: The American South, 1920–1960* (Louisiana State University Press, 1987), 359.
22 Kirby, *Rural Worlds Lost*, 309, 320.
23 Kirby, *Rural Worlds Lost*, 360.
24 Gisolfi, *The Takeover*, 61, 51–52.
25 Psyche A. Williams-Forson, *Building Houses out of Chicken Legs: Black Women, Food, and Power* (University of North Carolina Press, 2006), 32–33.
26 Paloma Maria Carroll, "A White Man's County: Racial Violence, Vigilante Terrorism, and Black Flight in Forsyth County, Georgia" (MA diss., University of Georgia, 2018), 21–22.
27 Mark Ellis, "Racial Unrest and White Liberalism in Rural Georgia: Barrow and Oconee Counties in the Early 1920s," *Georgia Historical Quarterly* 97, no. 1 (Spring 2013): 31.
28 Gisolfi, *The Takeover*, 32–33.
29 John Michael Vlach, *The Planter's Prospect: Privilege and Slavery in Plantation Paintings* (University of North Carolina Press, 2002), 41.
30 Williams-Forson, *Building Houses out of Chicken Legs*, 53.
31 Williams-Forson, *Building Houses out of Chicken Legs*, 66–67.
32 Williams-Forson, *Building Houses out of Chicken Legs*, 68–70.
33 James Cobb, "Beyond Planters and Industrialists: A New Perspective on the New South," *Journal of Southern History* 54, no. 1 (1988): 60, 66.
34 Gray, *We Just Keep Running the Line*, 20, 44, 57, 60, 111.
35 Gray, *We Just Keep Running the Line*, 110, 78, 111.

36 Gray, *We Just Keep Running the Line*, 108, 98.
37 Gray, *We Just Keep Running the Line*, 65, 87, 86.
38 Hope Shand, "Billions of Chickens: The Business of the South," FacingSouth.org, 1983; C. R. Daniel et al., "Trends in Meat Consumption in the USA," *Public Health Nutrition* 14, no. 4 (2011): 577.
39 Gray, *We Just Keep Running the Line*, 84, 120; Isaac Arnsdorf, "How a Top Chicken Company Cut Off Black Farmers, One by One," ProPublica, June 26, 2019.

Chapter 22: From Killing Fields to Kill Lines

1 Leon Fink, *The Maya of Morganton: Work and Community in the Nuevo New South* (University of North Carolina Press, 2003), 42, 20.
2 David McCreery, *Rural Guatemala, 1760–1940* (Stanford University Press, 1994), 173–74, 269, 187–88.
3 McCreery, *Rural Guatemala*, 188.
4 John Soluri, *Banana Cultures: Agriculture, Consumption, and Environmental Change in Honduras and the United States* (University of Texas Press, 2021), 70–71.
5 Jonathan Blitzer, *Everyone Who Is Gone Is Here: The United States, Central America, and the Making of a Crisis* (Penguin, 2024), 77–78.
6 Blitzer, *Everyone Who Is Gone Is Here*, 82.
7 Blitzer, *Everyone Who Is Gone Is Here*, 31–32.
8 Blitzer, *Everyone Who Is Gone Is Here*, 92–93; Stephen Kinzer, "Efraín Ríos Montt, Guatemalan Dictator Convicted of Genocide, Dies at 91," *New York Times*, April 1, 2018.
9 Fink, *The Maya of Morganton*, 61, 36.
10 Alberto Alonso-Fradejas, "Life Purging Agrarian Extractivism in Guatemala: Towards a Renewable but Unlivable Future?," in *Agrarian Extractivism in Latin America*, eds. Ben M. McKay, Alberto Alonso-Fradejas, and Arturo Ezquerro-Cañete (Routledge, 2021), 147.
11 Fink, *The Maya of Morganton*, 42; Mary E. Frederickson, *Looking South: Race, Gender, and the Transformation of Labor from Reconstruction to Globalization* (University Press of Florida, 2011), 186; LaGuana Gray, *We Just Keep Running the Line: Black Southern Women and the Poultry Processing Industry* (Louisiana State University Press, 2014), 129, 131.
12 Fink, *The Maya of Morganton*, 54.
13 McCreery, *Rural Guatemala*, 284.
14 Fink, *The Maya of Morganton*, 66.
15 Jan Eeckhout, *The Profit Paradox: How Thriving Firms Threaten the Future of Work* (Princeton University Press, 2021).

16 "Big Chicken: Poultry Growers Fight for Fairness," Farmaid.org.
17 Isaac Arnsdorf, "How a Top Chicken Company Cut Off Black Farmers, One by One," ProPublica, June 26, 2019.
18 Fink, *The Maya of Morganton*, 12.
19 Isabelle Taft, "Trump's Big Immigration Raid Snared Them. They're Still in Mississippi," *New York Times*, November 4, 2024; Ann Rogers, "Slain Guatemalan Migrant Leaves Behind Legacy of Faith in Two Counties," *Angelus News*, March 29, 2021; Associated Press, "11 Ex-Police Officers Sentenced in 2021 Killings of 17 Migrants and 2 Others in Northern Mexico," November 14, 2023.
20 Arnsdorf, "How a Top Chicken Company Cut Off Black Farmers, One by One."

Chapter 23: Caindo na Cana

1 Documentário, "Brazil—The Troubled Land" (1964), https://www.youtube.com/watch?v=jWq4__898mg.
2 A. J. Langguth, *Hidden Terrors* (Pantheon Books, 1978).
3 Thomas D. Rogers, *Agriculture's Energy: The Trouble with Ethanol in Brazil's Green Revolution* (University of North Carolina Press, 2022), 49–52; Herbert Klein and Francisco Vidal Luna, *Feeding the World: Brazil's Transformation into a Modern Agricultural Economy* (Cambridge University Press, 2019), 2.
4 Nelson Lichtenstein, "The Return of Merchant Capitalism," *International Labor and Working-Class History* 81 (2012): 15; Langguth, *Hidden Terrors*, 159; Naomi Klein, *The Shock Doctrine: The Rise of Disaster Capitalism* (Holt, 2007), 78; Wolfgang Streeck, *Buying Time: The Delayed Crisis of Democratic Capitalism* (Verso, 2017), 25–27.
5 Rogers, *Agriculture's Energy*, 67, 71.
6 Nick Cullather, "The Foreign Policy of the Calorie," *American Historical Review* 112, no. 2 (2007): 337–64.
7 Raj Patel, "The Long Green Revolution," *Journal of Peasant Studies* 40, no. 1 (2012): 1–63.
8 Rogers, *Agriculture's Energy*, 61, 78; Ryan Nehring, "The Brazilian Green Revolution," *Political Geography* 95 (2022): 6; Klein, *The Shock Doctrine*, 73.
9 Klein, *The Shock Doctrine*, 112–13; Langguth, *Hidden Terrors*, 193.
10 Rogers, *Agriculture's Energy*, 109, 183.
11 Rogers, *Agriculture's Energy*, 89–95.
12 Rogers, *Agriculture's Energy*, 69.
13 Rogers, *Agriculture's Energy*, 137, 121, 119, 115.
14 Rogers, *Agriculture's Energy*, 131, 121, 126, 179–81.
15 Rogers, *Agriculture's Energy*, 185–86, 189.

16 Rogers, *Agriculture's Energy*, 170; Barbara Nunberg, "Structural Change and State Policy: The Politics of Sugar in Brazil Since 1964," *Latin American Research Review* 21, no. 2 (1986): 78; Klein and Luna, *Feeding the World*, 316–18.
17 Austin Frerick, *Barons: Money, Power, and the Corruption of America's Food Industry* (Island Press 2024), 40–41.
18 Tania Salerno, "Cargill's Corporate Growth in Times of Crises: How Agro-Commodity Traders Are Increasing Profits in the Midst of Volatility," *Agriculture and Human Values* 34 (2017): 213; Frerick, *Barons*, 39.
19 Mike Davis, *Planet of Slums* (Verso, 2017).
20 McKenzie Funk, *Windfall: The Booming Business of Global Warming* (Penguin, 2015), 145; Ray Bush and Giuliano Martiniello, "Food Riots and Protest: Agrarian Modernizations and Structural Crises," *World Development* 91 (March 2017): 193–207; "FAO Food Price Index in Nominal and Real Terms," https://www.fao.org/worldfoodsituation/foodpricesindex/en/.
21 Peter Kingstone, "Is Brazil's Economy Too Commodity-Dependent?," *Americas Quarterly* (Summer 2012): 18, 20.
22 Lilia Moritz Schwartz, *Brazilian Authoritarianism: Past and Present* (Princeton University Press, 2022), 44; Sérgio Sauer and George Mészáros, "The Political Economy of Land Struggle in Brazil Under Workers' Party Governments," *Journal of Agrarian Change* 17, no. 2 (2017): 397–414; Ben M. McKay, Sérgio Sauer, and Roman Herre, "The Political Economy of Sugarcane Flexing: Initial Insights from Brazil, Southern Africa, and Cambodia," *Journal of Peasant Studies* 43, no. 1 (2015): 201.
23 Akenya Alkimim and Keith C. Clarke, "Land Use Change and the Carbon Debt for Sugarcane Ethanol Production in Brazil," *Land Use Policy* 72 (2018): 65–73; "Global Ethanol Production by Country or Region," Alternative Fuels Data Center; Timothy Mitchell, *Carbon Democracy: Political Power in the Age of Oil* (Verso, 2023), 233; Funk, *Windfall*, 2–3, 152.
24 "Sucre Industriel: spectre du travail forcé," *Le Monde*, January 2, 2023, 17.
25 Klein and Luna, *Feeding the World*, 62–63, 335. For reference, the largest private landowner in Iowa farms 162,000 hectares.
26 *Energy News*, "BP to Broaden Sugarcane Crushing Capability in Brazil's Tocantins," August 9, 2024; Ben C. McKay, Alberto Alonso-Fradejas, and Arturo Ezquerro-Cañete, "Introduction," in *Agrarian Extractivism in Latin America*, eds. Ben M. McKay, Alberto Alonso-Fradejas, and Arturo Ezquerro-Cañete (Routledge, 2021), 1–2.
27 McKay et al., "Political Economy of Sugarcane Flexing," 199.
28 Frerick, *Barons*, 34–41; Brian Garvey and Maria Joseli Barreto, "At the Cutting Edge: Precarious Work in Brazil's Sugar and Ethanol Industry," in

Neoliberal Capitalism and Precarious Work: Ethnographies of Accommodation and Resistance, eds. Rob Lambert and Andrew Herod (Edward Elgar Publishing, 2016), 173; Gerson Freitas Jr., "Brazil Sugar King Moves Closer to Gaining Railway Control," *Bloomberg*, April 16, 2014.

29 Annelies Zoomers, "Globalization and the Foreignisation of Space: Seven Processes Driving the Current Global Landgrab," *Journal of Peasant Studies* 37, no. 2 (2010): 435; Loka Ashwood et al., "What Owns the Land: The Corporate Organization of Farmland Investment," *Journal of Peasant Studies* 49, no. 2 (2022); Simon Romero, "TIAA-CREF, U.S. Investment Giant, Accused of Land Grabs in Brazil," *New York Times*, November 16, 2015.

30 Wolfgang Streeck, *Buying Time: The Delayed Crisis of Democratic Capitalism* (Verso, 2017), 113.

31 Vann Newkirk II, "The Great Land Robbery: The Shameful Story of How 1 Million Black Families Have Been Ripped from Their Farms," *The Atlantic*, September 2019.

32 Will Wade and Dina Bass, "Microsoft AI Needs So Much Power It's Tapping Site of US Nuclear Meltdown," *Bloomberg*, September 20, 2024.

33 Joseph Fargione et al., "Land Clearing and the Biofuel Carbon Debt," *Science* 319, no. 5867 (2008): 1235–38.

34 Fargione, "Land Clearing and the Biofuel Carbon Debt."

35 Peter Dauvergne and Kate Neville, "Forests, Food, and Fuel in the Tropics," *Journal of Peasant Studies* 37, no. 4 (2010): 637. Other estimates were considerably lower. Ben White and Anirban Dasgupta, "Agrofuels Capitalism: A View from Political Economy," *Journal of Peasant Studies* 37, no. 4 (2010): 593–607; "Press Release: Biden-Harris Administration Announces $239 Million to Increase Access to Clean, Affordable Domestic Biofuels as Part of Investing in America Agenda," October 29, 2024.

Coda: Burying Ground

1 Stephanie M. H. Camp, *Closer to Freedom: Enslaved Women and Everyday Resistance in the Plantation South* (University of North Carolina Press, 2004), 118.

2 Marc Parry, "Buried History: How Far Should a University Go to Face Its Slave Past?," *Chronicle of Higher Education*, November 2017.

3 Parry, "Buried History."

Image Credits

26 Records of the Court of Common Pleas, S136007, Writs of partition, box 3, 1777–1792, folder 10A, South Carolina Department of Archives and History, Columbia, SC.

31 A topographicall [Description and] Admeasurement [of the yland of] Barbados in t[he West Indyaes] with the Mrs. [Names of the Seuerall plantacons]. Antiqua Print Gallery / Alamy Stock Photo.

49 Image courtesy of the Gibbes Museum of Art/Carolina Art Association. Gift of Alice Ravenel Huger Smith.

59 *Harper's Weekly*, January 5, 1867, 8. Alpha Stock / Alamy Stock Photo.

62 Moore, Henry P, photographer. Seabrook's Flower Garden. Edisto Island South Carolina United States, 1862. Photograph. Reproduced from the Collections of the Library of Congress.

82 Mount Vernon in Virginia / Alexander Robertson delineavit; Francis Jukes sculpsit. London: Pub'd by F. Jukes No. 10 Howland Street, 1800 March 31st. Reproduced from the Collections of the Library of Congress.

108 William Tatham, *An Historical and Practical Essay on the Culture and Commerce of Tobacco* (London, 1800), facing p. 29. Slavery Images.

147 Denis Diderot, *Encyclopédie, ou, Dictionnaire Raisonné des Sciences, des Artes et des Metiers . . . Recueil de Plances, sur les Sciences . . .* (Paris, 1762), vol. 1, plate IV. Chronicle / Alamy Stock Photo.

147 Denis Diderot, *Encyclopédie, ou, Dictionnaire Raisonné des Sciences, des Artes et des Metiers . . . Recueil de Plances, sur les Sciences . . .* (Paris, 1762), vol. 1, plate I. Les Archives Digitales / Alamy Stock Photo.

153 Débarquement de la Flotte Française a Saint-Domingue (Paris, [1820]), foldout, facing title page. Slavery Images.
168 Corcoran Collection (Gift of the American Art Association). Public domain.
170 "The Tobacco Market at Richmond," *Harper's Weekly*, vol. 9 (November 11, 1865), 709. Pictorial Press Ltd / Alamy Stock Photo.
173 Photograph by Marc Ferrez. Getty Research Institute Digital Collections.
188 James Buckingham, *The Slave States of America* (London, 1842), vol. 2, facing p. 553. Slavery Images.
195 Loading Steamboats at New Orleans, the New Orleans Historic Collection, Edwards, J. D. (Jay Dearborn), 1831–1900, Object Number 1985.238.
197 *Harper's New Monthly Magazine* (1853–54), vol. 8, p. 456. (Copy in Special Collections Department, University of Virginia Library.) The Reading Room / Alamy Stock Photo.
204 *Harper's Weekly*, July 4, 1863. Photograph, www.loc.gov/item/2014645368. Reproduced from the Collections of the Library of Congress.
225 "A Spring Scene Near Richmond, Virginia," *Harper's Weekly* (May 21, 1870), p. 321. Reproduced from the Collections of the Library of Congress.
227 *Harper's Weekly* (March 14, 1868), vol. 12, p. 173. Slavery Images.
242 Located in The Hershey Story, 63 West Chocolate Avenue, Hershey, Pennsylvania 17033.
246 Interior of a sugar factory in La Havana (Cuba). 1857. Engraving. 19th century. Madrid, National Library of Fine Arts. Author: Eduardo Laplante (1818–c. 1860). Location: BIBLIOTECA NACIONAL-COLECCION, MADRID, SPAIN. Album / Alamy Stock Photo.
268 *Informe Sobre Censo de Cuba*, 1899, 535. United States War Department / University of Urbana-Champaign / Internet Archive.
271 Hum Images / Alamy Stock Photo.
284 T. J. Woofter Jr., *Landlord and Tenant on the Cotton Plantation* (Negro Universities Press, 1969) [orig. published 1936 by U.S. Works Progress Administration], 5.
288 Lange, Dorothea, photographer. Plantation overseer. Mississippi Delta, near Clarksdale, Mississippi. Mississippi United States Clarksdale Coahoma County, 1936. June. Photograph. Reproduced from the Collections of the Library of Congress.
292 Map reproduced by Michael Borop from Aiken, *The Cotton South Since the Civil War*, 6.
308 Theodore Rosengarten.
322 Vachon, John, photographer. Parkin vicinity, Arkansas, 1936. Jan.?. Photograph. Reproduced from the Collections of the Library of Congress.

Image Credits

320 Annie R. Mitchell History Room, Tulare County Library, Visalia, California.

342 Lange, Dorothea, photographer. Company housing for cotton workers near Corcoran, California. Corcoran California King County United States, 1936. Nov. Photograph. Reproduced from the Collections of the Library of Congress.

345 Caravan of striking cotton pickers south of Tulare, California. California United States Tulare Tulare County, 1933. Oct. Photograph. Reproduced from the Collections of the Library of Congress.

352 U.S. Bureau of Reclamation / David Rumsey Map Collection, David Rumsey Map Center, Stanford Libraries.

375 U.S. Department of Agriculture, *Atlas of American Agriculture*, part 5, sec. A (Government Printing Office, 1918), 17.

383 Edward King, *The Great South* (Hartford, Conn., 1875), 650. Slavery Images.

391 Patricia Goudvis Photograph Collection, Amistad Research Center, New Orleans, Louisiana.

402 Homeland Security Photo / Alamy Stock Photo.

Index

Page numbers in italics refer to figures and tables.

A&P grocery chain, 378
abolition
  of the British slave trade, 18, 137, 244, 256
abolitionism
  in Cuba, 244, 247, 251, 252, 256
  in Mexico, 199
  in the U.S., 201, 205, 228, 335
Acala cotton, 339–40
Adams, John, 163–64
Adams, Wirt, 235
Africa
  Central Africa, 5–6
  Cubans of African descent, 19, 274, 276
  foodways and agricultural knowledge, 15, 38–40, 41, 63–65, 155
  Gold Coast of, 180
  origins of the Southern "swept yard," 65, 203, 298, 318
  "Rice Coast" of, 38–40, 203–4
  Senegambia, 40, 113
  slave forts of, 180
  in the slave trade, 16, 30, 34, 37–38, 45, 71, 76, 94, 99–101, 112–13, 118, 124–25, 139
  spiritual traces from, 68
  See also São Tomé
"aggregators," 285
"agribusinesses," 332, 353, 395, 403, 412

Agricultural Adjustment Administration (AAA), 321, 348–49, 377–78
Agricultural Labor Bureau of the San Joaquin Valley, 341
Agricultural Wheel, 308
agriculture
  agronomy, 38, 269–70, 299, 302–3, 338–39, 353, 366, 408–10
  compound plows, 337
  "crop mastery," 107–14, 117, 129–30, 214, 224, 269–70
  diversification, 130, 170, 193–94, 209, 284–85, 304, 313, 314, 373, 382
  fertilizer, 12, 285, 291, 302–6, 309, 314–15, 354–55, 363, 373, 374, 411
  Indigenous strategies of, 88–90
  industrial food agriculture in California, 359–64
  irrigation, 39, 41–43, 46, 338, 340, 344, 351–56, *352*, 409
  mechanization of, 246–48, 303, 321–22, 334, 338, 360–64
  pest control, 65, 193, 270, 354–55, 364
  small-scale cultivation, 19, 40, 45, 70–71, 157
  soil fertility, 22, 195–96, 303–4, 313, 354–55, 369
  "upland" crops, 26, 46–47, 183, 212

477

478 Index

agriculture *(continued)*
 wage work in, 341, 377–78, 388–89, 399–400
 weed control, 57–58, 60, 62, 155, 363, 369
 See also Black farmers; plantations; *specific crops and commodities*
Aguacatán, Guatemala, 393–94, 396–98
Aiken, William, Jr., 233
Airbnb, 8
Alabama, 73, 184–86
 the Black Belt of, 21, 186, 283, *292–93*, 299
 cotton in, 171, 199, 279, 296, 303, 361
 poultry industry in, 371, 400, 402–3
 slavery in, 189, 195–96
 Tuskegee Institute, 299, 304–5, 319
"Alabama Settlement, the" 336
Alamo, Battle of the, 199
Albertson grocery chain, 399
alcohol, 35, 67, 180
Alien Land Laws of 1913 and 1920 (CA), 340
All God's Dangers (Cobb), 307
Amador's Revolt, São Tomé, 2–4, 23, 149
Amazon (company), 399
"American Century, the," 11
American Cotton Council, 361, 365
American Dream, 325
American Revolution, 16–17, 32, 64, 85, 124, 131–37
 constitutionalism and the plantation, 137–42
 Native American lands during the, 133, 184–85
 trade on the eve of the, 120–21, *122*, 124–25, 130
American Sugar Refining Company (ASRC, "the Sugar Trust"), 11, 244, 251, 264, 273
Anglo-Dutch wars, 29
Angola, 4–6, 113
"anti-enticement" laws, 287
Antigua, 119
Antwerp, 4
Appomattox, 216, 225
Arab Spring, 414
Arango y Parreño, Francisco de, 160–62, 165
Arawak people of the Caribbean, 29
Arax, Mark, 333–35, 352, 368

Arbenz, Jacobo, 395
Argentina, 408, 409
Arizona, 200
Arkansas, 171, 194, 290, 311, *322*, 332, 387, 389, 398, 400
Army of Northern Virginia, 215–16
Arnold, Benedict, 134–35
Arnsdorf, Isaac, 400
artificial intelligence (AI), 420–22
asiento monopoly, 160
Associated Farmers of California, 345
Atkins, Edwin, 243, 249, 252
Atlanta, GA, 212, 214, 281, *293*, 315
Atlantic world, 27–34
 the Atlantic consumer economy, 76, 123–25, 250
 the British in the, 29, 181–84, 193, 244
 credit flows in the, 139
 the French in the, 144–45, 149, 157
 risk in transatlantic trade, 44–45
 the slave trade in the, 18, 21, 29, 37, 45–46, 102, 113, 137
 the Spanish in the, 161–63
Audubon Sugar School, Baton Rouge, LA, 270
Austen, Jane, 121
Austin, George, 40, 41
Australia, 206
authoritarianism, 323, 410
autonomy
 of the colonial subject, 36, 90, 252
 of the enslaved, 53–54, 60, 232
 family autonomy and self-sufficiency, 19, 219, 252
 of free Black people, 283, 297, 314, 326, 382–85
 the importance of dwellings, 201–3, 211, 213, 214, 237
 See also bodies

Bacon's Rebellion, 92–95, 97–98, 132, 186–87
Bahamas, 182
Bakersfield, CA, 345, 347
Baldwin Hall, University of Georgia, 424–45
Ball, Charles, 41, 49–50, 54, 59, 61–62, 71, 79, 189
Ball, Elias, 41, 55, 71
Ball, Harry, 290
Baltimore, MD, 172, 175–76, 250, 251

bananas, 155, 268–69, 394, 395
Bandera, Quintín, 243, 254
Bank of America, 339–40, 367
Baptist, Edward, 184
Barbados, 6, 14–16
   economic crisis of the 1670s, 99
   migration of planters to the Carolinas, 37–40, 44–51
   minority rule and resistance in, 37, 53
   slavery and the slave trade in, 40–44, 76, 99–100, 180, 250, 417
   sugar plantations of, 27–33, *31*, 182
   the task system in, 60–61
   yellow fever in, 103
barrels/barrel-making, 33, 66–67, 249
Barrios, Justo Rufino, 394
Bartram, William, 47–48
Batista, Fulgencio, 410
beans (feijão), 155, 412–13
Bear Flag Revolt of 1846, 334
Beckert, Sven, 181
beet sugar, 250, 263
"Being Kind to the Soil" (Carver), 304–5
Belgium, 255
Bentley, Milo, 319
Berkeley, William, 93–95
Berlin, Ira, 92
Berman, David, 365
Bernice, LA, 387
Berringer, Benjamin, 27–28
Berringer, Margaret, 27–28, 37
"best poor/white man's country," 95, 111, 186–87
Beverley, Robert, 129
Biden, Joe, 422
Bilbo, Theodore, 321
biofuels, 22, 410–22
bird flu, 399
Black communities
   Alabama's Black Belt, 21, 186, 283, *292–93*, 299
   autonomy of free Black people, 283, 297, 314, 326, 382–85
   Black outmigration from the South after the New Deal, 316, 320, 321
   Black Republicans, 212, 237, 257
   in Cuba, 19, 274, 276, 277
   disfranchisement, 51, 239–40, 276, 286, 309

   fears of a Black surplus, 78, 326–27, 334
   free Black people's relationship to common lands, 224–25, *227*, 231–32, 233
   fugitive slaves, *31*, 69, 105, 139, 105, 150–51, 206, 154, 215, 221, 335
   "Great Migration," 323–24
   majority-Black, minority-white, 15, 17, 53, 57, 70, 77, 106, 133, 151, 162, 190, 257
   "maroons," *31*, 69, 150
   minority-Black, majority-white, 106, 128, 129, 376–77
   newspapers, 309
   stereotypes of Black people, 248, 385–86
   veterans, 153, 223, 232, 236
   white fears of Black self-determination, 159
Black farmers, 21–22, 420
   African foodways and agricultural knowledge, 15, 38–40, 41, 63–65, 155
   "crop mastery," 107–14, 117, 129–30, 214, 224, 269–70
   landownership after the Civil War, 291, 294, 296, 298–99
   organizing among, 307–12, 314
   outmigration from the South, 320, 321–22, 324, 385
   in poultry, 382, 384–85, 387, 403
Black Jacobins: Toussaint Louverture and the French Revolution, The (C. L. R. James), 159–60
Black Reconstruction in America (Du Bois), 238–39
Black women, 100, 101
   during the American Revolution, 217
   the "cake wenches" of Savannah, 66–67
   during the Civil War, 217–19
   enslaved women, 66–67, 116–18, 202–3, 216–17
   household affairs and, 299–300
   poultry processing workers, 386, 387–88
   rape, 237, 384, 396
   reproductive labor of enslaved women ("increase"), 116–18, 124, 136, 146
   the waiter-carriers of Virginia, *383*, 383–84
black-eyed peas, 38
Blackstock, Tom and Velva, 377
Bland, Richard, 282

Blitzer, Jonathan, 395
Blue Ridge Mountains, 177
bodies
   adornment and freedom, 135–36, 218
   as "surplus sinks," 365–67
   the torture of, 3, 14, 53–54, 68, 70, 84, 112, 114, 396, 410
   as value-generating machines, 146, 170, 304, 305, 408
   See also violence
"boias frias" ("cold lunches," temporary farmworkers), 411–12
boll weevils, 21, 194, 291, 312–15, 322, 324, 339, 347, 384
Bolzius, Johann, 54, 74, 77–78
Bonaparte, Napoleon, 152–54, 164
borax, 355
Borlaug, Norman, 408
Boswell, James G., 21, 332–33, 339, 341, 343, 349, 353, 360, 367
BP (British Petroleum), 22, 417, 421, 422
Bracero program, 21, 356–59, 364
Brazil, 4–6, 10, 22
   biofuel plantations of, 22, 410–22
   coffee plantations of, 171–78, *173*
   cotton plantations of, 285, 368
   dependence on imports, 174–78
   escaped slaves, 69
   independence from Portugal, 173
   Landless People's Movement, 239, 407
   São Paulo state, 411–13, 416
   slavery in, 10, 172–73
   sugar plantations of, 22, 405–10
Breen, Timothy, 129
Britain
   during the English Civil War, 28, 29
   establishment of the Bank of England, 44
   the Industrial Revolution, 10, 18, 180, 181, 191
   the London financial markets, 30, 34, 43–45, 77, 87, 92–93, 109–10, 124, 129–30, 207, 250
   Parliament, 29, 44–43, 127–28, 137–40, 206
British Empire
   abolition of the British slave trade, 18, 137, 244, 256
   Anglo-Dutch wars, 29
   British Army, 182–83

Cape Coast Castle, West Africa, 180
   colonial North American charters, 28, 85, 88, 90
   Council of Trade and Plantations, 33
   empire of free trade, 250
   encroachment on Indigenous peoples, 34–36
   in New England, 14, 32–34, *122*, 139
   the plantation in the, 14–15, 25–80
   in the West Indies, 10, 20, 32–33, 34, 44, 45, 73, 75–77, *122*, 124, 135, 144
   See also American Revolution; Barbados
British Royal Society, 38
Broderick, Margaret, 101
Brooks, Robert P., 297, 298
Brown, John (abolitionist), 207
Brown, John (author and former slave), 58–59, 68, 189
Brown, Kathleen, 103
Bryan, Jonathan, 47–48
Bureau of Agricultural Economics, 303
Burge, Dolly, 214
Burling, Walter, 192–93
Bush, George W., 397
"business plantations" of the Delta, 282
Butler, Pierce, 58, 66
Byrd, Otway, 120
Byrd, William, I, 94, 104–5
Byrd, William, II, 83–84, 105, 110–14, 119, 134, 155, *168*
Byrd, William, III, 119–20

Cahuilla people of California, 338
"caindo na cana" (falling back into cane), 417
"cake wenches," 66–67
calicos, 179
California, 21, 200, 331–49, 351–56
   abolitionism in, 335
   the Bracero program, 21, 356–59, 364
   the Central Valley, 351–53, *352*, 360, 367–69, 409
   conquest and statehood, 335–39
   the cotton plantations of, 331–35, 338–47
   droughts, 338, 367
   gold rush, 206
   industrial food agriculture in, 359–64
   irrigation and hydrology in, 351–56
   oil crisis and, 367–69

Index 481

the Okies migrating to, 347–49, 357, 360
"one-variety" laws, 339, 361, 365
the San Joaquin Valley, 21, 332–43, 346, 358–62
Tulare Lake/Tulare County, *330*, 337–38, 343, *345*, 353, 360, 368
wheat craze in, 353
California Department of Industrial Relations, 344
California Farm Bureau Federation, 340–41
calories, 408–9, 412
Camp, Wofford, 338–40, 345, 346, 348–49, 360–61
Campbell, Tunis, 232–33
canals and roads, 43
Cannery and Agricultural Workers' Industrial Union (CAWIU), 343, 346
Cape Coast Castle, West Africa, 180
capital offenses, 88, 173
capitalism, 6, 8–11, 16–17, 22, 30
   in the American style, 9–11, 264–65, 407
   in colonial America, 44–45
   fossil capitalism, 355–56, 363, 366–67
   plantationizing tendencies of, 11–14, 283, 358, 375–76, 411
   "slavery's capitalism," 246–47
   vertical integration, 265, 378–79, 387–88
Caradeux, Nicolas, 145
carbon dioxide, 421
Cárdenas, Lázaro, 347, 407–8
Cargill, 22, 418, 422
Caribbean Sea. *See* West Indies
Carolina colony, 15–16, *26*, 28–29, 31–36, 50–51. *See also* Lowcountry Carolina rice; North Carolina; South Carolina
Carolinas Campaign, 213, 222
Carter, Harlon, 358
Carter, Landon, 113–16, 117, 282, 385
Carter, Robert, III, 103, 130, 137
Carter, Robert, IV, 116
Carver, George Washington, 38, 299, 304–6, 324
Case Farms, Morganton, NC, 393, 398–99
Casey, Matthew, 267
Casiano, Ramón, 358
Castro, Emiliano Rodríguez, 396
Castro, Fidel, 410
Castro, Paulino López, 398
Catawba people of the South, 35, 80

Catesby, Mark, 38
cattle, 38, 162–63, 196, 214, 231, 342, 365, 421
Central American Free Trade Agreement, 397
Central Valley Project (CVP), 352–53, *352*, 367
centrales in Cuba, 248–57, 266–68, 271–72, 277
CEPA (corporate-led, external input-dependent, plantation agriculture), 417–18
chain restaurants, 379, 386
Chaplin, Joyce, 42
Charles II of England, 98
Charleston, SC, 55, 6, 205, *293*
   during the Civil War, 205
   elites of, 43, 47, 53, 64, 132, 166
   slave auction at, 41, 44–45
   workhouses in, 47, 56
chattel slavery, 16, 50, 95, 141, 154, 181, 202, 246, 248, 302
Chavez, Cesar, 360
"chemicalization and chemurgy," 334, 362–63, 365–66
Cheney, Paul, 145
Cherokee people, 35, 80, 186, 195, 372
Chesapeake Bay, 10, 89, 90, 102, 106, 124. *See also* Virginia
Chicago, 323, 409
chiggers, 59
Chile, 239, 409
China, 46, 148, 208, 368, 397, 405, 414, 418
Chinese immigration, 247, 266–67, 335, 340–41
chlorine, 355
chloropicrin, 354
Christianity, 48, 86, 100, 104
Christophe, Henri, 154–55, 156
"churka"-style cotton gins, 183–84
CIA (Central Intelligence Agency), 395, 406, 410
Civil War (American), 10, 18, 20, 193–94, 201–19, 335
   Appomattox and after, 216, 225–26
   Army of Northern Virginia, 215–16
   blockade runners, 205, 211, 233
   Carolinas Campaign, 213, 222
   enclosure after the, 226–32
   "second front" of enslaved women, 216–17
   Sherman's Reserve, 221–26, 234

Civil War (English), 28, 29
Claire, Theo, 351
Clark, John, 186
Clausen, A. W., 397
Clinton, Bill, 413
coal, 148, 169, 181–82, 245, 421
Cobb, Howell, 213–14
Cobb, Ned, 300–301, 306, 307–8, *308*, 316–20, 326–27, 360
Cobb, Viola, 300, *308*, 316, 319
Coca-Cola, 252
coffles, 169, 187–89, *188*
Cold War politics, 11, 316–17, 332, 343, 395–96, 405–10, 414
colonos (voluntary permanent workers), 249, 252, 266, 394
Colorado, 200, 206
Colored Farmers' Alliance (CFA), 308–12
Colored Farmers' Home Improvement Lodge, 308
Colored Methodist Episcopalian Church, 203
Comanche raiding parties, 199
Commodity Futures Modernization Act of 2000, 413–14
Commodity Index Funds, 414
common lands, *62*, 224–27, *227*, 232
   free Black people's relationship to, 224–25, *227*, 231–32, 233
   white entitlement over, 111–12, 226–27, 231–32
   See also enclosure/fencing; land; property rights
communism, 316–17, 343, 395–96, 405–10
Communist Party (U.S.), 316–17
company stores/company scrip, 253, 267, 290–91, 341–42, 376
"Company, the," 332–33
concentration camps, 255–56
Confederacy, 201–2, 208–16
   blockade runners, 205, 211, 233
   Commissary Department, 210–11
   the hubris of the, 208
   navy of the, 203, 205
   pardons of the, 226
   surrender of the, 18–19, 223–25
   women of the, 216–19
Congress, 139
   debates over slavery and statehood, 165, 185
   on "Indian Removal," 187
   planter class influence in, 205–6
   Reconstruction and, 226, 233, 237, 335
   repeal of the Glass-Steagall Act, 413–11
   sugar interests in Cuba, 244, 260, 263
Conkin, Paul, 302
conservation, 232, 351–52, *352*
Continental Congress, 132, 138
convict-lease system, 288–89, 309
cooks, enslaved, 15, 40, 65, 135
"coolie" laborers, 247
"Coon Chicken Inn" chain restaurants, 386
Copersucar, 417–18, 421
Corcoran, CA, 332–33, *342*, 343–44, 367–69
corn, *26*, 29, 86–87
   during the Civil War, 209, 214, 218, 224–25
   Indigenous and colonial, 35, 86, 88–91, 115
   industrial, 266, 397, 412, 417, 421, 422
   plantation self-sufficiency and, 115, 155, 177, 190–91
   as ration, 61, 79
Cornwallis, Lord, 134–36
Cortès, Hernán, 85
Cosan sugar conglomerate, 418, 419
cotton, 10, 18, 21–22
   Acala cotton, 339–40
   boll weevils, 21, 194, 291, 312–15, 322, 324, 339, 347, 384
   "cotton famine" of the Civil War, 285
   "domestic" suppliers of, 182, 338
   prices, 312, 343, 346, 373, 377
   varieties of, 183, 191–94, 192, 212, 338, 339–40
Cotton Belt, 18, 22, 142, 191–92, 195, 238, 282, 290, *292–93*, 282
Cotton Mechanization Project, 361
cotton plantations, 10, 18, 21, 45, 165, 120, 179–200, *284*
   "aggregators," 285
   agricultural science and, 299–306
   in the "Boone's Lick" region of Missouri, 209
   in Brazil, 285, 368
   in California, 331–35, 338–47, 368–69
   cotton gins, 183–84, 192, 193, 206, 213, 283, 290, 311, 339, 377, 399
   export of slaves to the Deep South, 187–91
   former plantations after cotton's decline, 267, 367, 374, *375*, 376–78

of the Jim Crow South, 281–306
in the Natchez District of Louisiana, 192, 193–94, 284
land hunger and westward expansion, 184–87
overproduction and incentives for control, 364–67
plow-up of 1933, 364
now "Prison Alley," 368–69
self-sufficiency and the frontier character of, 190–200
tenancy and standing renters, 281–99
cotton textiles, 169–70, 179–82, 183, 192–93, 249, 302
cottonseed oil, 283, 290, 365
counterinsurgency, 90, 255–56, 277, 308, 396–97, 407
Creek people, 35–36, 80, 185–87
Creek War of 1812–1814, 185–87
criminality, 88, 100–101, 112, 145, 173, 223, 231, 264, 278, 287, 356, 360
Criollo, Felipe, 253
Cromwell, Oliver, 309–10
crop diversity, 130, 170, 193–94, 209, 284–85, 304, 313, 314, 373, 382
crop liens, 286–87, 380
"crop mastery," 107–14, 117, 129–30, 214, 224, 269–70
Crown rule. *See* British Empire
Cuba, 20, 160–64, 243–61, 277, 405, 410
American sugar companies in, 263–69, 273–78
Army of Liberation, 19, 247, 253–54, 259–60, 273–74
the *centrales*, 248–57, 266–68, *268*, 271–72, *273*, 277
constitutionalism in, 258–59, 261, 276
Havana, 160, 162, 245, 247, 258–60, 275
Spanish-American War, 257–61
sugar refining, 269–73
Cuba Company, 275
Cuban American Sugar Company, 264–65, 267
Cugoano, Quobna Ottoba, 143–44, 152
Currency Act of 1764 (UK), 127–28
Currier & Ives, 385
Custis, John, 109–10
cyanide gas, 355

d'Auberteuil, Michel René Hilliard, 146
D'Avila, Delfino, 346
Dahomey, 180
Dale, Thomas, 88
Dallas, TX, *292*, 365
Daniel, Pete, 321
Daniels, Josephus, 257, 278
Dark Town series, 385
Davis, Angela, 219
Davis, Jefferson, 209, 212, 215–16, 235
Davis, Mary, 169–70
DDT, 364
de Carli, Euclides, 419
de Charlevoix, Pierre-François-Xavier, 145
de Crèvecoeur, Hector St. John, 32
de la Fuente, Alejandro, 276
de la Sagra, Ramón, 247, 267
de Laborde, Jean Joseph, 144
debt
colonial indebtedness, 102, 119, 127–28
company stores/company scrip, 253, 267, 290–91, 341–42, 376
Congressional control of state debt, 139
crop liens, 286–87, 380
foreclosure, 373
Indigenous indebtedness, 35
industrialization and land hunger, 194–95, 198
migration and, 394
mortgages, 43–44, 340, 347
national, 397, 413, 415
poultry farming, 380–82, 402–3
profit margin of slavery, 146
sharecropping and, 285–87, 290, 294, 297, 304, 316, 323, 341, 373, 376–77
Declaration of Independence (Haiti), 153
Declaration of Independence (U.S.), 44, 131
decolonization, 253, 408
deerskins, 34–36, 45, 93
Defoe, Daniel, 179
defoliants, 363
Delaware people, 133
Delgado, Santiago, 332–33
delousing, 364
Delta Council, 361
Delta Pine and Land Company, 291
Democratic Party, 200, 237, 257, 288, 316, 323, 336, 348
Dent, John, 374

depopulation, 30, 35, 45, 315
Dessalines, Jean-Jacques, 153, 154–55
"destined vortex" of the plantation system, 9, 170, 198
Deutsche Bank, 416
Deyle, Steven, 187–88
Dickens, Charles, 169–70, 182, 188–89, 198
diminishing returns, 5, 18, 43
Dixon, Harry St. John, 336–37
Dockum plantation, 41, 65
Dominican Republic, 278
Domino sugar, 273
Douglass, Frederick, 9, 170, 228
Drayton, John, 54, 61, 64, 67–68
Drayton, Richard, 42, 46, 47, 50
Drayton, William, 166
Dred Scott decision of 1857, 206
drivers, 15, 47, 54–57, 60, 115, 148–51, 188, 312
Du Bois, W. E. B., 238–39, 305–6
Dubois, Laurent, 149
Dunbar, William, 192–93
"Dunmore's Proclamation," 131, 133
DuPont, Samuel Francis, 205
Dutch Empire, 5–6, 22, 29, 120. *See also* Brazil
"dwellings," 201–3, 211, 213, 214, 237

earthworks, 42, 58–59
East India Company, 179–80, 183
economic development
  diminishing returns, 5, 18, 43
  economic weakness and underdevelopment, 13, 141, 157, 282–83, 285, 315, 380
  economies of scale, 19, 91, 123, 409–10
  modernizing philosophies, 19–20, 227, 240, 407, 408–9, 410
  planning, 11, 19–20, 407–8, 413
Edelson, Max, 39, 47
Edwards, Hattie, 383
Edwards, Laura, 216
Edwards, Richard, 423
Edwards, Sam, 289
egalitarianism, 91–92, 151, 157, 160–61, 185
Egypt, 204, 285, 323, 333, 338–39
Eisenhower, Dwight D., 358
El Caney, Haiti, 277
El Paso, TX, 357

Elaine, AR, 312
Ellis Island, 20
Emancipation Proclamation, 283
enclosure/fencing
  barbed wire, 344
  in Brazil, 419, 411
  after the Civil War, 226–32
  according to the enslaved/newly free, 62, 64, 202–3, 222–24, *225*, 236, 253
  "open range," 112, 196, 231, 232
  according to the planter class, 89, 111–12, 128, 195–96, 203, 209, 219, 226–27, 231–32
  during the New Deal, 321
  after Reconstruction, 298, 313–14, 324
energy
  biofuels, 22, 410–22
  coal, 148, 169, 181–82, 245, 421
  fossil capitalism, 355–56, 366
  measured in calories, 408–9, 412
  petroleum, 353–56, 361, 364–69, 411, 414
"engrossment" of individual estates, 75, 98
Enlightenment, 145–46, *147*, 152, 158
enslaved people
  in coffles, 169, 187–89, *188*
  as cooks, 15, 40, 65, 135
  as drivers, 15, 47, 54–57, 60, 115, 148–51, 188, 312
  enslaved women, 66–67, 116–18, 202–3, 216–17
  "increase," 116–18, 124, 136, 146
  manumission, 70–71, 92, 137
  See also slavery/slave trade
entailment, 102, 127, 129, 138
EPA (U.S. Environmental Protection Agency), 354–55
equality. *See* inequality
Erickson, McCann, 406–7
"Erosion March, The" (Flanagan), 325
ethanol, 22, 411–13, 415, 417, 418–22
Ethiopia, 160
ethnic cleansing, 186, 337, 384
European Union, 415–16
"eviscerators," 387–89
Exodus (biblical), 204

Farmers' Alliance, 309–11
Farmers' Improvement Societies, 308
fast food, 371, 385, 388

Index 485

Faulkner, William, 301, 302
Federal Extension Service, USDA, 321
feed and fodder, 196, 38, 211, 365
feed conversion contracts, 379–81, 401–2
fencing. *See* enclosure/fencing
Ferro-carril Central, 275
fertilizer, 12, 285, 291, 302–6, 309, 314–15, 354–55, 363, 373, 374, 411
Fick, Carolyn, 150
Field Order 15, 222, 223
Fifteenth Amendment, 336–37
Fifth Amendment, 140
"financialization of food," 414
Fink, Leon, 397
firearms and guns, 34, 35, 180, 208
fire-coppicing, 88–89
First National Bank, 264
Fithian, Philip Vickers, 102–4, 109, 130
Fitzhugh, George, 207–8
Fitzhugh, Henry, 127, 138
Fitzhugh, Rosamond, 118
Fitzhugh, William, 97–99, 101, 102, 109, 116–18, 207, 258, 275
Flanagan, Thomas Jefferson, 325
Flemming, Arthur, 379–82, 390, 402
"floating of the meadows," 41
Florida, 69–70, 186, 222, 294
flour milling, 169–71, *170*, 174–78
food
    African foodways and agricultural knowledge, 15, 38–40, 41, 63–65, 155
    "agribusinesses," 332, 353, 395, 403, 412
    fast food, 371, 385, 388
    "financialization of food," 414
    grocery chains, 366–67, 378, 379, 399
    industrial food agriculture in California, 359–64
    Koch Foods, 371, 400–3
    prices, 414–15, 420–22
    "progging," 116, 155, 225, 233, 344
    See also cattle; hogs/pigs; poultry
Ford Foundation, 409
foreclosure, 373
Forrest, Nathan Bedford, 235, 236
fossil capitalism, 355–56, 366
"founding gardeners" of the Lowcountry, 64
Fourteenth Amendment, 337
France, 149, 151, 160, 208. *See also* French Empire

Franklin and Armfield of Alexandria, VA, 189
Frazier, Garrison, 221–22, 235
"free homes," 218
Freedmen's Bureau, 218–19, 222, 228–33, 238, 372
freedom, 19
    adornment and, 135–36, 218
    defined and denied, 218–19, 253
    freedom seekers and fugitive slaves, 67–70, 79–80, 150–54
    in England and colonial America, 29, 43–44, 51
    land ownership and, 202, 221–24, 228, 296, 321, 380
    manumission, 70–71, 92, 137
    through military service, 94
    race conflated with, 100
    through revolution, 159–60
    See also autonomy; resistance
"freedom dues," 50
"Free-Soil" states, 335
French colonial system
    abolition of slavery in, 152
    Louisiana, 164–65, *292*
    in Mexico, 343
    Saint-Domingue, 17, 143–58, *153*, 159–65, 182, 277
    threatened invasion of Jamaica, 136
    in the West Indies, 10, 144, *147*, 148, 162, 182
French Revolution, 149, 160
Fresno scrapers, 337, 353
Fresno, CA, 333, 335, 336, 348
Friant-Kern Canal and Dam, 353
Friedlander, Isaac, 335–36
Friedman, Milton, 409
frontier, 11, 12, 18, 36, 42, 48–49, 100, 129, 132, 172, 195–96, 266, 331, 337
Frye, Berson, 333
fumigation, 354–55
Fundamental Constitution of the Carolina colony, 50
"furnishing" merchants, 283, 286–88, 298, 316, 317

Gainesville, GA, 371–72, 377–82
Galarza, Ernesto, 356
Garcia, Manuel, 344

Garner, James, 184
Garza, Elias, 342–43
George III of England, 121, 128, 137–38, 141
Georgia, 15, 21, 40–41, 73–80, 132, 133, 183–86
    Atlanta, 212, 214, 281, *293*, 315
    backcountry, 132, 133
    Civil War and Reconstruction, 201, 203, 212–16, 223, 229, 234–35, 286
    Department of Agriculture, 303
    mules and horses in, 300
    Native Americans in, 186–87
    poultry industry in, 378–79, 385, 398, 400
    railroads in, 302–3
    rice in, 71, 77
    segregation in, 322
    Settlement (organization), 311
    sharecropping in, 199, 283, 286, 294–96
    slavery in, 64, 66–67, 71, 78–80, 184, 121, 213–14
    Supreme Court of, 286, 380
    the Trustees of colonial Georgia, 73–78, 192
    University of Georgia (UGA), 321, 423–24
    Upcountry, 371, 372–82, 384–85
    village of Siloam, 283
    wealth inequality in, 120–21
German immigration, 74, 172
Germany, 45, 339
Gettysburg, Battle of, 216
Giannini, Amadeo, 339–40
Giffen, Russell, 368
Gilmore, Ruth, 368
"Ginstar" defoliant, 363
Gisolfi, Monica, 380
global markets
    competition in, 51, 61, 78, 91, 123–24, 181–82, 248, 323, 334, 374, 397
    crisis of 1973, 411
    import dependence, 51, 133, 172, 411, 413
    tariffs, 251, 259, 263, 270–72, 284
    See also Atlantic world; slave trade
Global North, 420
Global South, 400, 408, 414, 418–20
Glorious Revolution of 1689, 44
Glymph, Thavolia, 218
Gold Coast of Africa, 180
gold/gold rushes, 85, 87, 143, 206, 334–35

Gómez, Máximo, 244, 254, 277
Gone with the Wind, 314
Gonzalez, Johnhenry, 155, 156, 157
"Goose Creek men," 35–36, 43
Gordon, Lincoln, 406–7
Gordon, Thomas, 182
Gordonsville, VA, *383*, 383–84
Gore, Al, 415
Goulart, João, 406–7, 409
gourds, 63
gran toma, 239–40
Grapes of Wrath, The (Steinbeck), 345
Gray, Eula, 317
Gray, LaGuana, 388
Gray, Ralph, 317
Great Depression, 21, 307, 315, 343, 346–47, 357, 367, 377, 379, 407–8
Great Houses, 7–9, 15, 64–65, *82*, 102–3, 105, 189–91, 201, 217, 348, 386, 423
"great merger movement," 264
"Great Migration," 323–24
"green manuring," 354
Green Revolution, 408–13, 414
Greenville, MS, 289–90
Gregg, William, 207
grileiros, 419, 420
grocery chains, 366–67, 378, 379, 399
Guantánamo Sugar Company, 264
Guatemalan asylum seekers, 393–98
guerrilla tactics, 133, 183, 209, 235, 396
"guestworkers," 267
Guiberson, G. W., 341, 356–57

Habersham, James, 40–41
hacienda comunera, 274–76
Hagar, Newton, 218–19
Haggard, Merle, 347
Haitian Revolution, 17, 148, 152–58, *153*, 159, 164–65
Hammond, James Henry, 208
Hampton, Wade, 235–36, 257
Harlem, 323
Harpers Ferry, 1859 attack on, 207
Harrell, Rose, 388
Harris, Jessica, 40
Harris, Judia Jackson, 311
Havana, Cuba, 160, 162, 245, 247, 258–60, 275
Havemeyer, Theodore, 264, 265

Index

Hawaii, 263
Hawkins, Roy, 386
headrights, 88, 92, 99
Henry, Nettie, 212
Henry, Patrick, 84–85, 129, 131, 133, 140, 184
herbicides, 363
Hernández, Dolores, 346
Hernández, Refugio, 343
Hershey's Chocolate, 19, *242*, 265
Hires Root Beer, 265
Hitler, Adolf, 159–60
hoes, 155–56
hogs/pigs, 62, 63, 111–12, 196, 224–25, 252
Honduras, 269
Hoover dam, 352
Hoppin' John, 40, 65
horses and mules
    control over, 252–53, 291, 296, 300–301, 306, 312
    the master's plow horse, 114, 136
    the South's import of, 208–9
    war horses, 136, 211, 214, 215
Horseshoe Bend, Battle of, 186
Howell, Thomas, 264
Hunter, Michael, 182
"hunting plantations," 232
Hurston, Zora Neale, 294, 295–96, 300
Hutson, Richard, 60
hydraulic engineering, 353–55
hydrogenation of food oils, 365

Illinois, 171, 371, 400
Immigration and Customs Enforcement (ICE), 400–401, *402*
Immigration and Naturalization Service (INS), 21, 347, 357
immigration, 172, 341, 357–59, 400–401, *402*
    the Bracero program, 21, 356–59, 364
    Chinese immigration, 247, 266–67, 335, 340–41
    German and Scandinavian immigration, 74, 172
    Guatemalan asylum seekers, 393–98
    Irish immigrants, 74
    Japanese immigration, 340
Imperial Valley, CA, 353
"in-between times," 66
Inconvenient Truth, An (film), 415

"increase," 116–18, 124, 136, 146
indentured servitude, 50, 91, 94–95, 99–101, 118, 247, 266–67, 335
India, 179, 183, 208, 285, 333, 414, 418
Indiana, 171
Indigenous people
    Arawak people of the Caribbean, 29
    farming strategies of, 88–90
    land theft from, 187, 394
    Maya people of Guatemala, 393–97, 399, 400–401
    slave-raiding nations, 34
    See also Native Americans
indigo, 44, 45, 46, *122*
industrialization, 5, 10, 207, 251, 283–85, 356
    industrial modernity, 252, 257–58
    the Industrial Revolution, 10, 18, 180, 181, 191
    "Second Industrial Revolution," 248
    See also energy; food; mechanization
inequality, 50–51, 130–31, 409, 413
inflation, 87–88, 367
information flows, 273, 287, 313
Ingrum, John, 401–3
inheritance, 101–2, 137–38
Inikori, Joseph, 180
innovation. *See* technologies
"integrators," 380–81, 386, 388, 400
Intergovernmental Panel on Climate Change, 415
International Harvester, 361
internment, 340
Iowa, 333–34, 409
Iraq, 415
Irish immigrants, 74
iron, 181, 208, 248
irrigation, 39, 41–43, 46, 338, 340, 344, 351–56, *352*, 409
Ixil Maya ethnic group, 396

Jackson, Andrew, 185–87, 190
Jackson, MS, 401–2, *402*
Jamaica, 30, 53, 77, 103, 121, *122*, 136, 146, 180, 182
James I of England, 85, 87, 90, 160
James II of England, 161
James, C. L. R., 159–60
James, Clifford, 318–19
Jamestown, 15, 85–95

Japanese internment, 340
Java (now Indonesia), 172
Jefferson, Thomas, 17, 84–85, 129, 131–35, 138, 233
   during the American Revolution, 140–41
   family of, 106, 109
   on the Haitian Revolution, 148, 164–66
Jewell, Jesse Dickson, 377–81, 387
Jim Crow South, 278, 281–82, 287–88, 296, 306, 307, 310, 382, 387
J-M Poultry Packing Company, El Dorado, AR, 387–89
Johnson, Andrew, 225–26, 229, 232–33, 234
Johnson, Anthony, 92, 100
Johnson, Nancy, 218
Johnston, Oscar, 321
joint-stock companies, 190
Jordan, Gloria, 388
Journey Through the Seaboard States (Olmsted), 228
Julião, Francisco, 405–6

Kalinago people, 29
Kansas-Nebraska Act of 1854, 206
kapoke (pokeweed), 64
Kaye, Anthony, 190, 194
Kemble, Fanny, 61
Kentucky, 129, 133, 135, 209, 334–35
Kesterton National Wildlife Refuge, 368
Kidder, Daniel, 174
kill lines, 387–91, *391*, 400
kin, the importance of, 54, 55, 68, 79, 198, 224, 227
King, Boston, 56, 66
Kingston, Maxine Hong, 61
Kirby, Jack Temple, 381
Kirkpatrick, Jeane, 396
Knights of Labor, 308
Koch Foods, 371, 400–403
Kongo people of Central West Africa, 64, 68
Kroger, 371, 399, 400
Kruger, F. G., 346
Ku Klux Klan, 236, 294, 321, 384
Kyoto Protocol (2002), 415

labor
   convict-lease system, 288–89, 309
   indentured servitude, 50, 91, 94–95, 99–101, 118, 247, 266–67, 335
   permanent labor surplus, 356, 358, 361
   productivity, 191, 362
   racialized labor exploitation, 11, 12, 20–22, 273, 278, 300, 332–33, 335, 359, 420
   strikes, 238–39, 308, 311, 343–46, *345*, 359–61, 367–68, *391*, 409, 413
   union organizing, 307–12, 316–19, *322*, 343–44, 360, 382, 389–91, *391*, 398, 407–8
   See also immigration; slavery/slave trade
Lacoste, Perfecto, 275
Lampkin, Josephine, 218, 219
land
   attempts at land reform, 234, 235, 254, 261, 347, 394, 409
   Black landownership after the Civil War, 291, 294, 296, 298–99
   Cuban taxes on land, 274–75
   "engrossment" of individual estates, 75, 98
   entailment, 102, 127, 129, 138
   "land companies," 184, 291
   land-grant colleges, 302, 303, 321; 409
   landlessness, 239, 291, 315, 407
   monopolies over land, 13, 15, 76, 99, 102, 111, 185, 222, 252, 269, 331, 407, 419
   ownership and "improvements," 50–51, 88–89, 97–98, 112, 132, 196–97, 266, 402
   property ownership and freedom, 202, 221–24, 228, 296, 321, 380
   racial equality through landownership, 274, 294
   redistributions of land, 222, 406–8
   share tenants and cash renters, 297
   sharecropping, 19–22, 238, 266, 282–90, *284*, 294–99, 310, 313, 315–17
   speculation on, 50, 98–99, 128–29, 133, 184, 211, 418–19
   standing renters, 21, 296–99, 300, 307, 312, 314, 315, 326
   tenant farmers in Cuba (*colonos*), 249, 252, 266, 394
   See also common lands; enclosure/fencing; Southern landscapes
Land Act of 1731 (UK), 43–44
Landless People's Movement of Brazil, 239, 407

landscapes. *See* Southern landscapes
Lanier, GA, 281
Lanterns on the Levee (W. A. Percy), 281
Latin America, 10, 172, 245, 407–8
Latino population, 341, 397–98
Laurens County, SC, 237
Laurens, Henry, 40–42, 44–45, 49, *49*, 54–55, 67, 77
"laying-by" period, 190
Lee Monument Association, 258
Lee, Fitzhugh, 258–59
Lee, Richard Henry, 134
Lee, Robert E., 212, 215, 222, 225, 258
Leflore County, MS, 309–10
liberalism, 50, 227
libertos (ex-slaves), 252–53
Lincoln, Abraham, 18, 43, 201, 207, 225–26
literacy, 54, 223, 299
livestock, *122*. *See also* cattle; hogs/pigs; poultry
local extension services, 303, 385
Locke, John, 50
Logum Logistica, 418
London financial markets, 30, 34, 43–45, 77, 87, 92–93, 109–10, 124, 129–30, 207, 250
"long fallow, hoe-and-hill culture," 38
Lopez de Santa Anna, Antonio, 199
López, Edgar, 400–401
Lords Proprietor of Carolina, 28, 34–36
Los Angeles, CA, 333, 339, 341, 354, 368
Lost Cause, 257–59
Louis Napoleon (Napoleon III), 208
Louisiana, 164–65, 171, 196, 222, *292*, 308, 387
    cotton plantations in the Natchez District, 192, 193–94, 284
    New Orleans, 172, 175, 189, *195*, 278
Louisiana State University, Baton Rouge, 270
Louverture, Toussaint, 152–54, 155, 159–60
Lowcountry Carolina rice, 37–51, 53–71, *122*
    in colonial capitalism, 44–45
    the lives of slaves growing, 53–70
    origins of, 37–40
    patrimony and the slave trade in, 40–44
    plantation sites and inequality, 45–52
    the planter class, 40–44
    slavery and the productivity of, 53–68
    the task system, 57, 60–61, 66, 79

Lubbar, Jack, 115–16
Luce, Henry, 10–11
Lula da Silva, Luiz Inácio, 415
lumber/timber, 11, 14, 33, 45–46, 66–67, *122*, 148, 163, 195–96, 232, 245, 249
lynchings, 257, 289–90, 305

Maceo, Antonio, 254, 256, 277
Madera Tribune, The (newspaper), 360
Madison, James, 17, 85, 139–41
malanga tubers, 274
malaria, 51, 60, 64, 76, 153
"Malcontents," 74–80, 90, 133
Mallory, Neysha, 389, 390
mandamiento forced labor system, 394
Mangorike plantation, 115
Mansfield Park (Austen), 121
Mansion, The (Faulkner), 301, 302
manumission, 70–71, 92, 137
Maranhão, Brazil, 419–20
Maranhão, Constâncio, 406, 411, 413
Maring, John, 90
"maroons," *31*, 69, 150
Marshall Plan, 407
Martí, José, 253–54, 274
Martin, Lydia, 390
Martin, Sylvia, 389, 390
Martyr, Peter, 86
Marx, Karl, 356
Maryland, 9, 59, 120–21, 189
Mason, George, 84–85, 134, 140, 258
Massachusetts Bay Colony, 32–33, 87
Massey, Samuel, 54–55
"Mastodon" cotton, 190
Mauldin, Erin, 285
Maxwell Wright & Co., 174–75
Maya people of Guatemala, 393–97, 399, 400–401
Mays, Trinity, 388
McAllum, Sam, 217
McCormick reapers, 178
McCusker, John, 32
McIlhenny, John, 278
McKinley, William, 257, 260
McMullen, John, 319
mechanization
    of agriculture, 246–48, 303, 321–22, 334, 338, 360–64
    assembly lines, 388

mechanization (*continued*)
　of the British textile industry, 180–81
　cotton gins, 183–84, 192, 193, 206, 213, 283, 290, 311, 339, 377, 399
　milling and refining, 176, 251
　of the poultry business, 380–81, 389, 414
　See also energy; industrialization
Menard, Russell, 32
Mepkin plantation, 49, *49*, 55
mercantilism, 29, 251, 385, 399
Methodists, 137, 203
methyl bromide, 354–55
Mexico, 199–200, 206, 239, 334, 343, 397, 407–9
　cotton, 191–93
　Mexican Revolution, 239, 343, 344
　migrants from, 341–47, 357–58, 360, 364
Microsoft, 421
Middle Passage, 14, 30, 41, 146, 173, 178, 267
Midwestern wheat farms, 171, 178, 191, 334, 337–38, 376, 377, 397
Miller & Lux, 338
Milling, Mary, 209
Milner, Estelle, 317
Mireles, Manuel, 344
Mississippi, 73, 171, 184–85, 195–96, 199, 287, 420
　cotton in, 195, 196, 222, 282, 286, 287, 331, 371, 400, 420
　poultry industry in, 371, *391*, *402*
　slavery in, 189–90
Mississippi Delta, 20, 43, 281, 282, 287–91, *289*, 294–97, 309–10, 312–15, 321, 326, 362, 382
Mississippi Valley Historical Association, 331
Missouri, 209
Missouri Compromise, 206
Mitchell, Hampton, and his family, 236
mocambos (escaped slaves), 1–3
modernity, 7, 9, 245–46, 252, 257–58
modernization. *See* economic development
Modyford, Thomas, 30–31
monocultural agriculture, 270, 325, 354, 376
　California cotton, 332–34, 353–55
　for consumer goods, 91, 95, 174
　Southern cotton, 193, 196, 303, 315, 361

monopolies
　over information/expertise, 114, 287–88
　over land, 13, 15, 76, 99, 102, 111, 185, 222, 252, 269, 331, 407, 419
　over local power, 286, 327
　Progressive-era antitrust enforcement, 264
Monroe, James, 137
Moreland, Moses, 374
Morgan, J. P., 265
Morganton, NC, 397–98
Morris, Robert, 184
mortgages, 43–44, 340, 347
Moses (biblical), 204
Mount Vernon, VA, *82*
mules. *See* horses and mules
Murray, J. S., 252–53
muscovado, 30
Mussolini, Benito, 160

Napoleon I, 152–54, 164
Napoleon III of France (Louis Napoleon), 208
Napoleonic Wars, 152, 163
Narrative of the Life of Frederick Douglass, 228
National Bank, 190
National Book Award, 307
National City Bank, 264
National Farm Labor Union, 360
National Recovery Administration, 346
Native American women, 35, 86
Native Americans, 34–35, 86–90
　anti-Indian violence, 93, 337
　the Cahuilla, 338
　the Catawba, 35, 80
　the Cherokee, 35, 80, 186, 195, 372
　the Creek, 35–36, 80, 185–87
　dispossession of, 41, 88–89, 94–95, 97–98, 111, 184
　enslavement of, 34
　Indian Wars in the American West, 256–57
　the Pamunkey, 94
　Powhatan Empire, 15, 80, 86–87, 89–90, 98, 141
　resistance by, 105–6
　the Savannah people, 36
　the Shawnee, 133, 135
　the Trail of Tears, 187

the Tuscarora, 35
the Yamasee, 34–36, 37, 41, 44, 45
the Yokut, 338
"Natural Limits of Slavery Expansion, The" (Ramsdell), 331
Navigation Acts (UK), 29
needs
   the balance of, 113, 203
   creating and commodifying new needs, 364–65
   in husbandry, 304, 326–27
   needfulness, 302, 306, 327
   needlessness, 78, 79, 300, 326, 388
Negro Home Demonstration Agents, 385
negros oficiales, 248
"neoplantations," 332
New Deal, 294, 364
   Agricultural Adjustment Administration (AAA), 321, 348–49, 377–78
   Black outmigration from the South and the, 316, 320, 321
   in California, 348, 349, 352–53, *352*, 367
   Central Valley Project (CVP), 352–53, *352*, 367
   exclusions of agricultural workers, 382
   Glass-Steagall Act, 413
   National Recovery Administration, 346
   regulatory order of the, 399
New England, 14, 32–34, *122*, 139, 228, 249–50
New Mexico, 200
New Orleans, 172, 175, 189, *195*, 278, *292*
New York Herald, The, 261
New York Stock Exchange, 207
New York Times, The, 419
Newkirk, Vann, 420
Nicaragua, 278
night riders, 236, 237, 384
nightwork/night walking, 68, 114
nitrogen, 302, 305, 355, 408
North Carolina, 120–21, 222, 257, 309, 393–94, 397–99, 400
Northrop, Lucius, 211
Northrup, Solomon, 189
Northwest Ordinances, 138, 185
Nova Era Bioenergia plantation, 416
nylon, 361

Occaneechee, 93–94
Ogeechee Home Guard, 223–24, 225, 234–35

Oglethorpe, James, 73–76, 192
Ohio, 171
oil, 353–56, 363–67, 408, 410–11, 414–15, 417
Okies migrating to California, 347–49, 357, 360
Oklahoma, 347–48
okra, 64–65
oligopolies, 20, 264, 268
Olmsted, Frederick Law, 228
"one-variety communities," 339, 361, 365
Opechancanough, 89–90
"open range," 112, 196, 231, 232
Operation Brother Sam, 407
Operation Wetback, 358
Opportunities in Cuba, 275
Organization of Petroleum Exporting Countries (OPEC), 367, 411
overproduction. *See* surplus
overseers, 47, 53–54, 106, 107, 109–14, 132, 288, *288*, 291, 374

Pacific R&H Chemical Corporation, 355
Pakistan, 418
Pamunkey people, 94
Panama Canal Zone, 396
Panic of 1819, 199
Panic of 1837, 190–91, 206, 207
Paquette, Robert, 56–57
Paraíba Valley, Brazil, 172, 175
Parke, Daniel, 119
Parker, Geoffrey, 6
Parker, W. S., 315–16, 317
Partido Independiente de Color, 277
Paschall, Walter, 281
patents, 193
paternalism, 47, 48, 73, 291
patriarchs of the South, 40, 41, 56, 101, 104, 114–15, 128, 137–38, 140, 201
patrimony, 116–19, 128, 129, 133, 137–40, 258
peanuts, 38, 305, 412
pellagra, 376
Pennsylvania, 14, 33, 204, 421
People's Party, 311
Pepper, Charles, 274
Percy, George, 88–89
Percy, LeRoy "the Gray Eagle," 286, 290
Percy, Walker, 406
Percy, William Alexander, 281, 286

Perdue Farms, 22, 381, 399
Pérez, Louis, 250
Perón, Juan, 408
Perry and Lane (UK), 124
pest control, 65, 193, 270, 354–55, 364
Petersburgh Express, 226
petroleum, 353–56, 361, 364–69, 411, 414
Philip II of Spain, 4
Philippines, 263
phosphate fertilizers, 304, 374
Piedmont region, 134, 142, 177–78, 196
    California transplants from the, 21, 333, 334, 349, 358
    during Civil War and Reconstruction, 212, 282–83, 285
    cotton in the, 285, 291, *292–93*, 296, 299–300, 307, 312–15, 361–62, 372–75
Pigford v. Glickman (1999), 321
Piggly Wiggly, 378
pigs/hogs, 62, 63, 111–12, 196, 224–25, 252
Pilgrim's Pride, 371, 399
Pillsbury, 381
Pinckney, Charles, 42, 230
Pitt, William, 121
plantations, 7–9
    of the American Empire, 172–79
    of the American hinterland, 169–71
    the antiplantation tradition, 13, 19, 115, 157, 219, 224, 240, 274, 299, 301, 306, 324–26
    birthplace of, 1–6
    boom-and-bust cycles of, 4, 13, 18–21, 28–29, 355, 368, 377, 379, 403
    of the British Empire, 14–15, 25–80
    capitalism's tendency toward plantation-izing, 11–14
    as central to American capitalism, 9–11
    during Civil War and Reconstruction, 18–19, 167–240
    "the destined vortex" of the plantation system, 9, 170, 198
    in early American history, 15–18, 81–166
    "edge cases" in the history of, 334
    the frontier plantation, 11, 12, 18, 36, 42, 48–49, 100, 129, 132, 172, 195–96, 266, 331, 337
    of the future, 21–22, 329–424
    as grand consumers, 7–23
    laboring in the unreconstructed Southern plantation, 307–27
    and the organization of space, 13, 65, 198–99, 203, 231, 283, 297–98
    "plantation complexes," 46, 48, 57, 67, 69, 125, 176, 184, 190, 273
    plantation homes (Great Houses), 7–9, 15, 64–65, *82*, 102–3, 105, 189–91, 201, 217, 348, 386, 423
    precarity of, 13–14, 17, 30–31, 51, 77, 233
    as quasi-feudal, 229
    self-sufficiency, 115, 155, 177, 190–200
    without slavery, 139–40, 154, 217–18, 241–27
    vertical integration, 265, 378–79, 387–88
planter class
    "absentee" planters, 109, 121, 231, 314
    the devil inside, 22–23, 61
    enclosure according to the, 89, 111–12, 128, 195–96, 203, 209, 219, 226–27, 231–32
    influence in Congress, 205–6
    in Lowcountry rice, 40–44
    patriarchs of the, 40, 41, 56, 101, 104, 114–15, 128, 137–38, 140, 201
    patrimony, 116–19, 128, 129, 133, 137–40, 258
Platt Amendment, 261, 265, 274–75, 276
pokeweed, 64
polarimeters, 271
Pollan, Michael, 365
Pope, Anne, 217
populism, 190, 310, 321, 407–8, 415
Populist Party, 257
"portfolio plantations," 332
Portuguese Empire
    Portuguese immigration abroad, 174
    São Tomé, 1–6, 10, 14, 23, 118, 149, 248, 420
    in the slave trade, 244–45
    See also Brazil
Post, James Howell, 264
poultry industry, 22, 371–91, 393–403
poverty, 13, 30, 267, 288, 304–6, 380–82, 408–9, 415–17
Powhatan Empire, 15, 80, 86–87, 89–90, 98, 141
precarity, 13–14, 17, 30–31, 51, 77, 233
Proálcool program, 411, 413, 422

"processioning," 111
"Proclamation Line," 128–29
"progging," 116, 155, 225, 233, 344
Progressive Era, 264, 387
property rights, 89, 219
   "dwellings," 201–3, 211, 213, 214, 237
   "improvements," 50–51, 88–89, 97–98, 112, 132, 196–97, 266, 402
   private, 111, 140, 224, 261
   See also horses and mules; enslaved people; land
Prosser, Gabriel, 137, 312
protectionism, 123, 250, 284. *See also* tariffs
Prunty, Merle, 298, 300
Puerto Rico, 263, 264, 270, 278
Puritans, 32, 87

Quakers, 137
Quintana, Ryan, 45–46

race and racism
   erasure, 326
   hypersexualized stereotypes, 166
   interracial communities, 235, 239–40, 255, 257–59, 274, 310–11, 324
   majority-Black, minority-white communities, 15, 17, 53, 57, 70, 77, 106, 133, 151, 162, 190, 257
   minority-Black, majority-white communities, 106, 128, 129, 376–77
   "natural" racial order, 148–49, 259
   race war anxiety, 159, 186, 254–56, 261
   "Race War" of 1912 (Cuba), 278
   racial discrimination in the USDA, 321–22
   racial equality through landownership, 274, 294
   "racial reckoning" of 2020, 8
   racialized labor exploitation, 11, 12, 20–22, 273, 278, 300, 332–33, 335, 359, 420
   stereotypes of Black people, 248, 385–86
   traitors to the race, 56
   white supremacy, 50, 54, 236, 257–58, 276, 310, 345, 348, 382, 385, 387
Radical Republicans, 226
railroads, 172, 181
   in California, 337
   coffles, 169, 187–89, *188*

   in Cuba, 245, 249, 252, 254–55, 265, 267–69, 271, 277
   in Guatemala, 394–95
   of the South, 206–7, 210, 213, 239, 281, 289, 290, 302, 309, 374
Raízen, 418
Ralston Purina, 377, 381
Ramsdell, Charles, 331–32
Randolph, Edmund, 138, 140, 166
rape, 237, 384, 396
Raynal, Abbé, 144
Reagan, Ronald, 395–96
recession, 127, 183
Reciprocity Act, 263
"reconcentration," 255–56, 260, 277
Reconstruction, 226, 227–28, 231, 232–40
   California during, 336, 338
   Freedmen's Bureau, 218–19, 222, 228–33, 238, 372
   the *gran toma* of, 239–40
   the rise of sharecropping, 283–90, 310, 313–14
red rice, 40
Red Shirts of South Carolina, 257
Red Sticks, 185–86
redistributions of land, 222, 406–8
Refugee Act of 1980, 393
Regional Foreign Labor Operations Advisory Committee (RFLOAC), 359
Renewable Energy Directive (EU), 416
reparations, 68–69, 234
Republican Party, 18, 139, 165, 207, 212, 226, 237–39, 257, 336
Research and Marketing Act of 1946, 364
Resettlement Administration, 321
resistance
   the antiplantation tradition, 13, 19, 115, 157, 219, 224, 240, 274, 299, 301, 306, 324–26
   of Black farmers, 21, 79, 232, 282–83, 315, 316–18
   guerrilla tactics, 133, 183, 209, 235, 396
   Haitian Revolution, 17, 148, 152–58, *153*, 159, 164–65
   of Native Americans, 105–6, 337
   Stono River uprising of 1739, *26*, 70–71, 74, 78, 90, 124
   in the workplace, 342, 398
   See also Haitian Revolution; violence

rice, 15, *26*, 35–36
  early colonial rice booms, 44–45, 50, 60, 69–70, 77
  in Georgia, 77–80
  Lowcountry Carolina rice, 37–51, 53–71, 91
  plantation rice in the slave trade, 45–46, 48, 120–21, 122
  the "Rice Coast" of Africa, 38–40, 203–4
Richmond, VA, 119, 134, 169–71, *170*, 174–78, 216, 258
"right to work," 389
Rights of Man, 151
Ring Fence Associations, 226
Ríos Montt, Efraín, 396
Roaring Twenties, 312
Rockefeller Foundation, 11
Rolfe, John, 87
Romero, Adam, 354
Roosevelt, Franklin D., 320–21, 348. *See also* New Deal
Root, Elihu, 261
Rothman, Adam, 185
Rowe, Katie, 218
Royal African Company, 30, 99
Royal Dutch Shell, 22, 417, 418, 422
Ruffin, Edmund, 198, 226–27
rum, 35, 75, 166
Russia, 368, 414

Sackman, Doug, 364
Sacramento, CA, 335, 336, 338
Safeway supermarkets, 366–67
St. Augustine, FL, 69, 70
Saint-Domingue, 17, 143–58, *153*, 159–65, 182, 277
salted fish, 14, 33, *122*, 148
Salyer, Fred, 332, 360, 367
San Francisco Chronicle, 338
San Jacinto, Battle of, 199
San Joaquin Valley, CA, 21, 332–43, 346, 358–62
Sanderson Farms, 388
São Martinho (company), 417
São Paulo state, Brazil, 411–13, 416
São Tomé, 1–6, 10, 14, 23, 118, 149, 248, 420
Sapelo Island, 232–33
Saunt, Claudio, 187
Savannah people of the South, 36

Savannah River Maroons, 69
Savannah, GA, 64, 66, 214–15, 221
Saxton, Rufus, 228–29, 231, 233–34
scalawaggery, 286
School of the Americas in Fort Benning, GA, 398, 410
"scientific farmers," 177–78
Sea Islands, 224, 228, 233, *293*
"seasoned" slaves, 37
"secession winter" of 1860–61, 159
"Second Industrial Revolution," 248
secret societies, 151, 156
seed breeders, 193
selenium salts, 367–68
self-dealing, 349
self-determination, 159, 260–61
"self-sufficiency," 95, 190–91, 197, 208–9, 408
"self-sustaining change," 181
Semple, Robert Baylor, 334
Senegambia, 40, 113
Seven Years' War, 77, 119, 124, 127
sharecropping, 19–22, 238, 266, 282–90, *284*, 294–99, 310, 313, 315–17
Shawnee people, 133, 135
Shell Oil Company, 354, 364
Sherman, William Tecumseh, 212–15, 221–24, 234, 235–36, 282–83, 372
Shiloh, Battle of, 216
Shine, Deena, 390
Sikh Americans, 340
Silver Jews (band), 365
"simbi" spirits, 68
Simril, Harriet, 237
Sinclair, Upton, 331
sitieros (Cuban farmers of African descent), 19, 274, 276, 277
1619 Project, 16–17
"skimming" husbandry, 13, 196–97, *197*, 210, 269
"slash and burn" husbandry, 195
slavery/slave trade
  arrival of the first enslaved Africans in 1619, 16–17, 91
  asiento monopoly, 160
  chattel slavery, 16, 50, 95, 141, 154, 181, 202, 246, 248, 302
  Middle Passage, 14, 30, 41, 146, 173, 178, 267

plantations without, 139–40, 154, 217–18, 241–27
"slave codes," 15, 31, 53, 70–71, 76
the slave quarters, 8, 62–63, 65, 116, 150, 201–2, 224, 237, 283
"slavery's capitalism," 246–47
statehood and, 165, 185
See also abolitionism; enslaved people
sleep deprivation, 68–69
Smith, John, 86
Smith-Lever Act of 1914, 303
social Darwinism, 258
social revolutions of the 1860s (in Brazil, Cuba, and the US), 224
soil fumigation, 354–55, 364
"Sons of Liberty," 138
sorghum, 38
South America, 173–76, 178, 410
South Carolina, 26, 51
   the backcountry, 132–34
   secession and the Civil War, 43, 80, 184, 203, 204, 208, 215, 223, 228–30, 233–34
   slavery/slave trade in, 37, 42, 43, 60–61, 180, 183–84
   Stono River uprising of 1739, 26, 70–71, 74, 78, 90, 124
   wealth inequality in, 120–21
   white terrorism in, 236–37, 257
"Southern food," 15, 38–40, 41, 63–65, 155.
   See also specific ingredients and dishes
Southern Historical Society, 258
Southern hospitality, 8, 49, 103, 128, 314, 319
Southern landscapes, 292–93
   the abandonments of, 324
   artificial landscapes requiring constant labor, 57
   the backcountry, 17, 48, 93, 95, 102, 132–33, 183
   Jim Crow, 278, 281–82, 287–88, 296, 306, 307, 310, 382, 387
   plantation tourism, 7–8, 49
   railroads across, 206–7, 210, 213, 239, 281, 289, 290, 302, 309, 374
   the "swept yard," 65, 203, 298, 318
   Tidewater region, 15, 39, 41–43, 46, 97–99, 109, 129–30, 139, 141, 177
   See also Lowcountry Carolina rice; Piedmont region; plantations
Southern Pacific Railroad, 337

Southern Railway, 374
"Southern Rights Party," 226
Southern Tenant Farmers' Union (STFU), 316–20, *322*, 360
Spanish Empire, 15, 29, 64, 160–63
   competition with the British, 85, 87, 152
   Florida under the, 69–70, 186
   search for gold, 143
   "sick man of Europe," 255
   in the slave trade, 160–61, 244–45
   tariffs, 259
   See also Cuba
Spanish-American War, 256, 258–61
speculation, 19, 338
   on commodities, 273, 275
   on land, 50, 98–99, 128–29, 133, 184, 211, 418–19
standing renters, 21, 296–99, 300, 307, 312, 314, 315, 326
"Starving Winter" of 1610, 15
state legislatures, 206, 335, 339
statehood, 185, 195, 335
steam power, 59, 169, 180–81, 194, *195*, 222–23, 206, 245, *246*, 248, 263, 283, 337
steel, 248–49, 268
Steinbeck, John, 345
Stono River uprising of 1739, 26, 70–71, 74, 78, 90, 124
Stowe, Harriet Beecher, 228
strikes, 238–39, 308, 311, 343–46, *345*, 359–61, 367–68, *391*, 409, 413
subsidies, agricultural, 303, 388, 397, 411, 414
sugar, 2–6, 166, 251
   beet sugar, 250, 263
   grains of different sizes, 272–73
   molasses, 4, 67, 250, 272, 288, 376
   plantations of Barbados, 27–33, *31*, 182
   plantations of Brazil, 22, 405–10
   plantations of Cuba, 263–73
   raw sugar, 144, 162, 248–51, 263–65, 270–72
   rum, 35, 75, 166
   sugar maples, 166
   sugar mills, 2–6, 77, 148, 150, 162, *246*, 247–49, 342, 389–90, 411–13, 417, 418
   See also Barbados
"Sugar Trust, the," 11, 244, 251, 264, 273
supermarkets, 366–67

surplus
  agricultural subsidies and, 303, 388, 397, 411, 414
  bodies as "surplus sinks," 365–67
  fears of a Black surplus, 78, 326–27, 334
  fertility, 369
Surprise, Kevin, 351
"swept yards" of the rural South, 65, 203, 298, 318

Tailfer, Patrick, 74–75
Tallapoosa County, AL, 315–17, 320
tariffs, 251, 259, 263, 270–72, 284
task system, 57, 60, 66, 79
Tatum, B. A., 381
taxes
  colonial taxes, 88, 101, 106, 128, 323
  in the Confederacy, 209–11
  Congress's power to levy, 139
  in crops, 90, 211
  land taxes in Cuba, 274–75
  regional poverty and, 288
Tayloe, John, 102–3, 109
Taylor, Alan, 53
Taylor, Paul, 344
technology, 11, 19, 180, 183–84, 248, 337–38, 420
  artificial intelligence (AI), 420–22
  milling and refining, 176
  plantation as frontier-conquering technology
  rational logic of business and, 229
  "world technologies," 193
  See also industrialization; mechanization
Ten Years' War, 244, 245, 253, 255
tenancy. *See* land
Tennessee, 371
Tenth Amendment, 140
terrorism, 19, 225–26, 237, 384, 409–10
Texas, 171, 194, 196, 199–200, *292*, 333, 334, 347, 360, 362
Thailand, 418
"thick skins" of Black people, 146
Thomas, William G., 213
Three Mile Island, Middletown, PA, 421
"through-and-through" cultivation, 297–98
TIAA-CREF pension fund, 22, 419–20
Tidewater region, 15, 39, 41–43, 46, 97–99, 109, 129–30, 139, 141, 177

TikTok, 8
Tillson, Davis, 229, 232–34
timber. *See* lumber
tobacco, 15–17, 29, 32–34, 38, 67, 80, 99
  cultivation and processing of, 107, *108*, 134, 170, *170*
  "gang system," 183
  plantations of Virginia, 15–18, 83–95, 97–106
  tobacco prices, 92, 97, 99, 102, 124
Tobago, 182
Tocantins, 417
Tomich, Dale, 194
Toombs, Robert, 286
torture, 3, 14, 53–54, 68, 70, 84, 112, 114, 396, 410
tourism, 7–8, 49
Townshend duties, 128
tractors, 321–22, 337
trade. *See* global markets; *specific commodities and trade goods*
Trail of Tears, 187
transatlantic trade. *See* Atlantic world
transportation. *See* railroads; steam power
"treadmill" of crop hybridization, 270, 363
Treaty of Guadalupe Hidalgo, 200
Trinidad, 77, 250
Troubled Land, The (documentary), 405, 407, 412
True and Historical Narrative of the Colony of Georgia in America, A (Tailfer), 74
Trump, Donald, 422
Trustees of Georgia, 73–78, 192
"trusties," 318
truth commissions, 396–97
Tucker, Sarah, 118
Tucker, St. George, 136–37
Tulare Lake/Tulare County, CA, *330*, 337–38, 343, *345*, 353, 360, 368
Tuscarora people, 35
Tuskegee Institute, 299, 304–5, 319
Twelve Years a Slave (Northrup), 189
"twenty-slave law," 209

U.S. Army, 187, 234–35, 337, 398, 410
U.S. Border Patrol, 21, 357–59
U.S. Civil War. *See* Civil War (American)
U.S. Constitution, 42, 138–41, 143, 336–37
U.S. Cotton Field Station, Shafter, CA, 353

U.S. Department of Agriculture (USDA), 11, 238, 313, 361–64, 369, 384
  Cotton Research Center, 339
  on feed conversion contracts, 380
  hearings on contemporary agribusiness, 402–3
  mechanistic worldview of, 302, 303
  racial discrimination by, 321–22
U.S. Department of Labor, 21, 359
U.S. Environmental Protection Agency (EPA), 354–55
U.S. Farm Bill of 1996, 413
U.S. Land Offices in the Mississippi territory, 184–85
U.S. Marines, 277, 278
U.S. Navy, 224
U.S. State Department., 401
U.S. Supreme Court, 206, 321, 335
Uncle Tom's Cabin, 228
unemployed masses, 356
"unimproved" acres, 89, 112, 132, 196–97
Union Carbide, 411
Union Navy, 205, 210
unions, 307–8, 312, 316–19, *322*, 343–44, 360, 382, 389–91, *391*, 398, 407–8
United Farmworkers (UFW), 367, 409
United Fruit Company, 19–20, 249, 265, 269, 394–95
United Nations (UN), 396–97
United States
  American-style capitalism, 9–11, 264–65, 407
  during the Civil War and Reconstruction, 18–19, 167–40
  interests in Latin America, 10, 407–8
  Louisiana Purchase, 164–65, *292*
  the Modernist city, 323
  New England, 14, 32–34, *122*, 139, 228, 249–50
  plantations in early American history, 15–18, 81–166
  plantations of empire, 172–79
  plantations of the American hinterland, 169–71
  during the Spanish-American War, 256, 258–61
  westward expansion, 36, 80, 142, 166, 184–85, 198
  "Yankees," 174, 201, 207, 212–14, 217

See also American Revolution; Civil War (American); New Deal; *specific agencies and departments*
University of California system, 344, 364, 409
University of Georgia (UGA), 321, 423–24
"Upcountry South," 20, *122*, 371, 372–82, 384–85
"upland" crops, 26, 46–47, 183, 212
USAID (U.S. Agency for International Development), 406
USS *Maine*, 260
Utah, 200

vagrancy, 287, 289, 356
Van Horne, William, 275–76
Vargas, Getúlio, 408
vertical integration, 265, 378–79, 387–88
Vicksburg, MS, 193
vigilantes, 19, 317, 337, 345
Villa, Pancho, 343
violence
  ethnic cleansing, 186, 337, 384
  lynchings, 257, 289–90, 305
  night riders, 236, 237, 384
  rape, 237, 384, 396
  terrorism, 19, 225–26, 237, 384, 409–10
  torture, 3, 14, 53–54, 68, 70, 84, 112, 114, 396, 410
  Wilmington Coup of 1898, 257, 278
Virginia, 15–18, 80, *82*
  during the American Revolution, 131–42
  Bacon's Rebellion, 92–95, 97–98, 132, 186–87
  colonial, 83–95, 127–31
  crop mastery and enslavement, 107–25
  Jamestown, 15, 85–95
  local government, 88, 100, 102, 119, 133, 138
  Piedmont, 177
  Reconstruction in, 222
  rice in, 38
  slavery in, 50, 189, 198
  tobacco plantations of, 15–18, 83–95, 97–106
  wealth inequality in, 120–21
  wheat, 174
Virginia Company, 87–88, 90, 102
"Vlangbengdeng" secret society, 156
Vodún, 148–49, 151

wages
- agricultural labor, 341, 377–78, 388–89, 399–400
- in Brazil, 405, 412, 416–17
- in Cuba, 267–68
- industrial, 356
- labor actions over, 308, 343–46, *345*, 360–61
- migrant labor and, 356–61
- minimum, 309, 348, 382
- mobility and, 267, 268, 287, 347
- relative regional wages, 210
- slaves on Sunday, 62
- wage work on the antebellum plantation, 221, 224, 228–30, 237–38, 283, 286, 287

waiter-carriers, *383*, 383–84
Walmart, 371, 399–400
Walsh, Lorena, 38, 124, 177
Warwick and Barksdale (company), 176
Washington, D.C., 188
Washington, George, *82*, 84–85, 123, 129, 134–37, 138–39, 140, 166
water. *See* irrigation
Watson, William, 38
wealth inequality, 129–30. *See also* planter class; poverty
Weber, Devra, 343, 348
weed control, 57–58, 60, 62, 155, 363, 369
Weems, Camilla, 385
Wesson's Vegetable Oil, 365
"West India Interest, the" 121
West Indies, 87, 103, 106, *122*, 124, 164–65
- British, 10, 20, 32–33, 34, 44, 45, 73, 75–77, 124, *122*, 135, 144
- French, 10, 144, *147*, 148, 162, 182
- Haiti, 17, 148, 152–58, *153*, 159, 164–65
- *See also* Barbados; Cuba

West, Vivian, 387, 389, 390
Westover Plantation, VA, 83–84, 105, 110–14, 119–20, 134, *168*
westward expansion, 36, 80, 142, 166, 184–85, 198
Weyler, Valeriano, 255–56
Whayne, Jeannie, 290
wheat, 130, 142
- California wheat craze of the 1880s, 353–54, 368
- combines, 337–38
- Midwestern wheat farms, 171, 178, 191, 334, 337–38, 376, 377, 397
- Southern "wheat bonanza" of the 1860s–1880s, 336
- Virginia wheat flour exports, 169–71, *170*, 174–78

Wheeler, Joseph, 259–60
Whigs, 200
white communities
- "best poor/white man's country," 95, 111, 186–87
- impunity before the law, 54, 79, 287, 346
- nonslaveholding whites of the South, 51, 372
- poor, 106, 129, 290, 310, 384
- theory of white deficit, 79–80
- white allies in the postwar South, 229
- white overseers, 53, 57, 114
- white sharecroppers, 302, 309, 347, 348, 376–77
- whiteness as a scarcity model, 79–80
- yeoman agrarian ideal, 15, 32, 47, 57, 190, 227, 233, 336
- *See also* planter class

white supremacy, 50, 54, 236, 257–58, 276, 310, 345, 348, 382, 385, 387
white women, 101–2, 216, 290, 384, 388
Whitefield, George, 74
Whitney's gin, 183, 193
widowarchy, 101–2
wildcat strikes, 308
Wilkinson, Joe, 110–11
Willard, A. J., 230–31, 232
Williams-Forson, Psyche, 383, 386
Wilmington, NC, 257, 278, *293*
Wilson, Robert E. "Lee," 290–91
Wilson, Woodrow, 278
Winthrop, John, and his son Henry, 32
Wisconsin, 171
Wisniewski, Alfonso, 409
women. *See* Black women; Native American women; white women
Wood, Betty, 66
Wood, Gordon, 120
Wood, Leonard, 260, 275
Workers' Party of Brazil, 415
World Bank, 397, 422
World War I, 263, 291, 312, 338–39, 384
World War II, 22, 334, 340, 357, 378, 386, 405
Wyatt, Francis, 89

Yamasee War, 34–36, 37, 41, 44, 45
"Yankees," 174, 201, 207, 212–14, 217
Yates, Wynton, 8
"yaws, the," 60
"Yazoo" land bonds, 184
Yeamans, John, 16, 27–29, 30, 31, 34–36, 51, 98
yellow fever, 60, 103, 153

yeoman agrarian ideal, 15, 32, 47, 57, 190, 227, 233, 336
Yokut people, 338
York County, SC, 237
Yorktown, Battle of, 135–36
Young Communist League, 317

Zapata, Emiliano, 343